RENEWALS 458-4574
DATE DUE

Multinational Corporations and the Emerging Network Economy in Asia and the Pacific

Multinational Corporations and the Emerging Network Economy in Asia and the Pacific delves into the ongoing rise of a global economy anchored in a web of inter-firm production networks and the role played by multinational corporations in the process. It considers the strategies and business models corporations have adopted lately to face today's highly competitive global markets, especially outsourcing and offshoring, focusing on the modalities observed in Asia Pacific and the Pacific Rim at large. Since their interception, corporations have undergone a series of fundamental changes; each has corresponded to a given era of industrial development and has given rise to a particular type of government policy response. The book addresses these timely issues and other such as the transformation of global production networks into global innovation networks, the link between corporate and national innovation strategies and movement up the global production value chain, and the fragmentation of production and the resulting increase in component and sub-assembly trade in the region. It also takes up the emergence of multinational corporations from developing countries and the efforts aimed at forging basic rules of corporate social responsibility and developing sound institutions for building a working framework of corporate governance in the Pacific.

Written by some of the region's most eminent and influential economists and political scientists, this volume will appeal to students and scholars working in the field of Asia Pacific studies as well as to businesspersons and policymakers taking decisions in the region.

Juan J. Palacios is Professor of Economics and Head of the Transnational Studies Program in the Department of Political Studies at the University of Guadalajara, Mexico.

Pacific Trade and Development Conference Series
Edited by Peter Drysdale, Australia–Japan Research Centre, The Australian National University

Titles published by Routledge in association with the PAFTAD International Secretariat and the Australia–Japan Research Centre, The Australian National University include:

Business, Markets and Government in the Asia Pacific
Edited by Rong-I Wu and Yun-Peng Chu

Asia Pacific Financial Deregulation
Edited by Gordon de Brouwer and Wisarn Pupphavesa

Asia Pacific Economic Cooperation/APEC: Challenges and Tasks for the 21st Century
Edited by Ippei Yamazawa

Globalization and the Asia Pacific Economy
Edited by Kyung Tae Lee

The New Economy in East Asia and the Pacific
Edited by Peter Drysdale

Competition Policy in East Asia
Edited by Erlinda M. Medalla

Reshaping the Asia Pacific Economic Order
Edited by Hadi Soesastro and Christopher Findlay

Challenges to the Global Trading System
Adjustment to globalization in the Asia–Pacific region
Edited by Peter A. Petri and Sumner J. La Croix

Multinational Corporations and the Emerging Network Economy in Asia and the Pacific
Edited by Juan J. Palacios

Multinational corporations and the Emerging Network Economy in Asia and the Pacific

Edited by
Juan J. Palacios

LONDON AND NEW YORK

First published 2008 by Routledge
2 Park Square, Milton Park, Abingdon, Oxon OX14 4RN

Simultaneously published in the USA and Canada by Routledge
270 Madison Ave, New York, NY 10016

Routledge is an imprint of the Taylor & Francis Group, an informa business

Publisher's note: This book has been prepared from camera-ready copy provided by PAFTAD International Secretariat.

© 2008 PAFTAD International Secretariat for selection and editorial matter; individual chapters, the contributors

Printed and bound in Great Britain by MPG Books Ltd, Bodmin

All rights reserved. No part of this book may be reprinted or reproduced or utilized in any form or by any electronic, mechanical, or other means, now known or hereafter invented, including photocopying and recording, or in any information storage or retrieval system, without permission in writing from the publishers.

British Library Cataloguing in Publication Data
A catalogue record for this book is available from the British Library

Library of Congress Cataloging in Publication Data
Library of Congress Cataloging-in-Publication Data
Multinational corporations and the emerging network economy in Asia and the Pacific / edited by Juan J. Palacios.
p. cm. — (Pacific trade and development conference series)
Includes bibliographical references and index.
1. International business enterprises—Management. 2. Business networks—Asia. 3. Business networks—Pacific Area. 4. Business enterprises—Computer networks—Asia. 5. Business enterprises—Computer networks—Pacific Area. I. Palacios Lara, Juan José. II. Title: Network economy in Asia and the Pacific.
HD62.4.M838 2007
338.8'885—dc22
2007015695

ISBN10:0–415–43332–0 (hbk)
ISBN10:0–203–94639–1 (ebk)

ISBN13:978–0–415–43332–7 (hbk)
ISBN13:978–0–203–94639–8 (ebk)

Contents

List of figures vii
List of tables and boxes viii
List of contributors xi
Preface xiii
List of abbreviations xvi

1 Multinational corporations and the economy of networks: an overview 1
   Juan J. Palacios

2 Eras of enterprise globalisation: from vertical integration to virtualisation and beyond 26
   Sandor Boyson and Chaodong Han

3 Innovation offshoring: root causes of Asia's rise and policy implications 58
   Dieter Ernst

4 Information and communication technologies and inter-corporate production networks: global information technology and local *guanxi* in the Taiwanese personal computer industry 89
   Kenneth L. Kraemer, Jason Dedrick, William Foster and Zhang Cheng

5 The creation of regional production networks in Asia Pacific: the case of Japanese multinational corporations 114
   Shujiro Urata

6 The internationalisation of firm activities and its economic impacts: the case of South Korea 139
   Sanghoon Ahn, Siwook Lee and Cheonsik Woo

7 The rise of Mexican multinationals: driving forces and limiting factors 163
   Víctor López Villafañe and Clemente Ruiz Durán

8	Emerging transnational corporations from East Asia: the case of mainland China *Edward K.Y. Chen and Ping Lin*	183
9	Multinational production networks and the new geo-economic division of labour in Pacific Rim countries *Prema-chandra Athukorala*	208
10	Multinational corporations and Pacific regionalism *Philippa Dee*	232
11	Governing multinational corporations in the Pacific *Robert Scollay*	267
12	Corporate social responsibility and capital accumulation *Djisman Simanjuntak*	283
	Index	306

Figures

2.1	The real-time supply chain IT architecture	36
2.2	The core model: real-time alignment of supply and demand	37
4.1	The PC industry value network	90
4.2	PC industry supply chain	94
4.3	ICT use in a supply chain	95
5.1	Japan's outward FDI	115
5.2	Japanese FDI outflow by region, 1989–2004	117
5.3	Japan's outward FDI by sector, 1989–2004	117
5.4	Overseas sales as a percentage of total sales by Japanese MNCs, 1993–2002	120
6.1	South Korean outward FDI, 1980–2003	144
6.2	Total South Korean outbound FDI, 2003, by destination	145
6.3	South Korean outbound FDI in manufacturing, 2003, by destination	146
6.4	FDI and trade in manufacturing	147
6.5	FDI and trade with China, 1990–2003	148
6.6	FDI and trade with the United States, 1990–2003	149
7.1	Mexico direct investment abroad	169
10.1	Inward FDI stocks into broad geographic regions	251
10.2	Inward FDI stocks into socioeconomic groupings of regions	251
10.3	Inward FDI stocks into 'geographic' groupings of regions	252

Tables and boxes

Box 2.1	Milestones in Ford's evolution across three eras of enterprise globalisation	28
2.1	Characteristics of two contrasting eras of enterprise globalisation	32
2.2	Impact of adopting the Toyota model, selected US companies	34
2.3	Re-engineering to real-time supply chains: two different approaches	39
2.4	Dell global supplier network	46
2.5	Problems with outsourcing information technology services	48
2.6	Three eras of enterprise globalisation: the relationship between key corporate behaviour and public policy responses	52
3.1	Intel's global innovation network	68
4.1	Extent to which notebook PC-makers outsource production to Taiwanese firms	91
4.2	Firm size in the notebook industry	93
4.3	List of firms interviewed	97
4.4	Use of ICT applications by PC-makers and ODMs	98
4.5	Information technology in tier 1 and tier 2 suppliers	100
4.6	Enterprise resource planning (ERP) systems of tier 1 and tier 2 companies	101
4.7	Electronic integration between ODMs and their suppliers	102
5.1	Sales of overseas affiliates of Japanese MNCs by sector, 1993–2001	119
5.2	Sales of overseas affiliates of Japanese MNCs: ratio of overseas sales to overseas sales plus sales in Japan, 1993–2002	120
5.3	Sales of overseas affiliates of Japanese MNCs by region	121
5.4	Sales patterns of foreign affiliates of Japanese firms, 1992 and 2001	122
5.5	Procurement patterns of foreign affiliates of Japanese firms, 1992 and 2001	124

5.6	Intra-firm transactions in sales of foreign affiliates of Japanese multinational corporations (percentage share in each sale), 1992 and 2001	128
5.7	Intra-firm transactions in procurements of foreign affiliates of Japanese multinational corporations	130
5.8	Intra-industry trade within East Asia, 1990–2004	133
5.9	Parts trade for East Asian economies: share of total	134
5.10	Intra-regional dependence in machinery production in East Asia, 1985–2000	135
6.1	Relationship between FDI and exports	152
6.2	Regression results for annual employment growth rates	155
6.3	Regression results for annual TFP growth rates	158
7.1	Entrepreneurship in Mexico, 1993–2004	163
7.2	Economic performance in perspective	165
7.3	Firms by size and industry level of technology	168
7.4	Alliances of the 500 largest companies in Mexico	170
7.5	Mexico's biggest multinational public companies	170
7.6	Largest multinational corporations in Mexico City and locations of their subsidiaries and businesses	172
7.7	Carso Global Telecom's reach	173
8.1	Outward FDI stock in selected countries	187
8.2	Outward FDI from China by destination country, 1979–2003	188
8.3	Outward FDI from China by destination region, 1991–2004	189
8.4	Major cross-border mergers and acquisitions by Chinese manufacturers, 2002–05	190
8.5	Chinese firms in the top 50 largest non-financial TNCs from developing economies in 2003	191
8.6	Presence of Chinese TNCs in 2005 Fortune Global 500 and Asian top 50 companies	192
9.1	World trade in parts and components, 1992–2004	213
9.2	Direction of manufacturing trade: total manufacturing, 1992–2004	215
9.3	Direction of manufacturing trade: parts and components, 1992–2004	216
9.4	Share of parts and components in bilateral trade flows, 1992–2004	217
9.5	Direction of China's manufacturing trade, 1992, 1996 and 2004	219
9.6	Intra-regional trade shares: total manufacturing, parts and components, and final trade, 1992 and 2004	221
9.7	Product fragmentation and the structure of manufacturing exports from China, 1994–2004	225
10.1	Expected signs of determinants of complex FDI from parent country to host country	236
10.2	Template for scoring cross-border trade in services	240

10.3	Template for scoring investment	243
10.4	Template for scoring movement of natural persons	246
10.5	Preferential trade agreements and average liberalisation scores	249
10.6	Econometric results for bilateral FDI stocks into broad regions	254
10.7	Econometric results for bilateral FDI stocks into socioeconomic groupings	255
10.8	Econometric results for bilateral FDI stocks into 'geographic' groupings	256
12.1	KLD ratings and indicators for the Domini Social 400 Index	294

Contributors

Sanghoon Ahn is a Fellow at the Korea Development Institute.

Prema-chandra Athukorala is Professor of Economics at the Research School of Pacific and Asian Studies, Australian National University.

Sandor Boyson is Research Professor, Logistics and Public Policy Department, and Co-Director, Supply Chain Management Center, Robert H. Smith School of Business, University of Maryland, College Park.

Edward K.Y. Chen is President and Sydney S.W. Leong Chair Professor of Economics, Lingnan University of Hong Kong.

Zhang Cheng is at the School of Management, Fudan University.

Jason Dedrick is a Senior Research Fellow at the Personal Computing Industry Center, The Paul Merage School of Business, University of California at Irvine.

Philippa Dee is a Visiting Fellow at the Crawford School of Economics and Government, Australian National University.

Dieter Ernst is a Senior Fellow at the East-West Center, Honolulu, Hawaii.

William Foster is at the Next Generation Internet Institute.

Chaodong Han is at the Supply Chain Management Center, Robert H. Smith School of Business, University of Maryland, College Park.

Kenneth L. Kraemer is Director, Personal Computing Industry Center, The Paul Merage School of Business, University of California at Irvine.

Siwook Lee is a Fellow at the Korea Development Institute.

Victor López Villafañe is a Professor at the Department of International Relations, Instituto Tecnológico y de Estudios Superiores de Monterrey.

Ping Lin is Professor of Economics, Lingnan University of Hong Kong.

Juan J. Palacios is Professor and Head, Transnational Studies Program, Department of Political Studies, University of Guadalajara.

Clemente Ruiz Durán is a Professor at the Graduate Studies Division, Faculty of Economics Universidad Nacional Autónoma de México.

Robert Scollay is Associate Professor at the Business School and Director of the APEC Study Centre, University of Auckland.

Djisman S. Simanjuntak is Executive Director and Professor, Prasetiya Mulya Business School, and a Fellow at the Indonesian Institute of Corporate Directors.

Shujiro Urata is Professor of International Economics, Graduate School of Asia-Pacific Studies, Waseda University.

Cheonsik Woo is a Fellow at the Korea Development Institute.

Preface

Launched in 1968, the Pacific Trade and Development Conference (PAFTAD) is an international cooperation forum and at the same time an active research network that groups distinguished scholars from countries around the Pacific Rim. To fulfil its mission, PAFTAD periodically holds international conferences where the most current and relevant issues on trade and economic development in the region are addressed by the PAFTAD academic community. After four decades of sustained effort, PAFTAD has become the most authoritative source of research products and policy orientations on those subjects in this part of the world.

Continuing that long tradition, the 31st Pacific Trade and Development Conference (PAFTAD 31) was held on 10–12 June 2006 in Guadalajara, Mexico, 32 years after the sixth meeting of this conference series had taken place in Mexico City, in January 1974. To date, Mexico is the only Latin American country that has played host to PAFTAD conferences.

The theme addressed at PAFTAD 31 was the multinational corporation and the role it is playing in the configuration of an economy of networks in Asia and the Pacific. Building on previous PAFTAD conferences that focused on related subjects such as foreign direct investment (FDI) and the so-called new economy, in Guadalajara we endeavoured to focus on multinational corporations (MNCs) proper, looking at them as corporate creatures that evolve through time in response to the technological changes they face and the economic and institutional environments in which they operate. The purpose was to examine their organisational structure, their operating logic and the strategies they have adopted lately to cope with those challenges, and on that basis to discuss the rules they should abide by and the social responsibilities they should observe in both national and international settings nowadays.

Many questions have emerged in recent years about the shift from vertical to horizontal corporate structures that became evident in the 1990s, as well as about the resulting transformation of corporations into networks and the contours of the highly interdependent, knowledge-based, networked economy such transformation is giving rise to. Other related issues raising questions that also beg for answers include the emergence of MNCs based in developing countries, the deployment of MNC operations across the Pacific via FDI, the impact of such deployment on regionalism and the regional international division of labour, and the quest for a regulating framework to harness MNC activity in the region. Such answers will enable both scholars and decision makers to discern the required policy responses.

PAFTAD 31 was convened to search for those answers. A committed group of noted specialists from countries around the Pacific Rim gathered in Guadalajara to discuss original work on the issues referred above. Once revised for publication, the papers presented and discussed at the conference became the substance of the present volume, which was assembled and edited with the rigour that has distinguished the PAFTAD series for the last four decades.

I want to express my sincere appreciation to each and every one of the participants in PAFTAD 31, especially the paper writers who came to Guadalajara to present their work and be part of the conference; their papers became the spinal column around which the activities of the conference were organised and developed. I refer to: Sandor Boyson, Dieter Ernst, Kenneth Kraemer, Shujiro Urata, Sanghoon Ahn, Edward Chen, Ping Lin, Victor López Villafañe, Prema-chandra Athukorala, Philippa Dee, Robert Scollay and Djisman Simanjuntak. I gratefully acknowledge too the useful input contributed by the discussants and the efficient work performed by the session chairs. I refer to: Hugh Patrick, Hadi Soesastro, Pang Eng Fong, Peter Petri, Peter Drysdale, Anantachoke Osangthammanont, Yung-Chul Park, Ralph Huenemann, Chia Siow Yue, Jenny Corbett, Yoshitomi Masaru, Akira Kohsaka, Renato Balderrama, Alfonso Mercado, David Hong, Josef Yap, Kyung Tae Lee, Myrna Austria, and Dinh Hien Minh. I also gratefully highlight the participation of Mr Gabriel Padilla, who delivered the inaugural address on behalf of Mr Sergio Garcia de Alba, Mexico's Minister of the Economy, and that of Mr Enrique Michel, former Mexican ambassador to Thailand, Vietnam, Cambodia and the Philippines, who acted as keynote speaker at the conference's formal luncheon.

Likewise, I want to thank the company managers and the representatives of both local industry associations and the Jalisco State Government who generously contributed their time and expertise by participating in the panel on the relationship between MNCs and small and medium-sized enterprises held on the last day of the conference. In particular, I am grateful to Mr Federico Lepe, Deputy Secretary for Economic Promotion, Jalisco State Government, and Mr Pedro Avalos, Chairman of the Western Mexico Office of the Electronics and Telecommunications Industry National Chamber (CANIETI), for the kind support they provided me with in the organisation of the panel and for their active participation in it. I also thank Professor Ralph Huenemman and Professor Peter Petri for contributing a learned introduction that set the framework for the fruitful exchange we held at the panel. This was the first time, as Professor Petri noted, that a session of this kind was included in the agenda of a PAFTAD conference.

Throughout the entire process of organising the conference and putting together the cast of participants, I benefited from the experience and consistent support of Professor Peter Drysdale, Director of the PAFTAD International Secretariat, and from the assistance of Mr Alberto Posso, executive officer at the secretariat, to whom I express my personal appreciation. I also gratefully record the institutional backing I received from the PAFTAD International Steering Committee, in particular from its chairman, Dr Hadi Soesastro, and from Professor Hugh Patrick who, when acting as chairman in previous years, actively promoted the idea of holding a PAFTAD conference in Mexico for the second time. Finally, I would not have been able to carry out the laborious tasks of coordinating and running PAFTAD 31 without the able assistance I received from Dr Maria Elena Romero and from my wife, Mrs Silvia L. Palacios; they efficiently dealt with the event's myriad logistics and operating details and kept it running day to day. I warmly thank them both.

Hosting PAFTAD 31 in Guadalajara was made possible by the generous and crucial financial support provided by Mr Sergio Garcia de Alba, Minister of the Economy of the Mexican Government, to whom I express my indebtedness and heartfelt appreciation. Dr Hector Gomez, Director General for Information Systems, Mr Jeffry S. Fernandez, Director General for Cultural Diffusion, and Dr Juan Manuel Duran, Dean of the Social Sciences and Humanities University Centre, all of the University of Guadalajara, in turn provided me with logistic, technical and material support in key aspects of the conference; I am grateful to them all too.

In like manner, I want to express my deep gratitude to the permanent donors who make possible the fulfilment of PAFTAD's long-term mission and, in particular, sustain the continuing operation of the PAFTAD International Secretariat. It is through the secretariat that these donors provided us with the other critical part of the funding for PAFTAD 31, including that required for the editing of the present volume. The donors include the Japanese Research Institute of Economy, Trade and Industry (REITI), the Asia Foundation, the Ford Foundation, the Australian National University, Singapore's Institute of Southeast Asian Studies (ISEAS), the University of Toronto, the University of Victoria, the Taiwan Institute for Economic Research (TIER), the Pacific Basin Economic Council (PBEC), Indonesia's Centre for Strategic and International Studies (CSIS), the Japanese Foundation for Advanced Information Research, the Japan Federation of Economic Organizations, the Kansai Economic Federation, the Rockefeller Brothers Fund, the Korea Development Institute (KDI), Japan's Ministry of Foreign Affairs, the Canada–Singapore International Development Research Centre, the Australian Agency for International Development (AusAID), the Philippine Institute for Development Studies (PIDS), the East–West Center, and Brandeis University.

Finally, I want to acknowledge the efficient work of Sue Mathews, who acted as the editor of this volume; of Minni Reis, who typeset the manuscript; and of Stephanie Rogers, who coordinated the editorial process on Routledge's end. They turned the original manuscripts into formal chapters and this book into a fine exemplar of high-quality publishing material. We hope it contributes to enhance interest among scholars and policymakers in the study of the network economy that is taking hold in the world at the dawn of the 21st century and the role MNCs are playing in that process.

Juan J. Palacios

December 2006

Abbreviations

$ is US dollar unless otherwise specified

2SLS	two-stage least squares regression
3G	third generation
9/11	11 September 2001
24 × 7	24 hours a day, 7 days a week
AFTA	ASEAN Free Trade Area
APEC	Asia-Pacific Economic Cooperation
ASEAN	Association of Southeast Asian Nations
ASEAN-4	Indonesia, Malaysia, the Philippines, and Thailand
ASEAN+3	ASEAN countries plus Japan, China and South Korea
ASEAN+4	ASEAN countries plus China, Hong Kong, Japan and South Korea
BIT	bilateral investment treaty
CAD	computer-assisted design
CD	compact disc
CDMA	code-division multiple access
CEO	chief executive officer
CITIC	China International Trust and Investment Corp
CPM	comparable profit method
CSR	corporate social responsibility
CNOOC	China National Offshore Oil Corporation
CNPC	China National Petroleum Corporation
DVD	digital virtual disk/digital video disk
EDI	electronic data interchange (also the name of a company)
ERP	enterprise resource planning
EU	European Union
EXIM code	Export–Import Bank code for industry classification (Korea)
FDI	foreign direct investment
FTA	free trade agreement/area
GATS	General Agreement on Trade in Services
GDP	gross domestic product
GIN	global innovation network
GPN	global production network

HS	harmonised system (trade classification)
ICN	International Competition Network
ICT	information and communication/s technology
IISD	International Institute for Sustainable Development
IPRs	intellectual property rights
ISO	International Organization for Standardization
IT	information technology
KIET	Korea Institute for Industrial Economics and Trade
KSIC	Korean Standard Industry Classification
LDC	less developed economy
M&As	mergers and acquisitions
MENA	Middle East and North African
MFN	most favoured nation
MNC	multinational corporation
MNE	multinational enterprise
MP3	MPEG-1 Audio Layer 3
NAFTA	North American Free Trade Agreement
NGO	non-government organisation
NIE	newly industrialised economy
NIEs-4	South Korea, Taiwan, Hong Kong, and Singapore
NOA	National Outsourcing Association
NPD	new product development
NTBF	new technology-based firm
ODM	original design manufacturer/manufacturing
OECD	Organisation for Economic Co-operation and Development
OLS	ordinary least square
PAFTAD	Pacific Area Forum on Trade and Development
PC	personal computer
PECC	Pacific Economic Cooperation Council
PPP	purchasing power parity
PRC	People's Republic of China
PTA	preferential trade agreement/preferential trading arrangement
R&D	research and development
RMB	renmimbi
S&E	science and engineering
SARS	severe acute respiratory syndrome
SITC	Standard International Trade Classification
SME	small and medium-sized enterprise
SOE	state-owned enterprise
TD-SCDMA	time-division synchronous code-division multiple access
TFP	total factor productivity
TI	Texas Instruments
TNC	transnational corporation
TSMC	Taiwan Semiconductor Manufacturing Company
UK	United Kingdom

UN	United Nations
UNCTAD	United Nations Conference on Trade and Development
UNIDO	United Nations Industrial Development Organization
US	United States
USITO	US Information Technology Office
WTO	World Trade Organization
XML	extensible mark-up language
Y2K	year 2000

1 Multinational corporations and the economy of networks: an overview

Juan J. Palacios

THE CORPORATION IN HISTORICAL PERSPECTIVE

Since its inception, the corporation has undergone a series of fundamental changes – in fact, complete metamorphoses – in its nature, legal status, institutional purpose, economic and social rationale, functional logic, and organisational structure, all as part of a dynamic and incessant process of corporate evolution that extends for more than four centuries. From the first joint-stock companies that started to emerge in the 16th century in England, beginning with the Company of the Mines Royal created in 1564 and the Company of Mineral and Battery Works constituted in 1565, corporations evolved into the more elaborate moulds of the large trading companies established in the 17th and 18th centuries, with the English East India Company, the Dutch West India Company, the Royal African Company and the Hudson Bay Company among the most important. These were the forerunners of the modern international enterprises that became a major symbol of the emerging industrial society of the 19th century, which in turn hatched what came to be the top economic icon of the 20th century, the multinational corporation. Multinational corporations (MNCs) started to take shape in 1914 and entered their maturation phase in the 1970s and 1980s (Gabel and Bruner 2003).

Each model of corporate organisation is qualitatively different from its predecessors from which, though, it stems. Sam Palmisano, CEO and chairman of the board of IBM, recently pointed out that 'the MNC of the late twentieth century had little in common with the international firms of a hundred years earlier, and those companies were very different from the great trading enterprises of the 1700s' (Palmisano 2006: 127).

The uninterrupted process of corporate evolution has intensified in the last two decades under the thrust of an unprecedented globalisation of communication signals, transport routes, and economic flows. Since the appearance of what Alvin Toffler (1984) dubbed the adaptive corporation in the early 1980s, a host of corporate creatures have emerged, including the hollow corporation, the network enterprise, the centreless corporation, the *ad hoc* corporation, the extended enterprise, the boundaryless organisation, the collaborative enterprise, the horizontal corporation, the minding organisation, and the knowledge-creating company (Palacios 2001b; DiMaggio 2001b). The latest exemplar is what Palmisano labelled as the globally integrated enterprise. A direct product of the spread of outsourcing, this new creature is said to differentiate itself from both the 19th century international firm and the 20th century MNC in that it inherently aims to supply the entire global market by integrating production and value delivery worldwide and in that it has become simply 'an array of specialised components: procurement, manufacturing, research, sales, distribution, and so on' (Palmisano 2006: 131).

In spite of their seeming diversity, though, all those corporate entities have come into being as a product of major changes along three lines of evolution: (a) a shift from rigid and clear-cut to blurred and porous boundaries between companies; (b) the flattening out of organisational structures and the related transition to more cooperative forms of management; and (c) the adoption of creativity, learning, and knowledge as firms' most valuable assets (DiMaggio 2001c). Firm boundaries have been gradually diluted by practices such as strategic alliances, joint ventures, mergers and acquisitions, and project-based collaborations. As a result, the coordination of production has migrated from within the setting of self-contained individual companies to the collective environment of inter-firm networks. In the language of Ronald Coase (1937), those corporate transformations signal the transit from a world where relationships between firms were coordinated through direct market transactions to a new one where that coordination takes place through network links and strategic associations. The problem is that, as Reinier Kraakman noted, the firms affiliated into networks 'are no longer governed by market transactions, but neither are they fully integrated into a single large firm' (Kraakman 2001: 148).

THE RISE OF OUTSOURCING AND OFFSHORING

The classic make-or-buy dilemma posed by Coase in the 1930s thus seems to have been solved in favour of the buy option. Outsourcing has been adopted by corporations around the world as a convenient and in fact necessary strategy to cope with the needs, threats and pressures stemming from the economic, social and institutional environments of the current era of globalisation and swift technological change. Its force and pervasive influence are such that it has given rise to the creature that, as noted above, embodies the latest stage of corporate evolution, the globally integrated enterprise.

Outsourcing finds its rationale in the advantages of a social division of labour where basic production complementarities are established among firms in a given industry, which thus specialise in particular segments of the industry's value chain. Such division of labour gives rise to horizontal corporate structures akin to flexible, segmented production schemes, while an internal division is consubstantial with vertically integrated and rigid corporate structures typical of mass production systems (Palacios 2005).

More specifically, the outsourcing of repetitive, non-essential operations enables companies to focus on their core competencies and thus make a more efficient use of costly assets; acquire manufacturing capabilities they do not have; reduce risks and costs by shifting heavy investments in a capital-intensive operation (manufacturing) to another company's books; acquire a virtually unlimited flexibility in production, design, and logistics; develop wide economies of scope; improve time-to-market standards and thus successfully cope with shorter product cycles; and realise economies of scale in procurement, enhance their procurement capabilities, and reduce inventory turnover rates and costs (Palacios 2001b).

Therefore, outsourcing is by no means a simple, optional cost-reduction tool; it is a sound and profitable business strategy. Accordingly, it is now a practice common among large corporations and increasingly adopted by medium-sized and smaller firms, to the extent that by early 2004 as much as 90 per cent of US businesses were outsourcing some of their operations (*BusinessWeek*, 11 March 2005).

Outsourcing deals soon extended beyond national borders, leading to the emergence of offshoring as outsourcing's most visible, and debated, modality. Offshoring has itself become a flourishing industry that accounts for about 15 per cent of the global information technology (IT) market (Betts 2006). Offshoring obtains when inputs and/or services are outsourced from providers located in overseas locations. In consequence, it is the vehicle through which corporations are building and/or hooking into continental and global production networks and even becoming global production networks themselves. Offshoring works on a global delivery model that allows companies to tap into competencies offered in offshore locations, providing them with unique advantages of time zones and ease of scaling up, in addition to significant savings stemming from differences in cost structure, wage levels, and economic environment (Palacios 2005).

The big dilemma now is not only whether to outsource or not, but also whether to do it onshore or offshore and whether to do it through a spin-off or through another company located in another country. Corporations have to look at every single activity in their entire value chain and ask whether they are the best at it in the world. If not, they have three options: invest to become the best in the business in question, outsource it to someone who is the best, or move it to a place where it can be done much more cheaply and with a higher quality (Gottfredson *et al.* 2005). In any case, the general rule is to source from the right source and on the right shore.

Therefore, the problem is, ultimately, to identify the functions that constitute the core of the firm – and even the core of the core – and that therefore must be kept in-house. In the last instance, the core of the core is the set of activities which a firm is the absolute best at, that is, functions that are highly proprietary and not common in the industry (Gottfredson *et al.* 2005).

In summary, as outsourcing practices have spread out, stronger linkages have developed among parent firms and their entire corporate ecosystem of partners, suppliers, and customers. This has resulted both in their integration along increasingly larger and more complex value chains and in the formation of more durable and extended production networks among the firms involved regardless of their geographic location. What is occurring ultimately is the gradual but seemingly inexorable replacement of freestanding, individual firms by inter-corporate business networks (Imai 1990; Castells 1996; DiMaggio 2001a) and, moreover, the transformation of the most advanced and forward looking companies into what Häcki and Lighton (2001) dub 'network orchestrators'.[1]

THE AGE OF NETWORKS AND THE NETWORK ECONOMY

All those trends and corporate transformations are key manifestations of the prevalence of a distinct economic order that is powered by microelectronics and information and communication technologies (ICTs) and predicated upon the adoption of flexible schemes of specialised and segmented production. More generally, those trends are part of an epochal shift that began in the mid-1970s and is still under way. It relates to the transition from the old industrial economy of mass production instituted by Henry Ford in the early 20th century to a new order that Alvin Toffler (1980) termed the third wave and others have dubbed the third technological revolution (Mandel 1978), the second industrial divide (Piore and Sabel 1984), the era of 'systemofacture' (Hoffman and Kaplinsky 1988), and even the Fifth Kondratiev (Amin 1994a). From a regulationist point of view, the shift in question corresponds to the transit from the old Fordist order to a post-Fordist regime governed by a new techno-economic paradigm that constitutes the foundation and working conceptual framework of the new economy of segmented production and flexible, demand-driven specialisation (Coriat 1979; Amin 1994b).

This epochal shift is taking place in the latest of the four ages into which human history can be divided according to Toffler (1980): nomadic, agricultural, industrial and informational. Unlike the industrial revolution, which engendered rigid bureaucratic organisational structures, the information revolution under way has given rise to networks as the dominant form of business and social organisation. This has occurred to such an extent that, as DiMaggio (2001c: 212) puts it: 'Today, the network is the central trope of organisational change, just as the assembly line was at the beginning of the twentieth century'.

The world has thus witnessed the advent of what has been termed the 'age of the network' (Lipnack and Stamps 1994). The top organising imperative of this age is to connect people, institutions, companies and organisations, regardless of distance, an endeavour made possible by the ICTs available today. The name of the game now is then 'to augment, amplify, enhance, and extend the relationships and communications between all beings and all objects' by means of a 'widespread, relentless act of connecting everything to everything else' (Kelly 1997: 1). In this context, decision making is being pushed down and out toward employees and customers; hierarchical corporate structures are flattening out and becoming more participatory; and flatter, network-enabled hierarchies are emerging everywhere.

The current epoch was therefore ushered in by the establishment of a powerful IT paradigm and the ensuing configuration of an information-driven, knowledge-based economic order where agency migrates from companies to business networks (DiMaggio 2001a). The basic organisational form of this emerging order, which Manuel Castells (1996) refers to as the network society, is the complex networks of transnational production that are forming around the largest and most technologically advanced MNCs, which are themselves internally organised in intra-firm decentralised networks that are in turn connected to broader inter-corporate production schemes.

The emergence of this new order was perceived by Peter Drucker as early as in the late 1960s when he detected the birth of the knowledge worker and foresaw the crucial role both knowledge and information were to play in the creation of wealth in the years to come (Drucker 1969).[2] He conceived of it as the knowledge economy; therefore, others like the informational economy, the new economy, and the network economy are but synonyms of Drucker's seminal term (Kenney 1997; Leydesdorff 2006).

This networked, knowledge-based economy is said to be governed by new rules that revolve around four realities of the present era: (a) wealth flows from innovation, not from optimisation (that is, it is gained not by perfecting the known but by imperfectly seizing the unknown); (b) the unknown is optimally cultivated by nurturing the nimbleness of networks; (c) the domestication of the unknown inevitably requires undoing the perfected; and (d) the find–nurture–destroy cycle occurs faster and more intensely than ever before (Kelly 1997). Accordingly, the rise of this new economy has been regarded as a revolution even more transcendental and far reaching than the information revolution itself, for it 'represents a tectonic upheaval in our commonwealth, a social shift that reorders our lives more than mere hardware or software ever can' (Kelly 1997: 1).

Acknowledging the already large and growing prevalence of this economy of networks and of the central role played in it by ICTs, the UN Secretary-General is calling for the development of a decentralised 'network of networks' on a world scale as the central goal of a 'Global Alliance for Information and Communication Technologies and Development' (Annan 2006). This initiative is part of the actions the international community is undertaking to build a working platform to carry out the immense, up to now unwieldy, task of governing the cobweb of production networks that are taking shape across the globe, that is, the task of managing globalisation.

MNCs AND GLOBAL PRODUCTION NETWORKS

The rise of a network economy is being driven ultimately by the powerful technologies in electronics, telecommunications and transport developed over the last two decades, which have induced an unprecedented increase in the geographic mobility of productive capital around the world. As noted earlier, the process is unfolding largely through the practice global companies are adopting these days of outsourcing and/or offshoring part of their operations. The resulting intensification of competitive pressures in international product and factor markets, particularly oligopolistic rivalry, in turn adds to the forces propelling the process.

Therefore, the agents guiding it all are the leading MNCs as the largest outsourcers, the primary sources of productive capital, and the top developers and users of leading-edge technologies in the world. Given such technological might and abundant productive assets, MNCs have been able to build a production infrastructure that cuts across national borders and can span the entire planet. In this way, they have become the main weavers of transnational production networks and the drivers and carriers of economic globalisation itself, which is in fact predicated upon the existence of a worldwide assemblage of cross-border, intercorporate production networks.

Global production networks are 'reciprocal structures of co-operation and risk sharing' that entail deeper and closer relationships among territorially non-adjacent, independent economic actors (Karlsson and Westin 1994). More specifically, these networks allude to complex and dynamic business schemes that are built along an integrated value chain, combine the scale economies of large transnational firms with the flexibility and efficiency of decentralised networked enterprises, and have internal matrix relationships coexisting with horizontal links with other firms in the network (Ernst 1997).[3]

Although transnational production networks potentially have a global reach, they tend in practice to take hold in regional settings. A distinct international division of labour is established in each region – mainly in North America, Europe and Pacific Asia ('the Triad') – with lead firms based in high-cost countries coordinating operations in affiliates based in low-cost locations (Ernst 1994; Linden 1998).

MNCs thus play a dominant role not only in the formation and shaping of cross-border production networks but also in the globalisation of world production. As early as the mid-1990s the United Nations Conference on Trade and Development (UNCTAD) observed that globalisation 'is ultimately the product of decisions taken by [global] firms' (UNCTAD 1994: 158). A decade later, Medard Gabel and Henry Bruner, both members of the 'Mapping the Multinational Corporations Project', whose advisory board includes some of the most noted specialists on MNCs,[4] went further to assert that 'Globalisation and global corporations are as interrelated as the chicken and the egg' (Gabel and Bruner 2003: x).

In effect, MNCs have been one of the most influential players on the international economic stage at least over the last half a century. Their influence is not only economic but also technological, political, social and even cultural, so much so that they have been regarded by observers like Gabel and Bruner as the leviathans of our time. Major multilateral economic institutions like the World Bank and the International Monetary Fund, international agencies like UNCTAD and the United Nations Industrial Development Organization (UNIDO), major international non-governmental organisations, and large regional development banks (for example, the Inter American Development Bank and the Asian Development Bank) are highly influential but tend to play a coordinating, supporting role.

As the sources of the productive capital that roams across the globe igniting growth and creating employment, and as the foundries where leading-edge technological innovations are forged every year, MNCs have a pervasive presence and play a truly central role in today's global economy. Of the world's 100 largest economies, at least 53 are MNCs; these large corporations command more resources and exert a stronger influence than nearly three-quarters of the nation-states in place today (Gabel and Bruner 2003: vi). The three largest – General Electric, Vodafone, and Ford Motor Company – jointly own $877 billion in foreign assets, which accounts for nearly 19 per cent of the total foreign assets of the top 100 MNCs (UNCTAD 2006: 31).

The proportion of world economic activity accounted for by foreign direct investment (FDI) – the currency used by MNCs to shop and set up shop around the world – increased steadily from 4.4 per cent in 1960 to 8.5 per cent in 1991 (UNCTAD 1994: 130). The stock of FDI in the world reached $9 trillion by 2004 (UNCTAD 2005: xix).

The number of parent corporations increased from 37,000 in the early 1990s up to 70,000 in 2004 and 77,000 in 2005. In turn, the number of affiliates abroad increased from 170,000 in the early 1990s to 690,000 in 2004 and to 770,000 in 2005 (UNCTAD 2005: 13; UNCTAD 2006: xviii). The number of employees in foreign subsidiaries has grown dramatically as well, from 19 million in the early 1980s to 53 million in 2002, while the volume of sales increased sevenfold during the same period.[5] In 2005, MNCs' foreign affiliates generated $4.5 trillion in value added, employed some 62 million workers, and exported goods and services valued at more than $4 trillion (UNCTAD 2006: xviii).

By deploying affiliates and contracting the services of myriad suppliers in locations around the world, MNCs have established an international portfolio of locational assets interlinked by functional relationships along their respective value chains (Palacios 2001b; UNCTAD 1993b). In this way they have propelled the formation of an integrated international system of shared production that is giving way to a much deeper geographical and functional integration of national economies than that produced by simple commercial transactions. It is this integrated system that constitutes the working framework for economic globalisation, which literally stands for the process where 'a growing number of national economies become mutually interconnected through cross-border flows of goods, services and factors of production' or, alternatively, 'a qualitative process of governing an increasingly complex pattern of cross-border linkages' (UNCTAD 1994: 118).

Altogether, the above processes are giving way to the configuration of a global economic architecture that functions through and relies on the existence and workings of a worldwide web of cross-border production networks which, as observed above, take hold along regionally differentiated patterns across the world. This is an unprecedented phenomenon that has come to constitute the most tangible manifestation of the emerging – in fact, already prevalent – information-driven, knowledge-based economy of networks.

THE EMERGENCE OF A NETWORK ECONOMY IN PACIFIC RIM COUNTRIES

Of the world's major regions, the Pacific Rim is the one where the tendency for global production networks to take hold in regional settings has manifested itself most clearly. A distinct international division of labour has been established in this transcontinental region, where trade and investment flows have intensified steadily since Japan and, subsequently, South Korea, Taiwan, Hong Kong and Singapore (the Four Little Dragons), emerged as fledgling economic powers in the 1960s and 1970s. The economies on both sides of the Pacific Ocean have grown increasingly connected and interdependent as a result, and the region has become more and more integrated as the web of trans-Pacific trade routes and production networks has grown in extension and complexity over the years.

The international division of labour has grown more complex too. This occurred particularly on the western fringe of the Pacific Rim, where that division took shape as a hierarchical arrangement of the sort predicted by Kaname Akamatsu's theory of the flying geese pattern of development,[6] as Bruce Cummings characterised it in the mid 1980s,[7] with Japan at the top of the hierarchy. This was due to the fact that such an arrangement was largely moulded by Japanese MNCs in the electronics and automobile industries in the course of the aggressive expansion of their operations across Pacific Asia in the late 20th century, all driven by a quest to achieve ambitious goals such as Mitsubishi's project of building the Asian car (Steven 1989; Palacios 1993). The flock has evolved over the past decades as more flying geese (China, India, and Vietnam) have joined in and others have moved ahead in the formation (Thailand and Malaysia).

The rise of China as an industrial powerhouse in the 1990s further added to the complexity of the geo-economic division of labour in Pacific Asia and the Pacific Rim at large. Over the past several years, massive investments have poured into China as companies from all latitudes have set up shop and innumerable production projects have migrated to plants operating in China from subsidiaries based in countries around the Pacific Rim. The web of economic linkages in the region grew increasingly intricate in consequence, and trading relationships among the economies of both sides of the ocean became 'thicker'.

In this context, it seems that the flying geese model is being replaced by a 'flying dragon' model in which the more dynamic networks woven by Chinese companies will give rise to a different division of labour in the region and China will eventually become the leader of the flock (Edgington and Hayter 2005). In fact, the flying geese metaphor was questioned in the mid-1990s on the basis that it fails to grasp the complexities of East Asia's economic integration, in particular the globalisation of production networks and the rapid pace of technological change as the main forces driving this process (Bernard and Ravenhill 1995).

Significantly, both economic integration and the changes in the regional division of labour in Pacific Asia have occurred largely regardless of the subscription of free trade agreements or other formal arrangements between national governments. This derives from the fact that economic integration and the changes in the regional division of labour have been driven by a pragmatic business logic that is not guided by diplomatic formalities as it refers to the sinking of productive capitals that vie for profitable locations wherever they happen to be around the world (Palacios 2001a). The point to note is that the corporate alliances and business partnerships through which capitals are invested create economic linkages that are more solid and lasting than those involving punctual trade deals and day-to-day commercial transactions. This circumstance has further reinforced the role of inter-firm deals as an effective vehicle for inducing a deep and solid economic integration like the one that has taken place in the last few decades in much of Pacific Asia. Those linkages are precisely the substance inter-corporate production networks are made of.

In sum, the Pacific Rim is the only part of the world where the emergence of a network economy has adopted such unique features. This occurs because of the intense interaction and close interconnections that have developed among the economies located around its vast geographic expanse, a circumstance that is explained by the fact that this transcontinental region is home to the economies that have been the most dynamic in the world for at least the past two decades. An in-depth study of the way the process actually unfolds in this region will thus permit us to grasp the essence of the way a network economy is taking shape on a global scale.

CONTENTS AND THEMATIC SEQUENCE OF THIS BOOK

The present volume endeavours to contribute a first advance in that direction. Taking as its reference framework the trends and developments referred to in the foregoing sections, the book seeks to examine the way an interconnected, information-driven, knowledge-based economy is emerging in the Asia Pacific region at the dawn of the 21st century and the role played by MNCs in the process. It also aims to identify the kinds of policy orientations the development of this phenomenon demands from governments and international organisations in the region.

Studying the MNC has been a relevant endeavour at least since Peter Drucker identified it as a distinct conceptual entity in his seminal *Concept of the Corporation* first published in 1946 (see Drucker 1993). Since then, the study on MNCs has been recognised as a separate academic discipline and is now as relevant as ever when MNCs are playing a central, dominant role on the global economic scene as the leading agents in the creation of material wealth in today's world. In this volume, we probe into the nature of the MNC as it stands today, in order to uncover its functional logic, its corporate physiognomy, and the strategies it is adopting to face today's fiercely competitive markets.

To attain those objectives, this volume brings together a collection of 11 essays written by distinguished specialists in the respective topics from countries around the Pacific. The essays can be grouped into five thematic sections.

Broad trends

The first section discusses broad trends and issues such as globalisation and offshoring in relation to the evolution of MNCs' structure and organisational models, including the rise of production and innovation networks in Asia Pacific. First, Sandor Boyson and Chaodong Han examine the distinct organisational morphology and strategies adopted by MNCs in each of the eras of industrial development they identify, in a study that challenges conventional wisdom on the recent evolution of MNCs, including Boyson's earlier account on the extended enterprise (Boyson *et al.* 1999). They argue that the current transition toward highly networked, highly outsourced enterprises cannot be taken as a trend that can be extrapolated into the future, given the risk of 'predicting the past' that such an exercise implies and the fact that the world is in the midst of a larger transition into the third of a series of enterprise transformations.

The first transformation occurred in what Boyson and Han identify as the 'era of vertical integration', characterised by the spread of the vertically integrated enterprise – epitomised by Ford Motor Company – as the dominant model of industrial organisation which entailed a rigid, centralised control over the entire value chain. Boyson and Han suggest that the second transformation has occurred in what they label the 'era of viral virtualisation', which is presently under way and is already reaching its maturation point. In this era, IT and what Boyson and Han refer to as 'viral outsourcing' have enabled the pooling of assets and capabilities into corporate virtual networks that extend beyond the traditional boundaries of single enterprises. In this context, they hold, a new era of revitalised command has already arisen and is currently taking shape, where the risks and limitations of the over-extended, over-outsourced enterprise have become apparent and a new metamorphosis in enterprise structure and strategy is taking place. In this emerging era, enterprises are becoming more risk-averse, less likely to over-extend themselves through alliances, and more likely to seek direct control over assets within their networks though also to re-strengthen their core. This trend is evidenced by the unprecedented intensification in cross-border mergers and acquisitions.

Boyson and Han argue that each era of enterprise transformation leads to a set of government policy responses with a particular array of instruments, incentives and regulations through which governments in host countries seek to regulate, extract value from or adapt to MNCs. Although the responses pertaining to the emerging era of revitalised command are still in flux, the authors anticipate that, given the increasing interlacing of transnational supply chains, not only MNCs but also host-country governments may seek to assert eminent domain over the operations along those chains. A question arises, though: to what extent can this environment accommodate and be consistent with Palmisano's concept of the globally integrated enterprise outlined above?

In another groundbreaking chapter, Dieter Ernst examines offshoring and its role in the formation and development of production and innovation networks as vehicles of deeper economic integration in Asia Pacific. An authority on this theme, Ernst formulates a new concept – innovation offshoring – which provides a more precise interpretation of Asia's spectacular industrial development. He conceives of innovation offshoring as a practice that goes far beyond the migration of relatively routine services to encompass the creation of new products and processes. It is driven, he posits, by MNCs and in particular by the changes in innovation strategies they are introducing in response to the globalisation of markets for both technology and knowledge workers. By increasing their investment in research and development (R&D) abroad, MNCs seek to integrate geographically dispersed innovation clusters into global networks of production, engineering, development, and research. In this way, Ernst argues, global production networks are being transformed into global innovation networks.

Global innovation networks combine the relocation of innovation operations (offshoring) and changes in the boundaries of firms (outsourcing). By offshoring given stages of their innovation processes to Asian specialised partners and to their affiliates in Asia, MNCs tap into the region's pool of lower-cost and specialised knowledge workers and thus induce their integration into both intra-firm and inter-firm global innovation networks.

On the policy side, Ernst argues that Asia needs to move beyond its traditional role as the world's primary 'global factory' by developing solid national innovation systems that facilitate the development of innovative capabilities at the firm level. In order to benefit from innovation offshoring, he proposes, Asian countries will have to eliminate barriers to trade and investment and establish a robust intellectual property rights regime; at the same time they will have to implement sound policies that effectively attract MNC investment in R&D by ensuring an adequate supply of well-educated technicians, engineers, managers and scientists and, in addition, by creating an enabling business environment that reduces opportunity costs for innovation offshoring deals and enables Asian firms to develop their own innovation capabilities.

In sum, as in previous works, Ernst makes a significant contribution to advancing knowledge on the workings and evolution of global production networks, in this case by providing a first description of the more complex forms the latter are transmuting into (global innovation networks) and the kind of government policies required to both facilitate and foster the upgrading of firms, Asian and otherwise, so as to enable them to successfully insert themselves into broader transnational corporate structures.

Building production and business networks

The second section of the book examines from three perspectives the way in which East Asian MNCs are building their production and business networks, particularly in Pacific Asia. Kenneth Kraemer, Jason Dedrick, William Foster and Zhang Cheng address the role played by ICTs and local *guanxi* in that process in the case of the Taiwanese notebook industry. They contend that the personal computer (PC) industry as a whole is fast advancing toward vertical disintegration as its constituent firms increasingly focus on their core competencies and outsource their non-core functions to other firms specialised in those functions at home or in overseas locations, thereby giving rise to global business networks. Branded PC-makers, the authors hold, become vertically disintegrated through their interaction with subcontractors on a global basis, which leads to the global integration of their supply chains through the use of ICTs; in this way, branded PC-makers are turning into truly networked corporations. In this context, ICTs become the backbone of the global integration of production processes.

Ideally, Kraemer and his colleagues observe, networked corporations rely on real-time digital networks linking customer demand to all the supply-side segments of the value chain. However, the authors challenge that very assumption by asking to what extent that ideal prototype matches reality, a question they set out to respond to by studying the notebook PC industry supply chain. They find that the ideal prototype applies in the case of the relationships between branded PC-makers and their original design manufacturer (ODM) partners. In the segments of the supply chain below the ODMs, though, what occurs is the formation of 'neural networks' of firms that make a very limited use of ICTs and instead rely on personal relationships, more precisely *guanxi*, which constitute the networks' organising principle. In the latter case, the two-way digital supply chain between branded PC-makers and ODMs becomes a narrow one-way stream which completely disappears when coordination between ODMs and lower-tier suppliers relies on social networks and *guanxi* relationships.

Transactions between PC-makers and lower-tier suppliers therefore take place in a system characterised by a high degree of uncertainty which compounds the problems posed by the weakness and complexity of the Chinese legal system. In addition, while ICTs can speed up and improve the efficiency of inter-firm communications, taking people out of the loop can slow the responsiveness of production networks. Therefore, the supply chain tends to become quite obscure for branded PC-makers beyond their immediate ODM and component suppliers.

In general, Kraemer and his colleagues shed new light on the intricacies of the process of network formation in the notebook industry. As to the latter, they found that it consists largely of Taiwanese companies whose high-end activities (management, R&D, product development, IT) are concentrated in Taiwan while their lower-end operations (manufacturing, process engineering, technical support) are largely located in the Yangtze River Delta on China's mainland. Their findings extend those reached in previous studies by Kraemer and Dedrick (Dedrick and Kraemer 1995, 1998, 2005) and constitute a valuable contribution to the understanding of the way a network economy is actually forming in Asia and elsewhere.

From a different viewpoint, Shujiro Urata further contributes to that understanding by providing a detailed empirical analysis of the way Japanese MNCs have developed their production and distribution networks in East Asia, considering their overseas operations in North and Latin America as contrasting evidence. He reports that, contrary to the convention that FDI is undertaken by only large corporations, as much as half of Japanese FDI is carried out by small and medium-sized enterprises (SMEs). Since Japanese MNCs tend to involve domestic SMEs in the construction of their production networks in Japan, the conclusion is that the networks they develop in other countries include those same Japanese SME partners. This implies that Japanese MNCs tend to create enclave-like industrial clusters consisting almost exclusively of Japanese companies in the host countries where they set up shop; a good example is the cluster established by Toyota in Tianjin, China.

Urata also reports that Japanese MNCs first created distribution networks for their products in several countries and subsequently established production bases in those locations, where their affiliates tended to import parts and components from their parent firms in Japan. That occurred because there was often a lack of local suppliers. As suppliers improved their capability for producing inputs whose quality was acceptable to their Japanese customers, and as the number of Japanese affiliates increased, local procurement networks started to develop between the affiliates and indigenous firms. As this type of network expanded and multiplied, larger regional production networks were built in East Asia via arrangements such as technology alliances, production consignment, outsourcing, and other international subcontracting schemes.

In this way, Japanese MNCs have become more dependent on intra-firm rather than inter-firm relationships within their value chain; as a result they have expanded and intensified their operations abroad on a regional rather than on a global basis. This reveals the importance of geographical proximity and intra-firm interactions for the coordination of Japanese MNCs' increasingly fragmented production and distribution processes, and confirms Urata's earlier finding that Japanese MNCs are less globalised and less open than US or European corporations (Brimble and Urata 2006).

Urata concludes that Japanese MNCs face two major challenges: (a) intensified competition from both MNCs and local companies in East Asian host countries as the technological advantages they used to enjoy have been quickly slipping away; and (b) a shortage of skilled workers and the resulting increase in wages in Japan, which make it difficult for Japanese MNCs to maintain key operations such as R&D and the formulation of corporate strategies at home. Urata proposes the use of inter-firm linkages to employ foreign workers both at the MNCs' headquarters and at their overseas affiliates; the formation of technical and managerial talent pools by both East Asian and the Japanese governments; and the development of local parts and component suppliers in East Asian host countries.

Complementing the contributions made by Urata and Kraemer *et al.*, Sanghoon Ahn, Siwook Lee and Cheonsik Woo examine overseas investments by South Korean firms, assessing the economic impact of outbound FDI on trade, productivity, and employment. They depart from the observation that the financial crisis of 1997–98 entailed three fundamental changes in Korea's economic landscape. The first was the transformation of Korea's industrial structure from one dominated by a handful of large *chaebol* with very limited links with foreign firms and domestic SMEs, to one where a host of foreign MNCs entered the Korean market commanding a large influence in many critical nodes of the respective supply chains. This implied a massive restructuring and downsizing of Korea's leading conglomerates, the adoption of outsourcing and offshoring strategies, and the rise of a group of technology-based SMEs which became one of the pillars of the Korean economy.

The second major change produced by the crisis, Ahn *et al.* continue, was the upgrading of Korean firms as they turned from manufacturing to higher value-added activities, thus strengthening Korea's innovation network. The third change was the leap outward into the global market by a small group of vanguard firms in Korea's flagship industries such as semiconductors and automobiles. Although Korea has become more fully connected with global markets, Ahn and his colleagues point out that it continues to be a small open economy with a large external sector, so it has remained critical for Korean firms to seek ways to capitalise on the vast opportunities provided by global markets through FDI and trade.

The authors found no meaningful relationship between outbound FDI and trade, although some appears to exist in the case of high-tech and medium-high-tech industries. On the other hand, they found that outbound FDI in general tends to have a positive effect on employment and total factor productivity, whereas outward FDI into China exerts a negative effect which tends to be suppressed in the case of industries trading heavily with Japan.

As the foregoing chapters show, Asian firms are major weavers of transnational production networks not only in Pacific Asia but also in Pacific Rim countries as a whole. However, this has been changing over the last decade with the emergence of MNCs in countries on both the Asian and the Latin American fringes of the Pacific. In fact, the rise of MNCs in developing economies in general is one of the most recent and significant phenomena in the evolution of multinational firms; accordingly, it is the subject matter of the third section of the book.

The rise of MNCs in developing economies

The emergence of MNCs in developing economies began in the early 1990s when major domestic firms in developing economies started to invest overseas and thus joined the universe of MNCs (UNCTAD 1993a). It is well known that most FDI originates in developed countries, where most MNCs are based: nearly 90 per cent of FDI outflows are accounted for by firms headquartered in the United States, the European Union, and Japan (UNCTAD 2005: p. xix). In recent years, however, the number of developing-country-based firms on the list of the top 50 largest MNCs has increased; in 2001, the list already included four – Hutchinson Whampoa, Singtel, Cemex, and LG Electronics – all based in developing countries around the Pacific Rim. These companies were in turn the four largest of the top 50 non-financial MNCs from developing countries and Central and Eastern Europe in that year.[8] This trend is likely to continue as a growing number of firms in developing economies increasingly internationalise their operations.

This timely issue is examined from two perspectives. Edward K.Y. Chen and Ping Lin approach it from the perspective of the predictions of Akamatsu's flying geese theory, noting that Japan was the first industrialised country to pass on mature industries such as textiles, clothing and electronic products to the then newly industrialising economies of Hong Kong, Singapore, Taiwan, and South Korea. They also point out that Hong Kong was the first developing economy to pass its mature industries on to other developing economies, in the 1970s. On that basis, Chen and Lin examine Chinese outward FDI, identifying the rationale behind Chinese MNCs' investment decisions abroad and their impacts in the respective host economies and the world economy at large. They identify two generations of MNCs based in less developed economies (LDCs) in Asia: (a) those that emerged in the late 1960s in Hong Kong, Taiwan, and South Korea; and (b) those that appeared in China in the 1990s, such as Haier, TCL, Huawei, and Lenovo.

On the other hand, Chen and Lin distinguish four types of Chinese outward FDI: resource-seeking, market-seeking, efficiency-seeking, and strategic asset-seeking investment. They note that strategic-asset-seeking investment is the dominant type. This is because Chinese international firms have to compete with leading western MNCs in the foreign markets where they operate, complement their cost advantages, enhance their competitiveness, and import advanced technology. While it is early for a systematic assessment of second-generation Chinese MNCs, given that they are still at an early stage of development, the authors note that they all strive to become global players. The inference is, therefore, that MNCs from developing countries in general have become potential competitors and so a real threat for MNCs based in advanced economies.

From that perspective, Chen and Lin question the validity of existing theories on FDI and identify three major characteristics of MNCs based in LDCs. One is that, unlike MNCs based in developed countries, LDC MNCs prefer to establish joint ventures with local partners rather than wholly-owned subsidiaries and, more recently, have preferred to go into mergers and acquisitions to gain majority or complete control of the respective ventures. The second is that, whereas MNCs from advanced economies tend to establish subsidiaries worldwide and operate mostly in their home regions, MNCs from LDCs tend to invest within their home region, invest in other LDCs outside their region, or invest in developed countries at earlier stages of development. The third major characteristic of LDC MNCs is the less advanced and less capital-intensive technologies they tend to transfer to host countries.

Finally, Chen and Lin also identify first- and second-generation Asian LDC MNCs. First-generation companies include those from South Korea, Taiwan and Hong Kong, which went abroad with the full support of and protection by their governments. Second-generation companies are represented mainly by Chinese MNCs which started to invest abroad because of the severe competition at home imposed by both domestic and foreign firms; this indicates that such investment decisions are driven by market forces rather than by government protection.

On the other hand, Clemente Ruiz Durán and Víctor López Villafañe examine the rise of MNCs in developing countries on the eastern (Latin American) side of the Pacific, specifically in Mexico. They argue that Mexican MNCs emerged as a result of the evolution of some of Mexico's largest private corporations, which had prospered under the shelter provided by a series of protectionist policies implemented by the successive governments in the long period from the late 1940s to the early 1980s. That protection was counteracted by a series of economic crises that erupted over that period, leading to a deterioration of Mexico's business environment in general. This was compounded by the fact that Mexican companies had little export experience and in addition had to face an overwhelming and direct competition from US MNCs following the enactment of the North American Free Trade Agreement (NAFTA) in 1994. As a result, Mexico did not enjoy the benefits of a flying geese model of development like the one that has prevailed in Pacific Asia, which has facilitated the industrialisation of successive groups of countries in that region from the late 1960s on.

Ruiz Durán and López Villafañe observe that the emergence of Mexican MNCs was part of a new wave of entrepreneurial energy propelled by the enactment of NAFTA, the opening up of the Mexican economy, and the collapse of protectionist government policies, one of whose manifestations was the near doubling of Mexico's business population between 1994 and 2004. In spite of this expansion, total factor productivity sharply declined in the face of heightened competition from countries like China, especially after its accession to the World Trade Organization (WTO). In consequence, Mexico's international position has grown increasingly vulnerable: while the country is still viewed as a low-cost location, cost levels are not as low as in China; on the other hand, however, Mexico begins to be regarded in international circles as a producer of higher value-added goods compared to China and other low-cost economies in Asia and elsewhere.

Despite all the above, a small but growing group of Mexican corporations have been able to extend their operations beyond their national borders. All of them are located in Mexico City's greater metropolitan region or in Monterrey, Mexico's third largest city and one of its industrial centres *par excellence*. In the case of those located in Mexico City, Ruiz Durán and López Villafañe report on Telmex, Mexico's national phone and telecommunications company; Grupo Televisa, Latin America's leading media company; Grupo Bimbo, one of the oldest corporations in Mexico's bakery industry; and ICA, the largest construction firm in Latin America. In the case of Monterrey, the firms they discuss include Cemex, the largest cement producer in both

Mexico and the United States and the only one based in a developing country; Gruma, with plants producing Mexican food products in 13 countries, including Australia, China and, soon, Malaysia, Indonesia, and Africa; Vitro, Mexico's largest glass maker; and Femsa, which owns Coca-Cola's second largest bottling plant in the world. The main factors driving those companies and conglomerates to go abroad, the authors argue, are the search for larger and more profitable markets and at the same time the high costs and the lack of government incentives they face in Mexico.

Development of production networks in the Pacific

The fourth section of the book takes up the analysis of the aggregate results of the actions of MNCs geared to the development of production networks in the Pacific. The links between network building and emerging phenomena such as the appearance of segmented international trade, as well as the interconnections among MNC activity, trade regimes and Pacific regionalism, are key phenomena that are assessed in this section.

First, Prema-chandra Athukorala examines the growth of the international fragmentation of production under way and its effects on trade patterns in the Asia Pacific, as well as the challenges posed by the international division of labour produced by such fragmentation for the flying geese pattern of growth in East Asia. Athukorala observes that trade in parts and components – what he calls fragmentation-based trade – used to be associated with FDI but that fragmentation practices recently began to spread beyond the domain of MNCs. This has occurred as MNCs have begun to subcontract some activities with local firms, as other firms outside the MNCs' networks have begun to procure components globally as well, and as other MNCs in electronics and related industries are relying increasingly on independent contract manufacturers for the operation of their global production networks.

Athukorala finds that the specialisation of countries produced by this fragmentation of production has become an integral part of East Asia's economic landscape, as trade in parts and components has been expanding more rapidly than conventional final-good trade. He notes that the degree of dependence on this new form of international specialisation is larger in East Asia than in Europe and North America. In this context, the rapid integration of China into East Asia's regional division of labour via its participation in regional production networks defuses the widespread fear that its integration into the global economy will deprive other countries of opportunities for international specialisation.

Athukorala concludes that what he calls network-related trade in parts and components has strengthened interdependence among East Asian economies, though it has not lessened their dependence on the global economy. As a result, he argues, the dynamism of the region as a whole will continue to depend on trade in final goods with the rest of the world. He also asserts that East Asian countries should pursue policies that promote economic openness, because trade-distorting effects of the rules of origin included in free trade agreements (FTAs) are more detrimental to fragmentation-based trade than to conventional final-good trade. Finally, Athukorala argues that a multilateral liberalisation along WTO lines is the best policy Pacific countries can adopt to reap the benefits offered by such fragmentation-based division of labour for trade expansion. This is because product fragmentation strengthens the case for a global, rather than a regional, approach to trade and investment policymaking.

Addressing a related issue, Philippa Dee sets out to determine empirically whether there is a unique regional model of FDI in the Asia Pacific region and to assess the role the 'complex network behaviour' of MNCs plays in its configuration. In addition she seeks to determine empirically the influence of investment provisions in preferential trade agreements (PTAs) on MNCs' regional investment behaviour in the region.

Dee observes that, unlike in previous decades, it is now well recognised that both FDI and trade respond to the forces of economic geography: those that tend to promote geographic concentration of production and those that tend to do the opposite. She adds that it is MNCs that make the decisions that determine trade and investment patterns. She argues that previous theories of MNC behaviour that distinguish market-seeking horizontal and factor-seeking vertical FDI, including those combining the two kinds of motivations, look too simplistic in light of experiences like that of Hong Kong clothing and textile entrepreneur Victor Fung, whose company behaves in a way that Dee believes is better described in network terms, rather than as simple horizontal or vertical FDI.

In general, Dee finds that there is in fact a pattern of investment unique to the Asia Pacific region, because FDI in the region responds clearly to the forces of economic geography. Comparative advantage is an important driving force but it is mitigated by economies of scale and transport costs. This pattern, Dee says, emerges most neatly for the ASEAN+4 grouping (ASEAN countries plus China, Hong Kong, Japan and South Korea) and is absent in the APEC region as a whole.

On the other hand, Dee reports that FDI into Asian countries adopts network characteristics to the extent that the PTAs between source countries and third-party economies facilitate investment linkages when the corresponding economic interactions take place within a network. In general, though, Dee notes that when FDI and trade are sufficiently driven by fundamentals – as it occurs in the Asia Pacific region – in a way where both FDI and trade benefit from comparative advantage but subject to considerations of economies of scale and transport costs, the resulting network patterns of investment are not necessarily boosted by investment provisions of PTAs. These network patterns can be sufficiently strong to insulate a country from investment diversion when the FDI source countries sign PTAs with third parties. Therefore, Dee's conclusion is that the investment provisions of PTAs pose neither a threat nor a promise to FDI in Asia. In contrast, when FDI and trade are not sufficiently driven by fundamentals, as is the case in Latin America, the investment provisions of PTAs signed by host countries with source economies have little real effect, as in the case of NAFTA.

Corporate governance and corporate social responsibility

The fifth and last section of the book addresses two timely issues that are the object of heated debate and discussion in both scholarly and corporate circles nowadays, namely corporate governance and corporate social responsibility (CSR). First, Robert

Scollay addresses the former with particular reference to the Pacific Rim, focusing on three aspects – competition policy, taxation and investment agreements – and touching upon CSR as a fourth relevant aspect for this theme.

The possibilities for instituting global or multilateral rules and agencies that can address issues relating to cross-border operations and the impacts of anti-competitive practices of MNCs are not large, Scollay reports, adding that the attempt to introduce competition policies into the agenda of the WTO has failed so far. The prospects are particularly dim in the Asia Pacific region given the existence of several distinct models of MNC structure and operation and the wide differences in legal traditions, capacities, and business cultures prevailing in the region; thus an alternative 'principles-based' approach seems to be the only acceptable option. What prevails in the world then, he says, is a situation where it is in the economic interests of the major players (the United States and the European Union) to prefer bilateral cooperation over global arrangements. This situation creates an adverse environment for small and powerless countries.

Scollay observes that bilateral investment treaties (BITs) have proliferated in recent years, as have PTAs which increasingly include investment provisions. He also notes that both BITs and PTAs fall short of imposing standards of conduct on foreign investors. The Asia-Pacific Economic Cooperation (APEC) forum upholds a set of non-binding investment principles which state that the regulation of foreign investor behaviour remains the competence of host governments and, where relevant and appropriate, of home governments. The author notes that some progress is likely to be made in this direction with the introduction of CSR provisions and obligations in BITs. The problem is that those provisions have not been accepted by home-country governments because if they are enforceable they may be onerous for potential investors and thus discourage FDI, while if they are non-enforceable they may lack any real practical effect.

As to taxation, Scollay focuses on the strategies to combat transfer pricing by MNCs, observing that if these practices are not restrained governments lose their autonomy in taxation matters and a 'race to the bottom' in tax rates ensues. In this case, governments can opt for the arm's-length approach endorsed by the Organisation for Economic Co-operation and Development (OECD), or for a profit-oriented approach which allows governments to adjust the profits of MNCs according to their taxation policies. In either case, Scollay holds, government cooperation promises to produce a more favourable outcome; the problem is that the required incentives for cooperation do not always exist.

Therefore, Scollay concludes, formal regulation of MNC activity will continue to depend on the enforcement of corporate governance regulations by national governments in both home and host countries. Regular consultations and the sharing of information, experiences and ideas among governments can provide some scope for informal cooperation to improve those practices. Competition in international capital and product markets and the activities of NGOs can also help to make progress in that direction.

Complementing Scollay's analysis, Djisman S. Simanjuntak addresses the complex and multidimensional theme of CSR proper. He does it from the perspective of corporations' central mission and *raison d'être*, profit making, which he equates to capital accumulation. Deeming the latter as the corporation's pivotal responsibility around which CSR elements rotate, Djisman points out that in today's environment, where firm boundaries have become blurred, MNCs have to meet other bottom lines in addition to profit maximisation. He notes that in past decades MNCs were questioned for abuses related to labour rights and for their involvement in corruption practices, but that today they are also questioned for their actions in relation to issues that range from environmental degradation to greenhouse gas emissions and over-fishing abuses; therefore they have to reinvent themselves in order to harmonise their interests with those of their stakeholders.

It is in that context that CSR has come to the fore as an increasing demand on corporations. First conceived of in the 1970s when developing countries strove to institute a code to restrict MNC activity as part of a 'new international economic order', CSR principles were first adopted by the OECD in its Guidelines for Multinational Enterprises issued in 1976, and later by the United Nations in the so-called 'Global Compact' launched in 2000. Djisman defines CSR as corporations taking responsibility for their actions or inactions and being accountable not only to their shareholders but also to a very wide range of stakeholders, including employees, customers, suppliers, subsidiaries and affiliates, joint-venture partners, local communities, and neighbourhoods.

Though the concept of CSR still meets with resistance, Djisman reports, a large and growing number of corporations have embraced CSR principles, especially in the United States and Europe; more than half of the Fortune Global 250 largest firms issue CSR reports in addition to their annual financial reports. In Pacific Rim countries, governments on the western side of the region have done more than those on the eastern fringe to push for progress in both CSR and corporate governance, particularly after the crisis of the late 1990s. This push occurred, the author contends, as a result both of a major transfer of asset ownership from governments to corporations so that the responsibility of MNCs now stretches far beyond the bottom line of profit making, and of the globalisation of MNC operations itself. Further progress, Djisman posits, requires actions and initiatives that need to be undertaken simultaneously. Above all, governments should introduce CSR priorities into national laws and regulations both unilaterally and through regional and global institutions; at the same time, governments should create within these institutions incentives for voluntary observance of CSR principles by business associations, the corporate community, the press, and NGOs.

KEY MESSAGES AND TOPICS FOR FUTURE RESEARCH

Collectively, the analyses contained in the 11 chapters reviewed in the foregoing paragraphs present conceptual insights and empirical evidence that provide the reader with an informed and essential understanding of both the process of network formation and the ways in which an economy of networks is emerging in the Asia Pacific region, all from the perspective of the role played by MNCs in this ongoing process. In particular, long-needed light is shed on the increasing fragmentation of production processes that occurs in the region thanks to the boundless possibilities opened up by MNCs' use of outsourcing as a strategy to contract out a growing number of corporate functions to specialised providers located at home or abroad. The distinct geographic patterns described by those processes, shaped by the spread of the resulting production segments in locations throughout the Pacific Rim, are also illuminated in the book.

The migration of myriad production and design projects from advanced economies around the Pacific to low-cost hotspots like China, Vietnam and some Central American countries further contributes to the growth and intricacy of trans-Pacific corporate production networks, as examined in these pages. In that context, younger MNCs are sprouting in the more advanced developing economies on both sides of the Pacific. As a result of it all, the international division of labour in the region as a whole has undergone major changes and rearrangements, thereby growing in complexity and extension in every sense.

Japanese MNCs largely shaped that division of labour and set major standards for corporate development in Pacific Asia. But although they tend to expand on a regional rather than a global basis, we find that product fragmentation tends to strengthen the case for a global approach to the formulation of investment and trade policies. In fact, one of the general messages in the book is that a bilateral or even a regional approach is not well accepted for orientating policies aimed at promoting cooperation and collective policymaking in the region; instead, a multilateral, principles-based approach to collective action seems to be the most suitable and acceptable option, especially for reaping the benefits offered by a trade fragmentation-based division of labour like the one prevailing in Pacific Asia. Another key message is that the opposite occurs regarding the enforcement of corporate governance rules and CSR standards, where a unilateral approach seems to be the only feasible course of action.

Therefore, the most sensible approach appears to be one that leads to the construction and refinement of an institutional framework that rests on a set of non-binding rules and regulations consistent with a multilateral approach, which at the same time can accommodate the pre-eminence of national governments in the management of corporate governance and CSR matters. In principle this conclusion strengthens the case for APEC, but insofar as the latter is a regional organisation, it is questionable whether it will continue to be an effective mechanism for advancing cooperation goals in the Pacific region in light of Scollay's and Djisman's findings just referred to.

Such a multilateral approach is also in line with the prediction of Boyson and Han that in the current era of revitalised command host-country governments will tend to assert eminent domain over the segments of the global supply chains – that is, the inter-firm production networks – that operate in their territories. The question emerges though as to who actually governs each network taken as a whole across national and firm boundaries. For the time being, this question remains unanswered and thereby defines a most relevant research area within this theme.

Other research endeavours are needed too. One is a comprehensive assessment of the international division of labour actually prevailing nowadays in both Pacific Asia and the Pacific Rim at large. Such an assessment should provide an up-to-date characterisation of that division and a new classification of Pacific economies according to their production and technological capabilities as well as of the role each plays in the region's economic apparatus. It should also permit us to determine to what extent the current arrangement matches the flying geese pattern predicted by Akamatsu's theory and in this way to test the latter in the context of the early 21st century. This is a relevant endeavour in view of the charge that this theory fails to take account of the globalisation of production networks and therefore fails to grasp the complexities of economic integration in Pacific Asia today. The analysis should also include an assessment of the actual gains and potential disadvantages entailed by the hierarchical arrangement envisaged by that theory for developing countries in the Pacific Rim area.

In addition, a particular research effort should be devoted to mapping out the transnational production networks that have been formed across the Pacific Rim along the supply chains of the most significant and dynamic industries operating in the region. This effort should include detailed studies on the geographic distribution of the production facilities deployed in Pacific Asia by the companies in each industry and their connections with plants located in the Americas. A separate effort to measure and map out offshoring arrangements is also in order, with specific studies by sub-region – for example, Northeast Asia, Southeast Asia, North America, Latin America – and for the Pacific Rim as a whole.

Regarding the agents in charge of those processes, further work is needed on the factors driving domestic firms in developing countries around the Pacific Rim to go multinational, including the obstacles they have to overcome in each case. Such research should be done in a comparative fashion so as to assess the influence of national environments on the efforts of developing country firms to extend their operations beyond their national borders and thus discern the policy measures required in each setting to support and regulate those efforts. Also required is a study of the various modalities adopted by MNCs in the region in order to identify their differences and similarities in each sub-region. This will allow us to see whether it makes sense to talk about Japanese, Chinese, Korean, Taiwanese, Australian, Mexican or US multinationals as well defined national corporate prototypes. Finally, equally needed is an assessment of the extent to which MNCs in advanced Pacific countries have become close to Palmisano's prototype of the globally integrated enterprise (Palmisano 2006), with an eye to determining whether this latest exemplar of corporate evolution embodies the full materialisation of the ongoing conversion of corporations into networks, first predicted by Ken'ichi Imai in 1990.

All those studies would jointly provide a solid empirical platform and a sound conceptual framework for a more detailed and comprehensive account of both the modalities adopted and the extent reached by the economy of networks in this region. After all, the Pacific Rim is in many respects the most eloquent and significant showpiece of the manifestations of this overarching trend that is taking hold in regional settings around the world at the dawn of what for long has been known as the 'Pacific Century'.

NOTES

1. Network orchestrators, of which Cisco and eBay are typical examples, tend to build a 'gated network' of contract manufacturers and suppliers, which they govern through their own proprietary extranets. Thus, network orchestrators own fewer assets, leverage more efficiently the resources of partner companies, require less capital, and return higher revenue per employee than conventional companies (Häcki and Lighton 2001).
2. Three decades later Drucker argued that the knowledge economy is giving way to a new society whose key productive resource is knowledge and where knowledge workers are the dominant group in the workforce. It is supposed to be a highly competitive, borderless society because knowledge moves faster than money or productive resources; it will facilitate upward social mobility because formal education will be available to everyone; and, therefore, through knowledge, it will provide anyone with the means to succeed or to fail (Drucker 2001).
3. A typical global production network includes a lead firm, its subsidiaries and affiliates, its joint ventures, its suppliers and subcontractors, its marketing and distribution channels, and its technological allies. The lead company bases its position on 'the intellectual property and know-how associated with setting, maintaining and continuously upgrading a *de facto* market standard' (Ernst 1997: 20).
4. They include professors John Dunning, Stephen Kobrin, Geoffrey Jones, and Mira Wilkins.
5. See <http://globstat.UN-DTCI.org>.
6. Akamatsu's first formulations were written in Japanese in the 1930s and published in English in the early 1960s (Kalotay 2004; Akamatsu 1961). Akamatsu's model has been applied and further elaborated in other studies such as those by Kojima (1973, 2000), Hayter and Edgington (2004), and Kalotay (2004). Its expanded version states that as host countries industrialise and upgrade their economies, the character of investments from home countries changes and those investments are directed to higher-end processes; thus, lower-end activities are gradually transferred from those industrialised host countries to newcomers.
7. Cummings argued that national economies in this region follow a development trajectory where each one replicates the model and strategies adopted by those ahead in the formation, which has been regarded as a product cycle explanation of East Asian industrialisation by commentators like Bernard and Ravenhill (1995).
8. See <http://globstat.UN-DTCI.org>.

REFERENCES

Akamatsu, Kaname (1961) 'A theory of unbalanced growth in the world economy', *Weltwirtschaftliches Archiv*, 86(2): 196–217.

Amin, A. (1994a) 'Post-Fordism: models, fantasies and phantoms of transition', pp. 139 in A. Amin (ed.) *Post-Fordism: A Reader*, Oxford: Blackwell Publishers.

—— (1994b) *Post-Fordism: A Reader*, Oxford: Blackwell Publishers.

Annan, K. (2006) 'Translate vision of global information society into reality', remarks by the UN Secretary-General on a new global alliance, New York, United Nations Headquarters, September 27; see <http://www.un.org/News/Press/docs/2006/sgsm10662.doc.htm>.

Bernard, M. and J. Ravenhill (1995) 'Beyond product cycles and flying geese: regionalization, hierarchy, and the industrialization of East Asia', *World Politics*, 47(2): 171–209.

Betts, M. (2006) 'Offshoring: not a passing phase', *Computerworld*, 22 February, <http://www.computerworld.com>.

Boyson, S., T.M. Corsi, M.E. Dresner, L.H. Harrington and E. Rabinovich (1999) *Logistics and the Extended Enterprise*, New York: John Wiley & Sons.

Brimble, P. and Shujiro Urata (2006) 'Behavior of Japanese, Western, and Asian MNCs in Thailand: lessons for Japanese MNCs', paper presented at the International Workshop on MNCs' Activities, Japan Center for Economic Research, 1 June.

Castells, M. (1996) *The Rise of the Network Society*, Oxford: Blackwell Publishers.

Coase, R. (1937) 'The nature of the firm', *Economica*, 4: 386–405.

Coriat, B. (1979) *El Taller y el Cronómetro: Ensayos sobre el Taylorismo, el Fordismo y la Producción en Masa* [The Workshop and the Robot: Essays on Taylorism, Fordism, and Mass Production], México: Siglo XXI Editores.

Dedrick, J. and K.L. Kraemer (1995) 'National technology policy and computer production in Asia-Pacific countries', *The Information Society*, 11: 29–58.

—— (1998) *Asia's Computer Challenge: Threat or Opportunity for the United States and the World?*, Oxford: Oxford University Press.

—— (2005) 'The impacts of IT on firm and industry structure: the personal computer industry', *California Management Review*, 47(3): 122–142.

DiMaggio, P. (ed.) (2001a) *The Twentieth-First Century Firm: Changing Economic Organization in International Perspective*, Princeton: Princeton University Press.

—— (2001b) 'Introduction: making sense of the contemporary firm and prefiguring its future', pp. 3–30 in P. DiMaggio (ed.), *The Twentieth-First Century Firm: Changing Economic Organization in International Perspective*, Princeton: Princeton University Press.

—— (2001c) 'Conclusion: the future of business organization and paradoxes of change', pp. 210–243 in P. DiMaggio (ed.), *The Twentieth-First Century Firm: Changing Economic Organization in International Perspective*, Princeton: Princeton University Press.

Drucker, P. (1969) *The Age of Discontinuity: Guidelines to Our Changing Society*, New York: Harper and Row.

Drucker, P.F. (1993) *Concept of the Corporation*, Piscataway NJ: Transaction Publishers. (reprint of the 1946 edition)

—— (2001) 'The next society', *The Economist*, 1 November; see <http://www.economist.com/surveys/displayStory.cfm?story_id=770819>.

Edgington, D.W. and R. Hayter (2005) 'Japanese electronics firms in Southeast Asia and China: patterns of bargaining, cultural learning and embeddedness', paper presented at the 19th Pacific Regional Science Conference, 25–28 July, Nihon University, Tokyo.

Ernst, D. (1994) 'Carriers of regionalization? The East Asian production networks of Japanese electronics firms', *Working Paper # 73*, Berkeley Roundtable on the International Economy, University of California at Berkeley.

—— (1997) 'From partial to systemic globalization: international production networks in the electronics industry', *Working Paper # 98*, Berkeley Roundtable on the International Economy, University of California at Berkeley.

Gabel, M. and H. Bruner (2003) *Global Inc.: An Atlas of the Multinational Corporation*, New York: The New Press.

Gottfredson, M., R. Puryear and S. Phillips (2005) 'Strategic sourcing: from periphery to the core', *Harvard Business Review*, 1 February, HBR OnPoint Article, No. 8878.

Häcki, R. and J. Lighton (2001) 'The future of the networked company', *The McKinsey Quarterly*, 3; see <http://www.mckinseyquarterly.com/article_page.aspx?ar=1091&L2=21&L3=1&srid=17&gp=0>.

Hayter, R. and D.W. Edgington (2004) 'Flying geese in Asia: the impacts of Japanese MNCs as a source of industrial learning', *Tijdschrift voor Economische en Sociale Geografie*, 95(1): 3–26.

Hoffman, K. and R. Kaplinsky (1988) *Driving Force: The Global Restructuring of Technology, Labour, and Investment in the Automobile and Components Industries*, Boulder CO: Westview Press.

Imai, Ken'ichi (1990) *The Information Network Society*, Tokyo: Chikuma Shobo [cited in Castells, 1996, p. 165].

Kalotay, Kálmán (2004) 'The European flying geese: new FDI patterns for the old continent?', *Research in International Business and Finance*, 18: 27–49.

Karlsson, C. and L. Westin (1994) 'Patterns of a network economy: an introduction', pp. 1–12 in B. Johansson, C. Karlsson and L. Westin (eds), *Patterns of a Network Economy*, Berlin: Springer-Verlag.

Kelly, K. (1997) 'New rules for the new economy', *Wired,* 5.09, September; see <http://www.wired.com/wired/archive/5.09/newrules.html>.

Kenney, M. (1997) 'Value creation in the late 20th century: the rise of the knowledge worker', pp. 87–102 in J. Davis, T. Hirshl, and M. Stack (eds), *Cutting Edge: Technology, Information, Capitalism and Social Revolution,* London: Verso.

Kojima, Kiyoshi (1973) 'A macro economic approach to foreign direct investment', *Hitotsubashi Journal of Economics,* 14(1): 1–12.

—— (2000) 'The 'flying geese' model of Asian economic development: origin, theoretical extensions, and regional policy implications', *Journal of Asian Economies,* 11(4): 375–401.

Kraakman, R. (2001) 'The durability of the corporate form', pp. 147–160 in P. DiMaggio (ed.) *The Twentieth-First Century Firm: Changing Economic Organization in International Perspective,* Princeton: Princeton University Press.

Leydesdorff, L. (2006) *The Knowledge-Based Economy: Modeled, Measured, Simulated,* Macquarie Park, NSW: Universal Publishers.

Linden, G. (1998) 'Building production networks in Central Europe: the case of the electronics industry' *Working Paper # 126,* Berkeley Roundtable on the International Economy, University of California at Berkeley.

Lipnack, J. and J. Stamps (1994) *The Age of the Network: Organizing Principles for the 21st Century,* Essex Junction VT: Oliver Wight Publications, Inc.

Mandel, E. (1978) *Late Capitalism,* London: Verso.

Palacios, J.J. (1993) 'Inversión e integración regional en el Pacífico: entre los acuerdos y los procesos 'naturales' [Foreign investment and regional integration in the Pacific: between formal agreements and 'natural' processes], *Comercio Exterior,* 43(12): 1128–1138.

—— (2001a) 'Cooperation *cum* integration? The intricate dialectics of Asia Pacific regionalism', pp. 37–59 in Juan J. Palacios (ed.) *Regional Integration and Cooperation in Asia Pacific: Economic and Geopolitical Dimensions,* Guadalajara: Universidad de Guadalajara Press.

—— (2001b) 'Production networks and global supply chains: the rise of the horizontal corporation', pp. 141–152 in Hans-Jörg Richter (ed.) *Innovation und Wettbewerb in der Dienstleistungsgessellschaft-Aufbruch in das neue Jahrtausend* [Innovation and Competition in the Service Performance Society at the Beginning of the New Millennium], Rostock, Germany: Neuer Hochschulschriftenverlag.

—— (2005) 'Global trends in the electronics manufacturing industry: the explosion of outsourcing and offshoring', paper presented at the workshop Innovation Capabilities and Industrial Development: Sectoral Comparisons and Policy Challenges, Tijuana, B.C., 11–12 August.

Palmisano, S.J. (2006) 'The globally integrated enterprise', *Foreign Affairs,* 85(3): 137–136.

Piore, M.J. and C.F. Sabel (1984) *The Second Industrial Divide: Possibilities for Prosperity.* New York: Basic Books.

Shapiro, C. and H. Varian (1999) *Information Rules: A Strategic Guide to the Network Economy,* Cambridge MA: Harvard Business School Press.

Steven, R. (1989) 'Japan's MNCs: the new power in Southeast Asia', *Multinational Monitor,* 10(11): 15–17.

Toffler, A. (1980) *The Third Wave,* Toronto: Bantam Books.

—— (1984) *Adaptive Corporation,* New York: McGraw-Hill

UNCTAD (United Nations Conference on Trade and Development) (1993a) *Transnational Corporations from Developing Countries: Impact on their Home Countries,* New York: UNCTAD (Transnational Corporations Management Division).

—— (1993b) *World Investment Report 1993: Transnational Corporations and Integrated International Production,* New York: UNCTAD (Division on Transnational Corporations and Investment).

—— (1994) *World Investment Report 1994: Transnational Corporations, Employment and the Workplace,* New York: UNCTAD (Division on Transnational Corporations and Investment).

—— (2005) *World Investment Report 2005: Transnational Corporations and the Internationalization of R&D*, Geneva: UNCTAD (Division on Investment, Technology and Enterprise Development.
—— (2006) *World Investment Report 2006: FDI from Developing and Transition Economies: Implications for Development*, Geneva: UNCTAD (Division on Investment, Technology and Enterprise Development.

2 Eras of enterprise globalisation: from vertical integration to virtualisation and beyond

Sandor Boyson and Chaodong Han

INTRODUCTION

> There is a defect in the art of technology assessment: the lack of a sense of depth in time. It is understandable not only because most systems analysts are trained either in engineering or in the social sciences that normally take a flat contemporary view of phenomena, but also because the concrete problems set before systems analysts for solution look toward future action and discourage probing the genesis of things. (White 1974)

The current mainstream and academic debates on globalisation and enterprise re-engineering have largely focused on the recent transition of enterprises to highly networked and outsourced entities. Certainly, the meteoric and highly visible rise of China and India as first low-cost, then advanced manufacturing and service workshops has accelerated this enterprise transition. Information technology (IT)-enabled extended enterprise supply chains and an associated third-party logistics industry capable of executing elaborate global business choreographies have also attracted the attention of analysts. These realities have framed the debate about the future of the corporation.

Yet we run the risk of 'predicting the past' if we assume that this trend can be merely extrapolated into the future. We can make serious misjudgments if we base our analytical judgments on a static view of enterprise globalisation. In this chapter, we argue that we must step back from the particularly frenzied pace of today and recognise that we are in the midst of a larger transition. We are currently moving into the third of a series of enterprise transformations that have occurred within the last 100 years or so and that have focused on new modes of globalisation and new extensions of corporate value-generating capabilities.

The first era of enterprise globalisation was the era of vertical integration. It was characterised by the spread and dominance of the vertically integrated enterprise as the best-practice model of industrial organisation. This model provided senior management with a high level of strategic control over the end-to-end value chain.

The second era of enterprise globalisation has been the era of 'viral virtualisation'.[1] We are currently near the end of this stage. IT and pervasive, viral outsourcing have enabled the pooling of assets and capabilities into multi-enterprise virtual networks well beyond the formal/traditional boundaries of any single enterprise. This business model can drive cost efficiencies and operational flexibility across global enterprises when executed selectively and in a balanced way, but at the level of the corporate suite it has led to a heightened perception of eroded strategic command and control and loss of network coherence.

The next era – that of revitalised command – is already upon us. The emerging emphasis is on corporate risk management. Enterprises are re-calibrating their globalisation strategies and strengthening the core of their organisations as the risks of the over-extended and over-outsourced enterprise have come into sharper focus. Executives today are struggling to internalise the lessons of the present era, an era characterised by the disruptions of Y2K, 9/11, severe acute respiratory syndrome (SARS), the Asian tsunami and Hurricane Katrina.

Most of this chapter is a detailed analysis of the transformation of the enterprise business model in the past 100 years or so, focusing on the three eras mentioned above. Sections at the end of the chapter suggest how governments might apply the lessons learned to public policy, particularly in the Asia Pacific region.

THE ERA OF VERTICAL INTEGRATION

The Ford Motor Company[2]

The Ford Motor Company was perhaps the first and largest truly global industrial corporation. The way in which it organised its production and supply chain as a completely vertically integrated system in the early 1920s set the stage for many practices used by the modern corporation. Box 2.1 provides a timeline of major Ford activities. Here, we examine the first-generation multinational enterprise globalisation practices.

Manufacturing

In 1896 Henry Ford built a quadricycle in his Bagley Avenue garage in Detroit. He added a chassis and created the Model T in 1908. He moved into volume production at his first Highland Park plant, with assembly lines where parts were put together on sawhorses and where workers towed chassis by hand along tracks. By 1914, the Detroit, Michigan, manufacturing complex sat on 965 acres (390 hectares), including 205½ acres (83 hectares) under one roof. This plant or similar ones produced the Model T the world over, including in England, China, Japan and Indonesia. With over 54 miles (87 kilometres) of conveyer belts moving components along the assembly line, the Detroit manufacturing complex was the most modern and revolutionary of its time. It used a large-scale, quality-management technique of manufacture called mass production to produce Model T cars. Its metrics of performance were the benchmarks of the day: it took 48 hours from iron ore to completed vehicle; the innovation of the assembly line in 1914 resulted in a 550 per cent productivity improvement, to 7,000 cars a day in its Detroit manufacturing plant; and this productivity improvement enabled Ford to drop the Model T price from $800 to $500 and to increase hourly wages from $2.40 to $5.00.

Box 2.1   Milestones in Ford's evolution across three eras of enterprise globalisation

Year	Milestone
1903	Ford Motor Co. founded First Ford Model A produced Ford cars exported to Britain and Japan
1904	Opened operations in Ontario, Canada Made first foreign-made cars
1908	Opened sales branch in Paris
1911	Opened assembly plant in Manchester, England
1913	Signed contracts to sell Model T in China, Indonesia and other Southeast Asian countries
1916	Opened an assembly plant in Buenos Aires, Argentina
1917	Rouge plant under construction in Dearborn, Michigan, allowing the complete production of vehicles from raw materials processing to final assembly
1920	Bought DTI railroad to control transport of materials and supplies to its Rouge plant in Dearborn
1923	Bought thousands of acres of forestland for supplying lumber for Model T
1925	Formed Ford Japan to implement an assembly line in Asia, assembling about 10,000 vehicles a year with imported components until the 1930s (operations there ceased due to World War II but started again in the mid-1970s)
1926	Established an assembly plant in Berlin, Germany Founded Ford Australia
1928	Formed Ford Motor Company Ltd to better manage western European activities due to growing production and sales across the continent and Britain
1967	Formed Ford Europe to coordinate car and truck manufacturing and sales in Europe and Africa
1970	Formed Asia-Pacific Auto Operations in Melbourne, Australia
1971	Formed North American Automotive Operations to consolidate operations in the United States, Canada and Mexico
1974	Formed Ford Latin America in Mexico City
1975	Formed Ford Mideast and Africa Inc. in Dearborn, Michigan
1979	Made 25 per cent equity investment in Mazda of Japan
1986	Acquired 10 per cent interest in Kia Motors of South Korea
1987	Made 75 per cent equity investment in Aston Martin Lagonda; subsequently bought the remaining shares, achieving 100 per cent control of Aston Martin Lagonda in 1994
1989	Acquired Jaguar of Britain
1993	Established first formal dealerships in China
1994	Ford China Operations formed for manufacturing and assembly Ford vehicle assembly began in India
1996	Opened a sales and marketing office in Moscow to serve dealers in Russia Launched the new global mid-size family car (design had started in 1988)
1999	Launched Ford IKON, specifically designed for the Indian market Acquired Swedish Volvo passenger cars for $6.45 billion
2000	Purchased Land Rover from BMW
2001	Started to form joint ventures with Chinese car makers and established a global procurement centre in China
2005	Announced an initiative to halve the number of suppliers for 20 high-impact component systems, representing about 50 per cent of Ford annual production purchases globally

Source: Compiled from information on the Ford Motor Company website and annual reports.

Sourcing

The scope of Ford's vertically integrated global supply network in the early 20th century was remarkable. The company drew raw material from all over the United States and overseas into its plants in the United States, and into overseas branches in Japan (Yokohama), Ireland (Cork), Argentina (Buenos Aires) and Denmark (Copenhagen). The company established lumber camps in Michigan in 1917 and opened coal mines in Kentucky and West Virginia in 1920. In 1927 it established a rubber plantation on the Tapajos River in Brazil that included worker housing, schools, hospitals, testing labs, powerhouses, sawmills, a railroad system, docks, an aeroplane hangar, seaplanes, warehouses, telegraph and radio rooms and a cemetery.

Transport and distribution

To ship raw materials and components to his plants and to distribute components and finished products, Ford bought up inter-modal assets and knitted together a seamless global transport system. In 1920 he purchased the Detroit, Toledo and Ironton Railroad for freight transport; he also acquired the Lima Ohio Locomotive Works for the maintenance of railroads. In 1924 he acquired steamship lines, and he subsequently launched freighter vessels such as the *Henry Ford II* and the *Benson Ford*. Ford also operated dry docks and loading/unloading facilities. The Ford airport was built in 1924 with internal capability to deliver roadster parts from the Dearborn plant to the Chicago Ford branch starting on 13 April 1925 and administrative airmail flights starting in February 1926.

By 1925, Ford's Yokohama plant was assembling 10,000 Model Ts a year and distributing them around Japan. This branch plant template set the style for overseas expansion for many other multinational enterprises in decades to come.

Henry Ford was a visionary but the Model T manufacturing and supply chain was rather inflexible; for example, for many years you could buy only a black Model T. This led to a deterioration of Ford's competitive position. So did the rise of more agile and innovative competitors such as General Motors. This company, led by Alfred Sloan, pioneered the annual introduction of new car models and colours. Ford went from his garage to global corporate CEO to shutting the doors of his Model T manufacturing plant in 1927 – all within 25 years.

But Ford's R&D labs and engineering centres kept going, and by 1932 he had a new product: the first V-8 engine. By 1948, Ford was fully global and operated branches in Argentina, Australia, Belgium, Holland, France, Portugal, South Africa, Spain, Sweden, Uruguay, Brazil, Chile, Mexico, Canada, China, Denmark and Egypt. The pattern of overseas expansion was now fully established.

Transaction economics: driver of the first era of vertical integration

In her sweeping review of the evolution of the automobile industry, Susan Helper (1991) noted that Ford was driven to assume control over the end-to-end supply chain by the erratic performance and inconsistent quality of its suppliers, who had grown up as suppliers in the bicycle industry. The following extracts illustrate the problem.

At Ford during 1909–14, the Company was not then averse to purchasing virtually all of its materials and parts from independent producers. The automaker shared its growing management expertise with suppliers: Ford purchased materials for its components makers, reorganised their manufacturing processes, supervised their larger policies, and, in some cases, aided them in financing production. *The Company became so dependent upon the production of its specialised suppliers that its own operations were frequently within thirty minutes of suspension because of tardy deliveries of parts or materials* [italics added]. In a similar effort to assure supply, William C. Durant at General Motors persuaded parts makers such as Weston-Mott in Utica and Alfred Champion in Boston to move their operations close to his in Flint. Smaller assemblers were even more tightly linked with their suppliers; their designs were so specialised that the bankruptcy of one firm often meant the bankruptcy of the other as well (Helper 1991).

To overcome this dependence, Ford engineered a total supply chain vertical integration strategy designed to ensure continuous availability and the uninterrupted supply of raw materials of high quality free from market changes. (Ford Motor Co. Promotional Film, 1925, National Archive, Ford Production Collection)

Ford created the vertically integrated global enterprise reference model largely in reaction to the economic phenomenon known as spiralling transaction costs. The concept of transaction costs was first defined by Coase (1937), who noted there are ex-ante costs associated with searching for, locating, qualifying, contracting and monitoring external providers. According to van Alstyne (1997), transaction costs define the boundaries of the firm:

… at the point where the marginal cost savings from conducting operations within the firm equal the marginal costs of errors and rigidity. Hierarchies solve these problems by vertical integration and owning the assets they use.

Vertical integration became the dominant enterprise model for stability and control of the multinational enterprise's system of industrial manufacturing. Just as Ford extended its reach to Japan in the early 1920s and set up a mirror-image branch plant with little in the way of indigenous customisation, so other US multinationals established cloned cells in other parts of the world right up to the end of the 1980s. A classic example was in the US pharmaceutical industry, where multinationals established industry outposts in the Commonwealth of Puerto Rico and Ireland. In the former case, by 1988 over 50 per cent of the global profits of US pharmaceutical companies came from Puerto Rican manufacturing subsidiaries that were assigned the patents to the most lucrative, blockbuster drugs by their parent companies. These subsidiaries distributed drugs from the island to countries throughout the world; the retained earnings from the sales were deposited in the Puerto Rican banking system and transferred to the US parent corporations after five years tax free, under the umbrella of section 936 of the US Treasury's Tax Code. In the case of Ireland, the Irish outpost became a launching point for pharmaceutical product introductions into the European Union countries (Boyson 1988).

What shook this first-era vertically integrated reference model to its foundations was the rise of a new type of competitor from the east, a business network model composed of multiple enterprises working closely together in a highly flexible and powerfully efficient manner. Backed by a powerful group of interlocked enterprises (a *kereitsu*), Toyota emerged as the change agent and the template for a new enterprise globalisation reference model. Its mode of operations presented a stark contrast to the 'Ford Way'.

THE ERA OF VIRAL VIRTUALISATION

> The 'virtual enterprise': your new model for success. Vertical integration is out. Today´s markets require a broad fabric of alliances for managing the entire value chain. (Flaig 1993)

The Ford Model T global supply chain was the original concept for the vertically integrated corporation that evolved in the first era of enterprise globalisation. Its supply chain organised demand, production and supply management activities as interlocked chain links that extended across the world. The organisational sub-units and assets that Ford networked were internally owned and operated. Certainly, Ford's commitment to total chain ownership – from mines and lumber to network production facilities, dealerships around the world and its own fleet of ships and trucks – seems antiquated today. Contrast Ford's approach with the virtual supply chain model of companies like Sun Microsystems today. Sun never touches 90 per cent of the server computers it sells globally; rather, an outsourced Sun supplier base receives Sun customer order signals directly and ships orders to the global customer base via outsourced third-party logistics companies (Boyson *et al.* 2004). This contrast between supply chain models highlights the transition from the vertically integrated to the 'virtualised' supply chain described in Table 2.1.

The rapid rise to dominance of network enterprise structures

Whereas Ford and other vertically integrated companies sought to internalise value through increasing corporate asset ownership and through accumulating expertise in-house, Sun and other virtualised companies seek to capture value through a network of strategic alliances with other enterprises and are far more opportunistic in approach. This spirit of opportunism is captured well by Castells (1996). To him, the modern network enterprise is 'that specific form of enterprise whose system of means is constituted by the intersection of autonomous systems of goals' (Castells 1996: 556). After examining business networks in Japan, South Korea and China, he concluded that their networked organisations are more adaptable, better able to use information technology than counterpart corporations in the West and better suited to adopt some of the 'flexible features of the spirit of informationalism'. He defines this spirit as 'a culture of the ephemeral, a culture of each strategic decision, a patchwork of experiences and interests, rather than a charter of rights and obligations' (Castells 1996: 556).

Table 2.1 Characteristics of two contrasting eras of enterprise globalisation

	1900 to the 1980s: vertical integration	1980s to the present: virtualisation
Assets	End-to-end asset ownership	IT-enabled end-to-end asset coordination
Margin capture	Upstream shift in the value chain to higher corporate technical sophistication in products and services	Shift to speed in spotting niche opportunities Orchestration of external partnerships for products and services
Key challenge	Overcome inflexibility of owned assets/sunk costs in a rapidly changing market (the 'Model T trap')	Overcoming fragility and risk of just-in-time systems in an increasingly volatile marketplace (the 'fire at core supplier' trap)

Source: Authors' compilation.

While Castells emphasises the flexibility and opportunism of the networked model, particularly for models arising in Asia, van Alstyne (1997) emphasises the unity of purpose and commonality of structure and process among enterprises participating in the network:

> Network organisations are defined by elements of structure, process, and purpose. Structurally, a network organisation combines co-specialised, possibly intangible, assets under shared control. Joint ownership is essential but it must also produce an integration of assets, communication, and command in an efficient and flexible manner. Procedurally, a network organisation constrains participating agents' actions via their roles and positions within the organisation while allowing agents' influence to emerge or fade with the development or dissolution of ties to others. As decision-making members, agents intervene and extend their influence through association; they alter the resource landscape for themselves, their networks, and their competitors and in the process can change the structure of the network itself. Then, a network as an organisation presupposes a unifying purpose and thus the need for a sense of identity useful in bounding and marshalling the resources, agents, and actions necessary for concluding the strategy and goals of purpose. Without common purpose, agents cannot discern either the efficacy or desirability of association or know whether actions are directed towards cooperative gains. These three design elements – co-specialised assets, joint control, and collective purpose – distinguish network organisations from centralised

organisations, inflexible hierarchies, casual associations, haphazard societies, and mass markets. (van Alstyne 1997)

As mentioned earlier, the emergence of Toyota as a fiercely competitive network model in the 1980s signalled a sea change in industrial organisation. Unlike Ford, with its mass production techniques that focused on scale economies to produce commodity products for a homogeneous mass market, Toyota focused on a model of flow production: this combined flexible automaton and rapid design/product changeovers that could capture economies of scope and meet the fragmenting, diverse demands of a more sophisticated international consumer marketplace. The feature set pioneered by Toyota included the following elements:

- efficient cellular layouts with balanced material flow, whereby each cell produced an entire component, sub-assembly or finished product;
- flexible automation for reduction in set-up time, with changeover times of as little as 15 minutes between products;
- *kaisen* (also known as continuous improvement), which engaged workers in the cell in constant inspection of product rather than having end-of-the-line inspection using sampling techniques;
- multi-skilling of cell workers, who are exposed to all facets of integrated production;
- just-in-time, demand-based pull production rather than the supply-based push orientation of the Fordist model; and
- strategic and operational collaboration with suppliers, including having Toyota personnel work on site at supplier facilities.

Toyota's success was very influential. Its feature set quickly became the new enterprise globalisation reference model and was widely imitated by US enterprises seeking to maintain competitiveness in the face of the Japanese juggernaut. Adoption of Toyota practices had big impacts on enterprise performance, particularly on accelerating cycle times for delivery of goods to the customer and on reducing inventory stocks. This is shown in the results of a 1992 survey of US companies that had adopted the Toyota model (Table 2.2).

By the late 1980s, competition from Japanese car makers had triggered a wave of US auto industry restructuring, particularly of supplier relationships. This led Ford to a return to practices the company had abandoned and almost forgotten – practices buried deep in its own past. According to Helper (1991), Ford's 'revolutionary' approach to partnerships in the 1980s was rooted in an earlier cycle of industrial development at Ford:

> Dramatic changes are under way in U.S. automakers' relationships with their suppliers. Before these changes began in the 1980s, the automakers' dealings with outside suppliers had been characterised by short-term contracts (usually one-year), arms'-length relationships, and many (usually six to eight) suppliers per part. Since 1980, however, the automakers have been moving (albeit in fits and

Table 2.2 Impact of adopting the Toyota model, selected US companies[a]

Lead time	% of companies	Inventory	% of companies
No change	4	No change	18
Decreased < 25%	38	Decreased < 25%	30
Decreased 25–50%	30	Decreased 25–50%	33
Decreased > 50%	28	Decreased > 50%	19

Note:
a The companies were selected as part of a survey conducted by Ingersoll Engineers.
Source: Nyman (1992).

starts) toward a very different supplier relations system. In the new system, only a few suppliers provide each type of part, and information is interchanged extensively between buyer and supplier. Contracts with outside suppliers are increasing in length (three- to five-year contracts are now common), and the automakers are reducing their commitment to their own components divisions, ending such practices as guaranteeing them business and in some cases divesting them completely.

These changes seem surprising on several counts. First, the automakers' willingness to give up power over their outside suppliers in favor of long-term, often sole-source contracts appears to defy economic logic. Second, a reduction in vertical integration at a time when both the technology and the market structure of the industry are in flux seems to contradict the predictions of organisation theorists that vertical integration should rise with increasing uncertainty. Their reasoning is that vertical integration allows decisions to be made sequentially; as the state of nature is revealed, 'internal adaptations can be made by fiat'. In contrast, dealing with a financially independent supplier requires either a contract that provides in advance for every contingency or costly post-contract haggling. As uncertainty rises, so does the number of contingencies and therefore also the expense of contracting. Finally, the new supplier relations cannot be attributed to the discovery of some organisational form never before seen in the United States. In contrast to linear views of history, in which each change must represent a new, improved product, *the recent changes move the U.S. auto industry back to a supplier relations system seen earlier in the twentieth century, when relationships with outside suppliers were close and vertical integration was rare* [italics added]. (Helper 1991: 781)

As Helper rightly points out, the rapid diffusion of strategic alliances in the auto industry during a period of extreme market volatility raised transaction costs. This trend flew in the face of static transaction cost theory, which would have predicted increasing vertical integration. However, US auto makers understood that they were witnessing a transition to a new era and that they had to radically change their behaviour just to keep up with fierce new Japanese networked competitors.

Toyota has remained the benchmark for auto production. Between 2001 and 2006, its shares outperformed those of the US auto industry by 75 per cent. Currently, the value of its outstanding stock is greater than that of Ford and General Motors combined.[3] But Toyota is hardly resting on its laurels. Its president, Batsakis Watanabe (the former head of the corporate purchasing division), was appointed to his present position in June 2005; he took the occasion of his appointment to reaffirm a continued corporate commitment to a 'value innovation' initiative. This initiative seeks to integrate more closely with suppliers; and to streamline design to simplify platforms and reduce the number of sourced components.

Real-time technology: enabler of the networked supply chain

Starting in the mid-1990s, the networked business model was accelerated and enhanced by the development of the web, the deployment of high-speed, high-bandwidth telecommunications networks, and breakthrough integrated enterprise software suites. These developments led to increasingly real-time collaboration across global extended enterprise ecosystems and a quickening of the pulse of end-to-end supply chain management activities.

The Council of Supply Chain Management Professionals defines supply chain management as follows:[4]

> ... encompassing supply and demand management within and across companies and is an integrating function with primary responsibility for linking major functions and processes within and across companies into a cohesive and high-performing business model.

As a discipline, supply chain management provides corporations with three important tools. First, there is a holistic management concept stretching from the point of demand all the way back to the source of supply. Second, there is a process architecture or superstructure capable of efficiently absorbing assets and resources from a range of sources (both internal and external to the enterprise). Third, there are methods to systematically evaluate the costs/benefits and tradeoffs involved in outsourcing/insourcing decisions at each step along the value chain.

The real-time supply chain is the result of highly streamlined physical and relationship networks. It is the apex of intensive organisational investment over many years in innovations such as cross-functional process integration, physical asset network streamlining, inter-enterprise collaborative demand planning and automatic vendor replenishment.

Today, the real-time supply chain is built on the foundation of an integrated IT architecture that extends from sensors in the field of operations to fused transactions and planning applications and web portals that share critical cross-enterprise views among key actors. The IT architecture shown in Figure 2.1 enables information processing simultaneously among all partners – customers, distributors, manufacturers and suppliers (Boyson 2005).

A single event – a customer order – triggers multiple actions at once across the entire global supply chain. This compresses time and costs and can result in orders-of-magnitude performance increases.

An example is Wal-Mart. Wal-Mart's top 200 suppliers now have instant access to point-of-sales data from stores. They can respond in real time to replenish low inventory balances or fill stock-outs based on pre-agreed business rules. This has led to some fascinating supply alliances among competitors. For example, Wal-Mart has facilitated a virtual consortium of fresh tomato suppliers led by Del Monte with participation from CH Robinson, Pikachi and others. Demand signals from Wal-Mart distribution centres are sent electronically to Del Monte and software is used to compare needed quantities of tomatoes with available on-hand inventory balances at Del Monte. If Del Monte does not have enough supply on hand, then automated business rules re-route the demand signal to the next tier of supplier in the virtual consortium, and so on until sufficient supplies are secured and the demand signal is fulfilled.

The real-time supply chain is a fundamental feature of the viral virtualisation era. It is an enterprise technology and business process architecture that has arisen in response to coordination challenges stemming from a recent explosion of demand and supply channels. Customer demand signals today come not only from store purchases but also from phone, mail and website orders. To keep up with this disorderly rush of demand signals, there has been a simultaneous explosion of channels to and from an increasing, collaborative, multi-tiered supplier network. This supply base now

Figure 2.1 The real-time supply chain IT architecture

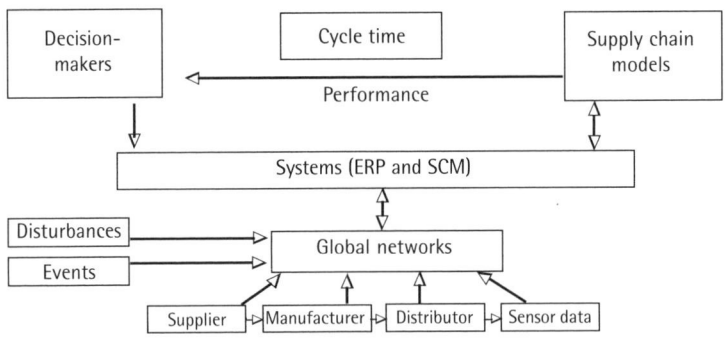

Note: ERP = enterprise resource planning; SCM = supply chain management.
Source: Boyson (2005).

includes core or strategic suppliers, alternative/contingency suppliers, commodity/spot market suppliers and e-sourced/virtual auction suppliers.

The real-time supply chain coordinates and aligns these demand and supply channels. Its alignment activities have been supported by an advanced outsourcing industry comprising third-party supply chain service and technology providers. This highly complex and dynamic multi-channel supply chain is depicted in Figure 2.2.

Imagine how a company such as Home Depot must adapt to this recent channel explosion. Traditionally, Home Depot's *modus operandi* has been to open retail stores across the United States and to focus on servicing the consumer base in the immediate geographic vicinity of the store. However, in the first few hours after opening its web store, its site received 8,000 hits from customers as distant as Asia and Africa. This sudden explosion in demand has required a significant change in mindset on the part of Home Depot supply chain executives. It has not been easy. Channels to and from the customers persist in remaining separate and apart. A refrigerator ordered online by a Home Depot customer in Rockville, Maryland, will not be delivered from the

Figure 2.2 The core model: real-time alignment of supply and demand

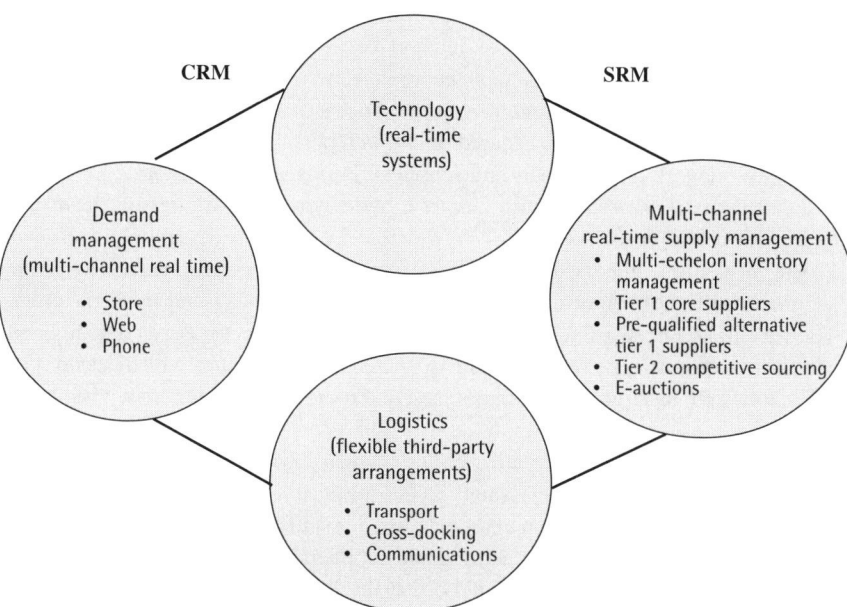

Note: CRM = customer relationship management; SRM = supplier relationship management.
Source: Boyson (2005).

Home Depot store only a mile away from the customer's home. Though this local store has available inventory and an installation technician on standby, the website customer order will be filled from a completely different warehouse and delivery system across the country.

This channel separation stands in contrast to best practices that create both multi-channel demand management repositories with single customer accounts spanning all channels, and multi-echelon virtualised inventory pools that span in-house and supplier inventories and optimise product sourcing and delivery. In fact, the Aberdeen Group (2005) found that 85 per cent of companies that have implemented a unified multi-channel demand management program have gained significant improvements: an average gain of 4.7 percentage points in gross profit margins (23.5–28.1 per cent); a 24 per cent gain in inventory turns (inventory holdings went from 39 per cent of sales to 30 per cent); and a 13-percentage point improvement in forecast accuracy. Similarly, it is typical for companies adopting a multi-echelon inventory solution to drive a 20–30 per cent reduction in on-hand inventory while improving service level reliability (Aberdeen Group 2005).

Some companies driven by competitive necessities have made the transition to best practice in the virtualisation era exceptionally quickly. Kurt Dowling, vice-president of supplier management, Sun Microsystems, said in 2004:[5]

> We went from building 100 per cent of our systems internally to building about 10 per cent of our systems internally in a span of three years.

In Sun's case, the impetus for this urgent, accelerated transformation was survival: it was confronting a marketplace for its products that was characterised by extreme volatility. The dot.com crash reduced demand for Sun's servers almost overnight, with a plunge in demand of almost 400 per cent year to year. The company decided that it had to 'virtualise' and outsource to survive. To maintain organisational coherence, Sun has increasingly relied on a shared online web portal to create real-time channels among its network of customers and suppliers. This is shown in Table 2.3.

In other companies, the impetus to move to the new model of networked organisation and virtualisation has been driven by longer-term competitive needs. Procter & Gamble, the world's largest consumer goods company, is seeking greater alignment with the promotional strategies of Wal-Mart and its other chain customers. The current lack of alignment has been quite costly: the firm carries a company-wide just-in-case inventory of 65 days worth of materials and product, which ties up some $3 billion daily in rapidly depreciating assets. Procter & Gamble's new vision is to become a consumer-driven supply network with 'no lost time, never-empty store shelves, and no stationary inventory'.[6] The company wants to use actual consumer purchasing information to increasingly replace unreliable forecasting data and trigger 'real-time, simultaneous movement of relevant demand data to all network partners – store, warehouse, retailer, manufacturer, and suppliers'.[7] This is shown in Table 2.3.

Finally, let us consider the case of Ford again. It has served as a sentinel example of how far and fast the virtualisation trend has proceeded. Ford's steel supply chain

Table 2.3   Re-engineering to real-time supply chains: two different approaches

Product	Sun Microsystems high-tech electronics	Procter & Gamble consumer products
Supply chain challenge	Need to react to year-to-year spikes or plunges of up to 400% in demand for services	Need for 10–15% average stock-out rates in retail stores
Re-engineering goal	To create a virtual supply chain that can adapt instantaneously to market volatility	Becoming a consumer-driven supply network, with a 72-hour product-to-consumer cycle
Key technology	The single worldwide enterprise resources planning system software, which contains all corporate transactions information and is linked to a huge data warehouse for knowledge management A 50,000-user online supply chain links customers, suppliers, distributors and transporters in real time	Online capabilities give 80% of suppliers visibility into the manufacturing process
Key business practice	Enabling goods to flow directly from outsourced production agents to customers (Sun never touches 90% of what it sells) Reducing the planning cycle from 15 to 5 days and halving inventory levels	Collaborating with chain stores and suppliers to 'sense and respond' to consumer demand, in recognition of the fact that events and promotions by customer store chains generate 50% of sales but cause two-thirds of errors in corporate forecasts

Source: Boyson (2005).

has evolved from a closed, vertically integrated chain in the 1920s to an open, multi-tier network comprising Ford's in-house procurement group, steel producers, and large and small contract manufacturer stampers. This network now involves more than 1,200 participants across hundreds of companies. Currently Ford procures millions of tonnes of steel and more than 2,600 unique parts and components annually, worth more than $1 billion. Ford partners with Newview to host a steel supplier portal through which the demands of the steel stamper supplier community are aggregated. These stamper contract manufacturer suppliers of all sizes can obtain volume discounts through the portal and can share product specification and quality control information with Ford in real time.

Rise of the global outsourcing industry

The growth of outsourcing has been inextricably linked to the emergence and maturation of the real-time supply chain as the top multi-enterprise business model of the second era. This model has become established (in Carlotta Perez's resonant phrase) as 'a new commonsense among managers' (Perez 1983).

Boyson *et al.* (1999) tracked the organisational innovations and the best practices of multinational enterprises in the 1990s that formed the foundation of today's supply chains. They found that virtualisation and the accompanying global outsourcing are part of a larger strategy of supply-chain-wide optimisation enabled by extensive 1990s corporate re-engineering initiatives that set up headquarter supply chain planning and management hubs to consolidate inbound (procurement) and outbound (distribution) flows to gain scale economies in transportation and purchasing; orchestrate business ecosystems (extended enterprise relationships that span thousands of component suppliers and customers); and interact with and strategically control increasingly capable third-party logistics providers for segmented or whole outsourcing of global logistics chains. They also interact with and strategically control other types of globalisation intermediaries, such as production agents (e.g., Li & Fung). These intermediaries have insider knowledge of labour/regulatory regime cost differentials across opening economies in Asia, Latin America and eastern Europe. They provide product design guidance and quality assurance of suppliers and they oversee production for multinational corporation clients.

As a premier production outsourcing agent, Li & Fung organised a far-flung network of external contractors and subcontractors. Li & Fung manage the whole supply chain process and its inter-linked stages: yarn is sourced from South Korea, dyed in Thailand, woven in Taiwan, cut in Bangladesh and assembled in Mexico where zippers sourced from Japan are added on. Final products are shipped to global retail distribution centres. Logistics functions connect these stages and quality control is maintained throughout the entire process (Hagel and Brown 2005). The network, which emerged to prominence in the 1990s, is an example of a loosely linked outsourced and 'virtualised' global supply chain. It had advantages in lowering overall production cost structures and increasing supply chain flexibility for apparel industry producers. It enabled producers to literally turn over their logistics and supply chains and focus on higher-value competencies such as channel marketing and design.

The mid-1990s also saw the emergence of daring, new, end-to-end transport logistics outsourcing providers such as Menlo Logistics, which assumed complete coordination of the entire global supply chain of National Semiconductor. Menlo conducted 'milk runs' to National Semiconductor suppliers around the world, picking up components, delivering them to factories, and then picking up finished goods and delivering them to distribution centres worldwide.

It is useful to recall the degree of scepticism about outsourcing's relevance in the mid-1990s. Many questioned the gains generated from outsourcing. However, not all shared this view. In 1996, the Supply Chain Management Center at the University of Maryland conducted a survey of 500 corporate logistics managers experienced in outsourcing (including 114 Fortune 500 companies). The principal investigators found that savings from outsourcing appeared to be significantly greater and more sustained if a strategic approach to supply chain outsourcing was taken than if only individual functions were outsourced. Survey respondents indicated that the savings from total supply chain outsourcing averaged 21.3 per cent in the first year, with additional annual average savings of 15.1 per cent in years 2, 3 and 4. This compares with 10.54 per cent savings in the first year and 9.44 per cent average savings in years 2, 3 and 4 for outsourcing the freight payment/auditing function, which shows the best cost savings performance for an individual function. The results accurately anticipated the business acceleration of outsourcing and the unfolding of rapidly broadening scope at such startling speed over the ensuing decade (Boyson *et al.* 1999: 135–138).

Pronouncements and breathless headlines signalling a massive global outbreak of outsourcing have been common in the trade press, as the following examples show.

> Subcontracting as many non-core activities as possible is a central element of the new economy. *We live in an age of outsourcing* [italics added]. Firms seem to be subcontracting an ever expanding set of activities, ranging from product design to assembly, from research and development to marketing, distribution and aftersales service. Some firms have gone so far as to become 'virtual' manufacturers, owning designs for many products but making almost nothing themselves. (*Financial Times*, 31 July 2001: 10)

> The pace is picking up across such industries as retailing, consumer goods, software, electronics, autos and medical devices. In many realms, the time it takes to bring a product to market has been cut in half during the past three or four years. At Nissan Motor Company, the development of new cars used to take 21 months. Now the company is shifting to a ten-and-half-month process. In the cell phone business, Nokia, Motorola and others used to take 12–18 months to develop basic models. Today: 6–9 months. Of course, speed has always been important in business ever since the California Gold Rush. What's changed in recent years is that a slew of new techniques make it possible to get things done much faster. *Start with global outsourcing. A vast network of suppliers around the world stands ready to do anything from manufacturing products to drawing up legal contracts. This helps companies create supply chains that are faster, more flexible and more efficient than ever before* [italics added]. ('Speed demons', *BusinessWeek*, 27 March 2006: 70)

> '*This is about how to redesign the supply chain*' [italics added], Girsh Paranjpe, president of Wipro Ltd, told *The Wall Street Journal*. Wipro is one of India's biggest outsourcing companies and recently picked up some additional American business as part of

a $7.5 billion computer services contract with General Motors. He is right; the outsourcing boom is simply evidence that the global supply chain is changing, evolving and becoming much more efficient. (Hollon 2006)

More serious survey research also found that the pace of outsourcing seemed to intensify during the millennial change. For example, among corporate respondents in a 2005 Deloitte survey 65 per cent said that they had outsourced manufacturing, 60 per cent said that they had outsourced engineering services, and 60 per cent said that they had outsourced distribution/logistics functions (Deloitte 2005). In a 2005 LTD Management Group survey, 42 per cent of 197 corporate respondents said that they outsourced at least half of their supply chains (LTD Management 2005).

Anantachoke Osangthammanont, of the Fiscal Policy Research Institute in Bangkok, distinguishes between two kinds of trajectories in outsourcing.[8] The first is efficiency-gain outsourcing: when functions of a firm (in both production and business processing) become a 'commodity' and do not have any strategic value, firms will outsource these functions to gain from cheaper labour costs. Except for very common functions, this outsourcing happens when firms understand their business well enough to standardise the functions. In other words, this process takes place at later stages of industry development or technology development. The second is complementary outsourcing: when firms are seeking new technology, best practices, strategic assets or more flexibility, they will outsource to acquire such strategic assets. This happens at an early stage of industry development when new technology is discovered.

Both kinds of outsourcing have increased in recent global supply chain management. Indirect evidence appears to support the claim that the pace of supply chain outsourcing has recently accelerated. One example is the market-driven expansion of the supply chain IT outsourcing provider industry. In June 2005, as part of a 'flurry' of recent activity by IT outsourcers, IBM added a new supply chain outsourcing unit to its business process transformation division, bringing together its existing 8,500 supply chain consultants and another 15,000 IBM employees who had worked on building IBM's own internal outsourcing arm.[9] In July 2005, IBM's CEO asked Bob Moffat (the senior vice-president of IBM's integrated supply chain group) to reorganise the global services supply chain in the same way he had reorganised the physical supply chain. He was charged with 'tightening the services supply chain'. To get the right people to the right place at the right time, he has launched the 'Professional Marketplace', a database of skills, location and availability of 250,000 IBM services, software, sales and distribution personnel worldwide. This will avoid sending over-qualified people to customer sites and ensure that lower-cost employees in Brazil and India are well utilised, thus lowering IBM's service cost structure.

These were only the latest in a series of strategic moves by the world's largest IT outsourcer into supply chain management, going back to Moffat's appointment as senior supply chain vice-president for IBM in 2002. His group now oversees some $40 billion of annual spending, on everything from raw material sourcing to logistics and customer support; his span of control covers 19,000 people and 33,000 suppliers.

He has re-engineered the supply chain away from traditional functional silos to a more horizontal structure, and he reported $7 billion in productivity gains in 2003.[10]

Smaller IT-oriented supply chain outsourcing players are also seeking to expand their markets. The India-based start-up company Aegis InterWorld has used software and services technology purchased from InterWorld Holdings to form a platform for internet-based order and workflow management. With the new platform launched in the summer of 2005, Aegis has already begun working with customers such as Verizon Wireless, Okidata and clothing retailers Ann Taylor and Joseph A. Bank. CEO Mark Skoda said that Aegis will help give customers 'the ability to design and carry out business process improvements in real time, bringing cost savings of 15 to 30 per cent over existing processes'.[11] Aegis's outsourcing services target all sizes of enterprises in sectors that include high tech, retail, and auto manufacturing; services range from supply chain application hosting to inbound call centres, transportation management, sourcing, purchase order processing, order delivery and transportation management.

Aegis's activities are attempting to capitalise on some early wins by multinational enterprises. The Standish Group found[12] that customers saved 49 per cent by outsourcing their supply chain applications management. For example, Kvaerner Pulping Inc., a division of Kvaerner Group, reduced its inventory by almost $1 million and shaved a massive 31 per cent off the company's annual IT budget by outsourcing its supply chain management software.

In fact, it seems that the entire third-party logistics industry that enables supply chain outsourcing is booming all over the world. In Japan, the third-party logistics business has been growing rapidly, driven by deregulation in the logistics industry, fiercer competition among service suppliers and the trend among shippers to outsource logistics for higher cost efficiency. Japan's third-party market will increase from about ¥1 trillion in 2003 to ¥1.8 trillion in 2013, according to Yano Research Institute Ltd.[13] Between 2003 and 2005, India's third-party logistics market expanded from $10 billion to an estimated $16 billion. A 2005 study by the Nankai Logistics Institute[14] identified over 30,000 third-party logistics companies in Tianjin, China's second largest port city. FedEx, the world's largest express transportation company, is creating an entire 'China Direct Strategy'; through its express hub in Shenzhen in south China's Guangdong Province, FedEx is able to provide customers in southern China with next-day delivery of products to cities across North America. This means that in some cases multinational manufacturers can ship direct from factories to consumers' doors and eliminate tiers of warehouses and associated inventory carrying costs.[15]

Thus, direct and indirect evidence appears to support the conclusion that the frenzied pace of corporate supply chain outsourcing might continue unabated. However, such evidence could be misleading. There are signs of a sea change in enterprise globalisation strategies and business models.

THE ERA OF REVITALISED COMMAND

We are once again entering a new era, where corporations are altering their strategies and changing their practice mix. Dell and Ford, sentinel examples of best supply chain practices in the previous era, have moved to drastically pull decision making and critical systems back from outsourcing providers. They are trying to recalibrate and revitalise their supply chains to remain competitive. In both cases, the companies have moved to dramatically strengthen strategic management command and control over key design, engineering and manufacturing activities and have launched initiatives for insourcing and localisation of assets.

The surge of insourcing across multiple industries

The auto industry: Ford's insourcing strategy

After 28 car recall campaigns in 2001, David Thursfield, Ford president – International Operations and Global Purchasing, admitted Ford may have been asking for too much. Caught up in the industry-wide trend toward outsourcing, Ford may have relied too heavily on suppliers for engineering, he said. To rectify the problem, Ford would reclaim some engineering responsibility. Ford then consolidated from 2000 to 200 suppliers and retook insourced engineering and manufacturing from such mega-suppliers as Lear Corporation and Johnson Controls. *'This is the biggest extreme we've ever seen'* says one brake supplier [italics added], 'Ford went from sourcing only brake components in the 1980s to sourcing complete systems in the late 1990s. And in just the past few months, the pendulum is swinging totally in the other direction.' 'It has been humbling for the company that pioneered mass production of the automobile to admit nearly 100 years later that it took its eye off the ball, that it sacrificed engineering prowess in what ironically was an attempt to make itself more efficient. This is the dark side of outsourcing, for it demonstrates that OEMs [original equipment manufacturers] run the risk of becoming subservient to the technical capabilities – or liabilities [–] of outsourcing agents.[16]

Ford is now examining a full spectrum of candidate systems for insourcing: seats, engine cooling, heating, ventilation, air conditioning, brakes, tyres, wheels and electric systems calibration. By re-applying its inherent system knowledge to more activities in production, Ford believes that it will regain control as well as gain new efficiencies. Ford is seeking to reassert its fundamental advantage in systems design and integration. Hobday *et al.* (2005) define this as a core capability of the modern corporation, albeit one that has been de-emphasised in the rush to outsourcing.

A recent survey[17] confirmed Ford's dramatic turnaround strategy, with 26 per cent of supplier respondents reporting that Ford was the most aggressive auto maker in bringing design and systems work back in house. But dissatisfaction with outsourcing is pervasive in the auto industry as a whole, and extends beyond Ford. More than 38 per cent of original equipment manufacturer respondents in the survey said that their companies had brought work that they previously outsourced back in house because a supplier had been unable to meet performance targets. Fully 70 per cent of original equipment manufacturer respondents said that some of their suppliers still shipped too much defective product. An even higher number (77 per cent) agreed that very few suppliers actually had full-service capability, despite claiming to have such capability.

The electronics industry's insourcing strategy

At the 2005 International Electronics Forum, Synopsys Inc. chairman and CEO Aart de Geus explicitly stated what had been on the minds of executive-level participants:

> We are at one of those switching moments again … when the wheels are coming off the electronics industry's 20 year long disaggregation train. (Yoshida 2005)

At the forum, both Sony Corp. and Matsushita Electric Industrial Co. revealed ambitious plans to again vertically integrate their semiconductor businesses. Sony announced plans to double the proportion of its own internally developed chips that are embedded in its systems from 20 per cent of the total chip content in value terms to 40 per cent over the next three to four years. This is an important development given that Sony annually accounts for purchases of $8 billion worth of chips, or 4 per cent of the worldwide semiconductor market. Similarly, Matsushita announced the roll-out of an internally designed 'scalable silicon architecture' named the 'Integrated Platform'. This platform will be incorporated in Panasonic products such as digital televisions, cameras, DVD recorders, MP3 players and cell phones. In both companies, the apparent goal is to develop differentiated products that can separate them from low-cost producers of commoditised chips in Asia. Matsushita executives called their new strategy a 'back to customisation' movement that would enable them to move up the value chain from the commoditisation sinkhole of the PC/Wintel platform.

At a more fundamental level than even fears of commoditisation, there is a pervasive perception by managers in the electronics industry that strategic management command and control are being eroded. The Electronics Supply Chain Association conducted a survey of 121 key electronic brand owners in December 2005.[18] Sixty-nine per cent of respondents claimed that they now have less control over critical supply chain processes such as order promising, risk analysis and management, inventory management and forecasting than they did previously. The extent of outsourcing has been identified as a major factor in loss of perceived control (Littleson 2006). It is within this context that a return to more active orchestration of supply chain systems and greater internalisation of design, engineering and logistics management appears to be a bid to re-exert strategic command and control over the factors that influence competition.

Logisticstoday.com recently named Dell as one of the ten best supply chains in the world. This was only the latest in a string of such honours for Dell, which is often cited as a sentinel example of a company gaining competitive leadership by exploiting the trend to global outsourcing. The extent of Dell's global outsourced network is shown in Table 2.4.

Yet the Dell model has been so tightly managed and the company has had such a strong hold over its outsourced supplier network that it averages 91.25 inventory

Table 2.4 Dell global supplier network

Components and materials	Suppliers	Supply location
Printed circuit boards	SCI, Celestics	Asia, Scotland, Eastern Europe
Drives	Seagate, Maxtor, Western Digital	Asia (mainly Singapore)
Printers	Lexmark (formerly Hewlett-Packard)	Europe (Barcelona)
Monitors	Philips, Nokia, Samsung, Sony, Acer	Europe, Asia
Box builds	Hon Hai/Foxteq	Asia, Eastern Europe
Chassis and cases	Hon Hai/Foxteq	Asia, Ireland
Sheet metal and plastics	Trend Tec, APW	Europe
Services	*Service provider*	*Service location*
Inbound logistics	Suppliers' hubs must be within 30 minutes travel of Dell	Ireland, Eastern Europe, Middle East, Africa
Outbound logistics	Eagle Global, FedEx, UPS	Strategically located to serve regional markets
Call centres	Dell-run but moving abroad	Round Rock (Nashville, USA); Bangalore (India); Limerick (Ireland)
System integration	EDS	Global
Information technology	Agile Software, Ariba, GT Nexus (2 Technologies, Oracle, V3 Systems, PartMiner)	Global
Services and field repair	IBM, Unisys, Wang, Banctec	Global
Consulting	Arthur Andersen, Gen 3	Global

Source: Kraemer and Dedrick (2002); Dell website; <Logisticstoday.com>.

turns a year; keeps only four days of inventory on hand in its own plants; and has nine days of inventory on hand in its aligned third-party managed warehouses. Dell also uses its leverage over external suppliers to throw off huge amounts of cash. Dell gets immediate payment from customers over its order management website, then delays payment to suppliers and enforces advantageous terms of trade through 60-day payment schedules; it has created a $4 billion float for itself from the accumulated interest.

Herein lies the paradox: though often touted as a virtual and fully outsourced company, Dell has held strict control over its outsourced network to survive and succeed. Given this outsourcing prowess, it was jarring to hear Dell CEO Kevin Rollins declare in 2004:

> Our model requires that we own the value chain (which includes manufacturing and parts procurement). We can't outsource. The issue has become one of logistics. The cost of moving a personal computer around has become more expensive than the cost of labor.[19]

As if to emphasise the point, Ro Parra, Dell's senior vice-president for manufacturing, similarly noted[20] that there is only $11 of labour inputs in each Dell personal computer, too small a cost to justify wholesale outsourcing to China.

To support a strategy of pulling back from international outsourcing, Dell has invested heavily in next-generation local market capability. On 6 October 2005, only eight months after the ground was broken in a vacant lot, Dell opened a $100 million, 750,000 square foot (70,000 square metre) manufacturing facility in Winston–Salem, North Carolina. The facility is capable of producing a computer every five seconds. The computers will be distributed online throughout North America and marketed through Dell's own newly announced network of retail stores in the United States. These radical moves are being made to address a serious deterioration in Dell's stock value. According to the *New York Times*:[21]

> Between July 2005 and June 2006, Dell shares in the stock market have lost almost 42 per cent of their value.

Dell is crossing a rubicon into a third era of enterprise globalisation – the era of revitalised command – and is placing greater emphasis on strategic localisation and multi-channel ownership.

The IT service industry's insourcing strategy

As in the auto and electronics industries, there is ample evidence of a significant pullback in IT service outsourcing investments by multinational enterprises since 2003. The Bank of America cancelled its IT services outsourcing contract with TSYS and moved IT management back in house. Sainsbury (UK) ended its outsourcing contract with Accenture to take back/insource IT management. Cable and Wireless terminated its IT management contract with IBM, as did JP Morgan Chase, whose outsourcing agreement with IBM was worth $5 billion. Prudential shifted a substantial piece of its computer services management back in house. Deloitte Consulting reports that many firms are now favouring in-house management of IT services rather than outsourcing.

A National Outsourcing Association (NOA) survey indicates that only a small percentage of insourcing has resulted from poor outsourcing experiences; the majority result from positive, proactive deliberate company policies (Brownlow 2006). However, in a 2004 CIO Insight survey half of 604 chief information officers said that they had experienced problems from IT outsourcing. Table 2.5 shows the most cited problems.

The cost savings and financial returns on investment from outsourcing have been disappointing for many companies. This disappointment may stem from an inadequate calculation of the total cost factors involved in 'offshoring' IT support, particularly costs associated with due diligence, risk management and governance. Such costs can halve the projected savings from offshore outsourcing.

Our survey of recent developments in auto, electronics and IT services industry supply chains shows an emerging but pronounced tendency toward re-internalisation of assets and capabilities that were previously outsourced. The drivers appear to vary depending on the industry – pressures to maintain system quality in the auto industry; imperatives to retain higher value integrated system design advantages and/or logistics network advantages in the electronics industry; and a need to rein in IT costs in the business services industry.

Risk management and business continuity planning: cross-industry drivers of the insourcing trend in a post-9/11 world

We have identified real-time supply chains as key mechanisms of enterprise globalisation, building webs of interaction with customers, suppliers and producers across multiple borders. A recent body of work has focused on the effects of supply chain disruption on the multinational enterprise. Professor Vinod Singhal, at the College of Management, Georgia Institute of Technology, and Professor Kevin Hendricks, at the Richard Ivey School of Business, University of Western Ontario, have conducted an event study that presented evidence of the economic consequences of firm-level supply chain disruptions. The study monitored some 800 disruptions at publicly traded

Table 2.5 Problems with outsourcing information technology services

Type of problem	% of CIO respondents reporting the problem
Quality	65.1
Missed deadlines	42.9
Higher than expected costs	38.5
Didn't understand our business/market	36.2
Not enough value	30.9
Staff resistance	17.3
Security concerns	15.0
Lack of executive support	4.7

Source: CIO Insight, < http://www.cioinsight.com/category2/0%2C1568%2C1776844%2C00.asp>, CIO Insight Global IT Service Outsourcing Report (2004), accessed 15 November 2006.

firms. The findings showed (Singhal and Hendricks 2003) that, for firms suffering from supply chain disruptions, stock returns were 33–40 per cent lower than their benchmarks over a three-year period that started one year before and ended two years after the disruption announcement date. They also showed that disruptions negatively affected profitability. During the same time period there was a 107 per cent average decline in operating income; a 114 per cent decline in return on sales; a 93 per cent decline in return on assets; and 7 per cent slower growth in sales.

Against this backdrop of severe financial implications associated with supply chain disruption, some people have attempted to define more effective strategies and practices for managing global supply chain risk. For example, Sweden's Lund University has established a supply chain risk management forum to better differentiate among types and severity of enterprise-level operational risks. And multinational enterprises such as Wal-Mart and FedEx have created global situation rooms led by directors of business continuity to track and respond to emerging threats.

Currently there is a fierce debate about which form of global organisation is the best buffer against risks of disruption. Hagel and Brown (2005) and others argue that networked virtualised enterprises are far more resilient than classically vertically integrated companies. They point to the way in which Li & Fung, as a flexible network organisation, was able to dynamically shift production from its contracted supply base in Asia to Latin America when the SARS epidemic hit, thereby avoiding the disruption that caused $63 billion of business loss in Asia. Critics such as Barry Lynn (2005) take the opposite stance:

> Some supply chain experts argue that today's lean and flexible production systems are actually safer than the vertically integrated, company-delimited production organisation. But, as time goes on, such systems become more and more likely to witness collapse. The hyper-specialised production system that is emerging is, if we are honest, the natural outcome of what happens when globalisation and outsourcing are combined with an entire lack of regulations by government.

Lynn (2005) gives two examples. The first was a 1999 earthquake in Taiwan, which shut down two semiconductor companies in an industrial park and crippled global electronics production. The second was an explosion in a single Japanese chemical plant, which disrupted one-half of global capacity to produce a resin needed to make memory chips, doubled the price of memory chips and added $100 to the average cost of a laptop.

The Aberdeen Group (2005) recently conducted a survey of 180 global enterprises. Eighty per cent reported supply disruptions in the previous 24 months. Most expected risks to increase. The study found (Aberdeen Group 2005) that best-practice companies are taking a variety of measures to counteract risks – including the adoption of balanced sourcing methods. Such portfolio risk management activities will invariably lead multinational enterprises to reduce over-dependency on a few outside service and product suppliers; and will act as a constraint on the scope and intensity of future outsourcing. Signs of this trend are starting to emerge.

As corporations look out to the horizon, they see storm clouds of environmental, political and demographic risk. Companies are re-thinking their strategies and operations to take these factors into account. Friedman's popular monograph about globalisation (Friedman 2005) may be right – our new world may be flat – but the ground that corporations must traverse is hard and a strong wind is blowing.

CONCLUSIONS

Enterprise transformations

Shifts in OECD corporate strategy in a third era

We have defined a series of three major transitions in the organisational structure of the globalising multinational enterprise in the past 100 years or so. In the first era, the enterprise kept strictly to its vertically integrated form and sought end-to-end asset ownership. Its globalisation style was that of a resource predator, and its expansion overseas was a vehicle for sourcing industrial raw material and low-cost labour from 'sweatshop countries'. In the second era, virtualisation opened up the structure of the multinational enterprise and enabled it to serve more as an alliance partner and as a bridge to the global marketplace for nascent national outsourcing providers of all kinds. Multinational enterprise outsourcing investments in this period accelerated the overall growth of the 'technical workshop countries' (for example, China and India) that have provided increasingly advanced manufacturing and services support.

As we go forward into a third era of globalisation – that of revitalised command – we are witnessing yet another metamorphosis in enterprise strategy and structure. The multinational enterprise is becoming more risk-averse and less likely to over-extend itself through alliances, and is showing an emerging bias toward more direct absorption and control over assets in its network. This bias is clearly demonstrated in the recent intensification in outward US cross-border merger and acquisition activity as a preferred method of investment. It surged from $16 billion in 2002 to $29 billion in 2003 and nearly $31 billion in 2004 (Deloitte 2005).

Another key feature of this corporate search for heightened control in an era of rising transport costs and increased risks is an emerging tendency to locate higher value activities closer to home markets. In the United States, Dell's newly opened manufacturing centre in North Carolina is an example of this trend; and in Japan the Japanese External Trade Organisation has found that 'many Japanese companies are focusing on adding to higher-end production capacity in the home market'.[22]

Shifts in the distribution of global corporate power and investment

So far, we have discussed only the changes occurring in multinational enterprises based in Organisation for Economic Co-operation and Development (OECD) countries. Yet structural change in the Asian region is fast producing a set of worthy local competitors to the OECD multinational corporations – competitors who face many of the same challenges and opportunities as their OECD counterparts. These trends were highlighted at the PAFTAD conference on which this book is based. For example, Chen and Lin (Chapter 8 in this volume) showed that mainland China's emerging global enterprises already account for a third of developing country foreign direct investment outflow. Currently, this represents a stock of almost $40 billion in recently acquired strategic assets abroad. If Hong Kong corporate overseas investments are included, the current combined capital stock rises to $350 billion. At the same time, two-thirds of China's growth has been driven by foreign direct investment, demonstrating the deepening two-way ties that bind the regional and world economies.

Conference participants also presented evidence of an important parallel trend: deepening intra-regional production networking. They highlighted this phenomenon in two different but complementary ways. Prema-chandra Athukorala (Chapter 9 in this volume) tracked an overall increase in intra-regional components and sub-assemblies trade. Shujiro Urata (Chapter 5 in this volume) and Sanghoon Ahn and his colleagues (Chapter 6 in this volume) showed that Japanese multinationals were strengthening their intra-regional production networks – as were South Korean multinationals, through expansion into China.

Thus, Asia's indigenous multinational enterprise sector is experiencing a transformation in its ability to project out into world markets due to a transformed regional production platform capability.

Government policy responses

The context for public sector supply chain decision making

The transformations of the enterprise business model that have occurred over a century have triggered profound government reactions. Major host country policy restructuring has consistently attempted to adjust to or react against the contours of the emerging corporate paradigm. One can construct a paired and step-wise relationship between changes in multinational corporate behaviour and shifts in public policy responses, as shown Table 2.6.

Each era of enterprise transformation has provoked, and will continue to provoke, a specific set of policy responses, a regime of instruments, incentives and regulatory frameworks used by governments to extract value from or adapt to multinational corporations.

Since we are only at the beginning of the third era of enterprise globalisation, country policy regimes are still in flux. We can anticipate a lot more policy debate on increasingly interlaced cross-border supply chains, whose assets are so closely mingled and exchanged that national origins of corporate owners are becoming difficult to trace or tax. Perhaps we are witnessing the birth of an era where not only multinational corporations but also host country governments must seek revitalised command.

One scenario consistent with this aim consists of individual countries asserting supply chain eminent domain, seeking to extract value from or regulate the operations of transnational supply chains. One example is the Tianjin Development Area in China, where 13 square kilometres of ocean are being dredged to create a 'Logistics City' capable of helping China move beyond being a global manufacturing workshop to become a value-added global logistics services provider. This 'Logistics City' will

Table 2.6 Three eras of enterprise globalisation: the relationship between key corporate behaviour and public policy responses

	Stage 1: vertical integration	Stage 2: virtualisation	Stage 3: revitalised command
Key corporate behaviour			
Style	MNC seen as predatory, alien	MNC seen as partner and bridge to global markets	MNC seen as over-extended enterprise driven by cost economics and outsourcing to the limits of organisational coherence and seeking to rebalance
Demand	Demand largely restricted to OECD countries	Internationalisation of demand linked to income growth in developing countries	Demand in most industries spreads globally, creating sustainable regional markets
Supply	Internationalisation of supply	Broader international base of higher value supply	Emergence of more regional supply chain patterns, driven by high energy costs and heightened global supply chain risk
Effect	Rise of raw material and sweatshop countries	Rise of advanced manufacturing and service workshop countries	Increase in 'nearshoring', in step with increasing oil prices, enhancing the prospects for more intensively coordinated regional supply chains by the United States with Canada and Mexico; and by Japan with East Asian countries
Public policy response			
Priority/primary objective	Regulate MNCs	Deregulate and globalise the economy	Animate sustainable growth
Actions	Control domestic abuses

Create legislative and regulatory buffers against international capital's crushing impacts on local capital formation

Develop labour law protections and natural resource stewardship policies | Government builds policy bridges to international capital and 'incentivises' investments

Stimulation of demand through local capital formation/ownership

Formation of strategic partnerships between local companies and MNCs

Freeing up of domestic entrepreneurial energies through streamlined government processes and low-risk capital/incentives | Coherent national education and cultural preservation policies to help industries and workforces rapidly move up the value and skill chains and still maintain national identity/cultural coherence

Government incentives for localisation and acculturation of MNC supply chain activity

Emphasis on advanced physical and digital inter-modal logistics infrastructure creation (e.g. super-ports and super-portals) |

Note: MNC = multinational corporation; OECD = Organisation for Economic Co-operation and Development.

Source: Authors' compilation.

increasingly capture value from the global trade of automobiles, steel and so on that flow into and out of the Beijing and northern China industrial areas.

Or perhaps we shall see the emergence of a different scenario, a more sophisticated approach, where there is an intensive cross-national effort to preserve and strengthen specific supply chains that extend across borders. For example, the Mexico and US governments have worked hard to facilitate the cross-border supply chains of the US automobile industry and to enable rapid customs clearance of parts and assemblies. Another example is the livestock supply chain extending between the United States and Japan. Outbreaks of bovine spongiform encephalitis ('mad cow disease') have led to a joint effort to secure the United States–Japan beef supply chain and make improvements in disease surveillance. This was a decisive collaborative intervention in the transnational supply chain, and such actions will probably occur more often in the future.

These examples highlight the ways in which rapid globalisation and a shifting strategic landscape with greater emerging economic, political and ecological risks will drive governments – individually or collectively – to seek ways to strengthen and revitalise command.

Key challenges in the Asia Pacific region

A critical challenge in the Asia Pacific region is the mismatch between the intense pace of national economic activity and the lagging tempo of supply chain infrastructure build-out. The required degree of catch-up in supply chain infrastructure can be best understood by examining the case of China. Some 59 per cent of North American manufacturers currently source components or material from China (ASRIA 2006).

Although China is clearly the regional supply chain leader, as measured by volume of incoming investment and percentage of world exports, its supply chain infrastructure is not keeping pace with developments. China's logistics costs take up 18.5 per cent of nominal GDP, versus 10.1 per cent in the United States and 11.0 per cent in Japan, despite a logistics market that is about one-fourth the size of the US market (Hammond and Lee 2004, citing Peter van Laarhoven 2004). Such figures indicate the persistence of deeply embedded inefficiencies in the economy, caused by policy deficiencies and by deficiencies in communications and transport.

If we go deeper, we find that the supply chain infrastructure is under great stress from rapid growth and is experiencing significant blockages in the circulation of goods and services. According to Hammond and Lee (2004), who cite their original sources from *Business Times Singapore* (12 May 2003) and *Xinhua News Agency* (20 May 2003), in 1995, 1.5 million twenty-foot equivalent units (TEUs), a measure of freight volume, were handled in Shanghai; and 0.3 million TEUs were handled in Shenzhen. In 2002, 8.5 million TEUs were handled in Shanghai and 6 million TEUs were handled in Shenzhen. High congestion at Shanghai and Shenzhen ports due to 'astounding growth' is the main problem. Difficulties also arise due to the major bottleneck at the border between Shenzhen and Hong Kong and the need for repeated customs clearance because of inconsistent provincial regulations. However, congestion is being reduced by the construction of numerous ports and, in the eastern region, the construction of new expressways.

In many ways, China's problems are not unique in the region. As the World Bank (ASRIA 2006) noted:

> Although Asia has become a focal point for outsourcing by many global brands, in terms of sustainability performance supply chains in the region are considered by industry experts to lag those typical of developed economies. The reasons for this lack-luster performance include:
>
> - complexity of local laws, regulation and business practices
> - poor enforcement
> - lower environmental, labor, health and safety standards
> - governance issues including lack of accountability, transparency, disclosure and corruption
> - insufficient network and transport infrastructure
> - technology and awareness gaps
>
> On a country level, the more advanced Asian economies such as Singapore and Hong Kong with their highly developed infrastructure, legal frameworks and advanced technology, lead the pack in terms of supply chain competitiveness. Taiwan, Malaysia and Thailand follow, with China, although a growing haven for supply chains, notably lagging behind.

Clearly, the region tells a tale of two supply chains. Contrast China's logistics deficiencies with the practices of Singapore, the regional logistics leader. Singapore has invested heavily in digital commerce infrastructure as a competitive capability over the past 25 years. A cargo vessel still at sea can electronically report its cargo holdings via the public PortNet System. The data will be used to automatically program the positioning of cranes and other equipment to sequence and expedite the offloading and processing of cargo. In addition, through the public TradeNet system, a trader can get all necessary import/export approvals from 18 agencies involved in customs clearances within 15 minutes of submitting an electronic request – 24 hours a day, 7 days a week (Hanna *et al.* 1996).

As in the Singapore example, governments must use technology and advanced management practices to overcome national supply chain barriers and build sustainable logistics platforms to energise enterprises.

To sustain success, China and other regional players with lagging supply chain infrastructures must do more than merely hand physical goods over to global OECD multinational supply chains. Governments must continue to modernise and digitise infrastructure. They must work to support the creation of increasingly sophisticated national business ecosystems: high-speed, high-value service chains linking suppliers and customers in collaborative design, production, distribution, after-sales service and product reinvention. In the third era of enterprise globalisation, this is the core challenge faced by governments in the Asia Pacific region and by their business constituencies.

NOTES

1 Viral virtualisation is a term borrowed from viral marketing, suggesting that outsourcing increases exponentially.
2 Except where otherwise noted, the facts on Ford's operations are from primary research at the Ford Production Collection 1916–1954, US National Archives, College Park, Maryland. Sandor Boyson conducted the research in 2006.
3 See *Wall Street Journal*, 22 May 2006, p. R.1.
4 See <http://www.cscmp.org/Website/AboutCSCMP/Definitions/Definitions.asp>.
5 See <purchasing.com> website 2004.
6 This information comes from an interview between Sandor Boyson and Larry Kellam, of Procter & Gamble. It is reported in Tech Web, October 2003.
7 See <purchasing.com> website 2004.
8 He raised these comments as a reviewer at the PAFTAD conference on which the chapters in this book are based.
9 Chen and Lin discuss other aspects of IBM in Chapter 8 in this volume.
10 See *Fortune*, 5 September 2005: 132.
11 See <http://www.aegisinterworld.com/NewsEvents/NewsEventsPressReleases.htm#PressRelease3>.
12 See 'Aegis heats up supply chain outsourcing', *e-Week*, 7 September 2005; 'The ROI of application service providers', Standish Group, 2005.
13 See <http://www.jetro.go.jp/en/invest/newsroom/newsletter/pdf/ij_10.pdf>.
14 Unpublished report by Ling Wang, Nankai University, 2005.
15 Jetro, Invest Japan, No. 10, 2005; 'India's 3rd party logistics industry', IE Singapore, 2004.
16 See 'InSourcing Ford's quality control', *Ward's Auto World*, 1 May 2003.
17 See 'Survey confirms Ford insourcing', *Ward's Auto World*, 1 August 2003.
18 See <http://www.informationweek.com/shared/printableArticle.jhtml?articleID=174300572>.
19 CNET News, 19 October 2004.
20 In a speech at the R.H. Smith School of Business, University of Maryland, November 2006.
21 'Dell's world isn't what it used to be', *New York Times*, 13 May 2006, <www.nytimes.com/2006/05/13/technology>.
22 *Wall Street Journal*, 6 August 2006: A4.

REFERENCES

Aberdeen Group (2005) 'Supply risk management benchmark: assuring supply and mitigating risks in an uncertain economy', Boston MA: Aberdeen Group.
Alstyne, M. van (1997) 'The state of network organisation: a survey in three frameworks', *Journal of Organisational Computing and Electronic Commerce*, 7(3): 83–151.
ASRIA (Association for Sustainable and Responsible Investment in Asia) (2006), 'Introduction', in *Taking Stock: Adding Sustainability Variables to Asian Sectoral Analysis*, International Finance Corporation', Washington DC: International Finance Cooperation, World Bank.
Boyson, S. (1988) 'Technological change and development: the case of Puerto Rico', National Technological Transformation Project, World Institute of Development Economics Research, Helsinki, Finland.
—— (2005) 'Update for in real time: managing the new supply chain', Graduate Seminar for Real Time Supply Chain Management (BULM744), University of Maryland, College Park, February.

Boyson, S., T.M. Corsi, M.E. Dresner and L.H. Harrington (1999) *Logistics and the Extended Enterprise: Benchmarks and Best Practices for the Manufacturing Professional*, New York: John Wiley.
Boyson, S., L.H. Harrington and T. Corsi (2004) *In Real Time: Managing the New Supply Chain*, Westport Connecticut: Praeger.
Brownlow, D. (2006) 'Dealing a new hand', *International Banking Systems*, January, <http://www.ibspublishing.com/free_to_view/ccm_15.4.htm>.
Castells, M. (1996) *The Rise of the Network Society, The Information Age: Economy, Society and Culture*, Vol. I, Cambridge MA and Oxford UK: Blackwell [cited in F. Stalder (1998) 'The network paradigm: social formations in the age of information', *Information Society Journal*, 14(4): 301–308.]
Coase, R. (1937) 'The nature of the firm', *Economica*, 4(16): 386–405.
Deloitte (2005) 'Growing the global corporation: global investment trends of U.S. manufacturers', New York NY: Deloitte Touche Tohmatsu.
Flaig, L.S. (1993) 'The "virtual enterprise": your new model for success', *Electronic Business*: 153–155.
Friedman, T. (2005) *The World is Flat*, New York NY: Farrar, Straus and Giroux.
Hagel, J. and J.S. Brown (2005) *The Only Sustainable Edge: Why Business Strategy Depends on Productive Friction and Dynamic Specialisation*, Harvard Business School Press.
Hammond, J. and H. Lee (2004) 'China and the global supply chain', Thought Leaders Session at Dartmouth Tuck School, July 2004, see <http://mba.tuck.dartmouth.edu/digital/Programs/CorporateEvents/SupplyChainThoughtLeaders/session7slides>, accessed 25 September 2006.
Hanna, N., S. Boyson and S. Gunaratne (1996) 'The East Asian miracle and information technology: strategic management of technological learning', World Bank Discussion Paper No. 326, Washington DC: World Bank.
Helper, S. (1991) 'Vertical integration trends and supplier strategy in the history of the automobile industry', *Business History Review*, 65(4): 781–824.
Hobday, M., A. Davies and A. Prencipe (2005) 'Systems integration: a core capability of the modern corporation', *Industrial and Corporate Change*, 14(6): 1109–1143.
Hollon, J (2006) 'Outsourcing: get over it', *Workforce Management*, 13 March, p. 58, see <http://www.workforce.com/archive/article/24/29/50.php>, accessed 3 November 2006.
Kraemer, K. and J. Dedrick, (2002) 'Dell Computer: organization of a global production network', Center for Research on Information Technology and Organizations, University of California, Irvine.
Laarhoven, Peter van (2004) 'Mail, express and logistics in China: challenges and opportunities', paper presented at the conference 'China at the Crossroad of the Global Supply Chain', 14–15 April, Shanghai.
Littleson, R. (2006) 'Coordinating response across the virtual enterprise', *Response Management*, April: 41.
LTD Management (2005) 'Outsourcing offshore supply chain management: what it is and what it isn't', <http://www.webpronews.com/enterprise/crmanderp/wpn-15-20050610OutsourcingOffshoreSupplyChainManagementWhatItIsAndWhatItIsnt.html>, accessed 9 November 2006.
Lynn, B. (2005) *End of the Line: The Rise and Coming Fall of the Global Corporation*, New York NY: Doubleday (pp. 223–224).
Nyman, L.R. (ed.) (1992) 'Making manufacturing cells work', Society of Manufacturing Engineers.
Perez, Carlotta (1983) 'Towards a comprehensive theory of long waves', IIASA Meeting on Long Waves, Depression and Innovation, Siena, Florence, 26–29 October.
Singhal, V. and K. Hendricks (2003) 'Quantifying the impact on supply chain glitches on shareholder value: the significance of adaptive supply networks', SAP White Paper Series, see <www.sap.com/usa/solutions/business-suite/scm/pdf/BWP_Quantify.pdf>; accessed 3 November 2006.

White, L. Jr (1974) 'Technology assessment from the stance of a medieval historian', *American Historical Review*, 79(1): 1–13.

Yoshida, J. (2005) 'Electronics reconsiders vertical business model', *Electronic Engineering Times*, 9 May 2005, see <http://eetimes.com/news/latest/showArticle.jhtml?articleID=162800206>, accessed 2 November 2006.

3 Innovation offshoring: root causes of Asia's rise and policy implications

Dieter Ernst

INTRODUCTION

Much economic research on the role of Asia[1] in the global economy has focused on the impact of changes in macroeconomic parameters (for instance, financial and foreign exchange crises), but has neglected the issue of 'deeper economic integration'. The latter refers to transformations in markets for capital, goods, services, technology and labour that, to a large degree, result from changes in corporate strategies and organisation. 'Globalisation' is widely used shorthand for these transformations (Ernst 2005c). Barriers to integration continue to exist, of course, in each of these different markets, but there is no doubt that a massive integration of markets has taken place across borders that, only a short while ago, seemed to be impenetrable. And much of the action now is in Asia.

An important new development is the rise of Asia as a location for 'innovation offshoring'. Global corporations are at the forefront of these developments, experimenting with new approaches to the management of global innovation networks. But Asian governments and firms are playing an increasingly active role as promoters and new sources of innovation.

Innovation offshoring is therefore likely to accelerate. It is driven by fundamental changes in corporate innovation management in response to the globalisation of markets for technology and knowledge workers. Innovation offshoring thus creates a whole new set of challenges – and opportunities – across the Pacific Rim.

The main drivers of this change are global corporations that are increasing their overseas investment in R&D while seeking to integrate geographically dispersed innovation clusters into global networks of production, engineering, development, and research. This trend has added a new dimension to the traditional notion of global production networks (GPNs), transforming them into global innovation networks (GINs).

GINs combine the geographic relocation of innovation ('offshoring') with changes in the boundaries of the firm ('outsourcing'). Global companies 'offshore' stages of innovation to Asian affiliates to tap into the region's lower-cost pool of knowledge workers.[2] Equally important are the region's large and increasingly sophisticated markets. This has led to Asia's integration into intra-firm GINs. But global firms also 'outsource' some stages of innovation to specialised Asian suppliers, as part of complex inter-firm GINs.

It is time to correct earlier claims that only low-level service jobs will move offshore (Mann 2003) and that there is 'little evidence' of a major push by global companies to set up research operations in the developing world (Bhagwati 2004). Innovation offshoring goes far beyond the migration of relatively routine services like call centres, software programming, and business process support – the subject of current public debates on 'outsourcing'. Beyond adaptation, innovation offshoring in Asia now also encompasses the creation of new products and processes (Ernst 2006a).

Asia's integration into global innovation networks could facilitate knowledge diffusion and learning (Ernst 2002a, 2005c). But innovation offshoring also creates a competitive challenge of historic proportions. Asia needs to move beyond its traditional role as the primary 'global factory' for manufactures, software, and business services. It needs to develop strong national innovation systems to facilitate firm-level development of innovative capabilities.

Across the region, governments and domestic firms are all searching for strategies that would enable them to benefit from integration into GINs. China and India have clearly been at the forefront, but equally important are developments in South Korea, Taiwan, Singapore, and Malaysia.

In short, new strategies and policies are required across Asia to cope with these new opportunities and challenges. Yet, while the policy relevance of these developments is all too evident, there has been very little research on the root causes and impacts of innovation offshoring.

This chapter presents preliminary findings of research on root causes. It does not explore impacts of Asia's integration into GINs, for instance on knowledge diffusion, value added and productivity growth.[3] The analysis is based on an extensive micro study of developments in the electronics industry, which dominates East Asia's trade and foreign direct investment (FDI). The research is based on structured interviews with more than 150 companies in the United States, Asia and Europe.

The first part of the chapter reviews the foundations of Asia's rise as an important location for innovation offshoring, highlighting achievements and policies to cope with the decreasing returns to the export-led 'global factory' model. The second part analyses the forces behind the growing organisational and geographical mobility of innovation within GINs, and explores what this implies for innovation offshoring. The chapter concludes with generic policy suggestions for Asian governments to cope with the new opportunities and challenges of innovation offshoring.

FOUNDATIONS OF ASIA'S RISE

The global factory

Asia's rise as an important location for innovation offshoring owes much to the region's success as the primary 'global factory' in industries as diverse as textiles, footwear, agro-industries, electronics, steel, cars, machine tools, software and information technology (IT)-enabled business services.

Integration into GPNs provided a fascinating example of the catalytic role that linkages with foreign firms can play for industrial development (Borrus *et al.* 2000; Ernst 1997). It enabled Asian firms to access the world's leading markets, especially in the United States, and helped to compensate for the initially small size of their domestic markets. Network participation also provided access to leading-edge technology and best-practice management approaches, creating new opportunities, pressures and incentives for Asian network suppliers to upgrade their technological and management capabilities and the skill levels of workers (Ernst and Kim 2002).

Aggressive support policies by Asia's governments enabled local firms to cope with these opportunities and challenges and to improve their position in these networks. The result is one of the most impressive success stories of Third World economic development. During the first years of the new century, the region's rate of growth in gross domestic product (GDP), trade, and inward FDI has surpassed even the impressive pace it achieved during the decades of the 1980s and 1990s. Asia also has become an increasingly sophisticated market for an even wider array of goods and services.

No other industry reflects Asia's rise as well as the electronics industry. Asia's five leading exporting countries (China, South Korea, Taiwan, Singapore and Malaysia) today account for more than one-fourth of world electronics manufacturing output. These five countries occupy leading positions in global markets for digital consumer electronics, computers, and mobile devices, as well as for high-precision components, such as semiconductors and displays.

For instance, roughly 70 per cent of the output of the semiconductor industry is now based in Asia. In addition, India, which has firmly established itself as a global export production base for software and IT-enabled business services, is now emerging as the next frontier for offshore manufacturing in sectors as diverse as car components, electronic components and pharmaceuticals.

This process has culminated in China's emergence as the dominant 'global electronics factory'. Since 2004, China has been the world's largest exporter of electronic products, surpassing the United States – a dramatic increase from its position as number 10 in 2000. Noteworthy in particular is a rapid improvement in the country's export portfolio: digital consumer electronics and mobile telecommunications equipment have increased relative to commodity-type appliances and personal computers (PCs), and electronic components have now become China's second biggest electronics export item.

China's emergence as the second largest electronics importer (up from seventh in 2000) indicates the growing importance of Asia's rapidly growing and increasingly sophisticated markets for communications, computing and digital consumer equipment, and for the electronic components (especially semiconductors) required by Asia's global electronics factories. The main prize is the sheer size of China's market. In the electronics industry, China has become the main export market for the United States, Japan, Taiwan and South Korea. China is the world's largest market for telecommunications equipment (wired and wireless), as well as a test bed for advanced third-generation (3G) wireless communication systems. China is also one of the most demanding markets for computing and digital consumer equipment. As most of that equipment is produced in China, the country has become the world's third largest market for semiconductors.

Upgrading through technology diversification

Asia's role as the 'global factory' will continue to be an important source of economic growth and capability development. However, both the 1997 financial crisis and the downturn in the global electronics industry in 2000 have brutally exposed the downside of that model. A country is more vulnerable to external disturbances, the higher the share of electronics in its exports, the greater its integration into GPNs, and the more it depends on exports to the United States (Ernst 2001).

In addition, there are decreasing returns to the 'global factory' model (Ernst 2004). As the capital intensity of such investment increases, it generates less new employment. Local spillovers to domestic suppliers also decline as global contract manufacturers, such as Flextronics, provide integrated manufacturing services, increasing their share of global factory production. And much of the 'global factory' investment has remained 'footloose', leading to plant closures in established locations and relocation to new, lower-cost sites.

Furthermore, Asian firms heavily rely on American, Japanese and European firms as the dominant sources of new technology. This reflects the heavy concentration of R&D, innovative capabilities and intellectual property rights (IPRs), much of it centred on the United States.[4] For Asian firms, this has resulted in razor-thin profit margins owing to the hefty licensing fees charged by the global brand firms.

Across the region, a broad consensus has emerged that Asia's electronics industry needs to upgrade to higher value-added and technologically more demanding products, services and production stages and that this requires the development of strong innovative capabilities. To achieve this goal, Asian governments and leading electronics and software companies are seeking to develop and improve the skills, knowledge, and management techniques needed to create and commercialise successfully new products, services, equipment, processes and business models.

A remarkable achievement of these efforts is a pragmatic focus on what is feasible in view of the fact that the region continues to lag substantially behind advanced nations in the development of a broad-based science and technology system (Ernst 2005d). Instead of jumping right into 'technology leadership' strategies to compete head on with global technology leaders, the focus has been on 'technology diversification'. This arguably has laid an important foundation for the region's success in attracting innovation offshoring.

Technology diversification, defined as the expansion of a company's or a product's technology base into a broader range of technology areas, focuses on applied research and the development of products that draw on component and process technologies that are not necessarily new to the world or difficult to acquire (Granstrand 1998). This enables Asian firms to build on their existing strengths in manufacturing, process development and prototype development. They also can leverage their experience in providing knowledge-intensive support services required to raise money and to manage supply chains and customer relations, knowledge exchange and the development of human resources. Most importantly, technology diversification allows Asian firms to use their accumulated capabilities to implement, assimilate and improve foreign technologies, as technology diversification often requires the exchange of knowledge with foreign parties.

Achievements

The results of these efforts are impressive. Asian governments and leading electronics and software companies have mobilised substantial investments to improve infrastructure (especially for broadband communication) and to support leading-edge R&D programs in a few high-priority areas. South Korea, Singapore, Hong Kong and Taiwan, together with small Nordic countries in Europe, lead the world in broadband access and speed. A few regions in China and India that are attracting innovation offshoring are rapidly catching up (Fonow 2006).

In addition, gross domestic expenditures on R&D have substantially increased in Asia's five leading electronics exporting countries, with China and Singapore experiencing the fastest rise. This has led to a substantial growth in the output of scientific papers, in citation ratios of these papers, and in the number of patents invented in Asia granted by the US Patent and Trademark Office (Wong 2006; Hicks 2005).

As a result, new innovation clusters have emerged for broadband technology and applications in South Korea and Singapore; for mobile communications and digital consumer devices in South Korea, Taiwan and China; and for software engineering and embedded software development in India.

The concerted efforts by Asia's governments and leading companies to support research programs and alternative standards offer an intriguing example. In telecommunications, for example, South Korea's four leading players (Samsung, SK Telecom, KT, and LG) are all engaged in serious efforts to become major platform and content developers for complex technology systems, especially in mobile communications. These efforts can build on considerable capabilities, accumulated in public research labs, like the Electronics and Telecommunications Research Institute, as well as in R&D labs of the *chaebol*[5] to develop complex technology systems like switching systems and communication systems that are based on the code-division multiple access (CDMA) standard developed by Qualcomm.

Another important example is China's development of an alternative 3G digital wireless standard, called time-division synchronous code-division multiple access (TD-SCDMA), which the International Telecommunications Union approved in August 2000.[6] Datang Telecom, a Chinese state-owned enterprise, and the Research Institute of the Ministry of Information Industry developed the TD-SCDMA standard with technical assistance from Siemens.

To accelerate the implementation of this strategy, Datang formed a series of collaborative agreements with global industry leaders to develop China-based R&D. There is a joint venture with Nokia, Texas Instruments (TI), the Korean LG group, and Taiwanese original design manufacturers (ODMs), a joint venture with Philips and Samsung, and a licensing agreement with STMicroelectronics. These will provide the Chinese company with access to critical design building blocks. Such linkages illustrate the important role that such programs play in attracting innovation offshoring.

Skills and capabilities

Asia's greatest attraction for innovation offshoring results from substantial improvements in the region's talent pool. Building on existing strengths in volume manufacturing, Asian firms have developed a broad range of specialised skills and capabilities. These include quality control, and the management of resources, supply chains and customer relations.

But to remain in the GPNs, Asian firms had to move up into product development, and increasingly into system and integrated circuit design (Ernst 2005a). Proximity to Asia's vast electronics manufacturing base has been an important asset, because product development focuses on manufacturability and the production of commercial samples. Asian firms also made substantial progress in developing the specialised skills required for complex R&D projects.

Most importantly, as noted by the National Science Board (2004: chapter 1, overview, p. 8), Asia's leading electronics exporting countries:

> ... [have substantially expanded] their higher education systems and the high-technology sectors of their economies in an effort to develop internationally competitive centres of excellence. In the past, these ... countries have been the main source of internationally mobile scientific and technical talent, but recently some of them have developed programs designed to retain their highly trained personnel and to even attract people from abroad.

For instance, China now graduates almost four times as many engineers as the United States. South Korea – with one-sixth of the population and one-twentieth of the GDP – graduates nearly the same number of engineers as the United States (National Science Board 2004: Appendix 2–33). China is experiencing explosive growth in Ph.D.-level degrees in science and engineering (S&E), the critical indicator of a country's research capabilities. A recent report prepared for the National Bureau of Economic Research (Freeman 2005) shows that between 1995 and 2003, first-year entrants in S&E Ph.D. programs in China increased six-fold, from 8,139 to 48,740. The report concludes:

> At this rate China will produce more S&E doctorates than the United States by 2010! (Freeman 2005: 4)

Such rapid expansion will undoubtedly come at the cost of a declining quality of graduate education, at least outside a handful of élite universities. A recent McKinsey report (Farrell *et al.* 2005) argues that, if all negative factors are factored in, only 25 per cent of India's engineering graduates are suitable for work at global corporations, while the current share in China is only 10 per cent.[7]

But there are signs that the quality problem is being addressed aggressively. The McKinsey report shows that the current supply of suitable engineers in low-wage countries represents as much as three-quarters of the suitable engineering talent pool in higher-wage countries. This share is substantially higher than the 44 per cent share of low-wage countries in the total supply of suitable young professionals in higher-income countries. Furthermore, the supply of suitable young engineers is expected to grow much faster in low-wage countries than in higher-wage countries. McKinsey projects that by 2008, low-wage countries will supply the same number of suitable young engineers as high-wage countries.

Highly skilled knowledge workers are much cheaper in Asia (outside Japan) than in the United States. For instance, the cost of employing a chip design engineer in Asia is typically between 10 and 20 per cent of the cost in Silicon Valley (Ernst 2005a).[8] As coordinating cross-continental design teams is likely to add substantial costs, industry experts estimate the net advantage to be between 30 and 50 per cent. Cost savings of such magnitude obviously are quite significant for companies that are under constant pressure to improve their return on investment, and provide an important incentive for innovation offshoring.

Asia's growing exposure to innovation offshoring

Cost savings are certainly important for large global corporations that are acting as pacesetters for an increase in the offshoring of innovation to Asia. A recent survey of the world's largest R&D spenders (UNCTAD 2005) shows that the world's leading R&D spenders intend to increase both their intra-firm and inter-firm GINs in Asia.[9] And large global electronics firms report the most aggressive plans to expand Asia's role in both forms of innovation offshoring.

By 2004 China had become the third most important location for overseas R&D affiliates, after the United States and the United Kingdom, followed by India (sixth) and Singapore (ninth). More than half of the responding firms have at least one R&D facility in China, India or Singapore.

Leading global corporations also intend to expand their offshore outsourcing of R&D to Asian firms. China is now the third most important location – behind the United States and the United Kingdom, but ahead of Germany and France. India is ranked equal to Japan.

The UNCTAD survey projects that the pace of R&D internationalisation will accelerate – as many as 67 per cent of the respondents stated that the share of foreign R&D will increase; only 2 per cent indicated the opposite. In this new wave of R&D internationalisation, large US corporations are likely to play a critical role as they are planning to expand their reliance on R&D internationalisation. Furthermore, Japanese and South Korean firms are keen to move beyond their current low levels of R&D internationalisation.

Finally, Asia is expected to receive much of the future R&D internationalisation, with China being a more attractive location for future foreign R&D than even the United States and India. Leading global corporations also intend to expand their offshore outsourcing of R&D to Asian firms.

THE NEW MOBILITY OF INNOVATION

Only a decade ago, research on the geographical distribution of patents demonstrated that innovative activities of the world's largest firms were among the least internationalised of their functions (Patel and Pavitt 1991). This gave rise to the proposition that innovation, in contrast to most other stages of the value chain, is highly immobile: it remains tied to specific locations, despite a rapid geographic dispersion of markets, finance and production (e.g. Archibugi and Michie 1995).

Attempts to explain such spatial stickiness of innovation have highlighted the dense exchange of knowledge (much of it tacit) between the users and producers of the resultant new technologies. Research has thus focused on the *dynamics* of spatial agglomeration within localised innovation clusters (e.g. Feldman 1999; Porter and Solvell 1998; Jaffe *et al.* 2000).

Global innovation networks

There is no question that the demanding requirements of managing complex innovation projects tend to concentrate innovation in the home country. However, research on globalisation has clearly established that the centre of gravity has shifted beyond the national economy (e.g. Dunning 1998). International linkages proliferate as markets for capital, goods, services, technology and knowledge workers are integrated across borders (Ernst 2005c). While integration is far from perfect, especially in the latter two markets, it is nevertheless transforming the geography of innovation (Ernst 2002a).

Once globalisation extends beyond markets for goods and finance into markets for technology and knowledge workers, fundamental changes have occurred in corporate innovation management. A gradual opening and networking of corporate innovation systems is giving rise to GINs that cut across firm boundaries and national borders. Global corporations, primarily from the United States, are increasing their overseas investment in R&D while seeking to integrate geographically dispersed innovation clusters into global networks of production, engineering, development, and research. This trend has added a new dimension to the traditional notion of GPNs, transforming them into GINs.

There is an important element of continuity: GINs emerge as a natural extension of GPNs and hence share important characteristics with GPNs (Ernst 2006a). But, as we will see below, they also differ.

Global production networks

Let us first look at defining characteristics of GPNs and how they developed over time. Trade economists have explored the importance of changes in the organisation of international production as a determinant of trade patterns (e.g. Feenstra 1998; Jones and Kierzskowski 2000). Their work demonstrates that (a) production is increasingly 'fragmented', with parts of the production process being scattered across a number of countries, hence increasing the share of trade in parts and components; and (b) countries and regions which have been able to become a part of the global production network are the ones which have industrialised the fastest. And leading growth economists (e.g. Grossman and Helpman 2002) are basing their models on a systematic analysis of global production networking strategies.

Building on this work, I have developed a broader concept that emphasises three essential characteristics (Ernst 2002a, 2002b, 2003, 2005c):

- *asymmetry*: lead firms ('flagships') dominate control over network resources and decision making;
- *knowledge diffusion*: the sharing of knowledge is the necessary glue that enables these networks to grow; and
- *scope*: GPNs encompass all stages of the value chain, not just production.

GPNs differ from multinational corporations (MNCs) (as described in Boyson and Han, Chapter 2 in this volume) in three important ways. First, these networks cover both intra-firm and inter-firm transactions and forms of coordination: a GPN links the flagship's own subsidiaries, affiliates and joint ventures with its subcontractors, suppliers and service providers, as well as partners in strategic alliances. A network flagship like IBM or Intel breaks down the value chain into a variety of discrete functions and locates them wherever they can be carried out most effectively, where they can improve the flagship's access to resources and capabilities, and where they are needed to facilitate the penetration of important growth markets.

Second, GPNs differ from MNCs in that a great variety of governance structures is possible (see Dee, Chapter 10 in this volume). These networks range from loose linkages that are formed to implement a particular project and that are dissolved after the project is finished (so-called virtual enterprises) to highly formalised networks ('extended enterprises'), with clearly defined rules, common business processes and shared information infrastructures. What matters is that formalised networks do not require common ownership: these arrangements may or may not involve control of equity stakes.

Third, 'vertical specialisation' ('outsourcing' in business parlance) is the main driver of these networks (Ernst 2002b). GPNs help flagships to gain quick access to skills and capabilities at lower-cost overseas locations that complement the flagships' core competencies. As the flagship integrates geographically dispersed production, customer and knowledge bases into global production networks, this may well produce transaction cost savings. Yet the real benefits result from the dissemination, exchange and outsourcing of knowledge and complementary capabilities.

Over time, the focus of outsourcing is shifting from assembly-type manufacturing to knowledge-intensive support services, like supply chain management, engineering services, and new product introduction. Outsourcing may also include design and product development. This indicates that GPNs also differ from traditional forms of subcontracting – much denser interaction between design and production and other stages of the value chain require substantially more intense exchange of information and knowledge. Network flagships increasingly rely on the skills and knowledge of specialised suppliers to enhance their core competencies.

What distinguishes global innovation networks?

GINs share most of the above characteristics of GPNs, but they also differ. Take as an example changes in the methodology and organisation of chip design, a highly complex innovation activity (Ernst 2005a, 2005b).

Until the mid-1980s, global system companies and semiconductor firms did almost all their chip design in-house. Vertical integration focused on the design of an individual component to be inserted on a printed circuit board. Since the mid-1990s, however, there has been an upheaval in chip design methodology owing to intensifying pressures to improve design productivity combined with increasingly demanding performance features of electronic systems.[10]

'System-on-chip' design combines 'modular design'[11] and design automation to move design from the individual component on a printed circuit board closer to 'system-level integration' on a chip. Such design has fostered vertical specialisation in project execution, enabling firms to disintegrate the design value chain as well as to disperse it geographically. This has given rise to complex, multi-layered global GINs.

Three GIN layers can be distinguished. The first is the network core, which encompasses five strategic groups of firms. A 'system company' (like IBM) defines the concept, but may well outsource everything else. Chip design may take place within the 'system company', an integrated global semiconductor firm (like Intel), a 'fabless'[12] design house (like Xilinx), or a combination of these. Chip fabrication and assembly also may be outsourced to specialised suppliers. A secondary GIN layer consists of suppliers of tools for electronic design automation, verification, and chip testing. This layer also includes licensors of design building blocks (for example, ARM Ltd processors) and design implementation services. And a third layer may involve system contract manufacturers, such as Flextronics or Taiwan's Foxconn.

Initially, vertical specialisation loosened the bonds between design and fabrication. This process started with application-specific integrated circuit design, where the goal was to avoid the high cost and time required to design a full-custom chip.[13] The Taiwan Semiconductor Manufacturing Company (TSMC), established in 1987, was an important catalyst. TSMC provides contract chip fabrication ('silicon foundry') services for fabless design houses that outsource chip fabrication and target specialised niche markets. Until the early 1990s, global design networks were centred on the well-known symbiotic fabless–foundry relationship, and hence retained a relatively simple structure.

Over time, however, vertical specialisation has increased the number and variety of network participants, business models, and design interfaces, bringing together design teams from companies that drastically differ in size, market power, location, and nationality. In one interview I conducted, a GIN included the following participants:

- a Chinese system company, which defined the system architecture;
- a Taiwanese contract manufacturer, which produced the resulting electronic equipment;
- an American integrated global semiconductor firm, which provided a design platform; and
- a European firm, which provided an embedded processor as an important design building-block.

Additional network participants included:

- fabless design houses from the United States and Taiwan;
- silicon foundries from Taiwan, Singapore, and China;
- chip-packaging companies from Taiwan and China;

- tool vendors for design automation and testing from the United States and India; and
- design support service providers from various Asian countries.

Intra-firm versus inter-firm innovation networks

Global firms like Intel and TI expand their intra-firm GINs by investing in offshore R&D labs (Table 3.1).

Take Intel as an example. Its labs in Santa Clara, Folsom and Austin remain primary locations for core technology development and applied research, while Haifa (established in 1974) is focused on processor research and Nishny Novgorod on software development. However, most of the action now is in Asia. In addition to its existing seven labs in Asia, Intel is planning to expand rapidly both the number of labs and their headcounts. Bangalore, Intel's largest lab outside the United States, conducts leading-edge dual processor development. With a workforce of around 2,700, management is seeking ways of recruiting additional engineers. In Shanghai, Intel has recently expanded its R&D team to focus on applied research to identify new applications for emerging markets. The Bangalore lab of TI signals the speed and depth of innovation offshoring to Asia. Established in 1985, it is TI's largest lab outside the United States, with more than 2,500 employees. By 1989 it was able to develop ASIC CAD libraries. Since 1998, it has conducted integrated development projects

Table 3.1 Intel's global innovation network

Location	Site	Workforce	Function
US (11 labs)	Santa Clara, Folsom, Austin		Core technology development
Asia (7 labs, more planned)	Bangalore	2,700 (largest lab outside US)	Leading-edge processor development
	Penang	500	Design implementation
	Shanghai	100++	Linux-based solutions for telecoms; new applications for emerging markets
	Beijing	50++	Platform and architecture lab
Israel	Haifa	1,400 since 1974	Processor research
Russia	Nizhny Novgorod	200++	Software

Source: Interviews conducted by the author.

for highly complex system-on-chip design. Since 2000, it has had the global mandate for co-developing 3G wireless chipsets and wireless local area network chipsets.

Global firms also outsource some stages of innovation, especially those related to product development, to specialised offshore suppliers as part of complex inter-firm GINs. For instance, global brand leaders for laptops and handsets use design services provided by so-called ODMs, mostly from Taiwan, for new product development. ODMs either implement a detailed set of design specifications provided by the global brand leader or provide their proprietary integrated 'turnkey' solution to basic performance parameters requested by the global brand leaders. In addition, global system companies (like IBM) and integrated device manufacturers (like Intel) are outsourcing to Asian fabless design houses the development of specific design building blocks and design implementation services (Ernst 2005a, 2005b).

The result is that, instead of a few pre-eminent centres of innovation, like Silicon Valley in the United States, there are now 'multiple locations for innovation ... around the world, and even lower-order or less developed centres can still be sources of innovation' (Cantwell 1995: 172). In chip design, for instance, a handful of new, but rapidly expanding, clusters is emerging in Asia in places like Hsinchu, Taipei, and Tainan (in Taiwan); in Shanghai, the Yangtze River Delta, Beijing, Shenzhen, the Pearl River Delta and Xián (China); in Seoul (South Korea); in Bangalore, Noida, Chennai, Hyderabad, Mumbai, Puneh and Ahmedabad (India); in Penang and Kuala Lumpur (Malaysia); and in Singapore (Ernst 2005a).

Centrifugal forces

Moreover, there is a growing recognition that the balance is shifting from 'centripetal' to 'centrifugal' forces. In other words, the globalisation of markets, technology, competition, and strategy and the resultant opening of corporate innovation systems have boosted the forces for geographical decentralisation of R&D. 'Pull' factors that attract R&D to particular locations include demand-oriented and supply-oriented forces and policies. 'Centrifugal' forces can be stronger than 'centripetal' forces when the host country market is large, grows rapidly, and becomes more sophisticated.

Supply-oriented forces are especially important in high-tech industries like electronics (Dalton and Serapio 1999: 40; Ernst 1997). Proximity to global manufacturing bases matters. However, the search for lower-cost overseas R&D personnel and for new ideas and innovative capabilities is increasingly important. As the pace and cost of technological development escalate and as the sources of breakthrough general-purpose technologies proliferate, companies must seek access to a wider range of scientific and technological skills and knowledge than is available in the home market.

We need to distinguish between 'home-base-exploiting' and 'home-base-augmenting' overseas R&D labs (Kuemmerle 1996). 'Home-base-exploiting' overseas R&D has been around for a long time. Its *raison d'être* is to transfer knowledge from the corporation's home base for commercialisation in overseas markets. The key requirement for overseas R&D is the adaptation of products, services, and production processes to local needs and resource endowments.

By contrast, 'home-base-augmenting' overseas R&D has become considerably more important during the last decades of the 20th century. Its rationale is 'external knowledge sourcing' – that is to say, tapping into new knowledge from an increasing number of overseas local innovation clusters, transferring that knowledge back to the home base (Kuemmerle 1997: 66), and combining these diverse technologies to create new products and processes (e.g. Granstrand *et al.* 1997). Hence, augmenting overseas R&D requires much more than adaptive engineering. It includes product development as well as applied and fundamental research.

Finally, what makes it possible to exchange complex knowledge among research teams that are located at distant locations? Research on the dynamics of global innovation networks shows that members of a specialised knowledge community – the people who share specialised skills like analog chip design – share rules and codes for exchanging knowledge. Even when dispersed far away in space, members of such communities 'will share more jargon and trust among each other than with any outsider within their present local communities. And even when meetings are required, their frequency will not necessarily be as high as to impose co-localisation as a necessary requirement for belonging to the epistemic community' (Breschi and Lissoni 2001: 991).

In short, for innovative activities that require complex knowledge it is now possible to create and connect teams of knowledge workers in distant locations, such as Silicon Valley, Seoul, Taiwan's Hsinchu Science Park, Beijing, Shanghai, Bangalore, Delhi and Hyderabad. The emergence of these kinds of multiple innovation clusters underlies the spread of innovation offshoring.

Driving forces

Innovation offshoring is driven by the same forces that gave rise to the offshoring of industrial manufacturing – liberalisation and technology (Dee, Chapter 10 in this volume; Ernst 1997, 2002b, 2005c). However, both forces have now reached a much higher level, pushing globalisation beyond markets for goods and finance into markets for technology and knowledge workers (Ernst 2006a).

Institutional change through liberalisation has played an important role in reducing constraints on the organisational and geographical mobility of innovation. Liberalisation includes four main elements: trade, capital flows, FDI, and privatisation. These different forms of liberalisation hang together. Trade liberalisation typically sparks an expansion of trade and FDI which, in turn, increases demand for cross-border capital flows. This increases pressure for liberalisation of capital markets, which forces more and more countries to open their capital accounts. This also encourages liberalisation of FDI and privatisation 'tournaments'.

The overall effect of liberalisation has been to reduce the cost and risks of international transactions and to considerably increase international liquidity. Global corporations have been the primary beneficiaries. Liberalisation provides them with a greater range of choices for market entry, be it via trade, licensing, subcontracting or franchising (*locational specialisation*); better access to external resources and capabilities that they may need to complement their core competencies (*outsourcing*); or fewer constraints on the geographic dispersion of the value chain (*spatial mobility*). Hence, liberalisation has acted as a powerful catalyst for the expansion of global production and innovation networks.

In addition, technology has played an important role in increasing the mobility of innovation. This is true in particular for the rapid development and diffusion of information and communication technology. The high cost and risk of developing IT have forced companies to search for lower-cost locations for R&D. Equally important is that IT and related organisational innovations provide effective mechanisms for constructing flexible network arrangements that can link together and coordinate economic transactions among geographically dispersed locations. IT-enabled network management reduces the cost of communication, helps to codify knowledge through software tools and databases, enables remote control, and facilitates exchange of tacit knowledge through audiovisual media.

This has substantially reduced the friction of time and space not only for sales and production, but also for R&D and other innovative activities. IT-enabled network management has facilitated the exchange of knowledge among diverse knowledge communities at distant locations that work together on an innovation project. In essence, IT has fostered the development of leaner and more agile production and innovation networks that cut across firm boundaries and national borders.

Liberalisation and IT have drastically changed the dynamics of competition and industrial organisation. Competition now cuts across national borders. The firm must be present in all major growth markets (dispersion). It must also integrate its activities on a worldwide scale in order to exploit and coordinate linkages between these different locations (integration). In addition, competition cuts across sector boundaries and market segments. Mutual raiding of established market segment fiefdoms has become the norm, making it more difficult for firms to identify market niches and to grow with them.

Vertical specialisation

To cope with the growing complexity of competition, global companies have had to adjust their strategies and organisation. Competitive success critically depends on vertical specialisation. Global firms selectively outsource certain capabilities from specialised suppliers and 'offshore' them to new, lower-cost locations. While vertical specialisation initially focused on final assembly and lower-end component manufacturing, increasingly it is being pushed into higher-end value-chain stages, including product development and research.

To make this happen, global firms have had to adopt collective forms of organisation, shifting from the multidivisional (M-form) functional hierarchy (Chandler 1977) to the networked global flagship model (Ernst 2002b).

The electronics industry has been an important breeding ground for this new industrial organisation model.[14] A massive process of vertical specialisation has segmented an erstwhile vertically integrated industry into closely interacting horizontal layers (Grove 1996). Until the early 1980s, IBM personified 'vertical integration.' Almost all ingredients necessary to design, produce, and commercialise computers remained internal to the firm. This was true for semiconductors, hardware, operating systems, application software, and sales and distribution.

Since then, however, vertical specialisation has become the industry's defining characteristic (Ernst 2003). Many activities that a computer company used to handle internally are now being farmed out to multiple layers of specialised suppliers. This has given rise to rapid market segmentation and to an ever-finer specialisation within each of the above value-chain stages. As firms accumulate experience in managing global distribution and production networks and learn from successes and failures in inter-firm collaboration, they have been able to expand vertical specialisation.

These adjustments were especially important in the choice of product and process specialisation, investment funding, and human resources management. As they feed into each other, small changes in any of these functions require adjustments in all the other aspects of the business model.

Vertical specialisation has been made possible by the spread of venture capital and related regulatory changes in the financial sector[15] that drastically changed corporate strategies of investment funding. US venture capital firms have provided access to a massive infusion of capital from US pension funds as well as hands-on industrial expertise. As a result, start-up companies in the electronics industry have been able to raise capital for high-risk innovation projects. At the same time, global industry leaders increasingly have used stock to attract and retain global talent and to acquire innovative start-up companies (Lazonick 2003).

This has led to a dramatically diminished commitment to long-term employment in the electronics industry. The result has been a substantial increase in the inter-firm and geographical mobility of labour, especially for highly skilled engineers, scientists, and managers. In the United States, the emergence of a 'high-velocity labor market' (Hyde 2003) for IT skills is driven by the proliferation of start-up companies, a drastic increase in the recruitment of highly educated foreigners, and the spread of lavish incentives (such as stock options) to induce job-hopping.

These practices have raised the cost of employing IT workers in the United States. For instance, between 1993 and 1999, computer scientists and mathematicians experienced the highest salary growth (37 per cent) of all US occupations (National Science Board 2004: chapter 3, p. 14). Average real annual earnings of full-time employees in California's software industry rose from $80,000 in 1994 to $180,000 in 2000, only to fall drastically to below $100,000 in 2002 after the bursting of the 'new economy' bubble.

But even in the midst of the IT industry recession, employees in the US IT industry continued to earn, on average, far more than workers in most other sectors of the economy, and between five and ten times more than their counterparts in Asia (outside Japan). In 2002, the average annual wage in the US IT industry was $67,440 ($99,440 in the software industry), compared with $36,250 in all private sector industries (US Department of Commerce 2003: appendix table 2.3). This has created a powerful catalyst for US IT firms to increase their overseas investment in R&D to tap into the growing pool of educated and experienced IT talent that is available in Asia at much lower wages.

Changes in innovation management

The above transformations in strategy and organisation have provoked fundamental changes in innovation management, further enhancing the mobility of innovation. There is a transition under way towards more open corporate innovation systems based on increasing vertical specialisation of innovation.

Corporate innovation management must address five tasks simultaneously: (a) develop and protect IPRs; (b) upgrade innovative capabilities (including R&D);[16] (c) recruit and retain educated and experienced knowledge workers; (d) adjust innovation process management (methodologies, organisation and routines) in order to improve efficiency and time to market; and (e) match all four tasks with the corporation's business model.

No firm, not even a global market leader like IBM, can mobilise internally all the diverse resources, capabilities and bodies of knowledge that are necessary to fulfil these tasks. As a consequence, both the sources and the use of knowledge have become increasingly externalised. Firms now must supplement the in-house creation of new knowledge and capabilities with external knowledge sourcing strategies. There are strong pressures to reduce in-house basic and applied research and to focus primarily on product development and the absorption of external knowledge (e.g. Chesbrough 2003).[17]

No longer does this externalisation of innovation stop at the national border. Firms increasingly need to tap sources of knowledge that are located overseas (Ernst 2002a). The result is that GINs cut across sectors and national borders (Ernst 2005b). According to the most recent *Science and Engineering Indicators 2004* report by the US National Science Board:

> ... the speed, complexity, and multidisciplinary nature of scientific research, coupled with the increased relevance of science and the demands of a globally competitive environment, have ... encouraged an innovation system increasingly characterised by networking and feedback among R&D performers, technology users, and their suppliers and across industries and national boundaries. (National Science Board 2004: Volume I, page IV-36)

Global markets for technology

Global firms have been able to move to an open innovation system because an increasing division of labour in innovation has given rise to global markets for technology (Arora *et al.* 2001). Global firms can now outsource knowledge needed to complement their internally generated knowledge. Furthermore, they can elect to license their technology and, hence, enhance the rents from innovation.[18]

There is now much greater scope for external technology sourcing. Global markets for technology imply that a firm's competitive success critically depends on its ability to monitor and quickly seize external sources of knowledge (e.g. Iansiti 1997). As demonstrated by Iansiti and West (1997), a company can leverage basic or generic technologies developed elsewhere. This allows it to focus on developing unique applications that better suit the needs of specific overseas markets.

Innovation offshoring helps global firms to hedge against failures of internal R&D projects or against slippage in capacity expansion. Innovation offshoring also makes it possible to multiply opportunities for technology diversification. There is a choice between 'building or buying' new business lines. Furthermore, global firms can accelerate the speed of the innovation cycle and reduce the very high fixed cost of investing in internal R&D.

Late entrants from Asia can also benefit from external knowledge sourcing. While they continue to trail behind industry leaders in their in-house technological capabilities, Asian companies can now use external technology sourcing to enhance their in-house innovative capabilities (e.g. Ernst 1997, 2000).

An important constraint to the emergence of global markets for technology is a set of unresolved issues related to the protection of IPRs. Fear of IPR theft has shaped corporate decisions on the location and nature of R&D centres. As discussed below, it also poses important challenges for government policies. There is broad consensus that global firms are unlikely to establish an R&D lab in a country that cannot guarantee effective IPR protection. The underlying assumption, supported by a vast literature (e.g. Teece 2000), is that a strong IPR Regime is critical to encourage innovation.

Note however that, despite weak IPR protection, Asian countries, and especially China, have been able to attract a massive inflow of R&D investments by global corporations. One possible explanation for this puzzle may be that IPR protection may be less important for adaptive and production support R&D or when products that result from overseas R&D in China are exported to the world market and not to the domestic China market. In this case, IPR theft by local firms may be less likely.

An additional explanation may be that vertical specialisation ('fragmentation') within GINs may allow global firms to navigate better the pitfalls of weak IPR regimes, especially for export-oriented R&D. 'Vertical specialisation' means that an innovation project consists of multiple building blocks that complement each other and that can only be used jointly. Global firms can establish R&D affiliates in countries with weak IPR protection (for example, China) to undertake R&D on technologies that require multiple complementary elements as part of a complex technology system. In this case, IPR theft for a particular technology is unlikely to generate economic rents for the perpetrator.

There is no doubt, however, that, over time, effective IPR protection will increase in importance, especially if Asian countries seek to attract more advanced foreign R&D projects and as domestic firms develop their own IPRs. As indicated below, this raises important policy issues for Asian governments that need to be addressed in future research.

Evolving global markets for knowledge workers

The growing availability of knowledge workers outside the dominant corporations and their increasing geographical mobility have been equally important for the gradual opening of corporate innovation systems. As demonstrated in the first part of this chapter, the supply of knowledge workers suitable for work in global corporations is growing substantially in Asia's leading electronics exporting countries. The same is true in eastern Europe and Latin America.

The result is an evolving global market for knowledge workers, which has created vast new talent sources. At the urging of American business, the US government responded to the changes in the knowledge worker market by allowing greater immigration of foreign students and professionals, especially for S&E. Until the turn of the century, the United States was the main beneficiary of the globalisation of knowledge workers.

A 1998 National Science Foundation study showed that more than 50 per cent of the post-doctoral students at the Massachusetts Institute of Technology and Stanford were not US citizens and that more than 30 per cent of computer professionals in Silicon Valley were born outside the United States (quoted in National Science Board 2004). Data from the 2000 US Census show that in S&E occupations, approximately 17 per cent of bachelor's degree holders, 29 per cent of master's degree holders, and 38 per cent of doctorate holders were foreign born.

This has enabled US start-up companies to pursue 'learning-by-hiring away' strategies. They could rapidly ramp up complex innovation projects by recruiting highly experienced personnel that were trained by other corporations or countries. But the main beneficiaries were major global US firms that were able to reduce the cost of research, product development, and engineering by shifting from national to global recruitment strategies.

Over the past few years, global firms have faced new challenges in global markets for knowledge workers. The shift to knowledge-intensive industries has increased the importance and scarcity of well-trained knowledge workers. At the same time, ageing populations are reducing the available working populations in Europe, Japan and the United States. With the exception of India, ageing is also a serious challenge for Asia's leading exporting countries.[19] As a result, the growth of global markets for knowledge workers is likely to slow down. This implies that, over the next decade or so, global electronics firms will find it increasingly difficult to attract – and retain – enough qualified workers, especially scientists and engineers.

Intensifying competition for knowledge workers also reflects negative side effects of the aforementioned changes in corporate strategy. For instance, in their quest to improve return on investment, global electronics firms have increased the use of temporary workers and have outsourced so-called non-core activities. The resultant downsizing of permanent workforces has increased the vulnerability of these companies to sudden shifts in demand.

Some global corporations pushed downsizing to the limits, especially after 2000. In the words of one expert, 'they're running themselves so lean that if they get a little sand in their gears, the whole organisation breaks down'.[20] If demand shifts to new product generations that require new technologies, these firms must search for specialised talent to fill the gaps caused by previous rounds of downsizing. As a result, crisis management has become the dominant concern of human resources managers.

Global corporations are responding to the intensifying competition for scarce global talent by moving R&D and engineering overseas, especially to populous countries like China and India that have emerged as important new sources of lower-cost S&E students and workers. For many high-tech companies, competing for scarce global talent has become a major strategic concern. As a result, global sourcing of knowledge workers now is as important as global manufacturing and supply chain strategies. The goal is to diversify and optimise a company's human capital portfolio through aggressive recruitment in global labour markets.

The demand for 'bottleneck skills', such as experienced design engineers for analog integrated circuits, has led to global 'auction markets' for knowledge workers. These 'auctions' enable knowledge workers to sell their talents to the highest bidder. Overall, however, the emergence of a global market for knowledge workers seems to have kept a tight cap on increases in remuneration (Lazonick 2005). This is because the leading global electronics firms can tap this market for workers who are readily available for hire and need not require extensive internal training or the inducement of lifelong employment.

By the same token, this market can be highly volatile and pose substantial risks. At any time, demand for knowledge workers may outstrip supply in some locations and supply will exceed demand in other locations. Especially for more senior and experienced engineers and project managers, demand continues to overshoot supply in Asia's major offshore locations.

In China, for instance, there is a paucity of project managers well versed in implementing state-of-the-art innovation process management. Competition for scarce talent (especially in S&E) has intensified, as large Chinese companies, such as Lenovo and Huawei, are now seriously competing for the best talent.[21] In India, it is less of a problem finding experienced project managers owing to India's long-established links with the United States and the roles played by non-resident Indians. But turnover rates are extremely high, and global firms are facing serious problems in establishing effective control and efficient processes (NASSCOM and McKinsey 2005).

The volatility of global markets for knowledge workers reflects a fundamental characteristic of innovation offshoring – its geographic dispersion remains concentrated in a handful of new clusters. This tends to prematurely exhaust the limited supply of suitable engineers in these clusters, giving rise to severe bouts of localised wage inflation and excessive turnover rates for key personnel. Global corporations are forced to constantly readjust and rebalance their location decisions and network management strategies and to continuously search for and experiment with new locations.

As a result, companies that have accumulated some experience in innovation offshoring are now shifting from 'labour-cost arbitrage' to strategies to reduce the extremely high turnover and retain scarce talent. In fact, in well-established offshore locations in Bangalore or Shanghai global firms are now willing to conduct 'exciting' R&D projects that can attract the best and brightest of the local talent pool.

At the same time, global firms are constantly seeking to identify new offshore locations with lower-cost populations of knowledge workers, such as lower-tier cities in China and India, or new locations in Vietnam, Romania, Armenia and Slovakia. But to develop these new locations, global firms must invest in the training of local knowledge workers.[22]

Implications for innovation offshoring

The transition to open innovation networks has changed the way in which global corporations are using their overseas R&D centres in Asia. A recent study about

R&D investment in China by major international companies illustrates this point (Armbrecht 2003). The study emphasises that, while cost savings matter, global firms are expanding their R&D in China primarily for strategic reasons. They want to tap into the vast pool of talent and ideas in order to stay abreast of competitors in the increasingly sophisticated markets of China and Asia. The Industrial Research Institute, which conducted the study, predicts a substantial increase in innovation offshoring in China.[23] The institute argues that the focus of overseas R&D labs is shifting from support and adaptation to the sourcing of China's emerging technologies and talent pools.

The following taxonomy (Ernst, forthcoming) helps to capture the evolution of R&D labs established by global electronics firms in China.

- 'Satellite' R&D labs, the least developed type of lab, combine elements of 'home-base-exploiting' and 'home-base-augmenting' R&D. These labs are of relatively low strategic importance, as evidenced by their vulnerability to budget cuts decided by headquarters.
- 'Contract' R&D labs describe the pure-play version of 'innovation offshore outsourcing'. For these labs, China's role is confined to the provision of lower-cost skills, capabilities and infrastructure. While dense information flows link these labs with R&D teams at headquarters and other affiliates, knowledge exchange remains tightly controlled, and highly unequal.
- The term '(more) equal partnership' labs is reserved for labs at the highest stage: those R&D labs of global firms that are charged with a regional or global product mandate. For these labs, barriers to knowledge exchange are supposed to be much lower, and may eventually give way to full-fledged mutual knowledge exchange.

Recent research documents the continued domination of satellite and contract R&D labs (e.g. von Zedwitz 2004; Gassmann and Han 2004; Li and Zhong 2003). However, there are also examples of (more) equal partnership arrangements, especially related to the development of China's alternative standards in mobile telecommunications, open source software, and digital consumer electronics (Ernst and Naughton 2005; Garcia and Burns 2006).

POLICY IMPLICATIONS FOR ASIA

This chapter demonstrates that innovation offshoring results from fundamental changes in business organisation. 'Vertical specialisation' is no longer restricted to the production of goods and services. It now extends to all stages of the value chain, including research and new product development. As the number of specialised suppliers of innovation modules increases, this provides a powerful boost to the organisational and geographical mobility of innovation.

Over the years, this process has taken on an increasingly international dimension – global firms construct GINs to improve the productivity of R&D by recruiting knowledge workers from cheaper, non-traditional locations.

Since the turn of the century, these networks have been extended to emerging new innovation clusters, especially in Asia. This trend is expected to provide global firms with a powerful new source of competitive advantage because they can now quickly generate more and higher-value innovation at lower cost.

Benefits and challenges

For Asian countries, innovation offshoring could provide substantial benefits, *provided* adequate policies and business strategies are in place. Equally important are the removal of barriers to trade and investment and the establishment of a robust IPR regime that combines protection with incentives for the creation of new intellectual property.

Case studies show that integration into global innovation networks could facilitate knowledge diffusion and learning, and that it could catalyse efforts by local firms to develop innovative capabilities (Ernst 2005c). To the degree that this would be translated into the creation and successful commercialisation of new products and services, this might help Asian efforts to counter the decreasing returns to the export-led 'global factory' model. It might also help Asian countries to move from extensive growth with diminishing returns to augmented growth with constant or increasing returns to investment.[24]

However, massive challenges must be mastered before Asian countries can exploit the above opportunities. To benefit from innovation offshoring, Asian governments now need to develop policies in three inter-related areas: by attracting and expanding R&D investments by global firms; reducing opportunity costs of innovation offshoring; and enabling Asian firms to develop their own innovative capabilities.

Most debates have focused on the first policy challenge. A combination of trade and investment liberalisation and state-supported incentives are widely used policy tools to induce foreign R&D investments. However, if Asia fails to meet the other two challenges, it is unlikely to reap sustainable benefits from innovation offshoring.

Creating an enabling environment

Countries and regions around the globe are fiercely competing to attract and expand R&D by global firms. The goal is to become better connected to GINs. As countries progress in their economic development, they increasingly rely on knowledge exchange through these networks.

As more and more countries become connected to these networks, there will be increased pressure on other countries to attract foreign R&D as well, in order to avoid being sidelined as pariahs in an increasingly inter-connected global innovation system. Hence, whether one likes it or not, integration into GINs seems to emerge as an increasingly important determinant of future prospects for economic development.

But there are also concerns that network integration may be a poisoned chalice. It is feared that integration into GINs may at best produce only short-term benefits and may not provide the means for upgrading the host country's industry to higher value-added and more knowledge-intensive activities.

Unfortunately, research on these issues is still at a very early stage: there are few robust data, and getting data on the offshoring of R&D is becoming more difficult, as global corporations are loath to disclose this sensitive information because it could negatively affect their stock market quotation (Ernst 2006a).

However, the literature does provide theoretical as well as empirical reasons to argue that, from a developing country's policy perspective, integration into GINs may provide substantial benefits (e.g. Lall 2000; Ernst *et al.* 1998). In a case study of Malaysia's electronics industry, Ernst (2004) demonstrates that attracting foreign R&D may do more than compensate for initial weaknesses of the domestic knowledge base. Such international knowledge sourcing may also facilitate the adjustment of business organisation and strategy to abrupt changes in technology and markets. Attracting R&D by global firms may also catalyse the development and the diffusion of innovative capabilities *ahead* of what the market would provide.

All of this implies that Asian countries cannot build their innovative capabilities by solely relying on their national innovation systems and by developing localised innovation clusters. For quite some time, these countries will have to draw primarily on foreign sources of knowledge as the main vehicle of learning and capability formation. However, in order to reap the potential benefits from innovation offshoring, Asian countries must have in place vigorous policies to reduce the potentially high opportunity costs that may result from 'brain drain' (both domestic and international), when global firms are crowding out the local market for scarce skills. Other costs include the possible deterrence effect on local R&D by the involvement of global labs; the acquisition by global firms of innovative local companies; and the disproportionately high benefits that may accrue to a foreign parent company.

In other words, innovation offshoring can produce sustainable long-term economic benefits for Asian countries only if policies exist to develop strong local companies that can act as countervailing forces to the accumulated strengths of global firms. But for Asia to cope with the complex challenges and opportunities of innovation offshoring, new policies are required that are very different from earlier top-down 'command economy' industrial policies that were typical for the 'East Asian development model'.

Recent research on the offshoring of chip design to Asia demonstrates the importance of well-functioning product and factor markets (Ernst 2005a). Market failures *per se* may not necessarily prevent global firms from investing in R&D, especially if this generates windfall profits. The main concern appears to be a certain degree of transparency and predictability that allows for the longer-term planning that is necessary for R&D. Host country policies can actually use idiosyncratic market characteristics to differentiate a particular location and to increase its attractiveness for foreign R&D.

For instance, differences in financial markets can lead to diverse approaches to investment finance (for example, debt, equity or retained earnings) that will influence the volume and direction of investment in complementary R&D activities by local firms. In addition, the examples of South Korea and China demonstrate that host country policies to define alternative standards (for example, for 3G mobile communication systems or open source software), combined with the use of government procurement, can be powerful tools in attracting foreign R&D.

In the final analysis, however, policies to attract R&D by global firms can succeed only if they fulfil two critical conditions: they need to balance effective protection of IPRs with incentives for knowledge diffusion to local firms; and they need to provide a sufficiently large pool of knowledge workers who possess the skills needed to benefit from innovation offshoring.

Policies on intellectual property rights

If Asian countries seek to attract more advanced foreign R&D projects, an effective protection of IPRs becomes as important as the development of their own IPRs.

Well-defined enforceable patents reduce transaction costs, and thereby help increase the mobility of knowledge. In theory, smaller firms (for instance, local Asian firms) are expected to draw the greatest benefits. It is assumed that a stronger IPR regime increases the returns from investments in technology development more substantially for smaller innovative start-up companies than for the larger integrated companies.

In reality, however, the market for patents displays important imperfections (von Hippel 2005; Merrill *et al.* 2004; Cohen and Merrill 2003). For instance, reaping the benefits of IPRs may be costly, and small firms may face greater difficulties than large corporations in patenting. Even more important is the so-called 'anti-commons' problem (Arora *et al.* 2001: 263 ff). It is unrealistic to assume that each patent is associated with one innovation only.

In the IT industry this is a serious problem, as innovative activities require highly complex knowledge. In complex technology systems, innovation is systemic and cumulative, requiring many different pieces of knowledge, some of which may be patented and owned by companies with conflicting interests. Typically, however, IPR protection is fragmented. The resulting constraints to innovation can be substantial. For instance, for the inventor, the cost of 'inventing around' blocking patents can be extremely high. And the higher these costs are, the weaker is the innovator's bargaining power in the licensing negotiations.

This raises two important, but very tricky, policy questions. How should different contributors be rewarded? And who is likely to capture most benefits? While institutional arrangements for IPR protection matter, the outcome is primarily determined by bargaining power. This indicates how difficult it is for Asian governments to find the level of IPR protection that balances the interests of global and local companies.

It is important to emphasise that the protection of IPRs needs to be complemented with policies that foster the exchange of knowledge embodied in these IPRs. One critically important aspect is the development of effective linkages between universities and public research institutes, on the one hand, and R&D establishments of private business on the other (e.g. Ernst and Mowery 2004). There is a widespread perception that US leadership in industrial innovation owes much to the capacity of its higher education system to provide multiple and dense interlinkages between university research and innovation in enterprises.

This explains why major developing nations have launched or are considering significant public policy initiatives to strengthen university–industry linkages, in many cases consciously modelling these efforts on the perceived 'success factors' in the United States. Many of these initiatives seek to spur local economic development based on university research. This includes, for instance, the creation of 'science parks' located near research university campuses; support for 'business incubators' and public 'seed capital' funds; and the organisation of other forms of 'bridging institutions' that are believed to link universities to industrial innovation.

An important challenge for public policy is to establish a legal framework and a set of regulations that can facilitate the exchange of IPRs. A second equally important task would be to assign IPRs to the results of research that the government funds. One policy initiative that has attracted considerable attention from governments elsewhere is the 1980 Bayh–Dole Act in the United States, which provided a framework for the encouragement of patenting and licensing of publicly funded R&D results by universities.

But within the United States, the effects and desirability of the Bayh–Dole Act remain controversial (Mowery *et al.* 2004). There are concerns that this approach may slow down the diffusion of useful basic knowledge to the rest of society. While US universities have been important sources of knowledge and other key inputs for industrial innovation, much of this economic contribution has relied on channels other than patenting and licensing. Such broader university–industry linkages include knowledge exchange through, for instance, publications, conference presentations and faculty consulting, as well as the movement of personnel between universities and industry.

It is necessary to explore under what conditions the US approach to university–industry linkages can serve as a useful framework for policy elsewhere. Unfortunately, very little scholarly research is available to guide policy debates on this important issue. Research on the role of universities in industrial innovation has focused on the United States, Japan and major European economies (see e.g. Branscomb *et al.* 1999). While there are a few pioneering studies on national innovation systems in Asian countries like South Korea, Taiwan, China and Malaysia (e.g. Kim 1997; Naughton and Segal 2002; Rasiah 1995), the role of university–industry linkages has not been at the centre of analysis. Most importantly, there is no systematic cross-national comparative research on the diverse development trajectories of developing countries' higher education systems and the diverse array of university–industry linkages (Ernst and Mowery 2004).

Policies on education and skill development

Finally, an important yardstick for policies to attract foreign R&D is the supply of well-educated and experienced technicians, engineers, managers and scientists at a cost that is substantially lower than their cost at the home country locations of global firms. This requires incessant efforts on a massive scale to continuously upgrade existing skills and capabilities.

The lack of depth and horizontal mobility in the labour markets that is typical of most Asian countries increases the risk of individual investment in specialised skills. This explains why in many of these countries mismatches between the supply and the demand of specialised skills persist. To reduce these mismatches requires well-thought-out policies.

A recent study on Malaysia's electronics industry (Ernst 2004) shows that policy-makers and industry executives realise the need for new policies to:

- re-skill and re-train production workers, technicians, and engineers;
- expose S&E students to best-practice methodologies and tools and adjust curricula development to evolving labour market needs;
- produce graduates, especially for electrical and electronics engineering, IT, communication technology and circuit design, who are able to combine hardware, software and application knowledge;
- produce experienced managers, especially for strategic marketing, upgrading management, and management of international linkages;
- provide incentives for entrepreneurs that combine street-wise commercial and financial instincts with analytic capacity for strategic decision making;
- develop a cadre of experienced and industry-savvy administrators who are willing to stick out their necks and to do more than just follow the rules (this, of course, requires some incentive alignment);
- align incentives for university professors and academics that encourage close interaction with the private sector (company internships and sabbaticals);
- encourage dense interactions with expatriate nationals who are based in the United States, Australia and Europe, or in Asia; and
- bring in at short notice specialised experts from overseas who can help bridge existing knowledge gaps and who can catalyse necessary changes in organisation and procedures required to develop these capabilities locally.

The last two policy objectives are critical for policies to upgrade Asia's pool of knowledge workers. As global markets for knowledge workers evolve, such policies of leveraging international knowledge communities are also becoming more feasible. In the electronics industry, for instance, these informal social networks link developing countries with the world's centres of information and communications technology (encompassing Silicon Valley and other centres of excellence in less well-known places like Helsinki, Kista/Stockholm, Grenoble, Munich, Tsukuba and Tel Aviv).

This provides Asian countries with invaluable knowledge on global market and technology trends in a way that addresses the needs of domestic firms much better than formal linkages with global firms (Ernst 2006c). International knowledge communities also provide entrepreneurs and venture capitalists that can function in both worlds. This has created alternative and robust mechanisms of knowledge exchange across geographic borders and firm boundaries.

NOTES

I owe Juan Palacios a great debt of gratitude for inviting me to present this paper at the 31st Pacific Trade and Development Conference and for his thought-provoking suggestions. I gratefully acknowledge ideas, comments and suggestions from Jenny Corbett, Ralph Huenemann, David Hong, Pang Eng Fong, Peter Petri, Shujiro Urata, and Alfonso Mercado. At the East–West Center, I am grateful to Charles Morrison and Nancy Lewis for supporting this research. I also thank Seiji Naya and participants at East–West Center seminars. The Volkswagen Foundation provided generous funding for research on the offshoring of chip design. Kitty Chiu, Peter Pawlicki and Rena Tomlinson provided excellent research assistance.

1 Throughout this paper, 'Asia' excludes Japan. Unless indicated otherwise, data are from the author's research (Ernst 2005a, 2005b, 2006a, and forthcoming).
2 'Knowledge workers' are defined to include science and engineering personnel, as well as managers and specialised professionals (in areas like marketing, legal services and industrial design) who provide essential support services to research, development and engineering.
3 Future PAFTAD conferences could help to develop the analysis of impacts of innovation offshoring. As emphasised by Ralph Huenemann at the conference, future research needs to explore whether there is diffusion of innovations from multinational corporation labs to extra-firm labs and identify the main mechanisms for technology diffusion (illustrative case studies can be found in Ernst 2006b, 2006c, 2006d). For one participant at the conference, Jenny Corbett, another important topic for the impact analysis is the connection between the development of GINs and productivity growth in Asia. Such an analysis can build on the findings of new growth theories to establish (a) whether GINs can lead Asia to move from extensive growth with diminishing returns to augmented growth with constant or increasing returns to investment; (b) whether this depends on the number of knowledge workers or the size of R&D expenditure; and (c) whether it depends on creating local capacity to initiate new technologies or on continuing to borrow. All of this indicates to what degree innovation offshoring and GINs are raising new questions for future theoretical and empirical research.
4 In 2000, 85 per cent of global R&D expenditures were concentrated in only seven industrialised countries. The United States occupied the leading position with 37 per cent (Dahlman and Aubert 2001: 34).
5 '*Chaebol*' is a Korean term for a business conglomerate.
6 The two dominant competing global 3G standards are wireless CDMA (W-CDMA) (compatible with existing 'Global System for Mobile Communications' (GSM) operations and supported by European firms), and CDMA 2000 (compatible with existing CDMA operations and supported by US firms).
7 See Farrell *et al.* (2005). 'Young professionals' are defined as university graduates with up to seven years of work experience, and include engineers, finance and accounting specialists, generalist professionals, life science researchers, and quantitative analysts.
8 This cost comparison includes salary, benefits, equipment, office space and other infrastructure.
9 The UNCTAD sample consists of the first 300 firms of the R&D scoreboard of the 700 top worldwide R&D spenders, published by the UK Department of Trade and Industry.
10 'Design methodology' is the sequence of steps by which a design process will reliably produce a design 'as close as possible' to the design target, while maintaining feasibility with respect to constraints.
11 'Modular design' is a particular design methodology in which parameters and tasks are interdependent within units (modules) and independent across them.
12 A 'fabless' company is one that outsources the manufacture (fabrication) of computer chips.
13 An application-specific integrated circuit typically is composed of standard building blocks called 'cells' that are designed to implement a specific customer application.
14 The biotech sector of pharmaceuticals, however, has made the most progress in pushing vertical specialisation into research and development. A senior R&D manager at Merck estimates that '99 per cent of the world's bio-medical research takes place outside our [big pharmaceutical company] research labs' (Ray Hill, quoted in 'Change of culture: how big pharma is picking the best of biotech as a sector starts to mature,' *Financial Times*, 12 January 2006: 13).
15 Important complementary changes in US financial institutions include the launch of the National Association of Securities Dealers Automated Quotations (NASDAQ) in 1971 (making it much easier for start-up firms to go public), the passage of legislation in 1978 that reduced capital gains tax from 49 per cent to 28 per cent, and the 1979 decree by the

Department of Labor that pension fund money could be invested not only in listed stocks and high-grade bonds but also in more speculative assets, including new ventures (Lazonick 2005: 23).

16 'Innovative capabilities' are defined as the skills, knowledge and management techniques needed to design, produce, improve and commercialise 'artifacts', that is, products, services, machinery and processes (Ernst 2002a).

17 Chesbrough's concept of 'open innovation' provides a useful stylised model of this gradual opening of corporate innovation systems (Chesbrough 2003). However, the model fails to address explicitly the international dimension – that is, the development of GINs.

18 The underlying assumption is that, once markets for technology exist, one can codify knowledge sufficiently and develop well-defined and protective IPRs (e.g. Kogut and Zander 1993). However, an excessive reliance on technology licensing may be risky because it cuts the company off from vital system integration knowledge that it needs for continuous innovation (e.g. Grindley and Teece 1997).

19 Ageing populations in China and other leading Asian exporting countries may constrain Asia's future supply of low-cost knowledge workers. In China, one of the by-products of the one-child policy is that in a decade or so many more people will be retiring than entering the workforce (Jackson and Howe 2004). In contrast, India is one of the few countries in which the working-age population is projected to grow for the next 40 years or so, keeping wages low.

20 J.A. Joerres, CEO of Manpower, quoted in Boehm (2005).

21 Until recently, managers working for global corporations could earn 50 per cent more than managers working for local Chinese companies. Now, however, leading Chinese companies offer competitive remuneration packages and aggressively headhunt Chinese managers employed at global firms.

22 This is somewhat ironic in light of the fact that the same firms are less willing to invest in training at home. But it is less puzzling in view of the fact that global firms often seek government support for training. The intensifying incentive tournaments among competing offshore locations suggest that they are quite successful in securing training assistance.

23 Members of the Industrial Research Institute include more than 240 leading global manufacturing firms that perform more than two-thirds of the industrial R&D in the United States.

24 But, as indicated in note 3, case study evidence needs to be complemented with systematic research that measures the incidence of learning and technology diffusion and that establishes the link between innovation offshoring and productivity growth in Asia.

REFERENCES

Archibugi, D. and J. Michie (1995) 'The globalisation of technology: a new taxonomy', *Cambridge Journal of Economics*, 19: 1.

Armbrecht, F.M.R. (2003) 'Siting industrial R&D in China: notes from pioneers', slide presentation, 12 March, Industrial Research Institute, Arlington VA.

Arora, A., A. Fosfuri and A. Gambardella (2001) *Markets for Technology: The Economics of Innovation and Corporate Strategy*, Cambridge MA: MIT Press.

Bhagwati, J. (2004) 'Why your job isn't moving to Bangalore', *New York Times*, 15 February.

Boehm, R.L. (2005) 'The future of the global workplace: an interview with the CEO of Manpower', *McKinsey Quarterly* (November).

Borrus, M., D. Ernst and S. Haggard (eds) (2000) *International Production Networks in Asia: Rivalry or Riches?*, London: Routledge.

Branscomb, L.M., F. Kodama and R.L. Florida (1999) *Industrialising Knowledge: University–Industry Linkages in Japan and the United States*. Cambridge MA: MIT Press.

Breschi, S. and F. Lissoni (2001) 'Knowledge spillovers and local innovation systems: a critical survey', *Industrial and Corporate Change*, 10 (4): 975–1006.

Cantwell, J. (1995) 'The globalisation of technology: what remains of the product cycle model?', *Cambridge Journal of Economics*, 19: 155–174.
Chandler, A.D. (1977) *The Visible Hand: The Managerial Revolution in American Business*, Cambridge MA: The Belknap Press of Harvard University Press.
Chesbrough, H.W. (2003) *Open Innovation: The New Imperative for Creating and Profiting from Technology*, Cambridge MA: Harvard Business School Press.
Cohen, W.M. and S.A. Merrill (eds) (2003) *Patents in the Knowledge-Based Economy*, Washington DC: National Academies Press.
Dahlman, C.J. and J.E. Aubert (2001). *China and the Knowledge Economy*, Washington DC: World Bank Institute.
Dalton, D.H. and M.G. Serapio (1999) *Globalising Industrial Research and Development*, Washington DC: Office of Technology Policy, US Department of Commerce.
Dunning, J.H. (1998) 'Globalization, technology and space', in Chandler, A.D., P. Hagstrom and O. Solvell (eds), *The Dynamic Firm: The Role of Technology, Strategy, Organisation, and Regions*, Oxford: Oxford University Press.
Ernst, D. (1997) 'From partial to systemic globalisation: international production networks in the electronics industry', report to the Sloan Foundation, published as *The Data Storage Industry Globalisation Project Report 97-02*, Graduate School of International Relations and Pacific Studies, University of California at San Diego.
—— (2000) 'Inter-organisational knowledge outsourcing: what permits small Taiwanese firms to compete in the computer industry?', *Asia Pacific Journal of Management*, special issue on 'Knowledge Management in Asia', August.
—— (2001) 'Catching-up and post-crisis industrial upgrading: searching for new sources of growth in Korea's electronics industry', in Deyo, F., R. Doner and E. Hershberg (eds), *Economic Governance and the Challenge of Flexibility in East Asia*, Lanham Maryland: Rowman and Littlefield Publishers.
—— (2002a) 'Global production networks and the changing geography of innovation systems: implications for developing countries', *Economics of Innovation and New Technologies*, XI(6): 497–523.
—— (2002b) 'The economics of electronics industry: competitive dynamics and industrial organisation', in W. Lazonick (ed.), *The International Encyclopedia of Business and Management, Handbook of Economics*, London: International Thomson Business Press.
—— (2003) 'Digital information systems and global flagship networks: how mobile is knowledge in the global network economy?', in J.F. Christensen (ed.), *The Industrial Dynamics of the New Digital Economy*, Cheltenham: Edward Elgar.
—— (2004) 'Global production networks in East Asia's electronics industry and upgrading perspectives in Malaysia', in S. Yusuf, M.A. Altaf and K. Nabeshima (eds), *Global Production Networking and Technological Change in East Asia*, Washington DC: World Bank and Oxford University Press.
—— (2005a) 'Complexity and internationalisation of innovation: why is chip design moving to Asia?', *International Journal of Innovation Management* [special issue in honour of Keith Pavitt], 9(1): 47–73.
—— (2005b) 'Limits to modularity: reflections on recent developments in chip design', *Industry and Innovation*, 12(3): 303–335.
—— (2005c) 'The new mobility of knowledge: digital information systems and global flagship networks', in R. Latham and S. Sassen (eds), *Digital Formations: IT and New Architectures in the Global Realm*, Princeton and Oxford: Princeton University Press for the US Social Science Research Council.
—— (2005d) 'Pathways to innovation in Asia's leading electronics-exporting countries: a framework for exploring drivers and policy implications', *International Journal of Technology Management*, special issue on 'Competitive Strategies of Asian High-Tech Firms, 29(1/2): 6–20.

Ernst, D. (2006a) *Innovation Offshoring: Asia's Emerging Role in Global Innovation Networks*, special report prepared for the East–West Center and the United States Asia Pacific Council, East–West Center, Honolulu HI, July.

—— (2006b) 'Developing innovative capabilities in chip design: insights from the US and Greater China', unpublished manuscript, East–West Center, Honolulu HI.

—— (2006c), 'Can Chinese IT firms develop innovative capabilities within global knowledge networks?', paper presented at the international workshop 'Greater China's Innovative Capacities: Progress and Challenges', co-sponsored by Stanford University and Tsinghua University, 20–21 May 2006, Beijing, China.

—— (2006d) 'Upgrading through innovation in a small network economy: insights from Taiwan's IT industry', paper prepared for SPRIE/ITRI Stanford workshop 'High Tech Regions 2.0: Sustainability and Reinvention', 13–14 November 2006, Stanford University.

—— (forthcoming) *Innovation Offshoring: Asia's Role in Global Knowledge Networks*, Honolulu HI: East–West Center.

Ernst, D. and Linsu Kim (2002) 'Global production networks, knowledge diffusion and local capability formation', *Research Policy*, 31(8/9): 1417–1429. [special issue in honour of Richard Nelson and Sydney Winter]

Ernst, D. and D. Mowery (2004) 'University–industry linkages in the Pacific Rim: public policy issues', unpublished manuscript, Honolulu HI: East–West Center (February).

Ernst, D., L. Mytelka and T. Ganiatsos (1998) 'Export performance and technological capabilities: a conceptual framework', in D. Ernst, T. Ganiatsos and L. Mytelka (eds), *Technological Capabilities and Export Success: Lessons from East Asia*, London: Routledge.

Ernst, D. and B. Naughton (2005) *China's Emerging Industrial Economy: Insights from the IT Industry*, paper prepared for the East–West Center Conference on China's Emerging Capitalist System, 10–12 August, Honolulu, Hawaii.

Farrell, D., M.A. Laboissiere and J. Rosenfeld (2005) 'Sizing the emerging global labor market', *The McKinsey Quarterly*, No. 3.

Feenstra, R. (1998) 'Integration of trade and disintegration of production in the global economy', *Journal of Economic Perspectives*, 12(4): 31–50.

Feldman, M.P. (1999) 'The new economics of innovation, spillovers and agglomeration: a review of empirical studies', *Economics of Innovation and New Technology* 8: 5–25.

Fonow, R.C. (2006) *The New Reality of International Telecommunications Strategy*, Washington DC: National Defense University.

Freeman, R.B. (2005) 'Does globalisation of the scientific/engineering workforce threaten U.S. economic leadership', NBER Working Paper 11457, Cambridge MA: National Bureau of Economic Research.

Garcia, D.L. and K. Burns (2006) 'Globalisation, developing countries, and the evolution of international communities of standard setting practice', paper prepared for 'China's Technology Standards Policy Workshop', Tsinghua University, Beijing, China, 6 January.

Gassmann, O. and Z. Han (2004) 'Motivations and barriers of foreign R&D activities in China', *R&D Management*, 34(4): 423–437.

Granstrand, O. (1998) 'Towards a theory of the technology-based firm', *Research Policy*, 27(5): 467–491.

Granstrand, O., P. Patel and K. Pavitt (1997) 'Multi-technology corporations: why they have "distributed" rather than "distinctive core" competencies', *California Management Review*, 39(4): 8–25.

Grindley, P.C. and D.J. Teece (1997) 'Licensing and cross-licensing in semiconductors and electronics', *California Management Review* 39(2): 8–41.

Grossman, G. and E. Helpman (2002) 'Integration versus outsourcing in industry equilibrium', *Quarterly Journal of Economics*, 117(1): 85–120.

Grove, A.S. (1996) *Only the Paranoid Survive: How to Exploit the Crisis Points that Challenge Every Company and Career*, New York: HarperCollins Business.

Hicks, D. (2005) 'Growth in Asian S&T capability and R&D offshoring', slide presentation at the Council on Foreign Relations, 24 May, New York.

Hyde, A. (2003) *Working in Silicon Valley: Economic and Legal Analysis of a High-Velocity Labor Market*, Armonk NY: M.E. Sharpe.
Iansiti, M. (1997) *Technology Integration: Making Critical Choices in a Dynamic World*, Boston MA: Harvard Business School Press.
Iansiti, M. and J. West (1997) 'Technology integration: turning great research into great products', *Harvard Business Review*, May–June: 69–79.
Jackson, R. and N. Howe (2004) *The Graying of the Middle Kingdom*, Washington: Center for Strategic and International Studies.
Jaffe, A.B., M. Trajtenberg and M.S. Fogarty (2000) 'Knowledge spillovers and patent citations: evidence from a survey of inventors', *American Economic Review*, 90, AEA Papers and Proceedings, 215–218.
Jones, R. and H. Kierzskowski (2000) 'A framework for fragmentation', in S. Arndt and H. Kierzkowski (eds), *Fragmentation and International Trade*, Oxford: Oxford University Press.
Kim, L. (1997) *Imitation to Innovation: The Dynamics of Korea's Technological Learning*, Boston: Harvard Business School Press.
Kogut, B. and U. Zander (1993), 'Knowledge of the firm and the evolutionary theory of the multinational corporation', *Journal of International Business Studies*, 24 (4): 625.
Kuemmerle, W. (1996) 'Home base and foreign direct investment in R&D', unpublished Ph.D. dissertation, Harvard Business School, Boston
—— (1997) 'Building effective R&D capabilities abroad', *Harvard Business Review*, March–April: 61–70.
Lall, S. (2000) 'Technological change and industrialisation in the Asian newly industrialising economies: achievements and challenges', in L. Kim and R.R. Nelson (eds), *Technology, Learning and Innovation: Experiences of Newly Industrialising Economies*, Cambridge: Cambridge University Press.
Lazonick, W. (2003) 'Stock options as a mode of high-tech compensation', Working Paper, INSEAD.
—— (2005) 'Evolution of the new economy business model', in E. Brousseau and N. Curine (eds), *The Economics of the Internet*, Cambridge: Cambridge University Press.
Li, Jiatao and Jing Zhong (2003) 'Explaining the growth of international R&D alliances in China', *Managerial and Decision Economics*, 24: 101–115.
Mann, C.L. (2003) 'Globalisation of IT services and white collar jobs: the next wave of productivity growth', Policy Brief 03-11, Institute for International Economics, Washington DC (December).
Merrill, S.A., R.C. Levin and M.B. Myers (eds) (2004) *A Patent System for the 21st Century*, Washington DC: National Academies Press.
Mowery, D., R.R. Nelson, B.N. Sampat and A.A. Ziedonies (2004) *'Ivory Tower' and Industrial Innovation: University–Industry Technology Transfer Before and After the Bayh-Dole Act in the United States*, Stanford CA: Stanford University Press.
NASSCOM (National Association of Software and Service Companies) and McKinsey (2005) *Extending India's Leadership of the Global Information Technology and Business Process Outsourcing Industries*, New Delhi, India: NASSCOM.
National Science Board (2004) *Science and Engineering Indicators 2004*, volume I, Arlington VA: National Science Foundation.
Naughton, B. and A. Segal (2002) 'Technology development in the new millennium: China in search of a workable model', in W. Keller and R. Samuels (eds), *Crisis and Innovation: Asian Technology after the Millennium*, Cambridge: Cambridge University Press.
Patel, P. and K. Pavitt (1991) 'Large firms in the production of the world's technology: an important case of non-globalisation', *Journal of International Business Studies*, 22(1): 1–21.
Porter, M. and Ø. Sølvell (1998) 'The role of geography in the process of innovation and the sustainable competitive advantage of firms', in A.D. Chandler, P. Hagström and Ö. Sölvell (eds), *The Dynamic Firm: The Role of Technology, Strategy, Organization, and Regions*, Oxford: Oxford University Press.

Rasiah, R. (1995) *Foreign Capital and Industrialisation in Malaysia*, Basingstoke: Macmillan.
Teece, D. (2000) *Managing Intellectual Capital*, Oxford: Oxford University Press.
US Department of Commerce (2003) *The Digital Economy 2003*, Washington DC: US Department of Commerce.
UNCTAD (United Nations Conference on Trade and Development) (2005) *UNCTAD Survey on the Internationalization of R&D* (Occasional Note), UNCTAD/WEB/ITE/IIA/2005/12, 12 December.
von Hippel, Eric (2005) *Democratising Innovation*, Cambridge MA: MIT Press.
von Zedwitz, M. (2004) 'Foreign R&D laboratories in China', *R&D Management*, 34: 4.
Wong, P.K. (2006) 'The role of global MNCs vs. indigenous firms in the rapid growth of East Asian innovation: evidence from US patent data', paper presented at the international workshop 'Greater China's Innovative Capacities: Progress and Challenges', co-sponsored by Stanford University and Tsinghua University, 20–21 May, Beijing, China.

4 Information and communication technologies and inter-corporate production networks: global information technology and local *guanxi* in the Taiwanese personal computer industry

Kenneth L. Kraemer, Jason Dedrick, William Foster and Zhang Cheng

INTRODUCTION

Globalisation and the need for competitive advantage are driving many firms and whole industries towards vertical disintegration. Firms focus on their core competence, from which they derive competitive advantage, and outsource their non-core activities to other firms who are specialists in these activities at home and abroad, thereby giving rise to global business networks. The personal computer (PC) industry is one such network, and might be a harbinger for other industries.

In the PC industry, the branded PC-makers concentrate on product design and marketing. They outsource production, distribution and after-sales service and source the major parts needed, components and assembly activities from specialised producers. Working with their main subcontractors on a global basis, the branded PC-makers are vertically disintegrated, yet globally integrated through the use of information and communication technologies (ICTs), which are the backbone of such global integration. The result is the so-called networked corporation.

Ideally then, the networked corporation is supported by a real-time digital network with unbroken links from customer demand to the last supplier in the supply chain. In it, the branded PC-maker and its suppliers have digital access to demand and supply information in order to achieve an optimal balance. This requires digital access to demand information from the end customer or the retailer so that the PC-maker can monitor demand, or even manage demand directly. It also requires access not only to the inventory and manufacturing capability of its subcontractors, but also to the inventory and manufacturing capability of companies further up the supply chain. In theory, these upstream suppliers are motivated to make use of the internet and related applications because they realise that they need to adopt the technology in order to serve global markets and better coordinate with their downstream customers.

But to what extent does the ideal vision of digitally enabled production networks match reality? We examine this question in detail, focusing on the notebook PC industry supply chain. We find that the picture is mixed. The digital production network is a fairly good characterisation of the information systems linking branded PC-makers with their original design manufacturer (ODM) partners, but the rest of the supply chain – the micro production networks[1] below the ODMs – is best characterised as a 'neural network' that is based on human and personal relationships with very limited use of ICT; hence the subtitle of this paper – 'Global information technology and local *guanxi*'. *Guanxi* refers to the personal relationships and obligations that underlie social and business interactions in the Chinese culture; given the concentration of the PC industry in Taiwan and China, *guanxi* is the organising principle for the industry's neural network.[2]

THE NOTEBOOK INDUSTRY VALUE NETWORK

The PC industry is a complex network of companies involved in different industry segments, from microprocessors and other components, to complete systems, operating systems, and applications. Firms tend to specialise in one of three categories of activities:

- *design or new product innovation*, including R&D, design, market research, and new product development (NPD);
- *production or operations*, including process engineering, manufacturing, logistics, information technology (IT), finance, and human resources; or
- *distribution and customer relations*, including marketing, sales, advertising, distribution, customer service, and technical support.

On the upstream (supply) side (Figure 4.1), the industry comprises branded PC-makers who focus on design, marketing, and sales; contract manufacturers and ODMs who focus on production; and a large array of suppliers who provide parts and

Figure 4.1 The PC industry value network

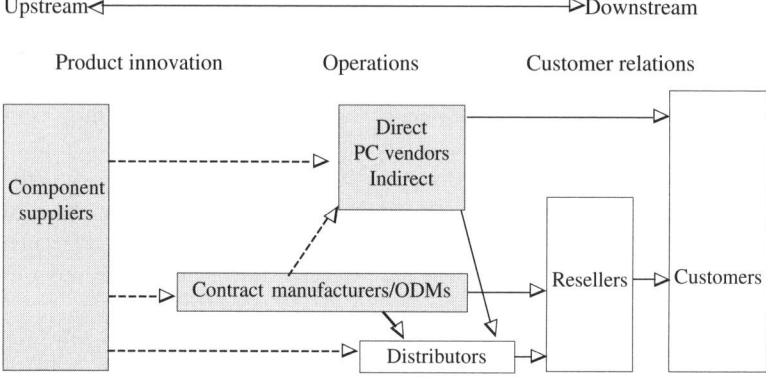

Notes:
--- Components, subassemblies, box-builds.
— Complete systems.

Source: Adapted from Curry and Kenney (1999).

components. This upstream network is multi-tiered and becoming more concentrated organisationally and geographically for economies. On the downstream side, the industry comprises logistics providers, a large array of distributors (wholesalers, retailers, resellers and systems integrators), and service and support. The downstream (demand) side is increasingly distributed in an effort to serve new markets. In this paper, we focus mainly on design and production activities of the PC-maker, the ODMs and upstream suppliers (Figure 4.1, shaded areas).

Division of labour

New product innovation in the notebook industry is led by US firms such as Dell, HP, Apple and Gateway, with competition from Japanese and Asian firms, notably Toshiba, Fujitsu, Sony, Acer and, most recently, Lenovo. Most notebook PCs are produced in the Yangtze River Delta of China by Taiwanese owned and managed firms (Table 4.1).

Together, the Taiwanese ODMs produce more than 80 per cent of the world's notebook PCs (MIC 2006), up from just 40 per cent in 1998 (Dedrick and Kraemer

Table 4.1 Extent to which notebook PC-makers outsource production to Taiwanese firms

Top 10 branded notebook companies	Subsidiaries in China	Estimated outsourcing to Taiwanese companies in January 2005[a] (% of world production)	Shipments by Taiwanese companies, April 2005[b] (% of world production)	Taiwanese ODM suppliers[c]
Apple		100	5.1	Quanta, Asus, Elite
Dell	Xiamen	92–93	21.6	Quanta, Compal, Wistron
HP	Shanghai	100	19.1	Quanta, Compal, Wistron, Inventec, Arima
IBM[d]	Shenzhen	40	4.2	Wistron, Quanta
Acer		100		Quanta, Compal, Wistron
NEC	Shanghai	100	5.3	Arima, FIC, Wistron, Mitac
Sharp		n.a.	n.a.	Quanta, Mitac, Twinhead
Sony	Wuxi	60	4.0	Quanta, Asus, Foxconn
Toshiba	Hangzhou	>70	9.6	Quanta, Compal, Inventec
Fujitsu-Siemens		50	4.0	Wistron, Mitac, Uniwill, Quanta, Compal

Notes: n.a. = not available; ODM = original design manufacturer.
a 'Taiwan notebook makers to curtail low-price strategy, extend global dominance', *Digitimes*, 20 January 2005, <http://www.digitimes.com/news/a20050119A7032.html>.
b Digitimes (2005), 'Taiwan's notebooks – 1Q 2005', *Digitimes*, Wednesday, 17 August 2005, <http://www.digitimes.com/Reports/Report.asp?datepublish=2005/6/3&pages=RI&rseq=400 9/2/05>.
c Yang and Hsia (2004) quote this table from a report by the Ministry of Economic Affairs, Taiwan (cited in Yang 2005).
d Prior to the acquisition of IBM's PC business by Lenovo.

2006). Now that IBM has sold its PC company to Lenovo, no US PC company produces its own notebooks. Lenovo now has its own notebook production but, like other Chinese notebook brands, also sources lower-end products from the Taiwanese ODMs.

Firm size in the production network

The notebook production cluster in China is a multi-tiered structure with ten key ODMs and hundreds of upstream suppliers. Moreover, at each level of the supply chain, there are a few large and many more small and medium-sized firms forming micro production networks (Table 4.2). Based on various reports in the literature, we estimate that, out of 1,200 Taiwanese firms in the Yangtze River Delta, around 200 are directly related to the PC industry.[3] Many of the other firms might also be upstream suppliers to the industry.

FRAMEWORK: DIGITAL AND SOCIAL NETWORKS

The digital networks of the global corporation overlie physical production networks and are complements to the social networks that plan and control operations. Digital networks enable global firms to improve the information flows from customers to suppliers and the information flows needed to manage the physical flows of material forward from suppliers to customers.

The key value of using IT in the supply chain is to substitute information flows for physical flows wherever possible and to provide 'integrated' information flows that reduce problems, or help to optimise the system. Consequently, research and practice have sought to create the 'ideal' integrated supply chain that would integrate information flows both internally and externally, and both upstream and downstream (White *et al.* 2004; Norris *et al.* 2000; Johnson and Whang 2002; Swaminathan and Tayur 2003; Sambamurthy *et al.* 2003).

During the 1990s, firms made major investments in upgrading internal IT through enterprise resource planning (ERP) systems, which were critical to integration in firms operating through multiple divisions or geographical locations. They enabled the firm to operate as a single enterprise, and also created a stable platform for inter-firm integration (Markus 2002; Markus *et al.* 2000).

With the advent of the internet, firms began to shift from firm-specific applications (electronic data interchange, EDI) to external integration, adding more flexible web-based applications for e-business, especially for e-coordination. Such applications automate business processes between a focal firm and suppliers, including e-purchase orders, online catalogues and online linkages with suppliers to exchange information regarding fulfilment (for example, order and inventory information).[4]

Moreover, firms have tried to extend these applications beyond a focal firm, such as the PC-maker and its ODM contractors, to the suppliers of the contractors, and to the suppliers of their suppliers further up the supply chain. Most new applications have been private networks driven by large firms for their own production ecology (for example, Dell and HP in the PC industry). Others have been promoted by industry associations; for example, the RosettaNet organisation in the PC industry creates standards for inter-firm business processes and promotes them to the industry.[5] Still

Table 4.2 Firm size in the notebook industry (2004 revenues, $ million)[a]

(a) Notebook-makers Top 10 companies	Revenue	(b) Original design manufacturers Top 10 companies	Revenue
Dell	49,205	Quanta	10,222
HP	79,905	Compal	6,660
Toshiba	54,543	Wistron	3,673
Acer	7,036	Asustek	2,459
IBM	96,293	Inventec	4,139
Fujitsu	44,512	Uniwill	682
NEC	45,375	Mitac	1,591
Sony	66,775	Arima	570
Apple	8,279	FIC	1,209
Asustek	2,459	ECS	525

(c) Suppliers (top Taiwanese PC suppliers by component category)

Supplier	Revenue	Supplier	Revenue
Memory		**Power supplies**	
Nanya Tech	1,277	DeltaElectronics	1,462
Winbond	984	Com2B	4,909
Mosel	818	LiShin	55
PSC	1,810	Potrans	51
LCDs		**Optical storage**	
AUO	5,186	Quanta Storage	315
ChiMei	3,230	Lite-On	1,532
ChungHwa	2,471	PanInternational	244
Quanta Display	1,834	BTC	416
HannStar	1,221	Ultima	n.a.
Motherboards		**Keyboards**	
Compeq	403	Sunrex	74
Unimicron	522	Darfon	148
Gold Circuit	311	Chicony	396
HannStar Board	85	Lite-On	1,532
Vertex	103	**Cases**	
Career Tech	218	Catcher	47
Tripod	286	Waffer	80
Connectors		Uneec	175
Foxconn[b]	13,285	Loyalty Founder	103
Speedtech	95		
Battery			
E-One Moli	64		
Simplo	284		
Solomon	255		
Gallopwire	69		

Notes: LCD = liquid crystal display; n.a. = not available.

a Foreign multinational suppliers such as Intel, Seagate, Western Digital are not included, although they manufacture in China or elsewhere in Asia, because their use of information and communication technology is similar to that of the PC-makers and they are not part of the China–Taiwan cluster.

b Hon Hai (Foxconn) is a major supplier in a number of categories, including connectors, motherboards, and cases, and is a major contract manufacturer for many electronic products. There are no data available on the breakdown of its revenues by product, but Foxconn connectors are shown separately here because FoxconnConnectors is listed on the Taiwanese Stock Exchange as a separate company.

Sources: For notebook-makers, the ranking and revenue are based on Daoud and Lovende (2005: Vol. 1, Table 8, p. 12) (4Q04 data). For original design manufacturers and suppliers, information is from Compustat (2004 sales); Hoovers (2004 sales: see <http://www.hoovers.com>; and Taiwan Stock Exchange Corporation (2004 sales: see <http://www.tse.com.tw/en/>).

others have been promoted by governments. For example, the Taiwanese government recognised that the complexity and costs of these digital networks were beyond the capabilities of most small- and medium-sized enterprises (SMEs) and created two plans (A and B) to create electronic information linkages using the RosettaNet system and XML between PC-makers and ODMs on the one hand (Plan A) and between the ODMs and their suppliers on the other hand (Plan B). The intended result of such efforts is a large digital network, created by linking the micro production networks of particular focal firms and their business partners with one another as illustrated in Figure 4.2.

Social networks

The digital networks described above rely on codified business processes and related information. However, much of what occurs to make production networks function is not codified but tacit, and relies on social networks and various kinds of personal and direct relationships: face-to-face communication, information sharing, negotiation, and development of personal regard and trust (Granovetter 1985). Moreover, reliance on social networks might be stronger where firm relationships are based on family

Figure 4.2   PC industry supply chain

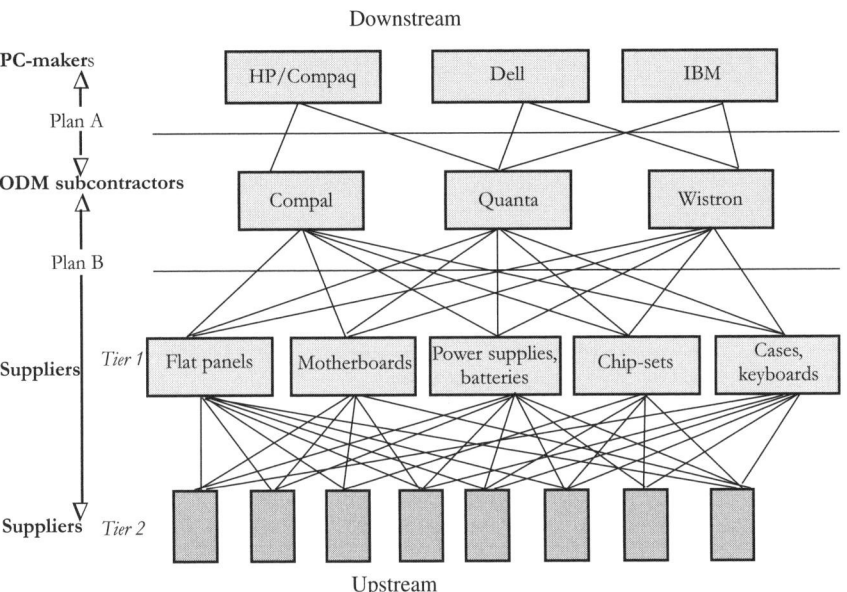

Note: ODM = original design manufacturer.

and personal relationships such as Chinese business networks versus formal and market-oriented relationships in Western firms. Consequently, it is important to examine the relative use of digital and social networks in global production chains.

Methodology

We do so by examining the notebook PC industry in Taiwan and China. The time-based nature of competition among firms and the industry's global footprint provide strong motivation for building digital networks both globally and locally (Dedrick and Kraemer 1998). The industry is unique in that it has been an early adopter of industry-wide standards (the RosettaNet system and XML) for inter-firm coordination. Thus, its experience might be a harbinger for other industries and might provide useful insights (Malakooty 2005).

We assess digital integration of the notebook industry supply chain indirectly by examining whether firms have in place ICTs that would provide capabilities for integration. Figure 4.3 presents a simplified picture of how internal systems such as ERP fit physically with internet-based applications or e-business technologies such as EDI, extranets or email.

In the middle of the figure is a focal firm's ERP system. It might include one or more modules such as purchasing, material management, production planning and

Figure 4.3   ICT use in a supply chain

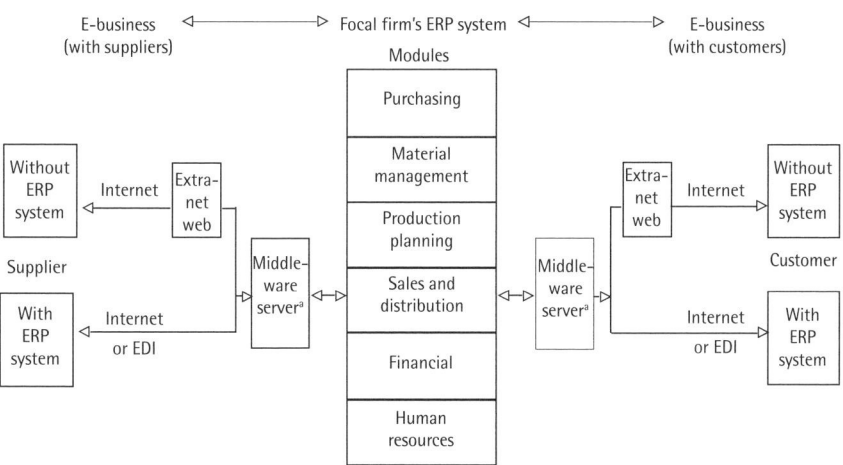

Notes: EDI = electronic data interchange; ERP = enterprise resource planning; ICT = information and communications technology.
a   RosettaNet, Standard and XML language.
Source: Adapted from Hsu and Kraemer (2006).

control, sales and distribution, finance, human resources and possibly others. On the supplier side, information generated by an ERP system can be shared via the internet directly with suppliers' ERP systems using middleware software that is based on industry predefined standards such as EDI or RosettaNet and the XML language. If a supplier does not have ERP or another internal system that can be linked, it can still receive and exchange business information through EDI, an extranet website or email. In the simplest case, an ERP system might generate an email notifying a customer or supplier of new information posted to a website. Thus, firms may have multiple levels of automation in place simultaneously: highly automated, semi-automated, web-based, fax-based, email, or manual systems.

We used the framework described by Figure 4.3 to develop a protocol for interviews with executives and information systems managers. We conducted 45 interviews in 20 companies across four tiers in the PC industry to gain an understanding of extant ICT capabilities for integration. We interviewed four branded PC-makers, five ODMs, ten tier 1 suppliers and two tier 2 suppliers (Table 4.3). The semistructured field interviews were conducted in 2004 and 2005 with PC-makers in the United States and with ODMs and suppliers on site in Taiwan and China. Many interviews were with information systems executives, although some were also with senior executives, product development managers, procurement managers, and sales managers. The researchers were accompanied by a local Chinese researcher who participated in the interviews and helped with translation when needed. Immediately after the interviews, each would write up a different interview and then check the others' write-up with their own notes. Differences were resolved through discussion or follow-up questions where appropriate. As part of the interview, respondents were shown Figure 4.2 delineating the tiers in the supply chain in order to establish a framework for the interview. Each firm was asked about its use of ICT internally, and about its use of ICT externally with customers and suppliers.

We compared the interview results with secondary data on the formal electronic linkages actually implemented in Taiwan's Plan A/B program (DOIT 2006), which focused on the Taiwanese ODMs and their suppliers. As will be seen later, our results are consistent with the final report on the Taiwanese plans. We further complemented the interviews with our previous interviews and studies of the computer industry (Dedrick and Kraemer 1998, 2005, 2006).

DIGITAL NETWORKS IN THE NOTEBOOK PC INDUSTRY

Great progress has been made in developing digital networks within the PC industry since 1990, but most of that progress has been internal to PC-makers and the ODMs, or between the PC companies and the ODMs. There has been much less progress in extending digital networks upstream from the ODMs to tier 1 and tier 2 suppliers. These suppliers are beginning to use ICTs internally, but traditional Chinese human and business networks appear to be more significant for external linkages. Thus, the supply chain can be said to be characterised by global ICT between the branded PC-makers and the ODMs, and by *guanxi,* or personal relationships, assisted by modest ICT use, in the local networks.

Table 4.3 List of firms interviewed

Name	PC-related business	No. of interviewees	Location
PC-maker			
IBM PC division[a]	PC-maker	4	US, Japan, China
Dell	PC-maker	4	US
HP	PC-maker	3	US, Japan
Lenovo	PC-maker	3	China
ODM/subcontractor			
Quanta	ODM	8	Taiwan, China
Compal	ODM	3	Taiwan, China
Arima	ODM	2	China
Wistron	ODM	3	Taiwan, China
Asus	ODM	2	China
Tier 1 supplier			
Western Digital	Disk drives	1	US
Acon	Cables and connectors	2	China*
Sinbon	Notebook FPD cable, connectors	1	China*
TWS(Total Wireless)	Battery packs	1	China*
ACeS International	Connectors	1	China*
Auras Technology	Thermal modules, CPU coolers	1	China*
Darfon	Keyboards	1	China*
Laird Technologies	EMI thermal interface, wireless antenna	1	China*
Unimicron	PCB-maker	1	China*
Delta	Power supply, batteries	1	China*
Tier 2 supplier			
Copartner	Cables and connectors	1	China*
Top Chem	Chemicals for PCB manufacturing	1	China*

Notes: CPU = central processing unit; EMI = electromagnetic interference; FPD = flat-panel display; ODM = original design manufacturer; PCB = printed circuit board.
a All interviews were prior to the purchase of IBM's PC division by Lenovo in December 2004.

Source: Interviews conducted in 2005 by William Foster and Z.C. Chang (interviews marked *) or (all others) Jason Dedrick and Kenneth L. Kraemer.

ICT in the PC-makers

As the PC-makers turned to outsourcing production, they mostly engaged in major efforts to install packaged ERP systems and focused on purchasing, supply chain management, and customer relationship management. Nearly all retained their internal, customised order management systems, which provided the digital interface between orders, supply, production and distribution. These were especially valuable as the PC-makers moved from in-house operations to outsourcing, because they helped to control the fulfilment of orders.

As they outsourced production, some PC-makers discontinued their own material management and shop-floor management systems, relying instead on the systems of the contract manufacturer or ODM. The shift to outsourcing also created a need for inter-organisational systems for sharing customer demand information with suppliers and receiving information on inventory and production so that the PC-makers could better manage new product introductions and fulfilment on ever shorter cycles.

The critical applications for PC-makers, however, are the order management and forecasting systems. These can be custom-built, such as the Dell Order Management System, or can be commercial enterprise applications such as SAP-F (fulfilment). They are the key systems for integrating internal operations. In turn, they may be integrated directly with customers and suppliers through ERP-to-ERP exchanges, through EDI or RosettaNet applications, or through web interfaces or extranets.

Results from the field interviews (see Table 4.4) with leading PC-makers show that such firms have implemented the key internal systems and that they use a variety of approaches to external integration. EDI is most widely used because it has been around the longest, but RosettaNet procurement applications are also used. Extranets for customers and suppliers are used by all, as is email and attached files for information exchange.

ICT in the original design manufacturers

The ODMs have followed the PC-makers in upgrading their internal systems (Table 4.4). Most ODMs implemented mainstream ERP systems in the late 1990s, but continue

Table 4.4 Use of ICT applications by PC-makers and ODMs

	PC-maker				*ODM*			
ICT applications	A	B	C	D	E	F	G	H
Internal								
Product data management	×	×	×	×	×	×		
Sales/order/distribution management	×	×	×	×	×			
Material/inventory management	×	×	×	×	×		×	
Production/shop floor management	×	×			×	×	×	×
Human resources	×	×	×					
Finance/accounting	×	×	×	×	×			
External								
Customer extranet	×	×	×	×		×	×	×
Supplier extranet	×	×	×	×	×	×	×	×
E-procurement (EDI/RosettaNet)	×	×	×	×	×	×	×	×
Email	×	×	×	×	×	×	×	×

Notes: EDI = electronic data interchange; ICT = information and communications technology; ODM = original design manufacturer. A blank in this table means 'no such application'.

Source: Interviews conducted by the authors in 2005.

to use their custom shop floor management systems. These systems helped the ODMs to internally integrate their new manufacturing operations in China with their headquarters in Taiwan. They also helped the ODMs to manage the sheer volume of notebooks that they were producing. For example, the largest ODM (Quanta) manufactured 15 million notebooks (1.25 million per month, 52,000 per day) in 2005.[6] This scale of operation cannot be maintained without considerable automation. In addition, most ODMs are manufacturing many different configurations for multiple customers, each configuration requiring multiple parts. Thus, most ODMs see ICT as essential to their operations, as do the PC-makers who rely on their capabilities.[7]

The external systems used by ODMs are shaped on the one hand by the requirements of the PC-makers and on the other hand by the limitations of their suppliers. On the downstream side, the ODMs need the capability to inter-operate with multiple IT systems because each PC-maker has different systems and the ODMs have to be able to communicate with each directly. However, our interviews indicate that the ODMs' internal ICT generally does not match that of the leading PC-makers; therefore most PC-makers do not allow the ODMs to perform tasks such as direct-shipping from the factory to the end customer.

The ODMs receive forecasts and orders from the PC-makers via EDI or the internet. Most ODMs are carrying out 2–4 procurement processes using the RosettaNet system. This is because RosettaNet has been required by some suppliers (for example, Intel) and PC-makers, and has been promoted by the Taiwanese government. In particular, the Plan A/B program provided financial inducement for ODMs to implement RosettaNet applications with their customers. ODMs say that they also use RosettaNet applications to communicate with their tier 1 and tier 2 suppliers, but actual use appears to be very limited, as will be seen below.[8]

On the upstream side, the ODMs realise that their small suppliers do not have the technical expertise to implement EDI or RosettaNet, even though RosettaNet is touted as a cheaper and simpler standard. Instead, most ODMs have developed a secure website that each supplier can access. The ODM places forecasts and orders for each on the web and the tier 1 and tier 2 suppliers access the information via the internet.

ICT in lower tier suppliers

Although a few foreign or large Taiwanese suppliers of components match the PC-makers and ODMs in their use of ICT (see 'Foreign firm' column, Table 4.5), most tier 1 and tier 2 suppliers are SMEs whose ICT use is far below that of the ODMs. They rely instead on face-to-face meetings and personal ties that they have developed over many years. Some consider ICT limiting:

> If the customer needs it, we can do things in the system. After the deal is over, we will return to normal operation. Western systems can cause Chinese companies to lose flexibility to respond to customers. (Authors' interviews with company B; see Table 4.5)

Most ICT used by tier 1 suppliers is focused on internal integration aimed at better linkages between their manufacturing operations in China and their design and headquarters operations in Taiwan. All tier 1 suppliers we interviewed either had ERP

Table 4.5   Information technology in tier 1 and tier 2 suppliers[a]

	Foreign firms[b]	Taiwanese firms										
	Tier 1	Tier 1									Tier 2	
ICT applications		A	B	C	D	E	F	G	H	I	J	K
Internal												
Product data management	×								×			
Sales/order/distribution management	×	×							×		×	×
Material inventory management	×	×	×						×		×	×
Production/shop floor management	×	×	×						×			
Human resources												
Finance/accounting	×	×	×	×	×	×	×	×	×	×	×	
External												
Customer extranet	×			×		×	×		×			
Supply extranet						×	×	×	×	×		
E-procurement (EDI/RosettaNet)	×											
Email	×	×	×	×	×		×		×	×	×	×

Notes: EDI = electronic data interchange; ICT = information and communications technology.
a   A blank means 'no such application'.
b   Foreign multinational corporation supplier of disk drives.
Source: Interviews conducted by the authors in 2005.

systems or were in the process of implementing them (Table 4.6). However, most do not have shop floor automation, material requirement planning, customer relationship management, or supply chain management applications in place (Table 4.5). The ERP systems are mainly limited to finance and used to help CEOs coordinate and manage the costs associated with multiple product lines being produced at multiple manufacturing sites.

Thus, tier 1 companies are using IT for internal operational management rather than for supply chain coordination. This is very different from the ODMs that have invested heavily in systems linked to the PC-makers and, to a lesser degree, systems linked to the tier 1 suppliers.

A few suppliers currently communicate with a select group of international customers using the RosettaNet standards, but generally tier 1 suppliers are not set up to implement EDI or RosettaNet because of the considerable cost and complexity involved.[9] Most of these suppliers have websites for showing their product availability, but they currently use fax and phone to transact business.

The tier 1 suppliers all used email for communicating on a daily basis, but distrusted it for orders from customers. They wanted a signature, so they tended to use a fax machine. Some used email to negotiate prices and receive orders from international

Table 4.6 Enterprise resource planning (ERP) systems of tier 1 and tier 2 companies

	Company	ERP system
Tier 1	A	Taiwanese ERP (Dingxin)
	B	Taiwanese ERP (Dingxin)
	C	SAP ERP
	D	Taiwanese ERP (DSC)
	E	Taiwanese ERP (DSC)
	F	BPCS with a lot of customising
	G	Taiwanese ERP
	H	Oracle ERP
	I	SAP ERP
Tier 2	J	PRC ERP
	K	No ERP

Source: Foster *et al.* (2006).

markets. In this case, the capability of email to transcend time and distance limitations outweighed its disadvantages. When buying from international suppliers, tier 1 companies generally ordered through the supplier websites.

ICT use in the two tier 2 suppliers was even less advanced than that in tier 1. One said:

> As far as the manufacture of cables is concerned, we usually find our new suppliers online. But after finding them, we will turn to the traditional communication method again – place orders by fax and then confirm by phone. (Authors' interviews with company J; see Table 4.5)

They said they negotiated prices in person because:

> I like to look in the eye of my suppliers when negotiating price. (Authors' interviews with company J; see Table 4.5)

And they placed orders to suppliers only by fax:

> We don't use IT when placing orders. We need signatures on orders. And if we use email, it will involve some legal problems. (Authors' interviews with company J; see Table 4.5)

The other tier 2 provider had a number of PCs and was content to run his business using spreadsheets. For email, he used a local Chinese portal (authors' interviews with company K; see Table 4.5).

ICT in the local network

Beyond efforts of the firms themselves, the governments in both Taiwan and China have sought further automation and linkages in the local network, including linkages with customs and tax authorities.

The local authorities in the Yangtze River Delta have been motivated to help the Taiwanese ODMs as a means of attracting more foreign direct investment (FDI) to their cities. Intensely competitive for FDI, several cities (Kunshan, Suzhou, Wujiang, Songjiang) have developed large industrial parks and implemented 24x7 customs operations and automated ICT systems for customs processing and tax collection in the export processing zones. These operations and ICTs enable clearance in several hours compared to several days elsewhere (Wang and Lee, forthcoming).

As mentioned above, the Taiwan Ministry of Economic Affairs developed the Plan A/B program in an effort to ensure Taiwan's place in global production networks.

Three foreign multinational corporations (MNCs) participated in Plan A (IBM, HP and Compaq) to implement automated procurement linkages. Fifteen Taiwanese firms (ODMs and large component suppliers) developed machine-to-machine electronic linkages with 3–22 suppliers, many involving the same suppliers (Anon. 2002; DOIT 2006). The linkages focused entirely on purchasing activities – requests for quotations, orders, order changes, and order cancellations (Table 4.7). Although there are claims that the two plans involve more than 4,000 participants, our field interviews indicated that most local linkages are to the websites of ODMs and the larger tier 1 suppliers rather than being automated linkages of business processes.

Table 4.7 Electronic integration between ODMs and their suppliers

Program B participating firms[a]	Number of tier 1 suppliers that ODMs link with electronically	Implemented PIPs[b]
ASUS	22	3A3, 3A7, 3A8
Mitac	12	3A3, 3A7
Tatung	12	3A3, 3A7, 3A8
Acer	10	3A3, 3A7
Delta	10	3A3, 3A7, 3A8, 4A4
Inventec	10	3A3, 3A7, 3A8
Twinhead	8	3A3, 3A7, 3A8, 3A9
Compal	5	3A3, 3A7
Sampo	7	3A3, 3A7, 3A8, 3A9
Microstar	15	3A3, 3A7, 3A8, 3A9
Compeq	6	3A3, 3A8, 3A9, 3C6
Primax	5	3A3, 3A7, 3A8, 3A9
ADI	3	3A3, 3A7
Arima	5	3A3, 3A7
First International Computer	5	3A3, 3A7
Total	135	

Notes: ODM = original design manufacturer.
a Most of these firms are ODMs, but a few are large component suppliers (Compeq, Tatung, Delta, Sampo, Microstar, Primax, ADI). Quanta, which is the largest ODM, did not participate.
b PIPs are 'partner interface processes': 3A3 = request purchase order; 3A7 = notify of purchase order; 3A8 = request purchase order change; 3A9 = request purchase order cancellation; 3C6 = notify of remittance advice; 4A4 = notify of planning release forecast.

Source: DOIT (2006). Data last updated 28 February 2002.

Promotion of RosettaNet has been extended to China, with the backing of China's Ministry of Science and Technology, but the take-up is not clear. A recent RosettaNet Global Conference in Beijing featured presentations by foreign MNCs such as Dell, HP, IBM, Intel, Sony, Arrow Electronics, Fairchild Semiconductor, and Nokia. There were presentations about a demonstration project for extending linkages among Taiwanese firms beyond the Plan A/B program to other levels and to money flows in addition to information flows (Liang 2005; Hainian 2005), but there was not a single project presented about mainland Chinese firms. Thus, the development of the lower tier linkages in the supply chain is still in the education and promotion stage.

In summary, there is a strong, sophisticated digital network between the global PC-makers and Taiwanese ODMs in China, but the digital network more or less stops at the ODM level. Most tier 1 suppliers access the ODMs' website for forecast information and exchange information via email and attached files (spreadsheets, CAD files, Word files), phone and fax. The tier 2 suppliers we interviewed rely mainly on phone and fax. Efforts to promote greater linkages in the local network by Taiwan and China authorities do not appear to have much traction as yet, but local authorities have created ICTs for customs and tax processing in the export processing zones to speed up logistics.

These findings are consistent with recent research that has described the production networks in China as 'institutionally embedded but technologically de-linked' (Wang and Lee, forthcoming). The quote is a reference to the fact that local Chinese officials and Taiwanese entrepreneurs have developed customs and tax processing procedures for facilitating logistics in order to meet the demands of global PC-makers, but there has been no technology transfer to mainland Chinese firms.

The same might be said about the digital networks of the notebook PC industry in China. The Taiwanese ODMs use internal ICT to manage operations in multiple locations. The tier 1 and tier 2 suppliers are also internally focused – on financial and shop floor management to meet ODM demands. The local Chinese officials focus only on ICT that is specific to their own industrial park and that facilitates customs processing for their clients and tax collection for their own reinvestment needs. Given the dynamism of the industry, no one is yet able to make ICT investments in the micro production networks, in developing ICT capabilities in the lower tier suppliers, or in a broader digital network as envisaged by Taiwanese and, recently, Chinese officials. Given the limited state of ICT, and the narrow focus of most applications, a key question is: what makes the local elements of global production networks work?

SOCIAL NETWORKS IN PC INDUSTRY PRODUCTION

Anne Stevenson-Yang, a long-time observer of the IT supply chain in China and Taiwan and former Director of the US Information Technology Office (USITO) in Beijing, characterised the China–Taiwan PC supply chain as 'a human neural network that optimizes production and minimizes costs' (Foster *et al.* 2006). She was referring to the way in which human and business networks interact with one another in Chinese production networks.

There are many aspects of social relationships in the PC industry that are common across the entire electronics industry: the importance of family, school and corporate ties; the linkages among overseas Chinese employed in foreign multinationals; the entrepreneurial culture; the financing of new firms by family members and industry leaders; the importance of *guanxi* in all relationships; and so on. However, we focus here on personal relationships, trust, and informal information sharing as substitutes for contracts, inter-organisational information systems, and formal information sharing. We refer to these as *guanxi,* or personal relationships, versus market-based relationships. We find that whereas more formal market-based connections characterise relationships between the PC-maker and ODMs, *guanxi* and informal information sharing characterise those between ODMs and suppliers.[10]

Relationships between PC-makers and ODMs

The relationships between PC-makers and ODMs for production activities are based on formal contracts, and thus can be considered market based. The PC-maker develops concepts and specifications for a new notebook and then formally requests bids for development and manufacturing. The branded notebook companies usually have three or four ODMs in their supplier list (Table 4.1) and divide their product line among the suppliers, who compete on price (Dedrick and Kraemer 2005). The result is uncertainty and risk for ODM notebook-makers, as the branded PC companies tend to routinely switch between vendors for individual products.

In addition, the largest PC-makers usually contract directly with suppliers for key components and have them consigned to the ODM. At least one PC-maker conducts reverse auctions for individual parts. They contract directly because their size gives them greater bargaining capability and market power with suppliers. In contrast, the smaller PC-makers tend to let the ODMs procure the components due to their greater buying power, but look for some sharing of the price gain from the ODM.

The relationships for design and development are also formal and contractual, although they depend on the role the ODM plays in design. We estimate that about 20 per cent (Apple, Toshiba, Sony and Lenovo) do much of their own design; another 20 per cent rely nearly completely on the ODM to innovate and to design the notebooks; and about 60 per cent co-design notebook models with the ODM. The major PC companies also have their own design personnel and product managers who monitor the ODMs during the development process.

Although these relationships are market based, there is still considerable personal interaction between the branded notebook company and the ODM when they co-design new products. The PC-maker's branded industrial design and knowledge of the market must be blended with the ODM's knowledge of new technologies, physical development possibilities and manufacturing realities. However, even these interactions are structured by a design process complete with gates, performance metrics, and potential penalties.

Relationships between ODMs and their suppliers

Social networks are much more important than formal contracts between the ODMs and tier 1 and tier 2 suppliers. One reason is that it is simply the culture of business in China. As one tier 2 provider said: 'I have known the President of [one of Taiwan's largest contract manufacturers] for 30 years; we look out for each other.' The ODMs expect their suppliers to provide them with whatever they need, but they also look out for their suppliers. They will collaborate to find cheaper materials and methods to meet the continual demands of the branded PC firms for price reductions. They will negotiate face to face on sensitive matters such as pricing and sharing of missed production, overstock, and warranty costs.

Another reason that personal relationships are so important is that the IT systems used by suppliers are all different and primitive. Whereas the ODMs have modern ERP systems, most suppliers use home-grown systems or highly customised local packages that cannot be linked easily (Table 4.6). One tier 1 supplier said:

> Our major problem is that different companies use different systems; they do not link together and we can't build the linkages due to cost and skill needed. (Authors' interviews with company A; see Table 4.5)

The number of linkages for tier 1 and tier 2 suppliers is usually large; there are usually 50–100 customers and suppliers rather than a few dozen as with the ODMs. Consequently, it is easier to use human-to-human interfaces aided by phone, fax, and email for collaboration than to build more automated inter-organisational ICT connections.

Still another concern of suppliers is security:

> We are afraid of secrets getting out. Turnover is high and some key person may know the password and get access to our system for a competitor and do something to hurt our company, so we worry about that. (Authors' interviews with company A; see Table 4.5)

Lastly, this same supplier said:

> … customers are more focused on quality, cost and capability, not IT. (Authors' interviews with company A; see Table 4.5)

In fact, as indicated earlier, suppliers use ICT for internal financial and production management rather than external linkages. They are content to use the ODMs' websites or extranets for demand information, and consider them superior to more automated forms (EDI, RosettaNet) because of their greater richness, detail, and time span.

Tier 1 suppliers must manage inventory in a manner that reduces costs but ensures that they can meet the needs of their ODM customers. They are more likely to keep raw materials in stock than finished products, as raw materials can be used for multiple products. They operate on a hybrid of build to stock and build to order. According to a tier 1 provider:

> For cable assembly we build to order as we follow different designs according to the customer's request; for standardised connectors we can build to stock to adjust production loading. But mainly we build to order for better production and financial control. (Authors' interviews with company A; see Table 4.5)

In general, the tier 1 suppliers are very flexible and will give the ODMs what they want when they want it even if it means that their employees will have to work 15-hour days instead of 10–12-hour days. Also, tier 1 suppliers are not hesitant to outsource work to the company of a trusted friend or relative in order to meet an ODM's requirement.

The tier 1 suppliers are generally small and centrally managed by an owner who relies on their own network of personal relationships to navigate and carve out their company's position in the supply chain. These hundreds of tier 1 and 2 suppliers interact like a neural network, matching demand with supply and making sure that there are no shortages in the supply chain. Due to the efficiency and effectiveness of this system, the ODMs are able to be very responsive, in turn, to the branded PC-makers.

How personal relationships work

Suppliers reduce risk due to volatility, competition and price pressure by developing personal relationships and business relationships based on proximity and face-to-face communications. As put by one supplier:

> If talking face to face, people can construct a closer relationship. It is not only the Taiwan way, but the Chinese way. (Authors' interviews with company A; see Table 4.5. Similar statements were made in interviews with companies B, F and J)

Establishing and maintaining these relationships carries through, with suppliers locating offices near major customers, with frequent sales contacts with customers, with face-to-face price and market share negotiation, and with changes occurring within this structure. To overcome the issue of location, one company

> ... sets up offices close to big customers ... and does the business in a traditional way. To avoid losing touch with customers, each salesman only deals with 3 major customers. (Authors' interviews with company B; see Table 4.5)

The purpose of such close contact is for the salesman to collect information, verify it with multiple sources and make the correct interpretation of its implications for the supplier:

> The salesman goes to the customer site almost daily. He visits sourcing, engineering, quality control, or production control to collect information, to validate messages from various sources for information that is true and valuable, and to increase our chances [to win the business]. For example, sometimes a buyer may ask for a lower price but promise you a larger order quantity in exchange, or ask you to prepare a large stock of inventory [as a hedge against the volatility of orders]. The salesman then may go to the customer's engineers to verify the offer by asking whether the company has received any big orders recently. (Authors' interviews with company B; see Table 4.5)

Beyond verification, the purpose of such close contact is to increase the chances that the company will actually receive an order. This involves ensuring that the company's product is qualified for procurement and negotiating price and market share. ODMs qualify at least two suppliers for any product, so the salesman and supplier's engineers provide information needed by the ODMs' engineers to qualify the product, and do so quickly lest they look for others. After qualification, the salesman will focus on price negotiation and market share. As put by this same company:

> At this time, a good relationship can make a big difference. With a good relationship, the customer may assign 60 per cent of their order with us. However, with a much closer relationship, the share can be 80 per cent. So the relationship is very important. (Authors' interviews with company B; see Table 4.5)

It turns out that such negotiations are fragile, however, when market conditions change. Here, personal relationships and face-to-face communication are important, first to just know about changes in time to act quickly and, second, to ensure a favourable outcome for the supplier:

> The market share may change quickly, so the salesman should keep in touch with customers, at least to know whether the true share changes or not. What we know from the order is the volume, but not the order share [of the customers' total volume]. With a good relationship and trust, the salesman can get the share information from the customer's buyer (maybe during a nice meal or by sending a small gift), or know about some pending changes (volume, requirements) in time. In this way, the company can react quickly to the change to avoid losing volume or market share. (Authors' interviews with company B; see Table 4.5)

Perhaps the most sensitive negotiation stems from price pressures after negotiation. Branded PC-makers often demand reductions from ODMs, which in turn demand reductions from the suppliers. But not all suppliers are equal. The ODM cannot pass on, say, a 10 per cent reduction to a key supplier such as Intel or Microsoft, so other suppliers with no market power may face a 20 per cent reduction. If the supplier knows about the coming change, it may try to negotiate for greater quantity at the expense of its competitor. Alternatively, the supplier may negotiate to substitute 'over-quality' material with cheaper material on the grounds that the original specification guarded against a quality defect that would rarely occur in practice. An example given by one supplier is a connector that was required to be pulled in and out 2,000 times without failure but that was rarely unplugged. The supplier said:

> When customers require lower cost, the companies can negotiate to change the spec but keep the function OK. In this way, the company and the customer share the benefit from changing materials. There are some situations where the customer might not know about this change, but eventually he will know. But, the customer usually accepts it since the supplier can help it cut down cost. (Authors' interviews with company A; see Table 4.5)

Finally, personal relationships are important during production in order to deal with demand fluctuation. The ODMs' suppliers must negotiate with their suppliers to give priority to their requirements over others in production, or to have the supplier work overtime. One interviewee said:

> When suppliers cannot supply in time, it is most efficient to call them directly or send staff there. Usually a factory has many orders from different customers to

fulfill. It is workable to change the order of batch production or to arrange overtime work to meet our needs. (Authors' interviews with company B; see Table 4.5)

We do the same for our customers. We had an order from BenQ that was 1.5 times our factory's manpower capacity. As solution, the whole factory worked from 8am to 1am for three months until enough workers were trained to pick up the additional workload. Chinese people are used to change pressure, and willing to work longer for more money. (Authors' interviews with company B; see Table 4.5)

Clustering and geographic location of activities

The direct, personal relationships that are part of the business culture in both Taiwan and Mainland China are facilitated by executives clustering in housing neighbourhoods and business associations and suppliers clustering around the ODMs.

In Taiwan, many of the presidents of the ODMs and lead suppliers live in the same neighbourhoods so it is relatively easy for them to meet informally. The headquarters of many ODM suppliers are near the Taipei–Hsinshu area, so many deals are done face to face. In China, executives and managers of the Taiwanese and foreign firms (customers and suppliers) tend to live in the same gated housing communities and belong to the same private clubs, thereby facilitating informal interaction among senior executives there.

The notebook production network, which was clustered in Taipei–Hsinchu, moved *en masse* to China after the Taiwan government removed investment restrictions in November 2001.[11] Although urged on by the branded PC companies, the ODMs were also seeking cheaper production labour, land and materials because their margins were very thin. In fact, the ODMs had already established some supplier networks in China ahead of the change in policy. Some had been in southern China since the early 1990s serving the desktop industry, and moved some production east. Others moved directly to the mainland ahead of the ODMs, and still others came with them (Yang and Hsia 2004; Chase *et al.* 2004). The key point is that their supply networks were in place as the ODMs moved.[12] Thus, the organisational network from Taiwan was fully in place, long-term relationships also remained in place, and Taiwanese executives, managers and professionals were able to continue to negotiate face to face.

At the factory level, personal relationships are further facilitated because suppliers must be no more than a few hours from their major customers. Related firms tend to cluster near their major customers at each tier of the supply chain. For example, a cable and wire manufacturer noted:

We make wires and cables from raw materials provided by upstream companies. Then the downstream companies will assemble what we made. Eventually they will then be assembled in PCs ... One of the reasons that we came to mainland China is that many factories in Taiwan have come here. One of the things we heard from other suppliers is that the biggest challenge in China is logistics. It is easier to produce overnight [have people work overtime], but it is harder to get the material to the factory. So a lot of suppliers locate their factories near the factories of their customers. (Authors' interviews with company A; see Table 4.5)

SUMMARY AND CONCLUSION

In the highly competitive notebook industry, the efficiency and effectiveness of its supply chain can make the difference between whether a PC-maker survives or thrives. Small differences in product quality, product costs, inventory costs and availability can be worth millions of dollars to the branded firms. In order to maximise the effectiveness and efficiency of the supply chain, PC-makers and their ODMs are using IT to minimise inventory and time to market, while ensuring that customers get the product they want at a competitive price. These companies use ICTs to support sales, order and distribution, procurement, material and inventory management, production planning and shop floor management, and finance and human resources.

Most ODMs use websites to provide tier 1 companies with forecast information and some push out orders through EDI, the RosettaNet system, or their website. However, there is a dramatic difference between the use of ICT in the ODMs and that in tier 1 and tier 2 suppliers. These suppliers primarily use ICT for financial controls to help them manage multiple production sites in China from their headquarters in Taiwan. Most communication takes place through face-to-face contact, phone, fax or email, or by accessing a website. Very few use EDI, XML or other more automated systems to interact.

The tier 1 suppliers are generally chosen by the ODMs not on the basis of their ICT capabilities, but rather on their ability to fulfil orders and on longstanding personal and business relationships. Most tier 1 and tier 2 suppliers do not feel pressured by the ODMs to invest substantially in ICTs, although they have received some support from the Taiwanese government for such investments.

In short, the structure of ICT in the notebook supply chain is asymmetric. The two-way digital supply chain that runs between the branded PC-makers and the ODM manufacturers becomes a one-way stream between the ODMs and tier 1 suppliers and is non-existent between tier 1 and tier 2 companies and further upstream.

Thus, the coordination of production among the ODMs and their suppliers is not very automated or even very digital – unless dialling the phone is considered digital. Instead, coordination relies on social networks and personal and business relationships. Many of these relationships go back 10–30 years and are based on a common identity. Thus, the notebook industry is a classic example of a Chinese business network, but in this case the network is based on a shared Taiwanese identity that was literally transferred intact from Taiwan to mainland China.

Even though most production is now done in the People's Republic of China (PRC), very few companies that are not Taiwanese or foreign owned and operated participate in this network. In particular, companies that are indigenous to the PRC are not part of the notebook manufacturing network. By comparison with societies such as the United States, Chinese society is characterised by a high level of mistrust (Fukuyama 1995); however, there is an exceptional level of trust in China if you have an in-group relationship. The notebook industry and the Taiwanese business networks that support it provide a way of coordinating production under a high degree of uncertainty and the weaknesses of a legal system that does not generally resolve contractual conflict well.

ICTs can increase the speed, efficiency, and precision of inter-organisational communications. However, by taking people out of the loop and replacing them with computers, ICT can dampen the responsiveness of a production network. Hundreds of manufacturers communicating continually via cell phones or in person with their suppliers, customers and each other create a very sensitive system. What is lost is the ability for PC-makers to have the kind of clear visibility up the supply chain that they would like to better ensure supply and quality and to control pricing. Beyond their immediate suppliers (ODMs and large component suppliers), the supply chain becomes quite obscure for the PC-makers.

In conclusion, the notebook industry relies on a production network consisting largely of Taiwanese companies whose activities are concentrated in Taiwan (management, R&D, product development, IT) and the Yangtze River Delta (manufacturing, process engineering, sustaining support). This network is connected to the branded PC-makers through Western-style business transactions, including formal contracts and heavy use of ICT. Among the Taiwanese network, however, there is much heavier reliance on personal and informal relationships, or *guanxi*, to coordinate production, logistics, development, and other activities.

NOTES

This paper is based on research supported grants from the Sloan Foundation and the U.S. National Science Foundation (Grant # 447681-21940) to the Personal Computing Industry Center at The Paul Merage School of Business at the University of California, Irvine. Any opinions, findings, and conclusions or recommendations expressed in this material are those of the author(s) and do not necessarily reflect the views of the National Science Foundation.

1. The concept of micro production networks was first articulated by Ernst and Kim (2002) to refer to the sub-networks below the lead or flagship firms and their immediate contractors – in our case the PC-makers and ODMs.
2. As pointed out by Myrna Austria at the conference, *guanxi* is not unique to the Chinese PC industry; direct and personal relationships are part of the business culture not only in China and Taiwan, but in East Asia in general. Thus, this work has implications more broadly.
3. Wang and Lee (forthcoming: Table 1, p. 27); TPI (2000a, 2000b, 2000c).
4. The information systems and operations management literature distinguishes three categories of e-business applications: e-coordination, e-sourcing and e-communities. While much of the literature (Johnson and Whang 2002) and press tends to focus on e-sourcing (auctions) and e-communities (electronic exchanges), there is actually far greater use of e-coordination (Johnson and Klassen 2005; Johnson and Leenders 2004).
5. The auto and aircraft industries have made similar efforts to develop standards and systems for inter-firm coordination.
6. Michael McManus, Taiwan Notebook Industry Overview, Digitimes Systems, Taipei, Thursday, 8 September 2005 (with reporting and research by David Tzeng, Joanne Chien and Huang Kung Tien).

7   According to a person from Gateway interviewed in 2004, PC-makers audit the ODMs' ICT capabilities before contracting with them.
8   As recently as mid-2005, inter-firm linkages with tier 1 suppliers via RosettaNet remain very limited. Most activity is still at the stage of pilot experiments involving a few firms and a few processes (see Hainian 2005).
9   The costs appear to be enormous for small firms. For example, one RosettaNet service provider whose estimate might be expected to be low put the total cost for a small firm to link to two back-end systems of a larger firm (for shipment notification and inventory report processes) at $310,000 over three years (see Hainian 2005). A supplier might need a dozen or more such linkages.
10 At the conference, Masaru Yoshitomi questioned how trust is generated among suppliers given that *guanxi* is sometimes considered identical to corruption in China and that the modular character and volatile market demand of the PC industry require open transaction relationships which make it difficult to establish relationship-based trust over time. We consider *guanxi* a feature of Chinese business culture whether in China, in Taiwan or elsewhere in East Asia. It is not necessarily identical to corruption, although we recognise that the media often use it that way. The key point, however, is that trust exists in the local supply chain because the firms have longstanding relationships with one another that they carried with them from Taiwan to China when the industry moved en masse around 2001. There are no domestic Chinese suppliers to the notebook industry; they are all Taiwanese firms that moved to mainland China and do business with one another as they did in Taiwan. The supply chain is more or less a closed system.
11 A similar pattern exists within the desktop PC industry, which is located mainly in the Pearl River Delta region of China, including the cities of Dongguan and Shenzhen near Hong Kong. In contrast to notebooks, which are lightweight and can be shipped to the end customer by air, final assembly of desktops is regionalised due to bulk, weight, and logistics considerations.
12 Foreign suppliers of batteries, optical drives and other components have also moved some production there. Thus, nearly all the industry's physical production network is in China. Although high-value components such as microprocessors, storage, memory and flat-panel displays are still imported, it may be only a matter of time before they too are produced locally. Although one observer at the conference suggested that extensive digital networks were also in place, we have not found this to be an accurate description of digital networks in the industry. Leng (2004) states: 'The innovative supply chain system allows major producers like Quanta to trade materials flow on a real-time basis and finish the products within 48 hours. Quanta has linked its database with the databases of more than 1,000 suppliers so they can easily coordinate with Quanta's order schedule'.

REFERENCES

Anon. (2002) 'Industrial Automation & electronic Business (iAeB) program', St-Pioneer, Vol. 90, June, <http://www.st-pioneer.org.tw/modules.php?name=magazine&pa=showpage&tid=1648>. [In Chinese]

Chase, M.S., K.L. Pollpeter, and J.C. Mulvenon (2004) *Shanghaied? The Economic and Political Implications of the Flow of Information Technology and Investment across the Taiwan Strait*, Santa Monica: Rand.

Curry, J. and M. Kenney (1999) 'Beating the clock: corporate responses to rapid change in the PC industry', *California Management Review*, 42(1): 8–36.

Daoud, D. and L. Lovende (2005) IDC Worldwide PC Market 1Q05 Review, #33692, Framingham MA: IDC.

Dedrick, J. and K.L. Kraemer, (1998) *Asia's Computer Challenge*, New York: Oxford University Press.

Dedrick, J. and K.L. Kraemer, (2005) 'The impacts of IT on firm and industry structure', *California Management Review*, 47(3): 122–142.

—— (2006) 'Original design manufacturing: control, trust and learning in a new organizational form', Working paper, University of California, Irvine.

DOIT (Department of Industrial Technology) (2006) 'ITAP IT applications promotion project: promoting e-business in Taiwan industries: projects ABCDE', Taipei: Taiwan Ministry of Economic Affairs, <http://www.itap.org.tw/group/application/tdp_itap/aboutus.php>.

Ernst, D. and L. Kim (2002) 'Introduction: global production networks, information technology and knowledge diffusion', *Industry and Innovation*, 9(3): 147–153.

Foster, W., Z.C. Chang, J. Dedrick and K.L. Kraemer (2006) 'Technology and organizational factors in the notebook industry supply chain', CAPS Research: Tempe, AZ.

Fukuyama, F. (1995) *Trust: Social Virtues and the Creation of Prosperity*, New York: Free Press.

Granovetter, M. (1985) 'Economic action and social structure: the problem of embeddedness', *American Journal of Sociology*, (91): 481–493.

Hainian, Jin (2005) 'China B2B hub: bridging the gap between global MNCs and SMEs in China', presentation at the RosettaNet Global Conference, Beijing, 20 April.

Hsu, Pei-Fang and K.L. Kraemer (2006) 'ERP and e-business integration in the extended enterprise: resource complementarities in business value creation', Center for Research on Information Technology and Organizations, University of California, Irvine.

Johnson, E.M. and S. Whang (2002) 'E-business and supply chain management: an overview and framework', *Production and Operations Management*, 11(4): 413–423.

Johnson, F.P. and R.D. Klassen (2005) 'E-procurement', *Sloan Management Review*, 46(2): 7–10.

Johnson, F.P. and M.R. Leenders (2004) 'Supply's organizational roles and responsibilities', Tempe AZ: CAPS Research.

Leng, Tse-Kang (2004) 'Global networking and the new division of labor across the Taiwan Straits', pp. 185–204 in F. Mengin (ed.), *Cyber China: Reshaping National Identities in the Age of Information*, New York: Palgrave Macmillan.

Malakooty, N. (2005) 'RosettaNet: the organization and the system', Working paper, Personal Computing Industry Center, The Paul Merage School of Business, University of California, Irvine.

Markus, M. Lynne (2002) 'Paradigm shifts: e-business and business/systems integration', *Communications of the Association for Information Systems*, 4(10): 1–44.

Markus, M. Lynne, C. Tanis and P. Fenema (2000) 'Multisite ERP implementations', *Communications of the ACM*, 43(40): 42–46.

MIC (Market Intelligence Center) (2006) 'The Taiwanese ICT industry outlook', PowerPoint presentation, Taipei, Taiwan, April.

Norris, G., J. Hurley, K. Hartley and J. Dunleavy (2000) *E-business and ERP: Transforming the Enterprise*, New York: John Wiley & Sons, Inc.

Sambamurthy, V., A. Bharadwaj and V. Grover (2003) 'Shaping agility through digital options: reconceptualizing the role of information technology in contemporary firms', *MIS Quarterly*, 27(2): 237–263.

Swaminathan, Jayashankar M. and S.R. Tayur (2003) 'Models for supply chains in e-business', *Management Science*, 49(10): 1387–1406.

TPI (Topology Research Institute) (2000a) 'A survey of Taiwanese IT industry layout in Kunshan', Taipei: TPI.

—— (2000b) 'A survey of Taiwanese IT industry layout in Suzhou', Taipei: TPI.

—— (2000c) 'A survey of Taiwanese IT industry layout in Wujaing', Taipei: TPI.

Wang, Jenn-hwan and C.K. Lee (forthcoming) 'Global production networks and local institutional building: the development of the information technology industry in Suzhou, China', *Environment and Planning A*.

White, W.J., A.C. O'Connor and B.R. Rowe (2004) 'The electronics supply chain', pp. 5-1–31 in *Inadequate Infrastructure for Supply Chain Integration*, Research Triangle Park NC: RTI International.

Yang, Y.R. and C.J. Hsia (2004) 'Local clustering and organizational governance of trans-border production networks: a case study of Taiwanese IT companies in the greater Suzhou area', *Journal of Geographical Science*, 36: 23–54.

Yang, Yung-kai (2005) 'Taiwanese notebook computer production network in China and the implication for the upgrading of Chinese electronics industry', unpublished Ph.D. thesis, Manchester Business School, University of Manchester.

5 The creation of regional production networks in Asia Pacific: the case of Japanese multinational corporations

Shujiro Urata

INTRODUCTION

Over the years, Japanese multinational corporations (MNCs) have increased in both number and the extent of their overseas operations. According to the World Investment Report 2005 (UN 2005), 4,149 MNCs, or 8.2 per cent of MNCs from developed countries, are headquartered in Japan. Among the world's top 100 non-financial MNCs, ranked by foreign assets, nine are Japanese MNCs. And Japan's Ministry of Economy, Trade and Industry reports (METI 2005) that the overseas sales of Japanese MNCs increased 1.5 times in the ten years from 1993 to 2002.

As the activities of Japanese MNCs expanded, the nature and extent of the linkages within MNCs and between MNCs and other firms changed. In the early stage of development, MNCs set up distribution networks for their own products, which were exported from their headquarters in Japan. With accumulated experience in overseas operations, MNCs set up production bases overseas, to benefit from locational advantages. Faced with the limited supply of parts locally, overseas affiliates of Japanese MNCs imported parts from headquarters and assembled them to produce finished products. At this stage, neither procurement nor sales networks with other firms were well developed. However, networks with local firms and with affiliates of Japanese MNCs were created over time, as local firms became more capable of producing parts of a sufficiently high quality for Japanese MNCs and as the number of affiliates of Japanese MNCs increased. A large number of Japanese MNCs followed their business customers in establishing affiliates. This type of procurement network was expanded and extended to result in the regional production network in East Asia today. In addition to production and distribution networks, Japanese MNCs have set up networks in such forms as technology alliance, production consignment, outsourcing and international subcontracting.

In light of these developments, this chapter attempts to examine empirically how Japanese MNCs have developed their production and distribution networks in East Asia. In the analysis, I examine Japanese MNCs' activities in North America and Latin America, mainly to discern the notable characteristics of their activities in East Asia.

The structure of the chapter is as follows. First, I give an overview of foreign direct investment (FDI) by Japanese MNCs and present and discuss basic information on Japanese MNCs. These two sections are intended to set the stage for the main analysis on networking by Japanese MNCs in the following sections. In these, I first examine the patterns of output sales and input procurement by Japanese MNCs and then analyse the presence of production and distribution networks using the data on international trade and those on international input–output tables. Finally, I present some concluding remarks.

JAPANESE FDI: AN OVERVIEW

Outward FDI by Japanese MNCs increased sharply in the latter half of the 1980s (Figure 5.1). This sharp increase was caused mainly by two factors: the sharp yen appreciation and the emergence of the bubble economy in Japan.[1] The rapid appreciation of the yen, which started in early 1985 and accelerated as a result of the Plaza Accord in September 1985, stimulated Japanese FDI through the relative price effect and the liquidity or wealth effect. The relative price effect reduced the international price competitiveness of Japanese products, reducing Japan's export volume. To cope with the new price structure, some Japanese MNCs moved their production bases to foreign countries, especially to East Asia, where production costs were lower. Yen appreciation promoted Japanese FDI through the liquidity or wealth effect. To the extent that yen appreciation made Japanese MNCs wealthier in the sense of increased collateral and liquidity, it enabled them to finance FDI more cheaply than their foreign competitors.

Another important factor was the emergence of the bubble economy in Japan. The liquidity effect discussed above was strengthened by the bubble economy, in

Figure 5.1   Japan's outward FDI ($ million)

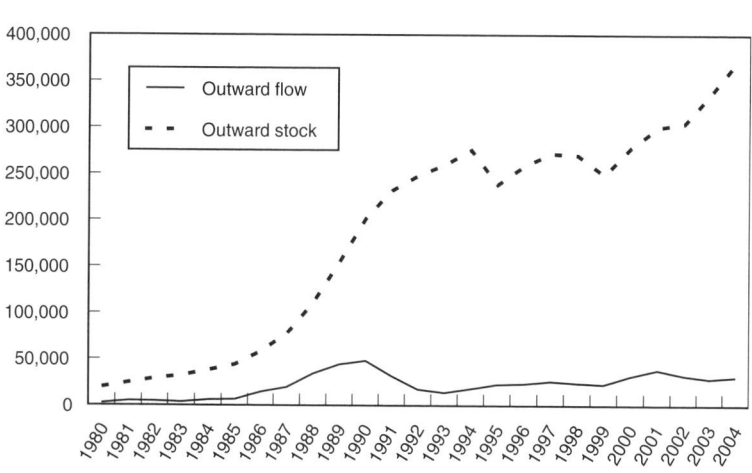

Source: UNCTAD Foreign direct investment database.

which the prices of assets such as shares and land increased enormously. The bubble economy was attributable to expansionary monetary policy pursued by the Bank of Japan, which tried to deal with the recessionary impact of the drastic yen appreciation. Active fiscal spending for the purpose of reflating the depressed economy was another factor leading to the bubble economy.

A general rise in Japanese MNCs' technological and managerial capabilities in international business – accumulated through past experience in exporting and FDI – was a natural factor underlying the surge in Japanese FDI. It is also important to note that a number of Japanese firms followed business customers that invested overseas. A case in point is FDI by subcontracting firms: in order to maintain their business, they followed parent companies that had undertaken FDI. Indeed, such 'follow-the-parent' type FDI contributed to the construction of production and distribution networks in East Asia, which will be discussed in detail below.

Japanese FDI declined in the early 1990s mainly because of the collapse of the bubble economy. The depreciation of the yen contributed to the decline. The mechanism set in motion in the latter half of the 1980s, leading to a substantial increase in FDI, reversed in the early 1990s. Japanese FDI began to rise after reaching a bottom in 1993 but the recovery was not so impressive. Japanese FDI through the rest of the decade remained at around the same level, largely as a result of the long recession. However, as Japan's FDI started to increase again in recent years, Japan's economy started to recover.

The 1990s and early 2000s saw substantial shifts in the regional destinations of Japan's FDI and in its sectoral distribution (Figures 5.2 and 5.3). Regional destinations shifted from North America to Europe and Latin America, as the share of Japan's FDI to North America declined from 46 per cent in 1989–96 to 29 per cent in 1997–2004 and the corresponding shares for Europe and Latin America increased from 21 and 8 per cent to 36 and 15 per cent, respectively. Asia's share remained more or less constant at around 17 per cent for both periods.[2]

Sectoral shares shifted from non-manufacturing to manufacturing as the shares for non-manufacturing and manufacturing in total changed from 68 and 31 per cent in 1989–96 to 58 and 41 per cent in 1997–2004, respectively.[3] Among the manufacturing sub-sectors, electrical machinery and transport machinery, which increased their shares during the 1989–2004 period, registered the two largest shares at 13 and 8 per cent of total FDI in 1997–2004, respectively. Food captured 5 per cent of the total and chemicals 6 per cent. Among the non-manufacturing sub-sectors, finance and insurance, which increased its share notably, accounted for the largest share, at 25 per cent of the total in 1997–2004. Other non-manufacturing sub-sectors that registered large shares include transportation services (9 per cent of the total in 1997–2004) and commerce (8 per cent of the total).

Before ending this section, let me note several characteristics of Japanese FDI that have implications for networking by Japanese MNCs. One is active FDI by small and medium-sized enterprises (SMEs). People usually pay more attention to FDI by large corporations than to FDI by SMEs. However, as Urata (2002) showed, SMEs are responsible for as much as half of FDI by Japanese MNCs in terms of the number of cases. This has important implications for networking by Japanese MNCs: Japanese

The creation of regional production networks in Asia Pacific 117

Figure 5.2 Japanese FDI outflow by region, 1989–2004 (¥ 100 million)

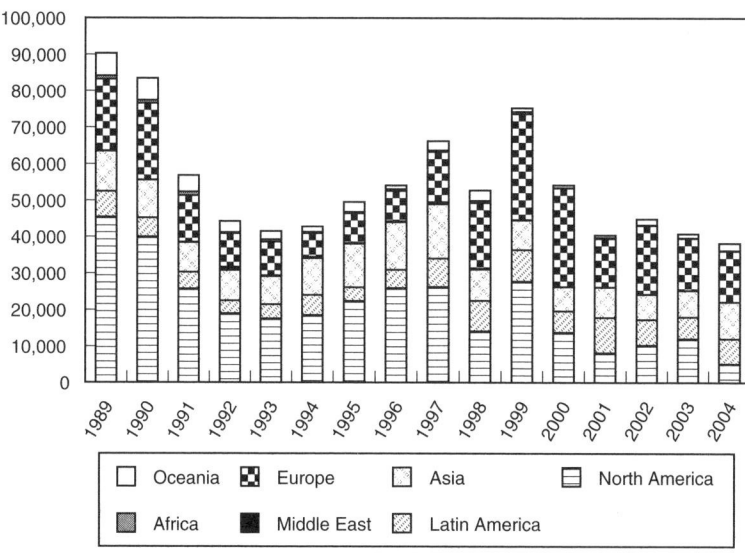

Source: Ministry of Finance.

Figure 5.3 Japan's outward FDI by sector, 1989–2004 (¥ 100 million)

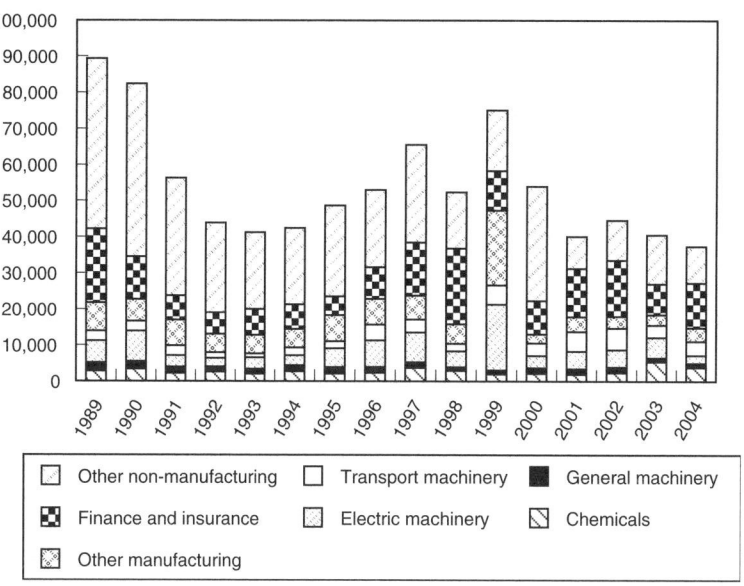

Source: Ministry of Finance.

MNCs which established networks in Japan by involving SMEs tend to set up overseas networks by involving the same SMEs that are involved in Japan.

Another notable characteristic of overseas affiliates of Japanese MNCs concerns the motive for their establishment. The motives for FDI by Japanese MNCs differ depending on the location of affiliates. Achieving low-cost production and expanding exports, particularly exports to Japan, are important motives for establishing affiliates in Asia, while expansion of local sales is the single most important motive for affiliates in North America. For affiliates in Latin America, the expansion of sales to third countries inside the region is an important motive (METI 2005). The motive to expand local sales is likely to increase in importance in the future for many developing regions, including Asia, as local demand for the products produced by the affiliates is going to increase as a result of rapid economic growth. And supplying parts to Japanese MNCs is an important motive for affiliates regardless of their location, with the exception of the affiliates in Latin America.

OVERSEAS ACTIVITIES OF JAPANESE MNCS

As seen above, Japanese MNCs increased their overseas operations in the 1990s, due to the continued expansion of their FDI. Here, I review recent developments in the overseas activities of Japanese MNCs to set the stage for an analysis of networking by Japanese MNCs.

Sales of overseas affiliates of Japanese MNCs increased 1.5 times in eight years from 1993 to 2001 (Table 5.1). In the manufacturing sub-sectors, the rate of increase was particularly high for machinery sectors and chemicals; in the non-manufacturing sub-sectors it was high for agriculture and mining. In 2001, among manufacturing sub-sectors, transport machinery and information technology (IT) equipment had large shares in the total overseas sales of Japanese MNCs, while in non-manufacturing sub-sectors wholesale and retail services accounted for a dominant share.

As a result of the increase in sales of overseas affiliates of Japanese MNCs, the share of overseas sales in overall sales (the overseas production ratio), which include not only overseas sales by the affiliates but also sales by MNCs' parents, increased over time. The overseas production ratio for Japanese MNCs which own overseas affiliates increased from 18.3 per cent in 1993 to 41 per cent in 2002 (Figure 5.4). For Japanese firms overall, including both MNCs and non-MNCs, the overseas production ratio is naturally much lower, but it also increased, from 7.4 per cent to 17.1 per cent in the 1993–2002 period.

Overseas production ratios differ among the manufacturing sub-sectors. Machinery sectors exhibit high values; transport machinery has the highest ratio, at 48 per cent, followed by electrical machinery, at 27 per cent (Table 5.2). The rate of increase in the overseas production ratio is particularly high for transport machinery: the ratio increased rapidly, from 17 to 48 per cent, from 1993 to 2002. As will be seen below, one reason for the rapid increase in overseas sales and the overseas production ratio for the machinery sector is the strategy of Japanese machinery MNCs to pursue efficient production by breaking up the production process into various sub-processes, which in turn are located in a country where the particular sub-process may be achieved

Table 5.1 Sales of overseas affiliates of Japanese MNCs by sector, 1993–2001

	Sales (billion yen)		Ratio	Share (%)	
	1993	2001	2001/1993	1993	2001
Total	91,738	137,973	1.50	100.0	100.0
Manufacturing total	29,040	64,563	2.22	31.7	46.8
Food	1,081	2,146	1.99	1.2	1.6
Textiles	626	922	1.47	0.7	0.7
Wood and pulp	314	590	1.88	0.3	0.4
Chemicals	2,349	5,583	2.38	2.6	4.0
Petroleum and coal products	827	286	0.35	0.9	0.2
Iron and steel	956	1,224	1.28	1.0	0.9
Non-ferrous metals	556	875	1.57	0.6	0.6
General machinery	1,530	3,045	1.99	1.7	2.2
Electrical machinery	8,567	3,441	2.12	9.3	2.5
IT equipment	–	14,738	–	–	10.7
Transport machinery	9,319	26,216	2.81	10.2	19.0
Precision machinery	433	1,415	3.27	0.5	1.0
Other manufacturing	2,482	4,083	1.65	2.7	3.0
Non-manufacturing	62,698	73,410	1.17	68.3	53.2
Agriculture	57	156	2.74	0.1	0.1
Mining	390	1,072	2.75	0.4	0.8
Construction	455	683	1.50	0.5	0.5
Communication and transport services	–	2,296	–	–	1.7
Wholesale and retail services	57,190	66,095	1.16	62.3	47.9
Other services	1,630	1,281	0.79	1.8	0.9
Other non-manufacturing	2,976	1,828	0.61	3.2	1.3

Note: IT = information technology; MNC = multinational corporation.
Source: METI (2005).

most efficiently. This type of strategy is generally characterised as a 'fragmentation strategy'.[4]

An examination of sales by the affiliates of Japanese MNCs shows different patterns depending on their location. The sales of affiliates in China increased remarkably fast – by 8.3 times – from 1993 to 2002. Affiliates in other East Asian countries, namely those in ASEAN-4 (Indonesia, Malaysia, the Philippines, and Thailand) and NIE-4[5] increased faster than those in other regions, although the rates of increase were significantly lower than those in China. The rates of growth were quite notable for affiliates in the Middle East and Africa, but the magnitudes of those sales were very small in the global context. However, there was a low growth of sales by affiliates in Europe, where sales increased by only 8 per cent in the nine years from 1993 to 2002, despite a relatively large expansion of Japanese FDI to Europe. The low growth of sales by European affiliates is attributable to a low economic growth rate in Europe compared to other regions.

Figure 5.4 Overseas sales as a percentage of total sales (overseas and home sales) by Japanese MNCs, 1993–2002

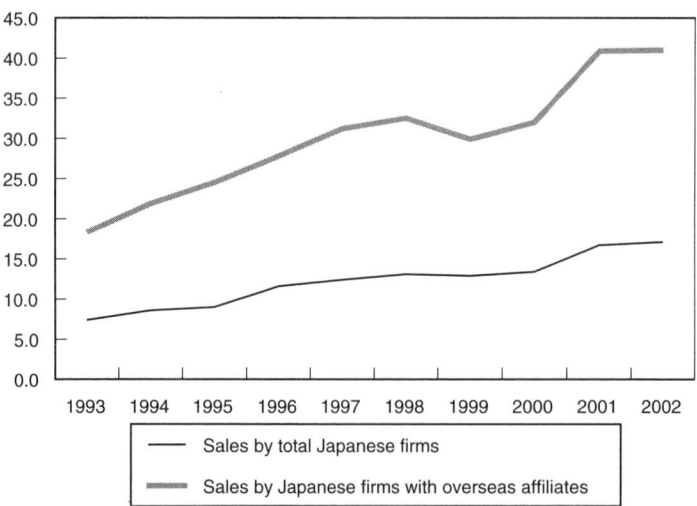

Note: MNC = multinational corporation.
Source: METI (2005).

Table 5.2 Sales of overseas affiliates of Japanese MNCs: ratio of overseas sales to overseas sales plus sales in Japan, 1993–2002 (per cent)

	1993	1997	2002
Manufacturing total	7.4	12.4	17.1
Food	2.4	2.8	4.8
Textiles	3.2	8.0	7.0
Wood and pulp	1.9	3.8	4.5
Chemicals	7.0	12.4	15.5
Petroleum and coal products	7.1	1.7	2.0
Iron and steel	6.3	13.1	9.8
Non-ferrous metals	6.5	10.9	11.3
General machinery	5.8	11.5	11.2
Electrical machinery	12.6	21.6	26.5
Transport machinery	17.3	28.2	47.6
Precision machinery	5.6	9.1	14.8
Other manufacturing	2.8	4.1	5.4

Note: MNC = multinational corporation.
Source: METI (2005).

The differences in the rate of growth of sales by affiliates in different regions obviously have impacts on the geographical distribution of affiliates' sales by Japanese MNCs. The share of Asia in overall affiliates' sales increased from 21 per cent in 1993 to 29 per cent in 2002, while the share of Europe declined from 28 to 20 per cent (Table 5.3). The share captured by North America remained the largest throughout the period, with the share maintained at 42 per cent.

NETWORKING BY JAPANESE MNCS: OUTPUT SALES AND INPUT PROCUREMENT PATTERNS

I now turn to a discussion of the geographical trading patterns of overseas affiliates of Japanese MNCs to discern the changing nature of networks involving Japanese MNCs. Tables 5.4 and 5.5 show the output sales and input procurement patterns for affiliates in Asia, North America and Latin America.

The tables indicate two common trends for both sales and procurement for affiliates in the three regions. One is a decline in the importance of the local market for both sales and procurement from 1992 to 2001, indicating that Japanese MNCs have expanded their networks beyond their host market.[6] This change is particularly notable for sales patterns. Despite differences in the importance of local sales in total sales among affiliates in the three regions – highest for affiliates in North America, followed

Table 5.3 Sales of overseas affiliates of Japanese MNCs by region

	Sales (billion yen)		Ratio	Share (%)	
	1993	2002	2002/1993	1993	2002
World	91,738	137,973	1.50	100.0	100.0
North America	38,913	58,683	1.51	42.4	42.5
United States	36,649	54,850	1.50	39.9	39.8
Latin America	3,320	5,383	1.62	3.6	3.9
Asia	19,547	40,067	2.05	21.3	29.0
China	619	5,142	8.31	0.7	3.7
ASEAN-4[a]	5,949	11,727	1.97	6.5	8.5
NIE-4[b]	12,726	22,024	1.73	13.9	16.0
Middle East	584	1,440	2.47	0.6	1.0
Europe	25,573	27,719	1.08	27.9	20.1
European Union	24,742	26,599	1.08	27.0	19.3
Oceania	3,631	4,011	1.10	4.0	2.9
Africa	170	669	3.94	0.2	0.5

Note: ASEAN = Association of Southeast Asian Nations; MNC = multinational corporation; NIE = newly industrialised economy.
a   Includes Indonesia, Malaysia, the Philippines and Thailand.
b   Includes Hong Kong, South Korea, Singapore and Taiwan.

Source: METI (2005).

Table 5.4 Sales patterns of foreign affiliates of Japanese firms, 1992 and 2001

1992	Asia					North America					Latin America			
	Local sales	Japan	Exports to			Local sales	Japan	Exports to			Local sales	Japan	Exports to	
			North America	Asia	Latin America			North America	Asia	Latin America			North America	Asia	Latin America
Manufacturing total	66.1	15.8	3.7	11.2	0.1	91.9	2.8	2.2	0.6	0.5	78.0	7.0	7.0	1.3	2.5
Food	46.0	26.5	3.1	4.9	0.0	78.7	18.5	0.1	0.6	0.0	27.8	15.4	14.9	8.9	5.7
Textiles	56.1	14.2	7.2	12.3	0.2	99.0	1.0	0.0	0.0	0.0	67.8	3.0	3.5	9.8	1.2
Wood and pulp	50.2	47.2	2.4	0.3	0.0	49.0	33.9	10.2	2.8	2.7	21.1	35.0	28.8	1.3	1.3
Chemical products	64.7	4.9	0.4	28.6	0.0	80.1	5.4	3.5	1.9	1.4	86.0	0.5	4.0	2.0	2.8
Iron and steel	85.5	2.1	3.0	8.6	0.0	98.0	0.6	1.1	0.0	0.3	100.0	0.0	0.0	0.0	0.0
Non-ferrous metal products	63.3	21.4	0.1	14.9	0.0	89.4	5.1	0.1	3.5	0.1	84.3	10.9	0.0	0.0	0.0
General machinery	53.0	23.6	2.1	11.3	0.0	86.1	0.8	7.5	0.4	0.9	74.4	0.1	0.3	0.0	24.3
Electrical machinery	45.7	27.2	5.3	19.0	0.1	89.2	2.6	2.8	1.4	0.6	96.3	0.2	1.6	0.1	1.3
Transport machinery	92.6	1.7	3.9	1.0	0.0	96.4	1.1	1.0	0.2	0.4	80.4	12.0	5.9	0.1	1.4
Precision instruments	36.9	51.8	5.2	1.9	0.0	94.7	3.6	0.5	0.2	0.2	100.0	0.0	0.0	0.0	0.0
Coal and petroleum products	55.9	0.0	43.9	0.2	0.0	68.9	7.1	0.0	16.8	0.0	99.6	0.0	0.0	0.0	0.4
Other manufacturing	78.6	9.4	2.6	5.6	0.1	94.8	2.8	1.1	0.1	0.2	61.2	3.0	35.7	0.0	0.1

2001	Asia					North America					Latin America				
	Local sales	Exports to				Local sales	Exports to				Local sales	Exports to			
		Japan	North America	Asia	Latin America		Japan	North America	Asia	Latin America		Japan	North America	Asia	Latin America
Manufacturing total	47.9	24.6	4.6	18.3	0.4	86.0	1.9	9.5	0.7	0.5	57.0	4.0	26.2	5.1	4.0
Food	80.2	7.6	1.1	8.9	n.d.	81.3	13.6	1.8	1.6	0.4	29.6	24.5	n.d.	n.d.	0.9
Textiles	40.3	35.3	5.6	14.5	n.d.	88.3	2.6	8.2	0.0	0.0	87.7	5.2	3.5	0.1	2.7
Wood and pulp	81.7	13.2	1.1	2.8	0.0	49.8	31.2	2.2	12.0	0.4	11.1	32.1	16.5	7.5	3.8
Chemical products	65.3	8.9	1.0	21.7	0.3	84.3	3.0	7.5	0.7	1.6	n.d.	0.4	n.d.	n.d.	40.0
Coal and petroleum products	26.8	52.1	0.0	17.9	1.2	40.3	1.2	50.8	5.4	n.d.	n.d.	n.d.	n.d.	n.d.	n.d.
Iron and steel	85.7	1.9	1.8	10.1	0.1	98.7	0.1	0.6	n.d.	0.1	72.5	6.0	0.0	0.0	0.0
Nonmetallic products	53.7	17.3	1.2	25.8	0.0	88.0	5.6	n.d.	n.d.	n.d.	66.5	n.d.	0.0	0.0	n.d.
General machinery	34.9	40.2	2.4	17.1	0.1	81.2	4.1	11.6	0.8	0.7	n.d.	0.5	n.d.	n.d.	n.d.
Electric machinery	34.5	28.0	13.6	16.9	n.d.	74.2	3.8	12.1	2.2	3.1	89.0	0.0	7.7	0.0	3.3
IT machinery	30.1	36.9	5.3	23.6	0.8	94.4	1.0	0.8	1.6	0.4	67.3	1.6	2.0	28.9	0.1
Transport machinery	66.1	8.1	2.9	16.4	n.d.	81.1	0.9	16.9	n.d.	0.3	n.d.	n.d.	42.2	0.1	3.6
Precision instruments	42.3	40.3	3.0	12.9	0.1	94.9	1.5	n.d.	n.d.	n.d.	n.d.	n.d.	n.d.	n.d.	n.d.
Other manufacturing	49.9	31.4	5.9	9.8	n.d.	93.7	2.7	2.4	0.2	0.4	56.4	19.1	6.0	0.0	0.1

Note: n.d. means that the data are not disclosed.
Source: MITI (1994); METI (2004).

Table 5.5 Procurement patterns of foreign affiliates of Japanese firms, 1992 and 2001

1992	Asia					North America					Latin America				
	Local sales	Japan	Imports from			Local sales	Japan	Imports from			Local sales	Japan	Imports from		
			North America	Asia	Latin America			North America	Asia	Latin America			North America	Asia	Latin America
Manufacturing total	48.5	37.9	1.8	8.9	0.7	51.5	41.7	1.3	4.0	0.6	58.9	33.2	2.9	2.2	1.2
Food	72.0	4.5	0.3	22.9	0.0	86.1	9.2	0.0	1.3	3.1	94.8	1.6	0.0	1.2	1.1
Textiles	40.7	22.4	4.7	12.1	0.0	81.7	18.3	0.0	0.0	0.0	69.1	12.0	18.9	0.0	0.0
Wood and pulp	83.7	13.2	0.9	0.3	0.0	93.0	5.9	1.0	0.1	0.0	100.0	0.0	0.0	0.0	0.0
Chemical products	71.4	16.9	3.7	3.5	0.0	70.3	28.1	0.5	0.0	0.0	84.9	0.4	3.7	0.0	1.3
Iron and steel	29.0	47.3	0.0	22.3	1.0	99.4	0.6	0.0	0.0	0.0	0.0	0.0	0.0	0.0	0.0
Nonmetallic products	64.8	9.2	0.4	6.2	7.4	73.8	12.8	0.4	0.9	3.9	87.0	7.1	0.0	0.0	5.8
General machinery	49.0	47.8	1.7	1.1	0.0	48.6	44.1	2.6	2.3	0.0	53.2	36.4	1.0	0.0	9.4
Electrical machinery	36.6	46.7	1.2	15.4	0.0	25.0	65.6	1.4	7.4	0.0	62.2	30.2	1.9	4.8	0.8
Transport machinery	52.9	43.8	1.8	1.1	0.0	57.3	36.3	1.4	3.8	0.9	31.5	62.4	4.2	0.4	0.6
Precision instruments	34.2	60.2	1.9	3.7	0.0	28.8	67.1	0.0	2.8	0.0	11.3	88.7	0.0	0.0	0.0
Coal and petroleum products	92.6	3.8	1.1	2.5	0.0	63.6	36.4	0.0	0.0	0.0	0.0	0.0	0.0	0.0	0.0
Other manufacturing	58.6	27.5	4.0	6.2	0.1	64.1	30.3	0.7	4.0	0.0	61.7	34.7	1.4	2.2	0.1

2001	Asia				North America					Latin America				
	Local sales	Imports from			Local sales	Imports from				Local sales	Imports from			
		Japan	North America	Asia	Latin America		Japan	North America	Asia	Latin America		Japan	North America	Asia	Latin America
Manufacturing total	43.9	36.1	1.2	17.4	0.1	50.4	42.3	8.8	1.8	0.4	44.7	38.3	8.8	5.6	2.3
Food	73.6	8.7	2.4	11.8	2.3	92.8	0.6	3.4	2.7	0.0	96.9	0.0	0.9	0.0	2.2
Textiles	58.5	25.0	2.1	6.9	0.2	86.2	8.2	0.0	5.6	0.0	81.2	3.4	6.1	2.3	1.5
Wood and pulp	90.0	6.2	0.3	2.2	0.0	99.1	0.9	0.0	0.0	0.0	100.0	0.0	0.0	0.0	0.0
Chemical products	60.3	17.1	4.8	16.1	0.0	67.5	29.4	1.0	0.1	0.1	52.6	11.7	16.0	0.0	19.6
Coal and petroleum products	35.9	2.7	1.5	56.1	0.0	24.6	9.8	55.8	0.0	0.0	n.d.	n.d.	n.d.	n.d.	n.d.
Iron and steel	27.1	63.2	0.0	8.7	0.1	51.6	29.2	0.9	18.3	0.1	94.2	5.8	0.0	0.0	0.0
Nonmetallic products	64.2	19.0	1.7	11.3	0.6	85.8	9.7	2.9	0.2	0.0	82.3	4.1	11.3	0.0	2.3
General machinery	59.1	36.2	0.3	4.3	0.0	43.3	52.5	0.8	0.6	1.7	53.8	43.0	3.2	0.0	0.0
Electric machinery	41.1	32.7	0.2	25.3	0.0	28.2	58.8	4.6	4.7	2.8	56.8	29.4	10.6	2.3	0.1
IT machinery	31.5	37.0	0.6	29.7	0.1	28.5	61.9	1.4	7.5	0.2	15.7	34.4	33.6	7.4	8.1
Transport machinery	47.4	46.4	1.6	3.9	0.0	56.7	38.5	3.1	0.3	0.5	38.0	51.5	2.9	7.4	0.0
Precision instruments	50.9	41.5	0.0	7.4	0.0	14.6	84.0	0.0	1.0	0.3	n.d.	n.d.	n.d.	n.d.	n.d.
Other manufacturing	43.9	40.8	0.6	12.4	0.1	54.1	36.7	0.6	8.5	0.1	81.1	15.4	3.5	0.0	0.0

Note: IT = information technology; n.d. means that the data are not disclosed.

Source: MITI (1994); METI (2004).

by those in Latin America and Asia – the share of local sales in total sales declined substantially for affiliates in the three regions. One reason may be that the host countries have opened up their trade policies and that affiliates responded to this as trade liberalisation led to an increased incentive for exports rather than domestic sales.

The other common trend is the increasing share of trade with countries in the same region. For example, for Asian affiliates the share of sales destined for other Asian countries under the category 'Asia' increased from 11.2 per cent in 1992 to 18.3 per cent in 2001. Increasing intra-regional trade by affiliates of Japanese MNCs appears to be the result of at least two forces. One is the establishment of regional trade agreements such as the North American Free Trade Agreement (NAFTA) in North America and the Mercosur arrangements in Latin America. Faced with lowered trade barriers for free trade agreement members, affiliates expanded trade with members.

Another factor is the emergence of a regional production and distribution network. MNCs break up the production process into several sub-processes and locate each sub-process in the country where it can be conducted most efficiently. This strategy to achieve a division of labour among different sub-processes has been adopted by many MNCs in electronics, transportation, precision machinery and textiles; it has increased intra-regional trade by MNCs. I examine the emergence of inter-process, intra-regional trade in East Asia below.

Having discussed the common trends observed for affiliates in the three regions, I turn to some differences in the sales and procurement patterns for the affiliates in the different regions and for the different sectors.

Let me begin with the sales patterns. The Asian affiliates show a higher export orientation than the North American or Latin American affiliates: for Asian affiliates the share of exports in total sales in 2001 was 52 per cent, compared with 14 per cent for North American affiliates and 43 per cent for Latin American affiliates. For the Asian affiliates, the importance of Japan and Asia increased from 1992 to 2001. As we will see later, for the Asian affiliates of Japanese MNCs Japan has become an important destination of finished products for the Asian affiliates while other Asian countries have become important destinations of parts and materials. These developments emerged as a result of the establishment of regional production and distribution networks by Japanese MNCs; they are particularly notable in the textile and machinery sectors, with the exception of transportation machinery.

In addition to increased intra-regional trade by North and Latin American affiliates of Japanese MNCs, there has been a rapid expansion of Latin American affiliates' exports to North America, led by the transport machinery sector. These exports, a large part of which appear to be Mexico's exports to the United States, are attributable to the establishment of NAFTA, under which freer trade has been achieved.

Turning to the input procurement patterns by the affiliates in Asia, North America and Latin America, one finds relatively small changes over time and small differences between and among affiliates in different regions. Therefore, only a few developments are notable. First, as noted above, intra-regional dependence on input procurement increased in all the regions. This was particularly notable in Asia, where the share of the procurement from Asia in total procurement increased sharply from 9 per cent in 1992 to 17 per cent in 2001. Second, the affiliates in the IT sector expanded their procurement of inputs from foreign countries, although substantial differences can be found for the sources of inputs. For the Asian affiliates, Japan and other Asian countries are two important sources, although the importance of other Asian countries is increasing while that of Japan is slowly declining, reflecting the development of regional production networks in Asia. For the North American affiliates, Japan remains the dominant source of input procurements. For the Latin American affiliates, North America increased in importance, possibly indicating the emergence of a regional production network involving the United States and Mexico.

An increasingly large portion of affiliates' transactions takes the form of intra-firm trade for affiliates in the three regions. The share of intra-firm transactions in overall transactions increased sharply from 1992 to 2001 (Tables 5.6 and 5.7). In 1992 intra-firm trade was substantial for the affiliates' trade with the home country, or Japan, indicating a strong relationship with parent companies in Japan. However, in 2001 intra-firm transactions amounted to a large part of affiliates' transactions not only in their trade with home countries but also in their transactions in host countries and with foreign countries. The increase in intra-firm transactions by the affiliates of Japanese MNCs appears to indicate the emergence of regional production networks involving Japanese MNCs, which has been made possible by the increase in the number of affiliates and by the expansion of their activities, as discussed above.

There is an interesting contrast between the importance of intra-firm sales and procurement in the host country on the one hand and those with Japan on the other hand. As for the sales patterns, more than 90 per cent of affiliates' exports to Japan went to their parent companies, while approximately one-half of their sales in the host or local market went to their affiliates. By contrast, the importance of intra-firm transactions is more important for the affiliates' local procurement than those from Japan. Indeed, for procurements from Japan, the importance of procurements from parent companies declined from 1991 to 2001 for Asian and North American affiliates. This decline appears consistent with the trend for procurement in Japan: the reliance on intra-firm transactions as well as *keiretsu* (inter-firm but intra-firm corporate group) transactions has been declining as Japanese companies have adopted a procurement policy to purchase inputs from the lowest-cost suppliers, regardless of their affiliation, in order to achieve efficient production. This type of procurement practice began in the mid-1990s, when Japanese companies were trying to achieve lowest cost operation in the middle of a long recession.

PRODUCTION AND DISTRIBUTION NETWORKS IN EAST ASIA

We have seen that Japanese MNCs have developed regional production and distribution networks. I now turn to the issue of regional production networks, which I analyse by examining the data on international trade and international input–output tables. I analyse trade data in two different ways. In one, I classify trade patterns into three types: inter-industry trade (one-way trade), horizontal intra-industry trade and vertical intra-industry trade. In the other, I classify trade into trade in parts and trade in finished products.

Let us begin with the first type of analysis on trade data. As noted, two types of intra-industry trade may be identified. One is horizontal intra-industry trade, where

Table 5.6 Intra-firm transactions in sales of foreign affiliates of Japanese multinational corporations (percentage share in each sale), 1992 and 2001

1992	Asia				North America				Latin America			
	Local sales	Japan	Exports to		Local sales	Japan	Exports to		Local sales	Japan	Exports to	
			North America	Asia	Latin America			North America	Asia	Latin America			North America	Asia	Latin America
	Local sales	Japan	North America	Asia	Latin America	Local sales	Japan	North America	Asia	Latin America	Local sales	Japan	North America	Asia	Latin America
Manufacturing total	6.3	84.2	62.4	44.4	11.3	24.4	73.5	39.0	60.7	37.4	5.0	20.6	49.8	3.3	12.2
Food	7.6	85.4	51.9	26.3	0.0	5.7	91.6	0.0	2.2	0.0	0.0	88.2	6.1	0.0	0.0
Textiles	4.3	36.1	1.1	23.0	0.0	0.0	100.0	0.0	0.0	0.0	0.3	67.6	13.6	0.0	0.0
Wood and pulp	0.0	57.9	0.0	0.0	0.0	2.8	92.6	0.0	0.0	0.0	0.0	0.0	0.0	0.0	0.0
Chemical products	2.4	49.0	11.5	3.2	2.0	14.0	71.5	54.1	93.9	92.2	21.2	36.5	0.0	0.0	0.5
Coal and petroleum products	0.0	0.0	0.0	0.0	0.0	0.0	100.0	0.0	100.0	0.0	0.0	0.0	0.0	0.0	0.0
Iron and steel	0.0	29.0	23.3	0.0	0.0	0.0	5.0	0.0	0.0	0.0	0.0	0.0	0.0	0.0	0.0
Nonmetallic products	0.8	82.6	0.0	55.1	0.0	29.8	93.0	37.6	19.9	0.0	7.6	100.0	0.0	0.0	0.0
General machinery	3.0	96.7	54.3	55.6	100.0	22.9	44.5	58.5	29.2	0.6	0.0	100.0	100.0	0.0	6.6
Electrical machinery	8.0	90.0	82.6	53.7	13.2	21.5	79.3	18.8	64.5	15.2	5.1	0.0	95.0	100.0	35.0
Transport machinery	7.2	73.9	71.2	57.9	20.2	34.0	44.9	55.8	96.9	69.3	0.0	0.0	98.2	100.0	25.9
Precision instruments	32.4	96.5	51.1	77.9	0.0	3.4	68.2	0.0	0.0	0.0	0.0	0.0	0.0	0.0	0.0
Other manufacturing	6.3	67.0	25.3	49.8	10.7	4.7	41.7	37.8	19.7	12.9	0.0	0.0	0.0	0.0	100.0

| | Asia | | | | | North America | | | | | Latin America | | | | |
| | Local sales | Japan | Exports to | | | Local sales | Japan | Exports to | | | Local sales | Japan | Exports to | | |
2001			North America	Asia	Latin America			North America	Asia	Latin America			North America	Asia	Latin America
Manufacturing total	49.6	96.0	73.8	70.2	90.7	46.5	92.3	86.2	72.6	51.3	51.5	100.0	55.5	86.3	100.0
Food	48.9	78.7	73.8	66.6	0.0	61.1	97.6	0.0	0.0	95.0	0.0	100.0	0.0	n.d.	0.0
Textiles	28.5	89.8	90.9	59.1	n.d.	0.0	100.0	0.0	0.0	0.0	2.2	45.5	100.0	0.0	0.0
Wood and pulp	26.3	82.8	0.0	100.0	0.0	100.0	97.3	100.0	100.0	0.0	0.0	0.0	0.0	0.0	0.0
Chemical products	41.2	77.1	92.8	50.5	96.6	27.3	96.4	84.7	50.4	43.9	0.0	100.0	n.d.	n.d.	0.0
Coal and petroleum products	88.9	100.0	0.0	99.4	100.0	0.0	100.0	0.0	48.9	0.0	0.0	n.d.	0.0	0.0	0.0
Iron and steel	8.0	86.6	100.0	27.9	0.0	6.1	100.0	100.0	n.d.	100.0	0.0	0.0	0.0	0.0	0.0
Nonmetallic products	19.5	97.8	100.0	65.4	0.0	0.0	60.2	0.0	n.d.	n.d.	100.0	n.d.	0.0	0.0	0.0
General machinery	61.8	98.7	98.9	91.8	90.3	48.5	31.8	90.1	26.8	4939.0	n.d.	100.0	n.d.	n.d.	0.0
Electric machinery	45.0	98.3	51.7	75.8	n.d.	31.8	94.0	15.0	27.3	21.4	86.6	100.0	100.0	0.0	0.0
IT machinery	56.9	95.5	80.3	80.8	99.3	22.9	97.6	25.7	78.6	99.9	42.3	100.0	89.9	23.8	100.0
Transport machinery	56.4	99.5	99.7	29.8	n.d.	54.4	102.0	88.2	n.d.	97.5	n.d.	n.d.	50.4	100.0	100.0
Precision instruments	58.7	99.5	92.3	93.7	100.0	9.8	98.2	0.0	n.d.	n.d.	n.d.	n.d.	n.d.	n.d.	n.d.
Other manufacturing	56.5	98.4	96.1	78.2	n.d.	19.3	97.9	93.6	55.5	100.0	0.0	100.0	100.0	0.0	0.0

Note: IT = information technology; n.d. means that the data are not disclosed.

Source: MITI (1994); METI (2004).

Table 5.7 Intra-firm transactions in procurements of foreign affiliates of Japanese multinational corporations, 1992 and 2001 (percentage share in each procurement)

1992	Asia					North America					Latin America				
	Local sales	Japan	Imports from			Local sales	Japan	Imports from			Local sales	Japan	Imports from		
			North America	Asia	Latin America			North America	Asia	Latin America			North America	Asia	Latin America
Manufacturing total	4.2	78.0	47.7	50.2	0.1	12.6	86.4	52.9	74.8	90.6	16.5	40.2	13.7	63.0	2.9
Food	0.2	75.8	14.3	48.8	0.0	8.3	98.6	0.0	100.0	100.0	0.0	39.9	0.0	75.5	0.0
Textiles	19.5	34.2	3.3	31.5	0.0	0.0	7.6	0.0	0.0	0.0	0.9	26.0	0.0	0.0	0.0
Wood and pulp	0.1	79.4	0.0	0.0	0.0	8.2	36.1	0.0	0.0	0.0	0.0	0.0	0.0	0.0	0.0
Chemical products	18.0	57.5	7.7	4.3	70.0	11.7	84.7	10.4	100.0	0.0	0.0	91.3	0.0	0.0	0.0
Iron and steel	5.2	1.1	0.0	0.0	0.0	0.0	40.6	0.0	0.0	0.0	0.0	0.0	0.0	0.0	0.0
Nonmetallic products	0.0	26.0	0.0	0.0	0.0	39.0	82.7	0.0	13.9	0.0	0.1	100.0	0.0	0.0	0.0
General machinery	4.5	93.9	80.3	84.8	0.0	45.0	87.6	24.2	75.9	100.0	0.0	97.6	84.6	0.0	3.3
Electrical machinery	2.0	84.6	86.6	59.8	100.0	30.3	80.5	46.2	62.8	100.0	42.0	17.6	24.0	60.0	8.0
Transport machinery	0.6	81.7	76.2	34.6	0.0	4.8	92.9	76.4	98.3	100.0	9.5	48.6	9.4	100.0	0.0
Precision instruments	17.5	85.6	0.0	100.0	0.0	0.0	57.4	0.0	0.0	0.0	0.0	0.0	0.0	0.0	0.0
Coal and petroleum products	0.0	100.0	100.0	10.0	0.0	0.0	100.0	0.0	0.0	0.0	0.0	0.0	0.0	0.0	0.0
Other manufacturing	7.3	64.1	0.7	61.8	0.0	5.2	78.4	3.9	6.8	0.0	0.0	19.5	100.0	36.8	100.0

2001	Asia					North America					Latin America				
	Local sales	Imports from				Local sales	Imports from				Local sales	Imports from			
		Japan	North America	Asia	Latin America		Japan	North America	Asia	Latin America		Japan	North America	Asia	Latin America
Manufacturing total	86.0	46.7	98.9	65.9	96.6	82.3	54.2	85.1	82.9	97.9	49.1	60.8	81.4	100.0	100.0
Food	98.4	52.3	100.0	24.2	0.0	100.0	63.1	0.0	37.5	100.0	0.0	0.0	100.0	0.0	0.0
Textiles	89.7	52.2	100.0	85.2	0.0	100.0	0.0	0.0	0.0	0.0	100.0	40.0	0.0	100.0	0.0
Wood and pulp	98.8	100.0	0.0	100.0	0.0	100.0	0.0	0.0	0.0	0.0	0.0	0.0	0.0	0.0	0.0
Chemical products	96.7	74.6	100.0	87.4	100.0	93.4	24.5	16.2	100.0	100.0	100.0	0.6	100.0	0.0	0.0
Coal and petroleum products	100.0	0.0	100.0	78.9	0.0	45.4	0.0	0.0	0.0	0.0	n.d.	n.d.	n.d.	n.d.	n.d.
Iron and steel	86.4	81.9	0.0	100.0	0.0	100.0	14.6	0.0	77.8	0.0	0.0	0.0	0.0	0.0	0.0
Nonmetallic products	66.3	54.7	81.1	87.8	0.0	100.0	96.9	0.0	0.0	0.0	100.0	100.0	0.0	0.0	0.0
General machinery	84.7	59.1	100.0	61.6	0.0	99.3	71.9	47.2	99.9	100.0	100.0	0.0	100.0	0.0	0.0
Electric machinery	89.3	27.7	67.1	29.8	71.7	99.1	73.4	64.7	91.8	100.0	100.0	100.0	100.0	100.0	100.0
IT machinery	89.8	44.3	100.0	72.6	100.0	97.9	11.0	29.3	84.3	78.3	100.0	71.0	56.4	100.0	100.0
Transport machinery	73.7	46.4	100.0	83.4	100.0	68.0	60.0	98.7	97.6	100.0	39.6	40.0	100.0	100.0	100.0
Precision instruments	96.6	50.9	79.0	89.2	0.0	100.0	4.8	0.0	99.6	100.0	n.d.	n.d.	n.d.	n.d.	n.d.
Other manufacturing	92.1	29.4	98.6	77.9	0.0	99.2	17.6	100.0	78.3	100.0	71.2	0.0	100.0	0.0	0.0

Note: IT = information technology; n.d. means that the data are not disclosed.

Source: MITI (1994); METI (2004).

people trade products of similar quality and price but with different design and other characteristics. Such trade may occur between countries with similar income levels, where consumers have similar tastes but also demand some variety. The other type is vertical intra-industry trade, in which people trade products of different quality and price. An example is trade in televisions: standard colour televisions and high-definition televisions are of different quality and price. Trade in parts and finished products is another example of vertical intra-industry trade. Vertical intra-industry trade tends to take place between developing and developed countries, where factor prices are very different.

A large part of intra-industry trade in East Asia is of the vertical type. Table 5.8 reports the results of the analysis to classify intra-regional trade in East Asia into three types, two types of intra-industry trade and inter-industry trade (or one-way trade).[7] The results show that the share of intra-industry trade increased notably from 1990 to 2004. For intra-industry trade, a large portion is vertical intra-industry trade, although both horizontal and vertical types increased over time.[8] Substantial presence of vertical intra-industry trade reflects inter-process division of labour pursued by MNCs from various countries, including Japan, the United States, the European Union, South Korea, and others.

I turn to the analysis of trade data by classifying the data into parts and finished products, to identify the nature of trade in East Asia. Table 5.9 shows the proportion of parts exports in overall exports for East Asian countries. The figures show a high share of parts exports in East Asia's exports to other East Asian countries for all the products under study. Furthermore, the shares concerning intra East Asia trade, that is trade from East Asia to East Asia, increased for all products except textiles and apparel. For example, for 2000–04, as much as 85 per cent of trade in electrical and apparatus was parts trade, while the remaining 15 per cent was trade in finished products. By contrast with intra East Asia exports, East Asia's exports to the United States and the European Union show a large share of finished products. Among East Asian countries, Japan's position in East Asia's exports is quite different from that of other East Asian countries: a relatively large portion of East Asia's exports to Japan consist of finished products. Indeed, like the United States and the European Union, Japan is an important destination for East Asia's exports of finished products.

The findings on international trade in parts and finished products are consistent with an earlier finding on the presence of vertical intra-industry trade and they appear to indicate the presence of an intra-regional production system in East Asia. However, an examination of trade patterns does not provide accurate information on a regional production system. To deal with this problem, I examine the regional production system explicitly by using information available from international input–output tables. The international input–output tables, which are constructed by the Institute of Developing Economies in Tokyo by linking national input–output tables, document flows of goods between sectors in different countries. The tables have been constructed for 1975, 1985, 1990, 1995 and 2000. I have used the international input–output tables for 1985 and 2000 to examine changes in the regional production system over time. The tables cover nine East Asian countries (Indonesia, Malaysia, the Philippines, Singapore, Thailand, China, Taiwan, South Korea, and Japan); the United States; the

Table 5.8   Intra-industry trade within East Asia, 1990–2004

Year	Inter-industry trade	Horizontal intra-industry trade	Vertical intra-industry trade
1990	42.5	3.3	54.2
1991	40.8	3.7	55.5
1992	23.8	11.7	64.5
1993	34.6	14.1	51.3
1994	33.0	13.7	53.3
1995	31.8	14.1	54.2
1996	31.0	15.4	53.6
2000	27.4	16.1	56.5
2001	25.5	14.0	60.5
2002	21.6	19.9	58.5
2003	23.4	16.4	60.3
2004	21.3	15.1	63.5

Note: Aggregation is based on six-digit HS1988. Computed using the method proposed by Fukao *et al.* (2003).

Source: Computed by the author using the UN Comtrade database.

European Union (2000 version only); and the rest of the world. Hong Kong is treated as a region involved only in trading, not in production. The tables adopted 7-sector aggregation and 24-sector aggregation; I used tables with the 24-sector aggregation. I would also have liked to investigate the patterns for machinery sectors such as electronic and transportation machinery, but the closest classification available in the 24-sector aggregation table is machinery, so this sector was the one I analysed.

Table 5.10 shows the changing importance of different sources of machinery inputs for the production of machinery goods for East Asian countries in 1985 and 2000. The sources are divided into local and foreign sources; the foreign sources are further divided into East Asia (including Japan); Japan; and East Asia (excluding Japan). For the East Asia total, the importance of foreign sources increased from 1985 to 2000, although wide variations in the patterns among different countries were observed. Reliance on foreign sources for the supply of machinery inputs is significantly high for developing countries when compared to Japan. Among developing countries, Association of Southeast Asian Nations (ASEAN) countries registered stronger reliance than NIEs or China. These findings are consistent with an observation that local component producers, or supporting industry, are underdeveloped in ASEAN countries, which thereby need to rely on foreign supplies.

The figures for East Asia excluding local sources show a substantial increase for many countries, indicating a deepening of the intra-regional production relationship. This pattern is clearly seen for all East Asian countries except Indonesia. Indeed, for many countries – including Malaysia, the Philippines, Singapore, Thailand and Taiwan – approximately half of the machinery inputs were imported from other East Asian

Table 5.9 Parts trade for East Asian economies: share of total (per cent)

	East Asia		ASEAN		NIEs		China		Japan		US		EU		World	
Exporting regions	90-94	00-04	90-94	00-04	90-94	00-04	90-94	00-04	90-94	00-04	90-94	00-04	90-94	00-04	90-94	00-04
Office and telecommunications equipment: (SITC 759 + 764) / (SITC 75+76)																
East Asia	58.2	66.7	65.3	76.4	47.6	61.5	70.8	80.7	49.4	45.8	41.0	43.8	38.2	43.7	44.5	54.2
ASEAN	56.9	62.3	68.7	76.2	39.0	54.9	73.7	64.7	42.6	43.5	33.7	39.1	24.8	38.4	38.3	49.2
NIEs	69.4	75.0	65.0	81.1	69.3	73.3	79.5	81.7	56.5	51.6	41.3	56.6	36.2	52.3	46.9	64.9
China	39.0	56.6	44.1	72.1	36.5	58.5			40.2	42.3	40.2	34.8	32.7	36.5	37.1	46.2
Japan	53.3	71.7	60.6	74.0	50.0	61.1	42.9	88.5	51.1		46.0	42.1	47.9	43.8	48.1	51.6
Electrical and apparatus: (SITC 771+772+773+776) / SITC 77																
East Asia	81.2	85.4	84.3	88.1	79.0	84.6	68.5	83.8	86.7	83.1	73.1	69.7	64.7	70.0	74.2	79.3
ASEAN	87.1	91.8	85.6	89.8	87.5	95.1	69.2	90.3	89.8	90.3	90.7	93.1	87.8	93.7	86.6	91.6
NIEs	82.3	87.2	87.3	91.8	83.8	88.9	68.4	84.6	85.1	83.4	67.9	69.1	56.5	68.0	71.5	80.9
China	56.3	72.2	63.2	76.2	52.4	72.4			77.4	68.2	33.9	37.0	27.6	35.8	47.2	55.9
Japan	79.4	80.2	81.7	84.9	78.5	77.5	69.0	77.9			68.7	60.2	59.3	59.6	71.3	73.1
Road vehicles: SITC 784 / (SITC 722+781+782+783+784)																
East Asia	48.7	53.9	45.0	48.8	63.2	58.4	20.6	46.4	94.9	92.7	21.5	19.5	13.2	18.8	23.3	23.6
ASEAN	67.7	78.1	58.3	68.5	56.7	89.0	64.9	86.0	91.4	87.3	97.7	98.3	19.0	40.2	55.8	58.5
NIEs	30.0	44.2	32.2	32.4	44.0	60.9	21.2	39.0	93.3	92.2	33.5	14.9	15.7	10.8	26.4	21.5
China	97.7	88.3	79.2	79.1	98.4	63.6			99.1	99.2	95.6	95.7		92.3	92.8	83.5
Japan	42.4	50.7	43.6	47.2	45.6	55.1	18.4	50.9			20.2	18.2	12.7	18.5	20.2	20.8
Textiles and apparel: SITC 65 / SITC (65 + 84)																
East Asia	62.6	56.0	84.9	79.8	64.4	56.9	91.1	83.0	21.8	18.5	14.1	16.6	21.7	23.8	44.5	43.8
ASEAN	63.3	62.5	73.1	74.8	77.8	71.2	94.0	91.1	29.1	37.2	9.2	6.3	23.0	18.5	32.7	29.8
NIEs	75.4	76.2	91.2	86.9	93.3	88.5	90.8	80.0	19.5	22.9	10.7	14.4	13.8	16.9	47.2	53.4
China	37.3	32.4	76.3	62.3	40.8	42.6			23.1	15.4	24.0	25.4	31.4	29.0	35.5	33.5
Japan	93.6	93.6	97.0	97.0	92.2	84.2	94.3	98.3			82.7	85.7	82.0	85.1	91.3	92.5

Note: ASEAN = Association of Southeast Asian Nations; EU = European Union; NIEs = newly industrialised economies; SITC = Standard International Trade Classification; US = United States.

Source: Computed by the author using the UN Comtrade database.

Table 5.10 Intra-regional dependence in machinery production in East Asia, 1985–2000

		Indonesia	Malaysia	Philippines	Singapore	Thailand	China	Taiwan	South Korea	Japan	East Asia	East Asia excluding Japan
Foreign sources	1985	84.5	86.2	103.7	85.6	58.3	11.1	46.7	45.6	4.4	12.5	37.0
	2000	76.4	89.4	96.9	67.7	84.1	28.2	63.0	48.4	13.4	36.0	52.8
East Asia	1985	52.3	55.8	42.9	62.9	85.8	97.9	81.3	80.2	96.6	93.7	84.8
	2000	60.3	69.0	62.3	83.6	71.0	90.9	80.3	80.3	95.1	87.7	82.2
East Asia excluding local sources	1985	36.8	42.0	46.6	48.4	44.1	9.0	28.0	25.8	1.0	6.2	21.8
	2000	36.7	58.4	59.3	51.3	55.2	19.1	43.3	28.7	8.4	23.7	35.0
Japan	1985	24.4	19.3	13.6	24.3	33.6	6.2	25.2	21.9	95.6	75.6	15.3
	2000	19.9	15.4	27.1	21.4	19.7	3.7	18.8	13.2	86.6	44.0	12.4
East Asia excluding local sources and Japan	1985	12.3	22.7	33.0	24.1	10.5	2.8	2.8	3.9	1.0	1.6	6.5
	2000	16.8	43.0	32.2	29.9	35.5	15.4	24.5	15.5	8.4	13.0	22.6

Note: The figures indicate proportions of inputs from respective sources in total inputs. Machinery products include agricultural machinery and equipment, specialised industrial machinery, ordinary industrial machinery, heavy electric machinery, engines and turbines, electronics and electronic products, and other electric machinery and appliances. The figure exceeding 100 for the foreign sources in the Philippines in 1985 is largely due to negative value for inputs from the Philippines recorded in the original table. An investigation on this unusual observation has to be pursued.

Source: Institute of Developing Economies, International Input–Output Tables 1985 and 2000.

countries in 2000. For East Asian developing countries, reliance on Japan for the supply of machinery inputs for the production of machinery products is still high but is declining. By contrast, East Asian countries other than Japan became increasingly important sources of machinery inputs for East Asian countries including Japan, indicating an expansion of intra-regional procurement networks in East Asia. The increased importance of East Asian countries other than Japan for the source of inputs is attributable to the successful development of the parts-producing sector, which in turn is partly due to the increased activities of MNCs.

CONCLUSIONS: THE CHALLENGES FOR JAPANESE MNCs

Japanese MNCs have successfully developed regional production and distribution networks for several manufactured products such as electronics products in East Asia through active FDI. Despite the substantial reduction in the cost of conducting international business at a global scale, thanks to technological progress and liberalisation in the communication and transportation sectors, Japanese MNCs have expanded and intensified regional business activities rather than global business activities. Furthermore, Japanese MNCs have increased their dependence on intra-firm rather than inter-firm relationships in their production network.

These observations appear to indicate that geographical proximity and intra-firm networks are important for Japanese MNCs in coordinating fragmented production and distribution processes. Indeed, in their study on MNCs in Thailand Brimble and Urata (2006) found that Japanese MNCs are less globalised and less open than those from the United States or Europe. It may be that Japanese MNCs rely on face-to-face communication and/or closer communication than their US or European counterparts to transmit detailed and subtle information regarding their just-in-time delivery of high-quality, high-precision inputs. One important question concerns the optimum level of business activities in terms of geographical and corporate boundaries for MNCs. Answering this question would require a detailed study of MNC operations and is beyond the scope of this chapter.

Japanese MNCs' operations in Asia have been more profitable than their operations in other parts of the world: in 2004, their profit-to-sales ratios for affiliates in Asia, North America and Europe were 4.3, 3.6 and 2.1 per cent, respectively. However, they must overcome various challenges if they are to achieve success in the future. First, intensified competition from MNCs from other countries and local companies in East Asia poses challenges to Japanese MNCs. Technological advantages enjoyed by Japanese MNCs have been quickly slipping away. Continuous improvement in technological and managerial capabilities is needed for Japanese MNCs to remain competitive.

Second, Japanese MNCs face a challenge at home, with a shortage of workers and a resultant increase in wages. Many Japanese MNCs would like to maintain important operations such as R&D and the formulation of corporate strategies at home, but the shortage of capable workers makes it difficult for them to achieve this objective. In the past, Japanese MNCs were quite successful in developing new products and production processes because R&D was closely connected to manufacturing activities.

Now that manufacturing processes are moving overseas, it is becoming difficult for Japanese MNCs to carry out effective R&D.

Japanese MNCs may use several strategies to deal with these challenges. One is the use of inter-firm or external linkages. Japanese MNCs must utilise foreign workers effectively, both in their overseas affiliates and in parent companies, in order to become more efficient in management and technological development. Several studies have shown that Japanese MNCs have not been successful in recruiting capable foreign workers. Indeed, there is a vicious cycle of limited job promotions for local workers and difficulty in recruiting capable workers in overseas affiliates.

A similar problem concerns inter-firm linkages. As we saw earlier, Japanese MNCs have become introverted as the share of intra-firm transactions in their overall transactions has risen in recent years. Certainly there are benefits from intra-firm transactions – for example, keeping important information like the technological properties of traded goods inside the firm. But there are costs in terms of limited competitive pressure and limited access to useful information. Japanese MNCs should formulate a long-term strategy to gain benefits by utilising inter-firm linkages, although building, maintaining and expanding inter-firm linkages may incur costs in the short run.

I have already discussed what Japanese MNCs should do to deal with the challenges. There are several policy measures that Japanese and East Asian governments can pursue in order for Japanese MNCs and their host economies to gain benefits. First, Japanese and East Asian governments should promote the development of human resources with technical and managerial capabilities. In particular, the Japanese government should invite students and promising business people to Japan to acquire useful skills with a view to Japanese MNCs employing these invited people when they have obtained the necessary skills. The Japanese government has been providing these types of programs, but more are needed and their quality should be improved. Second, Japanese and East Asian governments should promote the development of local parts and components suppliers in East Asia. Both governments can contribute to this cause by providing financial and non-financial assistance. Financial assistance includes the provision of funds for starting a business and preferential fiscal treatment such as exemption of business taxes for start-up firms; non-financial assistance includes technical assistance and the provision of information about markets. Financial assistance has to be given cautiously in a country where bureaucracy and the private sector are closely connected, as it can be a source of corruption. It should be emphasised that, when these policies are formulated and implemented, local and Japanese governments will need to communicate closely.

NOTES

The author is grateful for the comments of Professor Peter A. Petri and Dr David Hong.

1   The analysis of Japanese FDI in the 1980s and 1990s draws on Urata and Kawai (2000).
2   North America includes the United States and Canada; Latin America includes Mexico and other Central and South American countries.

3   The shares of manufacturing and non-manufacturing do not add to 100 per cent, because an item classified as 'branches' is not included in either manufacturing or non-manufacturing.
4   Kimura and Ando (2005) describe the fragmentation strategy of Japanese MNCs.
5   Newly industrialising economies (South Korea, Taiwan, Hong Kong and Singapore).
6   The decline in the importance of local procurement in total procurement is partly due to the increase in new affiliates. New affiliates tend to rely on parent companies for the supply of inputs because they have not created procurement networks yet. Kiyota *et al.* (2005) discuss this point further.
7   See Fukao *et al.* (2003) for the classification of three types of trade. Six-digit Harmonised System (HS) classification is used for the analysis.
8   This finding is consistent with Fukao *et al.* (2003). They also found that the extent of vertical intra-industry trade by industry is positively and strongly correlated with FDI.

REFERENCES

Brimble, P. and Shujiro Urata (2006) 'Behavior of Japanese, Western, and Asian MNCs in Thailand: lessons for Japanese MNCs', paper presented at an international workshop on MNCs' activities, Japan Center for Economic Research, 1 June.

Fukao, Kyoji, Hikaru Ishido and Keiko Ito (2003) 'Vertical intra-industry trade and foreign direct investment in East Asia', RIETI Discussion Paper Series 03-E-01, Research Institute of Economy, Trade and Industry.

Kimura, Fukunari and Mitsuyo Ando (2005) 'Two-dimensional fragmentation in East Asia: conceptual framework and empirics', *International Review of Economics and Finance*, 14(3): 317–348.

Kiyota, Kozo, Toshiyuki Matsuura, Shujiro Urata and Yuhong Wei (2005) 'Reconsidering the backward vertical linkage of foreign affiliates: evidence from Japanese multinationals', RIETI Discussion Paper 05-E-019, Research Institute of Economy, Trade and Industry.

METI (Ministry of Economy, Trade and Industry) (2004) *Wagakuni Kigyo no Kaigai Jigyo Katsudo* [*Overseas Activities of Japanese Firms*], No. 32, Tokyo: METI.

—— (2005) *Wagakuni Kigyo no Kaigai Jigyo Katsudo* [*Overseas Activities of Japanese Firms*], No. 33, Tokyo: METI.

MITI (Ministry of International Trade and Industry) (1994) *Wagakuni Kigyo no Kaigai Jigyo Katsudo* [*Overseas Activities of Japanese Firms*], No. 23, Tokyo: MITI.

UN (United Nations) (2005) *World Investment Report 2005*, Geneva and New York: UN.

Urata, Shujiro (2002) 'Engines of globalization: big and small multinational enterprises in the global era', pp. 35–59 in Kyung Tae Lee (ed.), *Globalization and the Asia Pacific Economy*, London and New York: Routledge.

Urata, Shujiro and Hiroki Kawai (2000) 'Intrafirm technology transfer by Japanese manufacturing firms in Asia', pp. 49–74 in Takatoshi Ito and A.O. Krueger (eds), *The Role of Foreign Direct Investment in East Asian Economic Development*, Chicago and London: University of Chicago Press.

6 The internationalisation of firm activities and its economic impacts: the case of South Korea

Sanghoon Ahn, Siwook Lee and Cheonsik Woo

INTRODUCTION

The Korean economy[1] has recovered markedly from the financial crisis of 1997 through concerted efforts to restructure its corporate and financial sectors. However, even as it managed to come out of the crisis with a better institutional foundation and macro fundamentals, Korea continues to face new challenges in maintaining its growth momentum and social integrity. Indeed, the financial crisis brought Korea into a new, distinctive phase of economic and social development, and the country is expected to continue to undergo deep and rapid structural changes, as it has over the past eight years.

The financial crisis ushered in at least three fundamental changes in the industrial dimension. The first pertains to the overall industrial landscape of Korea. Before the crisis, Korea's industrial landscape was dominated by a handful of *chaebol*-affiliated large firms, with a very limited role for foreign firms and small and medium-sized enterprises (SMEs). Following the crisis, however, a mass of global multinational enterprises (MNEs) entered the Korean market and came to have greater market influences in many critical nodes of the industrial supply chain, including core intermediate products. On the other hand, in the course of massive restructuring and downsizing efforts, Korea's leading conglomerates themselves pursued new business strategies, including outsourcing and offshoring, resulting in a serious undermining of traditional subcontract relations with SMEs. Although this put many traditional SMEs in deep trouble, a group of SMEs with independent technological capabilities managed to capitalise on new market environments, forging so-called NTBFs (new technology-based firms). As a result of all these changes, a new tripod structure of competitiveness has emerged in Korea, in which foreign MNEs and a group of NTBFs have come to the fore as two additional pillars of Korea's industrial competitiveness together with the *chaebol*-affiliated firms.

Second, the activities of Korean firms have been largely upgraded. In the corporate value chain, the focus has shifted from production to higher value-added activities such as marketing and R&D. Reflecting ever-maturing demand and supply conditions, and stimulated by variegated policy supports, inter-firm and inter-institutional transactions and collaboration have increased considerably amongst various agents comprising Korea's innovation network. Although these new developments were most pronounced among the large leading firms, many SMEs followed their lead, particularly the NTBFs. A substantial portion of SMEs increased investment in R&D and information technology (IT) as well as stepping up efforts to strengthen cooperation with overseas enterprises and enter foreign markets.

Third, in terms of market performance, a small group of vanguard firms in Korea's flagship industries such as semiconductors and automobiles are leaping forward in the global market, helped by a much-harnessed technological and financial base. In contrast, a majority of firms competing in the unsophisticated commodity markets are increasingly struggling in the face of ever-mounting competitive pressure from China. Overall, Korea has become more export-oriented, with a GDP share of exports amounting to 37 per cent in 2004, but a few vanguard firms lead this upward trend, with the rest lagging seriously behind.

Externally, the fierce forces of globalisation, technological change, and the surge of China and other late-industrialising countries will combine to exert greater competitive pressure on Korea, while bringing about profound structural changes in the global economy on the whole. Domestically, the regime shift in the Korean economy itself, entrenched in the wake of the crisis, is a powerful force that will make ongoing structural changes in the Korean economy sustainable into the future.

Essentially, Korea is in a great transition from its old model of semi-connected global development to a new model that is fully connected. In the coming decade or so, global market conditions will be very volatile. Korea is a small open economy with a large external sector, so it is all the more critical for Korean firms to proactively respond to such conditions in the global market, seeking a way to capitalise on the vast opportunities provided by the global market and production chain.

Outbound foreign direct investment (FDI) (overseas investment) and trade are two principal modes of global connection. There has been increasing interest in FDI into Korea, but overseas investment by Korean firms did not receive enough attention until recently. The volume of outbound FDI plunged right after the financial crisis, but as the volume of outbound FDI has rapidly increased, surpassing pre-crisis peak levels, policy attention has been renewed amid increasing concerns over a possible industrial 'hollowing-out' effect. Nonetheless, the economic impact of outbound FDI, especially its relation with trade and other industrial performance factors such as productivity and employment, remains as an under-explored research area in Korea, hampering sound policymaking. In this chapter, we aim to fill the gap.

The rest of the chapter will unfold as follows. In the following section, we will briefly survey the literature, including literature that directly addresses Korea-specific issues. We will then discuss the overall trends pertaining to outbound FDI and trade in Korea. Covering the period 1990–2003 and using three-digit industrial-level data, we will look into the trends and other salient features of Korea's outbound FDI and trade. We will give special attention to the identification of changes in outbound FDI and trade composition by region, by industry, and by firm size. In addition, we will examine the relationship between outbound FDI and trade through a simple regression analysis, so as to tell whether the relationship is subject to some systematic differences across different regions, industries, and time. We will subsequently describe an attempt to perform a rigorous regression analysis of the economic impacts of outbound FDI and trade in Korea. The focus will be the impact on total factor productivity (TFP) and employment in Korea's manufacturing sector. The final section summarises the main findings of the paper.

A SELECTIVE REVIEW OF RECENT LITERATURE ON FDI

FDI has grown remarkably over the last two decades, at a higher rate than trade in manufacturing, which has in turn increased faster than income. This has led to the emergence of considerable research on the fundamental characteristics and impacts of affiliate operations abroad. In this section, we provide a selective review of some of this existing literature. There is a large amount of literature on FDI, but we limit our focus to two issues.[2] First, we discuss a relatively recent and burgeoning strand of research which explains who chooses to serve foreign markets through FDI. Second, we present recent empirical studies regarding the economic impact of outbound FDI on domestic activities in home countries.

Who chooses to serve foreign markets through FDI?

The literature often classifies FDI as being horizontal or vertical according to firms' motives for affiliate operations abroad. Vertical FDI occurs where a firm pursues FDI in order to take advantage of international differences in factor prices, by locating its labour-intensive processing abroad and keeping capital-intensive input production and knowledge-intensive design and R&D at home. Horizontal FDI arises when a firm can reduce trade costs by setting up foreign affiliates replicating the parent firm. Hence, the literature of horizontal FDI emphasises the importance of trade costs and access to local markets as the main motives of FDI location decisions.

In recent years, economists have focused on explaining the conditions under which firms engage in investment abroad. For instance, Helpman *et al.* (2004) propose a multi-country, multi-sector general equilibrium model in order to explain whether the decisions of heterogeneous firms to serve in overseas markets are through exports or horizontal FDI. A basic idea of the model is that FDI involves higher sunk costs but lower per-unit costs than does exporting in the overseas market. The model suggests that only the more productive firms will choose to serve foreign markets and that the most productive firms among them will further choose FDI to serve the overseas market. In addition, the model predicts that the greater the heterogeneity of firms' productivity, the greater will be FDI sales relative to export sales. These predictions are strongly supported by data on US exports and sales of overseas US affiliates in 38 different countries and 52 sectors.

In a similar vein, Head and Ries (2003) develop and test a hypothesis that firms choosing FDI are more productive than firms choosing exports. Their findings, based on data for 1,070 large Japanese firms, show that firms using both FDI and exports to serve foreign markets are more productive than firms that rely exclusively on exports. Using a non-parametric test for first-order stochastic dominance, Wagner (2005) suggests empirical evidence for German firms, which is consistent with Helpman et al. (2004).[3] Specifically, he finds that the productivity distribution of foreign direct investors dominates that of exporters, which in turn dominates that of non-exporters.[4] Lee (2005) empirically analyses the choice of Korean firms in conducting foreign investments. He finds that Korean multinationals outperform their domestic counterparts in all dimensions; they are larger, pay higher wages and are more productive.

Using firm-level data on US multinationals' trade in intermediate inputs, Hanson et al. (2003) show that vertical production networks are shaping trade patterns between US parent companies and their foreign affiliates. From the patterns of trade in intermediate inputs by industry, they find that certain industries (machinery, transportation equipment, and electronics, including computers) appear to be good candidates for vertical production networks.[5] They point out that these industries share two common features. First, production tends to involve distinct stages that are physically separable; second, these production stages exhibit different factor intensities. As design activities and component production are more skill-intensive, while assembly activities are more labour-intensive, firms may have an incentive to locate labour-intensive activities in labour-abundant countries.

What are the economic impacts of FDI?

Given that the primary focus in this paper is the role of outbound FDI on Korea, our discussion is concentrated on existing empirical research on the effects of multinationals on home countries, rather than those on host countries. Specifically, we discuss the relationship between FDI and trade, on the one hand, and the economic impact of FDI on other domestic activities, including equipment investment, employment and productivity, on the other.

Outbound FDI and exports

Are foreign production and exports substitutes or complements? While standard trade theory predicts that they are substitutes, recent empirical work largely indicates a complementary relationship between them. As discussed in Blonigen (2001), there are several reasons to suggest both substitution and complementarity effects. Substitution between them arises if intangible assets specific to the firm, such as technology and managerial skills, may induce a firm to operate production facilities abroad rather than to export. It is often difficult to properly appropriate rents from such assets via contact with a third party, which leads the firm to establish its own facilities abroad. FDI also replaces trade when there are sufficient costs to external transactions such as exporting or licensing.

On the other hand, we expect a complementary effect when a firm's production presence in a foreign market with one product may increase total demand for all of its products. For instance, the presence itself may increase the firm's knowledge about the market and thus help tilt consumer preferences in the firm's favour. Furthermore, recent empirical evidence reveals that almost half of trade flows are parent-to-affiliate input trade. This may imply that foreign affiliate activities may increase exports of inputs to the host market from home countries.

Empirical tests regarding the extent to which FDI changes exports have been largely based on an FDI-augmented gravity model. By considering FDI patterns as an additional determinant of trade, a majority of research using this framework finds positive feedback from FDI to exports. Lipsey and Weiss (1981) and Blomstrom et al. (1997) are among the early studies adopting this approach.[6] By employing the detailed data of US multinational firms, Clausing (2000) finds complementarity between multinational activity and intra-firm trade. Hejazi and Safarian (2001) argue that US outbound FDI has a larger predicted positive impact on US exports than inbound FDI.

On the other hand, there has been growing research indicating that the impact of FDI on trade could vary depending on FDI type, data level, etc. For instance, Head and Ries (2003) suggest that horizontal investment tends to substitute for home production and exports, while vertical FDI expands home exports via intra-firm trade in intermediate inputs. In addition, Swenson (2004) argues that less substantial complementarities, and even substitution effects, are revealed as one moves from more aggregated industry FDI data to less aggregated data. Finally, Blonigen (2001) emphasises the importance of adopting the level of data aggregation appropriate for the hypothesis being tested. He finds a complementarity effect in the case of Japanese automobile parts for the US market, but a substitution effect using product-level data on Japanese final consumer products. He also finds evidence that, when firms locate production abroad, the substitution effects are large, one-time changes, not gradual steps over time.

Outbound FDI, trade and domestic activities

Another strand of FDI research that has attracted much attention from international economists is the relationship between FDI and domestic activities, especially employment, productivity and domestic investment. The recent surge of outward FDI has sparked debate on whether the home economy is hollowing out as productive capacity is moving abroad, thus hurting domestic growth and employment. So far, the FDI literature produces quite mixed results on this issue, and consequently it remains an open question.

Using firm-level data from US and Swedish multinationals, Blomstrom et al. (1997) examine the effects of affiliate net sales on employment of the parent companies. They find that US parent firms tend to substitute foreign production in developing countries for home employment, but this is not the case for foreign production in developed countries. On the other hand, in the case of Swedish firms, they provide evidence that foreign affiliate production raises the demand for home labour, regardless of FDI locations. In a different context, Feldstein (1995) provides aggregate level evidence that foreign investment diverts resources from domestic investment in Organisation for Economic Co-operation and Development (OECD) economies. On the other hand, Desai et al. (2005a) find that foreign and domestic investments are positively correlated for US multinationals.

Desai et al. (2005b) highlight the fact that foreign and domestic operations are jointly determined by other economic factors. This indicates that there are likely to be substantial questions of endogeneity in a regression of foreign operations on domestic activities, unless these determinants are explicitly controlled in estimation. In this context, Desai and his colleagues employ an instrumental variable approach in analysing the detailed affiliate-level data of US multinationals. They find that the estimated effect of foreign investment on domestic investment has a larger positive magnitude in the instrumental variables equation than does the corresponding estimated coefficient in the ordinary least square (OLS) equation. This result implies that omitted variables have the effect of making foreign and domestic investment look more like substitutes than is really the case.

THE RECENT PATTERN OF KOREAN OUTBOUND FDI

Korean outbound FDI began in 1968, but its size remained relatively small until the mid-1980s, due to various regulations to control foreign reserves and firms' inability to conduct investment abroad. Since then, outward FDI has grown steadily, particularly due to liberalisation policies first adopted in the mid-1980s.[7] As depicted in Figure 6.1, outbound FDI rapidly increased during the years 1993–96,[8] but there has been a relative slowdown subsequently. The share of total FDI stock in GDP increased from 0.2 per cent in 1980 to 5.7 per cent in 2003, even though it is still well below that of the United States (18.8 per cent) or of most developed countries (26.4 per cent on average).[9] This indicates that, as a late starter in conducting investments abroad, the importance of outbound FDI is ever increasing for Korea.

Figure 6.1 South Korean outward FDI, 1980–2003

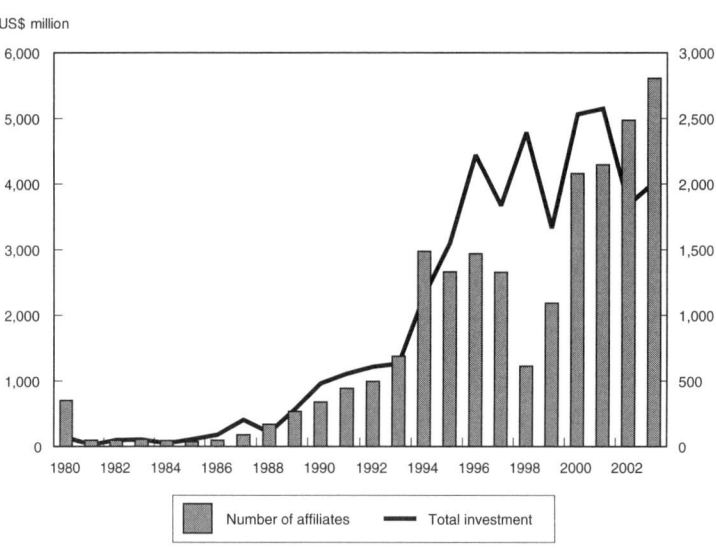

Source: Overseas Direct Investment Yearbook (Export–Import Bank of Korea).

Figure 6.2 shows the geographic distribution of outstanding FDI across countries or regions at the end of 2003. The United States accounts for 26 per cent of total outstanding investment, followed by Asia, China and Europe in order.[10] There has been a sharp increase in the amount of outbound FDI into China since 1998, notably by SMEs. As of 2003, China accounted for 19 per cent of the total FDI stock and 48 per cent of the total number of affiliates, respectively. This is quite a remarkable increase given that investments into China gained momentum only after 1992.

Investments destined for China have concentrated in manufacturing (84.8 per cent of total FDI stock into China at the end of 2003). Consequently, as of 2003, the share of net FDI stock into China relative to the total net stock in the manufacturing sector exceeded that of any other destination, as shown in Figure 6.3. On the other hand, in the case of Korean FDI into the United States, FDI in the service sector (55.8 per cent) is larger than that in the manufacturing sector (41.5 per cent).

Figure 6.4 contains recent trends in outbound FDI stock, exports and imports in manufacturing industries at different technology levels. Following the OECD (1997) approach in classifying manufacturing industries according to technology intensity, we divide manufacturing sectors into low, medium-low, medium-high and high technology industries. As depicted in the figure, the importance of high-tech and medium-high tech industries has substantially increased for outbound FDI as well as trade. This reflects the fact that major firms in leading export industries such as

Figure 6.2 Total South Korean outbound FDI, 2003, by destination (per cent)[a]

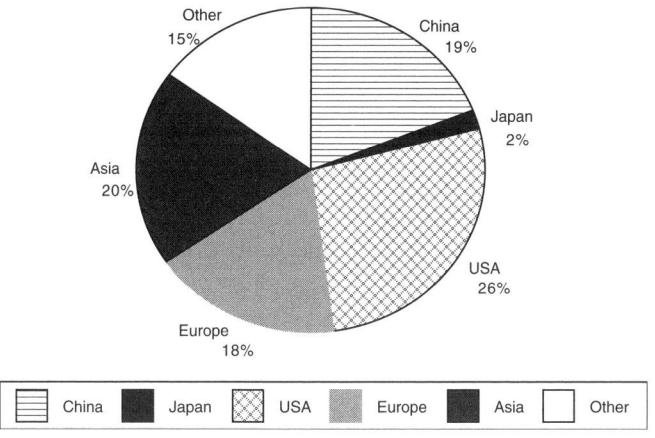

Note:
a   FDI share in whole industries (outstanding invested amount by 2003).

Source: Overseas Direct Investment Yearbook (Export–Import Bank of Korea).

Figure 6.3 South Korean outbound FDI in manufacturing, 2003, by destination (per cent)[a]

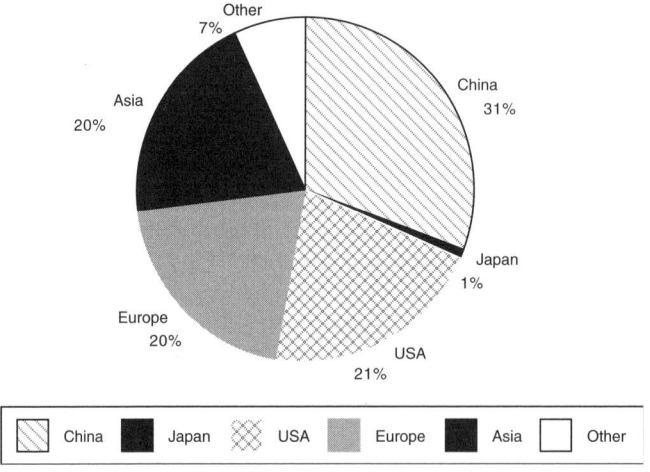

Note:
a FDI share in manufacturing (outstanding invested amount by 2003).
Source: Overseas Direct Investment Yearbook (Export–Import Bank of Korea).

computers, telecommunications equipment and automobiles have recently relocated some segments of their production lines and established new export bases, notably in China.

Figure 6.5 presents the recent trends in Korea's FDI into China and in bilateral trade between the two countries. Outbound FDI to China has grown substantially since the 1990s, at all levels of technology intensity. Imports from China followed a similar pattern. On the other hand, the rapid growth of exports into China was driven primarily by high-tech and medium-high-tech industries. A possible reason for this is that Korean multinational firms are vertically integrated, so production requiring relatively simple assembly processes may have been relocated abroad, while capital-intensive input production and knowledge-intensive designing and R&D were kept at home. This would result in the host country being used as an export platform for finished products through simple labour-intensive processing.

Finally, Figure 6.6 shows the patterns of FDI and trade with the United States. Unlike FDI into China, FDI into the United States is mostly concentrated in high-tech industries; FDI in less technologically advanced industries has remained relatively stable over time. As we would expect, the relative share of high-tech and medium-high-tech industries in both exports and imports is bigger than that of less technologically advanced industries.

Figure 6.4 FDI and trade in manufacturing ($ billion)

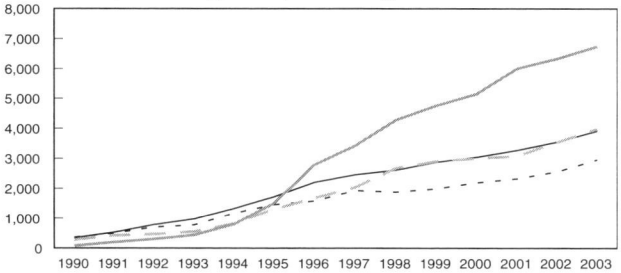

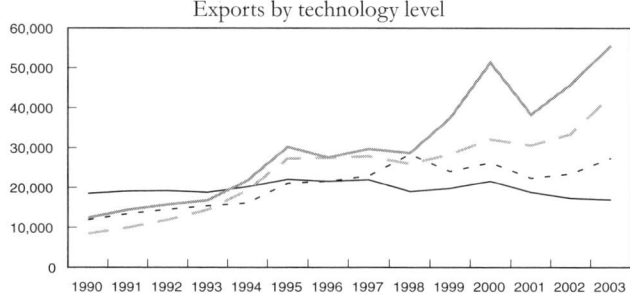

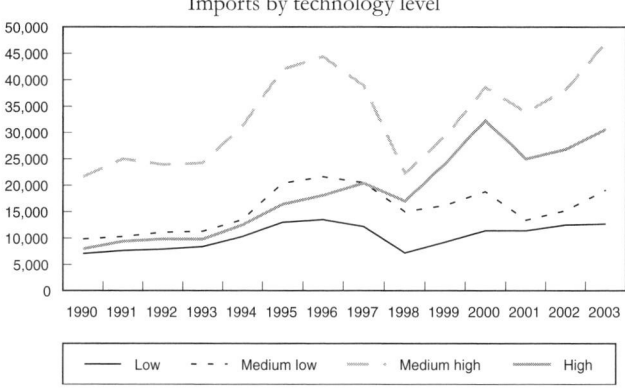

Note: High-tech industries are aircraft and spacecraft; pharmaceuticals; office, accounting and computing machinery; and radio, television and communication equipment.

Medium-high-tech industries are electrical machinery and apparatus not elsewhere classified; motor vehicles, trailers and semi-trailers; chemicals excluding pharmaceuticals; railroad equipment and transport equipment not elsewhere classified; and machinery and equipment not elsewhere classified.

Medium-low-tech industries are coke, refined petroleum products and nuclear fuel; rubber and plastic products; other non-metallic mineral products; building and repairing of ships and boats; basic metals; and fabricated metal products, except machinery and equipment.

Low-tech industries are manufacturing not elsewhere classified and recycling; wood, pulp, paper, paper products, printing and publishing; food products, beverages and tobacco; and textiles, textile products, leather and footwear.

Source: UN Commodity Trade Statistics Database (United Nations Statistics Division); Overseas Direct Investment Yearbook (Export–Import Bank of Korea).

Figure 6.5 FDI and trade with China, 1990–2003 ($ billion)

FDI trend by technology level (outstanding invested amount to China)

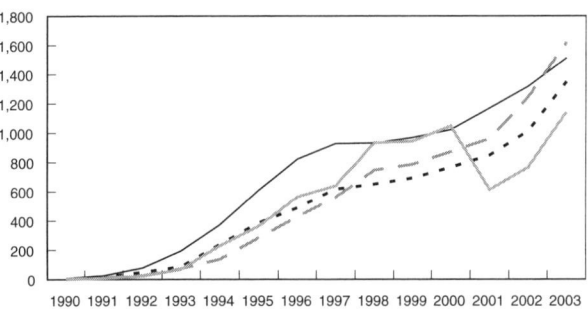

Exports to China by technology level

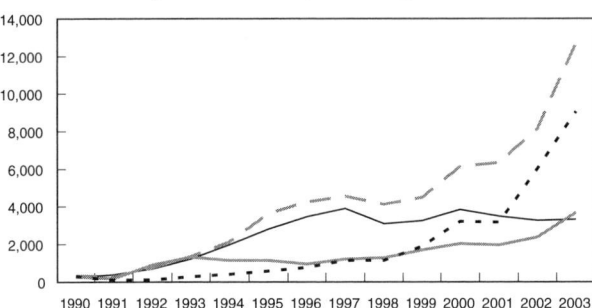

Imports from China by technology level

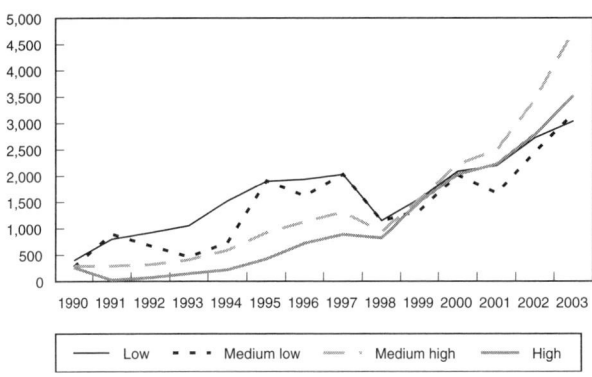

Note: See Figure 6.4 for a description of technology levels.

Source: UN Commodity Trade Statistics Database (United Nations Statistics Division); Overseas Direct Investment Yearbook (Export–Import Bank of Korea).

Figure 6.6 FDI and trade with the United States, 1990–2003 ($ billion)

FDI trend by technology level (outstanding invested amount to USA)

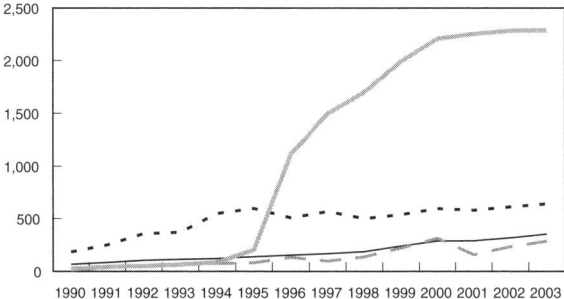

Exports to USA by technology level

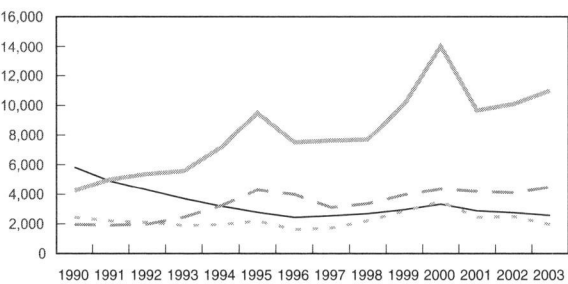

Imports from USA by technology level

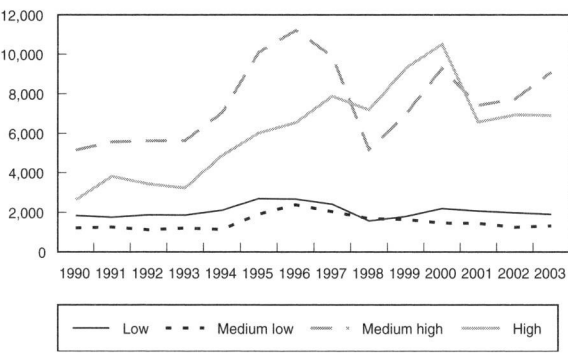

——— Low ▪ ▪ ▪ Medium low ⋯⋯ Medium high ≈≈≈ High

Note: See Figure 6.4 for a description of technology levels.

Source: UN Commodity Trade Statistics Database (United Nations Statistics Division); Overseas Direct Investment Yearbook (Export–Import Bank of Korea).

THE ECONOMIC IMPACTS OF OUTBOUND FDI AND TRADE: EVIDENCE FROM MICRO-DATA

Data description

For empirical analyses on economic impacts of outbound FDI and trade in Korea, we constructed a plant- and industry-level dataset for Korean manufacturing from 1990 to 2003. This dataset has three sources of information: the *Annual Report on Mining and Manufacturing Survey* (Korean National Statistical Office), the UN Commodity Trade Statistics Database (United Nations Statistics Division), and the *Overseas Direct Investment Statistics Yearbook* (Export–Import Bank of Korea).

The Korea National Statistical Office conducts the Mining and Manufacturing Survey annually. The survey covers all plants with five or more employees in mining and manufacturing industries and contains plant-level information on output, input, and a variety of additional information including the five-digit Korean Standard Industry Classification (KSIC) code assigned to each plant based on its major product. Variables such as plant-level employment growth, capital to labour ratio, non-production to production-worker ratio, labour productivity, and total factor productivity were calculated at the plant level based on information from this survey.

The UN Statistics Division compiles the *UN Commodity Trade Statistics Database* ('UN Comtrade'), which contains annual amounts of imports, exports, and re-exports in US dollars by commodity and by trading partners. Commodities are classified according to the Standard International Trade Classification (SITC: Rev. 1 from 1962, Rev. 2 from 1976 and Rev. 3 from 1988) and the 'Harmonised System' (HS) (from 1988 with revisions in 1996 and 2002). Imports from and exports to Korea's major trading partners by commodities based on the SITC Rev. 3 and on the HS system from 1990 to 2003 were downloaded from the UN Comtrade website.[11]

The Export–Import Bank of Korea is an official export credit agency providing comprehensive credit and guarantees for trade and overseas investment. Its *Overseas Direct Investment Statistics Yearbook* reports flows and stock of outbound FDI by industry and by destination. The Export–Import Bank has its own code for industry classification (the 'EXIM code'), which is by and large comparable to the three-digit KSIC code. For example, the total manufacturing sector consists of 71 industries according to the three-digit KSIC code and of 70 industries according to the EXIM code. Information on annual FDI flows and stock disaggregated by the EXIM code industries and by destination countries was downloaded from the bank's website.[12]

While the manufacturing survey contains plant-level information, the trade database and the FDI database do not provide plant-level information. When we put these three different sources of data together, therefore, we were able to link them only at a certain level of industry-wide aggregation. As the manufacturing survey and the UN Comtrade data have finer industry classification codes, we converted their industry classification codes and matched them to the EXIM code. In this way, we were able to construct our database with detailed unified industry-level information on production, trade, and FDI.

In the following sections, we report our main findings from regression analyses on: (a) the links between FDI and trade, (b) the impacts of outbound FDI and trade on employment growth, and (c) the impacts of outbound FDI and trade on employment growth. The first group of regression analyses on the links between FDI and trade are inevitably performed at the industry level due to the data limitations, yet information on the 70 industries over the 14-year period from 1990 to 2003 allows us to have as many as 980 observations. The second and third groups of regression analyses on employment growth and productivity growth take advantage of a still larger number of plant-level observations, at the order of magnitude of 100,000. Using plant-level information from the manufacturing survey, we ran regressions for plant-level employment growth and productivity growth on plant-level variables as well as on industry-level variables, including FDI and trade-related variables.

Relationship between FDI and trade: complements or substitutes?

In this section, we empirically examine the economic impact of outbound FDI on exports. Our estimations are based on 71 Korean manufacturing sectors for the period 1991–2003. Consider the following simple regression model:

$$Exports\_growth_{i,t} = \alpha_1 \cdot FDI\_growth_{i,t-1} + \alpha_2 \cdot Exports\_growth_{j,t-1} + v_{i,t} \qquad (6.1)$$

where $v_{i,t} = \alpha_{i0} + \xi T + \varepsilon_{i,t}$. α_{i0} represents an unobserved industry fixed effect affecting exports growth, T is a vector of year dummies, ξ is a parameter vector for time dummies and $\varepsilon_{i,t}$ is a white noise error term. The dependent variable is the annual growth rate of exports in sector i at year t, while the regressors are the one-year lagged growth rates of FDI and exports. All growth rates are calculated as annual changes normalised by dividing the averages of the beginning and ending years. Estimation results are reported in the first three columns of Table 6.1. Columns I and IV show estimations for all samples; columns II and V show only observations pertaining to low-tech and medium-low-tech industries; columns III and VI show only observations pertaining to medium-high-tech and high-tech industries. Heteroskedasticity-consistent standard errors are reported in brackets below parameter estimates.

As shown in Table 6.1, in relatively high-tech industries there is a complementarity effect between FDI and exports. The coefficient for FDI growth rates is statistically significant and positive. This result seems to support the hypothesis that, because Korean multinational firms are vertically integrated in these industries, production requiring relatively simple assembly processes was relocated abroad, the host country being used as an export platform for finished products through simple labour-intensive processing.

Equation 6.1 could have an endogeneity problem.[13] In the spirit of Desai et al. (2005b), we might expect that foreign production and exports are jointly determined by some common factors. For instance, the more productive firms might simultaneously produce more overseas and export more. Unless such common factors are properly controlled in the estimation, the causal relationship between FDI and exports might appear to exist when in fact it does not. As mentioned above, an FDI-augmented gravity model has been frequently used to investigate the substitution versus complementarity effects of FDI on exports. Unfortunately, the current empirical

Table 6.1 Relationship between FDI and exports (OLS and 2SLS estimations)

	OLS estimation			2SLS estimation		
	I	II	III	IV	V	VI
$FDI\_growth_{i,t-1}$	−0.0047	−0.0219)	0.0186	−0.1437	−0.2955	−0.0556
	(0.0096)	(0.0162)	(0.0101)*	(0.0602)**	(0.1479)**	(0.0641)
$Exports\_growth_{i,t-1}$	−0.1007	−0.1647	0.0577	−0.1183	−0.18380)	0.0448
	(0.0827)	(0.1031)	(0.1016)	(0.9010)	(0.1256)	(0.1160)
F-test						
Fixed effect	1.99***	2.20***	1.54**	2.25***	1.85***	1.00
Year effect	11.01***	5.91***	7.72***	7.80***	2.46***	6.88***
R^2	0.2819	0.2663	0.3602	–	–	–
No. of observations	642	315	327	626	308	318

Note: 2SLS = two-stage least square; OLS = ordinary least square; R^2 = ratio of regression variance to total variance.
*** significant at the 1% level; ** significant at the 5% level; * significant at the 10% level. Heteroskedasticity-consistent standard errors are reported in brackets below parameter estimates; see text for explanation of methodology.

Source: Authors' calculations.

literature, including that based on FDI-augmented gravity models, has paid little attention to this issue.[14]

In this context, we adopted an instrumental variable approach similar to that of Desai et al. (2005b) and re-estimated the effect of outbound FDI on exports for Korean manufacturing. In general, instrumental variables, which predict foreign investment but do not directly affect exports, could help us to identify the relationship between foreign investment and exports. That is because, if a host economy grows fast, multinationals like to expand foreign production in that country. As argued in Desai et al. (2005b), multinationals with prior local experience would have an advantage in expanding foreign production because they have better knowledge about the local market. Furthermore, local experience reflects unmeasured characteristics of firms that might allow them to serve a local market better than other markets. At the same time, an industry's initial distribution of foreign activity does not directly affect subsequent changes in exports.

In this respect, our instrumental variables procedure uses GDP growth rates of affiliate host countries and then aggregates them using weights equal to an industry's initial outstanding investment share in each host country, relative to that industry's total outstanding investment. We call the resulting variable MARKET. In addition, in order to include vertical FDI motives to take advantage of international differences in factor prices, we include the relative cost differences between home and foreign countries, proxied by the ratio of per capital GDP for Korea to that of host countries. Again, these cost differences are weighted by initial distribution of foreign activity. We define this variable as COSTS.

Our empirical strategy is as follows. At the first stage, we run a regression of the annual FDI growth rate on *MARKET* and *COSTS*:

$$FDI\_growth_{i,t-1} = \gamma_0 + \gamma_1 \cdot MARKET_{i,t-1} + \gamma_2 \cdot COSTS_{i,t-1} + \upsilon_{i,t} \quad (6.2)$$

Then predicted FDI growth rates in the first stage, defined as $\overline{FDI\_growth}_{i,t-1}$, are included as independent variables in the second stage equation:

$$Exports\_growth_{i,t} = \alpha_1 \cdot \overline{FDI\_growth}_{i,t-1} + \alpha_2 \cdot Exports\_growth_{j,t-1} + v_{i,t} \quad (6.3)$$

where $v_{i,t} = \alpha_{i0} + \xi T + \varepsilon_{i,t}$.

The results from this two-stage least squares regression (2SLS) estimation are reported in columns IV–VI of Table 6.1. In contrast to the OLS estimation shown in columns I–III, there is a strong substitution effect between FDI and exports.[15] The coefficients for FDI growth rates in the all-industry samples as well as in relatively low-tech samples turned out to be statistically significant and negative, indicating that foreign activities reduce exports. Our findings suggest that we could make a spurious inference about the effect of FDI on exports if the endogeneity problem is not properly dealt with.

Economic impacts of FDI and trade on employment growth

Does an increase in outbound FDI have a negative impact on job creation in a home country? To put the question another way, in which sector and under what circumstances could outbound FDI hinder domestic employment growth? This is a very important question for researchers and policymakers. However, answers to this question in the empirical literature are rather mixed, suggesting that the issue remains unsettled. South Korea, where outflows of both horizontal and vertical FDI surged in the 1990s, offers some useful evidence. Taking advantage of our rich micro-data, we try to shed light on the impacts of FDI and trade on employment in Korea from various angles. We pay special attention to heterogeneity in FDI outflows and in trade flows: by region, by industry, by technology level, by size of producer, etc. Using the same approach, we look into the impacts of FDI and trade on productivity growth as well.

Here, we report the results of various regressions on the determinants of plant-level employment growth. In the previous section, we showed that there were close links between FDI and trade. We therefore included both outbound FDI and trade growth (or, instead, export and import growth) as explanatory variables. As seen above, the major destination countries for outbound FDI from Korea are China and the United States, and major trading partner countries are China, Japan, and the United States. But the industry composition (especially whether the industry is high-tech, medium-tech or low-tech) varies substantially from country to country and over time. To take such variations into account, we included shares of major partner countries in FDI and trade as additional explanatory variables. The growth rates and country shares of FDI and trade were measured at a relatively detailed industry level based on the EXIM code, having 70 manufacturing industries.

Our regression equation for employment growth is:

$$\frac{L_{i,t+1} - L_{i,t}}{L_{i,t}} = \alpha_0 + \alpha_{Plant} \cdot X_{i,t} + \alpha_{Industry} \cdot Y_{j,t} + \alpha_D \cdot D_t + \varepsilon_{i,t} \quad (6.4)$$

where the left-hand-side variable is the employment growth rate in terms of the number of workers at plant i from year t to year $(t+1)$ and the right-hand-side variables are as follows:

- $X_{i,t}$, a vector of plant-specific variables for plant i in year t ($i = 1, ..., N_j$; $t = 1990$, 1991, ..., 2002), which includes the shipment growth rate, share of non-production workers, capital to labour ratio, and number of workers;
- $Y_{j,t}$, a vector of industry-specific variables for industry j to which plant i belongs in year t ($j = 1, ..., 70$; $t = 1990, 1991, ..., 2002$), including the industry-level non-production worker share, industry-level capital to labour ratio, outward FDI growth rate, shares of FDI to China and the United States, export growth rate, share of exports to China, Japan, and the United States, import growth rate, share of imports from China, Japan, the United States, etc.; and
- D_t, a vector of year dummy variables ($t = 1991, 1992, ..., 2002$).

We have run three sets of regressions using Equation 6.4. In the first set of regressions, the independent variable is the annual growth rate of employment for each plant in each year.[16] Each observation is pooled with year dummies to control for economy-wide year effects over the business cycle; then the OLS regression is applied. Table 6.2 summarises the results of the first set of regressions.

Columns I and II of Table 6.2 show the results of regressions for the whole sample (476,819 observations). Column I indicates that shipment growth, non-production workers' share, and capital to labour share at the plant level have significantly positive effects on employment growth at the plant level. On the other hand, the logarithm of the initial size of the plant measured by the number of workers has a negative effect on employment growth, reflecting a trivial fact that smaller plants will have more room for further growth than larger plants. At the industry level, we controlled for the capital to labour ratio and non-production workers' share.

We are now ready to focus on the major variables in which we are most interested. In column I, the growth rate of outbound FDI at the industry-level has a positive coefficient (0.012) with a very high heteroskedasticity-robust t-ratio of 5.49, suggesting that outbound FDI tends to have a positive effect on job creation. On the other hand, the estimated coefficient for the share of FDI to China is negative (–0.047) and statistically significant (its heteroskedasticity-robust t-ratio being –8.78), while the coefficient for the share of FDI to the United States is positive but statistically insignificant.

Estimated coefficients for trade-related variables (export growth, export share, import growth, and import share) are statistically insignificant for most variables in column I. Instead, trade (the sum of imports and exports) growth and trade share are

Table 6.2 Regression results for annual employment growth rates

Annual employment growth rates $(L_{i,t+1}-L_{i,t})/L_{i,t}$	Whole sample I	II	Large plants III	IV	Small and medium-sized plants V	VI
(Sales growth)$_{i,t}$	0.03687***	0.03687***	0.11128***	0.11148***	0.02678***	0.02677***
	(5.36)	(5.36)	(3.62)	(3.62)	(5.54)	(5.54)
(Non-production worker share)$_{i,t}$	0.00769***	0.00778***	0.00820***	−0.00785***	0.00977***	0.01000***
	(7.76)	(7.80)	(−3.10)	(−3.34)	(8.75)	(8.89)
(Capital-labour ratio)$_{i,t}$	0.00059***	0.00058***	0.00044**	0.00043**	0.00060***	0.00060***
	(9.27)	(9.26)	(2.40)	(2.34)	(8.33)	(8.34)
ln(number of workers)$_{i,t}$	−0.06183***	−0.06166***	−0.51762***	−0.50220***	−0.07390***	−0.07395***
	(−55.28)	(−54.89)	(−5.93)	(−5.94)	(−72.24)	(−71.63)
(Non-production worker share)$_{i,t}$	0.02443***	0.03498***	−0.11560	−0.11330	0.01628***	0.02282***
	(4.03)	(6.04)	(−1.41)	(−1.48)	(2.81)	(4.13)
(Capital-labour ratio)$_{i,t}$	−0.00009***	−0.00008***	−0.00031	−0.00051*	−0.00008***	−0.00010***
	(−4.51)	(−3.46)	(−0.98)	(−1.88)	(−4.23)	(−4.56)
(FDI growth)$_{i,t}$	0.01239***	0.01237***	0.12221***	0.09553**	0.00851***	0.00968***
	(5.49)	(5.67)	(2.84)	(2.45)	(3.81)	(4.59)
(FDI to China share)$_{i,t}$	−0.04702***	−0.03772***	−0.32073***	−0.30675***	−0.04738***	−0.03825***
	(−8.78)	(−7.36)	(−3.33)	(−3.33)	(−9.04)	(−7.74)
(FDI to US share)$_{i,t}$	0.00548	0.00022	0.12216	0.10677	−0.00151	−0.00502
	(1.10)	(0.04)	(1.32)	(1.19)	(−0.30)	(−1.02)
(Export growth)$_{i,t}$	0.00290		−0.00005		0.03294***	
	(1.36)		(−0.06)		(4.80)	
(Export to China share)$_{i,t}$	−0.03073***		−0.29375*		−0.03739***	
	(−3.43)		(−1.84)		(−4.38)	
(Export to Japan share)$_{i,t}$	−0.04706***		−0.15898		−0.04904***	
	(−6.90)		(−1.42)		(−7.36)	
(Export to US share)$_{i,t}$	−0.00033		0.38384		−0.00355	
	(−0.03)		(1.59)		(−0.39)	
(Import growth)$_{i,t}$	0.00484*		−0.00072		0.00303	
	(1.66)		(−0.11)		(0.43)	
(Import from China share)$_{i,t}$	−0.00214		−0.05092		0.01072	
	(−0.27)		(−0.27)		(1.43)	
(Import from Japan share)$_{i,t}$	−0.03759***		0.37032*		0.02926***	
	(−6.25)		(1.71)		(4.44)	
(Import from US share)$_{i,t}$	0.08426***		−0.07111		0.08836***	
	(5.39)		(−0.25)		(5.86)	
(Trade growth)$_{i,t}$		0.02966*		0.00204		0.08791***
		(1.80)		(0.58)		(5.57)
(Trade with China share)$_{i,t}$		−0.04214***		−0.02383		−0.02541***
		(−5.17)		(−0.11)		(−3.31)
(Trade with Japan share)$_{i,t}$		0.00833		0.23367		−0.03323**
		(0.58)		(1.07)		(−2.39)
(Trade with US share)$_{i,t}$		0.04482***		0.39562		0.06283***
		(3.85)		(0.94)		(6.03)
Intercept	0.18154***	0.17551***	3.46286***	3.33775***	0.20927***	0.20171***
	(25.60)	(26.85)	(5.69)	(5.75)	(31.25)	(33.18)
Year dummies	Yes	Yes	Yes	Yes	Yes	Yes
Number of observations	476,819	476,819	5,951	5,951	470,823	470,823
R^2 adjusted	0.11718	0.11705	0.50703	0.50669	0.08715	0.08716

Notes: *** significant at the 1% level; ** significant at the 5% level; *significant at the 10% level. The values in parentheses are heteroskedasticity-robust *t*-statistics.

Source: Authors' calculations.

used as industry-level explanatory variables for employment growth in column II. Trade appears to have a positive effect on employment growth (coefficient of 0.030) but is only marginally significant (robust *t*-ratio of 1.80). As with FDI, trade with China appears to have a negative effect (coefficient –0.042) while trade with the United States has a positive effect (coefficient 0.045).

It is often reported that a result of the impact of globalisation on domestic sectors is a tendency to create strong disparities in various dimensions, including disparities between large internationalised firms and SMEs. We have tried to detect such disparities by separating our sample into two groups: plants with more than 300 workers and plants with fewer than 300 workers.

Columns III and IV of Table 6.2 report the regression results for large plants (5,951 observations); columns V and VI give the results for small and medium-sized plants (470,823 observations). The observations that the growth rate of outbound FDI has a positive and highly significant coefficient and that the FDI to China share has a negative and highly significant coefficient remain robust across columns I–VI. However, the positive impact of FDI growth and the negative impact of China FDI on employment growth are much bigger for large plants. On the other hand, the positive impact of trade growth and the negative impact of trade with China on employment growth are more conspicuous for plants with fewer than 300 workers.

In 2003, the Korea Institute for Industrial Economics and Trade (KIET) carried out a survey of 706 Korean firms, asking about their motives for investing in China. Some 42.6 per cent reported low-cost labour as the most important motive (Kim *et al.* 2006). Only 33.0 per cent reported market access as the most important motive. If these results are accepted at face value, vertical FDI outweighs horizontal FDI as the major form of Korean firms' direct investment into China. Vertical FDI in search of low-cost labour aims to substitute foreign workers in the host country for domestic workers in the home country; it is therefore most likely to have negative impacts on job creation in the home country. Regression results summarised in Table 6.2 are consistent with this story. From the viewpoint of domestic workers, Table 6.2 suggests that the major channel for fierce competition with low-wage foreign workers could be either through the movement of domestic capital (that is, FDI) in the case of large enterprises or through the movement of goods (that is, trade) in the case of SMEs.

Impacts of FDI and trade on productivity growth

Extending our scope from job creation to productivity growth, we investigated the impacts of FDI and trade on productivity growth using the regression approach outlined above. Our regression equation for TFP growth is:

$$\ln TFP_{i,t+1} - \ln TFP_{i,t} = \beta_0 + \beta_{Plant} \cdot X_{i,t} + \beta_{Industry} \cdot Y_{j,t} + \beta_D \cdot D_t + \varepsilon_{i,t} \quad (6.5)$$

where the left-hand-side variable is the log growth rate of TFP at plant *i* from year *t* to year (*t* +1) and the right-hand-side variables are the same as those in Equation 6.1 except that $X_{i,t}$ here contains the level of ln *TFP* for a plant *i* at year *t* instead of the shipment growth rate.

Following Good et al. (1999), Aw et al. (2001), Hahn (2004) and Ahn et al. (2004), plant-level TFP is estimated by the chained-multilateral index number approach. It uses a separate reference point for each cross-section of observations and then chain-links the reference points together over time as in Tornqvist–Theil index. The output, input and productivity level of each plant in each year is measured relative to the hypothetical plant at the base time period. This approach allows us to make transitive comparisons of productivity levels among observations in a panel dataset. The productivity index for plant i at time t is measured in the following way:

$$\ln TFP_{it} = (\ln Y_{it} - \overline{\ln Y_t}) + \sum_{\tau=2}^{t} (\overline{\ln Y_\tau} - \overline{\ln Y_{\tau-1}})$$
$$-\left\{\sum_{n=1}^{N} \frac{1}{2}(S_{nit} + \overline{S_{nt}})(\ln X_{nit} - \overline{\ln X_{nt}}) + \sum_{\tau=2}^{t}\sum_{n=1}^{N} \frac{1}{2}(\overline{S_{n\tau}} + \overline{S_{n\tau-1}})(\overline{\ln X_{n\tau}} - \overline{\ln X_{n\tau-1}})\right\} \quad (6.6)$$

where Y, X, S and TFP denote output, input, input share and TFP level, respectively, and symbols with an upper bar are corresponding measures for hypothetical firms. The subscripts t and n are indices for time and inputs, respectively. Here, capital, labour, energy and real intermediate inputs were considered as factor inputs.

Again, we have run three sets of regressions using Equation 6.5. In the first set of regressions, the independent variable is the annual log growth rate of TFP for each plant in each year.[17] Each observation is pooled together with year dummies to control for economy-wide year effects over the business cycle; the OLS regression is then applied. Table 6.3 summarises the results of the first set of regressions.

Columns I and II show the results of regressions for the whole sample. The natural log of TFP level at year t is a so-called convergence term in a typical growth regression. In our regressions, the estimated coefficient was consistently negative. As with employment growth regression results, the non-production workers' share appears to have a positive effect on productivity growth. The logarithm of the initial size of the plant measured by the number of workers has a positive effect on TFP growth, reflecting economies of scale. At the industry level, we controlled for capital to labour ratio and non-production workers' share.

In column I, the growth rate of outbound FDI at the industry level has a positive coefficient (0.0058) with a sufficiently high heteroskedasticity-robust t-ratio (4.07), to suggest that outbound FDI tends to have a positive effect on productivity growth. On the other hand, the estimated coefficient for the share of FDI to China is negative (–0.0273) and statistically significant (heteroskedasticity-robust t-ratio of –8.42), while the coefficient for the share of FDI to the United States is positive (0.01178) and statistically significant (robust t-ratio of 3.81). Such patterns persist across all columns.

Among estimated coefficients for trade related variables (export growth, export shares, import growth, and import shares), both exports to and imports from Japan have shown significantly negative coefficients. Again, column II shows that trade with Japan has a negative effect on TFP growth (coefficient: –0.03859) while trade with China or with the United States has a positive effect (coefficients: 0.13198 and 0.14360, respectively).

Table 6.3 Regression results for annual TFP growth rates

Annual TFP growth rates $ln(TFP)_{i,t+1} - ln(TFP)_{i,t}$	Whole sample I	II	Large plants III	IV	Small and medium-sized plants V	VI
$ln(TFP)_{i,t}$	−0.54259***	−0.53687***	−0.36413***	−0.34760***	−0.54878***	−0.54126***
	(−276.09)	(−274.21)	(−19.74)	(−19.18)	(−269.57)	(−267.39)
(Non-production worker share)$_{i,t}$	0.01155***	0.01150***	0.00200	0.00200	0.01333***	0.01335***
	(12.75)	(12.60)	(1.58)	(1.60)	(13.95)	(13.80)
(Capital to labour ratio)$_{i,t}$	−0.00021***	−0.00021***	−0.00004***	−0.00003**	−0.00028***	−0.00028***
	(−7.25)	(−7.20)	(−2.70)	(−2.51)	(−7.46)	(−7.42)
ln(number of workers)$_{i,t}$	0.01391***	0.01396***	0.00698*	0.00269	0.01349***	0.01330***
	(27.02)	(27.07)	(1.66)	(0.67)	(24.45)	(24.22)
(Non-production worker share)$_{j,t}$	0.03517***	0.02651***	0.02938*	0.03565**	0.03686***	0.02810***
	(9.88)	(8.03)	(1.75)	(2.26)	(10.07)	(8.38)
(Capital to labour ratio)$_{j,t}$	−0.00001	−0.00001	0.00001	0.00003	0.00000	0.00001
	(−1.14)	(−0.70)	(0.15)	(0.88)	(0.22)	(0.59)
(FDI growth)$_{j,t}$	0.00577***	0.01764***	0.02558***	0.02661***	0.00834***	0.01688***
	(4.07)	(10.25)	(4.05)	(4.35)	(5.22)	(9.74)
(FDI to China share)$_{j,t}$	−0.02735***	−0.05867***	−0.09969***	−0.08032***	−0.02633***	−0.05651***
	(−8.42)	(−18.91)	(−5.22)	(−4.32)	(−8.02)	(−17.99)
(FDI to US share)$_{j,t}$	0.01178***	0.01269***	−0.03052	−0.01694	0.01867***	0.01318***
	(3.81)	(4.13)	(−1.52)	(−0.82)	(5.66)	(4.23)
(Export growth)$_{j,t}$	−0.00185		0.00081**		−0.04846***	
	(−0.66)		(2.06)		(−7.05)	
(Export to China share)$_{j,t}$	0.13532***		−0.03286		0.14890***	
	(25.14)		(−0.99)		(26.43)	
(Export to Japan share)$_{j,t}$	−0.11899***		0.09825***		−0.12904***	
	(−29.23)		(3.23)		(−31.43)	
(Export to US share)$_{j,t}$	0.12341***		−0.02060		0.12486***	
	(21.69)		(−0.57)		(21.70)	
(Import growth)$_{j,t}$	0.01557**		0.00106**		0.04505***	
	(2.55)		(2.04)		(8.38)	
(Import from China share)$_{j,t}$	0.02237***		−0.00327		0.02093***	
	(5.01)		(−0.12)		(4.59)	
(Import from Japan share)$_{j,t}$	−0.06058***		−0.07558***		−0.04665**	
	(−15.61)		(−3.03)		(−10.06)	
(Import from US share)$_{j,t}$	−0.00048		0.09788*		0.01513	
	(−0.05)		(1.86)		(1.59)	
(Trade growth)$_{j,t}$		−0.00453		0.00230***		−0.02322***
		(−0.75)		(4.54)		(−4.98)
(Trade with China share)$_{j,t}$		0.13198***		−0.05664		0.13074***
		(27.86)		(−1.62)		(27.51)
(Trade with Japan share)$_{j,t}$		−0.03859***		−0.07363**		−0.02344***
		(−6.20)		(−2.21)		(−4.16)
(Trade with US share)$_{j,t}$		0.14360***		0.04015		0.13696***
		(21.86)		(0.81)		(20.93)
Intercept	0.05702***	0.05409***	0.05657	0.07484**	0.05081***	0.05276***
	(16.73)	(17.54)	(1.62)	(2.20)	(14.29)	(16.28)
Year dummies	Yes	Yes	Yes	Yes	Yes	Yes
No. of observations	476,841	476,841	5,952	5,952	470,844	470,844
R^2 adjusted	0.31031	0.30718	0.22868	0.22279	0.31276	0.30886

Notes: *** significant at the 1% level; ** significant at the 5% level; * significant at the 10% level; The values in parentheses are heteroskedasticity-robust t-statistics.

Source: Authors' calculations.

Columns III and IV of Table 6.3 report the TFP growth regression results for the large plants; columns V and VI give the results for the small and medium-sized plants. Once again, the positive impact of FDI growth and the negative impact of FDI to China on TFP growth were much bigger for large plants. The negative impact of trade with Japan on TFP growth appears to be quite robust.

If a Korean firm can maintain competitiveness in the global market by hiring low-cost labour in China and reducing production costs, it has much less incentive to make extra efforts to improve productivity. Then, we can claim that outbound FDI to China tends to have a negative impact on employment growth and productivity growth for Korean producers. Nonetheless, previous regression results suggest that impacts of overall outbound FDI are positive both for job creation and for productivity growth.

CONCLUSION

This chapter analyses the economic impacts of Korea's outbound FDI, with a focus on its relation with trade and other industrial performance such as productivity and employment. We use trade, overseas investments and manufacturing survey data, which have been re-aligned consistently at a detailed (three-digit) industry level. We focus on three of Korea's major transaction partners, the United States, Japan, and China, and explore how the effects of transactions with these countries could differ across countries. In many cases, we group industries into four categories, depending on their technological attributes (OECD classification) and adopt typical large firm versus SME classifications to examine how technology level and firm size affected the relationship and effects concerned. The main findings of the chapter can be summarised as follows.

Relationship between outbound FDI and trade

The ultimate concern is whether these two factors are 'substitute' or 'complementary'. We analysed this issue using a simple aggregate OLS test for about 70 groups of industries over the period 1990–2003. When we lumped all industries together, our regression results showed no meaningful relationship between outbound FDI and trade. When the OLS analysis was conducted only with respect to high-tech and medium-high-tech industries, outbound FDI induced an increase in trade. However, the results may have been obtained simply because outbound FDI and trade are positively correlated with each other by a third, unspecified, factor. When we controlled for such an endogeneity problem by using an instrumental variable technique, we found that outbound FDI led to a decrease in trade for low-tech and medium-low-tech industries.

Impact of outbound FDI and trade on employment

According to the regression results for the employment increase effects for individual establishments (with both establishment and industry level data used as explanatory variables), an increase in the growth rate of outbound FDI in a certain industry leads to an average increase in employment growth of establishments in that industry.

However, the higher the share of outward FDI into China in certain industries the lower the average employment growth of establishments is in that industry. All these patterns are more pronounced among larger firms than among SMEs.

Impacts of outbound FDI and trade on TFP

According to the regression results on the TFP growth effects for individual establishments (with both establishment- and industry-level data used as explanatory variables), an increase in the growth rate of outbound FDI in certain industries leads to an average increase in the TFP growth of establishments in that industry. However, the higher the share of outward FDI into China in certain industries is, the lower the average TFP growth of establishments is in that industry. In contrast, the greater share of outward FDI into the United States has the opposite effect. All these patterns are more pronounced among large firms than among SMEs. The higher the share of trade with Japan in certain industries, the lower is the average TFP growth in establishments in that industry.

Overall effects of outward FDI on domestic activities in Korea

The existing literature is split as to the predicted direction of any effects of outward FDI on domestic activities in Korea. We find that, in general, outward FDI tends to affect employment and TFP positively whereas outward FDI into China exerts a negative effect. On the other hand, in industries trading heavily with Japan, employment and TFP growth for individual establishments tend to be suppressed.

Overall, the internationalisation of production, as captured by outbound FDI and trade, could have positive effects on the Korean economy. But their precise effects differ considerably, depending on the characteristics of industries, trading partners, and the size of business establishments concerned.

NOTES

An earlier version of this paper was presented at the OECD workshop *Globalization of Production and Value Chains*, Paris, 15–16 November 2005. Insightful comments and suggestions from Prema-chandra Athukorala, Jenny Corbett, Peter Drysdale, Dieter Ernst, David Hong, Kyung Tae Lee, Juan J. Palacios, Hugh Patrick, Peter A. Petri, Hadi Soesastro, Shujiro Urata and other participants in the PAFTAD Conference and the OECD workshop are gratefully acknowledged. All remaining errors are the authors' own.

1   In this chapter, South Korea is referred to as Korea, for the sake of brevity.
2   See Blonigen (2005) for a survey of recent empirical work on FDI determinants.
3   Given two cumulative distribution functions from independent random samples, a non-parametric test for first-order stochastic dominance provides statistical inference on differences in all moments of two samples. See Girma *et al.* (2003) for more details.
4   Girma *et al.* (2003, 2004) also employ a test for stochastic dominance for UK and Irish firms, respectively. While both find robust support for the hypothesis of Helpman *et al.* (2004), the latter does not indicate clear differences in performance between exporters and non-exporters.
5   Incidentally, the industries that Hanson *et al.* (2003) identified as good candidates for vertical specialisation are also the leading export industries of Japan and Korea. It seems obvious that outward FDI will become more and more important for Japanese and Korean firms.

6. On the other hand, Lipsey and Weiss (1984) find a strong complementary relationship between US affiliate production and US exports of intermediate goods, but no evidence for either complementarity or substitution in the case of the relationship between affiliate production of finished goods and exports of finished goods.
7. Lee (2005) explains several reasons for the surge of outbound FDI from Korea since the late 1980s. First, Korea opted for a liberalisation policy on outbound FDI in the mid-1980s. For instance, FDI up to $2 million has not required government approval since 1989. Second, the government began offering tax incentives, including a reserve for losses incurred by FDI. Third, the Korean Export–Import Bank provided subsidised loans for outbound FDI, financing up to 80 per cent of the investment.
8. The main reasons were rapid increases in real wage costs, the appreciation of the Korean won and the implementation of the liberalisation policy toward outbound FDI.
9. These figures are based on UNCTAD (2004).
10. Asia includes all the Korean FDI-hosting countries in the Asian region, except China, Japan and countries in the Middle East.
11. See <http://unstats.un.org/unsd/COMTRADE/>.
12. See <http://www.koreaexim.go.kr/en/>.
13. We plan to apply our approach in this section to an FDI-augmented gravity model in the near future.
14. The direction of causality is another issue. Aizenman and Noy (2005) find evidence that most of the relationship between FDI and trade can be explained by Granger causality from FDI flows to trade openness, but to a lesser extent it can be explained by Granger causality from trade to FDI.
15. We ran a similar regression for imports and did not find evidence of complementarity or substitution effects.
16. To check the robustness of the regression results, we performed the second and third sets of regressions. In both sets, we used the 3-year average annual employment growth rate for each plant in each year as the independent variable. In the second set, the average of the employment growth rate over the subsequent three years was calculated each year. In the third set, we avoided overlapping periods in averaging by choosing only years 1990, 1993, 1996 and 1999. The results of the second and third sets of regressions show that the main findings of the paper remain robust.
17. Once again, we have performed the second and third sets of regressions. In both sets of regressions, the 3-year average annual log *TFP* growth rate for each plant in each year was used as the independent variable. In the second set, the average of the *TFP* growth rate over the subsequent three years was calculated each year. In the third set, we avoided overlapping periods in averaging by choosing only years 1990, 1993, 1996 and 1999. The results of the second and third sets of regressions show that the main findings of the paper are not affected.

REFERENCES

Ahn, S., K. Fukao and H. Kwon (2004) 'The internationalization and performance of Korean and Japanese firms: an empirical analysis based on micro-data', *Seoul Journal of Economics*, 17(4): 439–482.

Aizenman, J. and I. Noy (2005) 'FDI and trade: two way linkages?', NBER Working Paper No. 11403.

Aw, B.Y., X. Chen and M.J. Roberts (2001) 'Firm-level evidence on productivity differentials, turnover, and exports in Taiwanese manufacturing', *Journal of Development Economics*, 66: 51–86.

Blomstrom, M., G. Fors and R.E. Lipsey (1997) 'Foreign direct investment and employment: home country experience in the United States and Sweden', *Economic Journal*, 107: 1787–1797.

Blonigen, A.B. (2005) 'A review of the empirical literature on FDI determinants', NBER Working Paper No. W11299.

Blonigen, A.B. (2001) 'In search of substitution between foreign production and exports', *Journal of International Economics*, 53: 81–104.
Clausing, A.K. (2000) 'Does multinational activity displace trade?', *Economic Inquiry*, 38(2): 190–205.
Desai, A.M., C.F. Foley and J.R. Hines (2005a) 'Foreign direct investment and the domestic capital stock', NBER Working Paper No. 11075.
Desai, A.M., C.F. Foley and J.R. Hines (2005b) 'Foreign direct investment and domestic economic activity', NBER Working Paper No. 11717.
Feldstein, M. (1995) 'The effects of outbound foreign direct investment on the domestic capital stock', pp. 43–63 in M. Feldstein, J.R. Hines Jr and R.G. Hubbard (eds), *The Effects of Taxation on Multinational Corporations*, Chicago: University of Chicago Press.
Girma, S., R. Kneller and M. Pisu (2003) 'Exports versus FDI: an empirical test', *Research on Globalization and Economic Policy*, 21.
Girma, S., H. Gorg and E. Strobl (2004) 'Exports, international investment, and plant performance: evidence from a non-parametric test', *Economics Letters*, 83: 317–324.
Good, D.H., M.I. Nadiri and R.C. Sickles (1999) 'Index number and factor demand approaches to the estimation of productivity,' pp. 14–18 in M.H. Pesaran and P. Schmidt (eds) *Handbook of Applied Econometrics: Microeconometrics*, Oxford: Blackwells.
Hahn, C. (2004) 'Exporting and performance of plants: evidence from Korean manufacturing', NBER Working Paper No. 10208.
Hanson, G.H., R.J. Mataloni and M.J. Slaughter (2003) 'Vertical networks in multinational firms,' NBER Working Paper No. W9723.
Head, K. and J. Ries (2001) 'Overseas investment and firm exports', *Review of International Economics*, 9: 108–122.
Head, K. and J. Ries (2003) 'Heterogeneity and the foreign direct investment versus exports decision of Japanese manufacturers', *Journal of the Japanese and International Economies*, 17: 448–467.
Hejazi, W. and A.E. Safarian (2001) 'The complementarity between U.S. foreign direct investment stock and trade', *Atlantic Economic Journal*, 29(4): 420–437.
Helpman, E., M.J. Melitz and S.R. Yeaples (2004) 'Export versus FDI with heterogeneous firms', *American Economic Review*, 94(1): 300–316.
Kim, Joon-Kyung, Yangseon Kim and Chung H. Lee (2006) 'Trade, investment and economic integration of South Korea and China', KDI Working Paper 2006-01.
Lee, H. (2005) 'The decision to invest abroad: the case of South Korean multinationals', mimeo, Korea Institute for International Economic Policy.
Lipsey, R.E. and M.Y. Weiss (1981) 'Foreign production and exports in manufacturing industries', *Review of Economics and Statistics,* 63(4): 488–494.
Lipsey, R.E. and M.Y. Weiss (1984) 'Foreign production and exports of individual firms', *Review of Economics and Statistics*, 66(2): 304–308.
OECD (Organisation for Economic Co-operation and Development) (1997), *Science, Technology and Industry: Scoreboard of Indicators*, Paris: OECD.
Swenson, D.L. (2004) 'Foreign investment and the mediation of trade flows', *Review of International Economics*, 12(4): 609–629.
UNCTAD (United Nations Conference on Trade and Development) (2004) *World Investment Report 2004*, Geneva: UNCTAD.
Wagner, J. (2005) 'Exports, foreign direct investment, and productivity: evidence from German firm level data', HWWA Discussion Paper 318, Hamburg Institute of International Economics.

7. The rise of Mexican multinationals: driving forces and limiting factors

Victor López Villafañe and Clemente Ruiz Durán

MEXICAN BUSINESS IN THE LAST 20 YEARS

Entrepreneurship in Mexico has become more dynamic as a result of structural reforms introduced in the last 20 years. The census data show (INEGI 2004) that 162,000 new businesses were created per year in the period 1993–2004, with the size of the business community increasing from 2.5 to 4.3 million, a net average annual growth rate of 5 per cent. This growth in new ventures was much higher than that in the rest of Latin America and was similar to that in East Asia. The figures mean that for each firm that already existed in the market, 0.68 new firms entered the market (Table 7.1).

This creation of new businesses was against all the odds. Government support for business creation was weak due to the collapse of the financial system in 1994. This dried up financial resources and pushed entrepreneurs to develop their own financial networks to create new ventures. The government provided only quite limited support, focusing mainly on training but with budget restrictions.

Table 7.1 Entrepreneurship in Mexico, 1993–2004 (No. of firms)

	1993	1998	2004	Change 1993–2004	Average annual change 1993–2004 (%)
Total	2,512,631	3,130,714	4,290,108	1,777,477	4.98
Manufacturing	288,562	361,579	481,084	192,522	4.76
Trade	1,280,922	1,497,526	2,120,483	839,561	4.69
Non-financial services	927,500	1,242,396	1,588,970	661,470	5.02
Other sectors	33,746	82,235	99,571	65,825	10.34

Source: Fuente INEGI, Enumeración Urbana de Establecimientos 1993, Enumeración Integral 1998, Mexico 1999, Censos Economicos 2004.

However, the lack of government support led to the formation of a heterogeneous business sector, with some highly modernised businesses, some traditional businesses and some businesses in the underground economy. The 2004 Economic Census found that output value in the manufacturing sector was an average of $5,000 for micro businesses and $29,000 for large businesses, a ratio of 1:5.8. Greater differences among firms become more clear-cut if we consider the average size of assets per business: micro firms averaged assets of only $167,000, small firms $643,000, medium-sized firms $4.4 million and large firms $30 million. The ratio of the assets of large firms to those of micro firms is 1,764:1.

The opening of the economy, the enactment of the North American Free Trade Agreement (NAFTA) and the collapse of central government promotion policies have encouraged entrepreneurship. The new entrepreneurial culture that has developed was based on the help-yourself philosophy, within the context of a changing attitude toward entrepreneurs as they became respectable figures in Mexican society. This has led to an increase in the political participation of businessmen, creating conditions for a political struggle that led to the collapse of the Partido Revolucionario Institucional – an authoritarian bureaucratic entity that ruled the country for 70 years. With the inauguration of a new administration in December 2000 there began a re-engineering period: new rules of the game were set and the public sector's role in the economy is being redesigned.

By many standards, Mexico is a strong economy. With a population of 105 million and a per capita GDP of over $6,230, Mexico's total GDP makes it the 10th largest economy in the world. It is the United States' second most important trading partner, after Canada; and it is competing with China, which is now the United States' third most important trading partner. Economic liberalisation has resulted in a dramatic transformation of both the quantity and the structure of trade: from 1980 to 2004, exports increased twelve-fold and there was a major shift from oil-related to manufacturing exports. However, despite the huge increase in exports, economic growth has been quite mediocre. During the 1980s (commonly referred to as Latin America's 'lost decade'), per capita GDP growth was negative. Despite the major liberalisation efforts taking place after 1985, growth rates in the 1990s were still less than half those of the 1960s and 1970s, and growth became even less dynamic at the turn of the century. This performance is even worse when compared to that of Mexico's primary trading partners and competitors. Mexico has consistently lagged behind its partners in the NAFTA area and some major East Asian competitors; its performance is generally similar to that of Brazil (Table 7.2).

One of Mexico's aims in signing up to NAFTA was to make manufacturing the driving force of the economy. Unfortunately, the behaviour of the Mexican industrial complex has been below expectations. Its average rate of growth was only 3.6 per cent during the period 1988–2003, due to a low productivity growth rate of 2.5 per cent. Even more concerning is decreasing total factor productivity (TFP). There are various ways to estimate TFP, but all of them indicate a sharp decline in TFP during the 1980s, and TFP remained relatively stagnant during the 1990s.

Table 7.2 Economic performance in perspective (GDP annual growth, per cent)

	1980–90	1991–2000	2001–04	1980–2004
Mexico	2.5	3.5	1.6	2.8
NAFTA partners				
United States	2.9	3.3	2.5	3.0
Canada	2.7	3.0	2.4	2.8
Main competitors				
China	9.2	10.1	8.4	9.5
South Korea	7.8	6.2	4.6	6.7
Brazil	2.3	2.7	1.6	2.4

Note: NAFTA = North American Free Trade Agreement.
Source: World Bank WDI online June 2005; 2004 data are from INEGI; Bureau of Economic Analysis; Statistics Canada; Korea National Statistics Office; IBGE.

Take, for instance, the performance of what can be considered a symbol of NAFTA: *maquiladoras*.[1] They registered yearly personnel increases for 37 consecutive years, and reached their maximum level of employment at 1.35 million in 2000. Yet, following November 2000, they shed 14 per cent of their workforce and closed 23 per cent of their plants. This could easily be dismissed as part of an adjustment due to the contraction of the US economy. Yet the underlying reasons are more structural than cyclical. An estimated 50 per cent of the *maquiladoras* that left the country moved elsewhere, mainly to Asian countries – particularly China. As long as foreign firms are located in Mexico for cost considerations, and there is little local content, they will be 'footloose', migrating to lower cost locations as relative wages start to increase.

As other countries, particularly China, join the World Trade Organization (WTO), Mexico's position becomes increasingly vulnerable. These countries are operating on global economies of scale rather than operating only in the North American region. Mexico is now considered to be a low-cost producer (though not as low as China) but is not considered to be a high value-added producer. It needs to move up the value chain.

Mexico has developed various pockets of excellence and high productivity associated with multinationals operating in high-tech and higher-middle-tech industries and national conglomerates operating in mature industries. These are no longer *maquila* operations (*maquiladoras*), as they employ many professionals and include in-house design and engineering. Yet often these pockets of excellence are still enclaves with few linkages to the rest of the economy.

This is Mexico's growth paradox: there is a promise of higher productivity, value added and wages; however this promise remains only very partially realised. The explanation for the paradox is that NAFTA-induced changes produced very little impact on firm-level learning and innovation. NAFTA gains are almost exclusively relegated to reallocation between and within sectors, rather than corresponding to an increase in technical efficiency (the 'within-plant effect'). Indeed, this is what economic theory would predict: first, reallocation effects based on changes in relative prices, then micro level increases in efficiency based on learning and innovation. A second-generation NAFTA agenda would focus on achieving dramatic increases in the 'within-plant effect' of rapid firm-level productivity growth.

Mexico is now at a crossroads: it cannot yet compete on the basis of knowledge assets (unlike, for example, Organisation for Economic Co-operation and Development countries), yet its traditional comparative advantage is being eroded by low-cost competitors. Both government and industry leaders are extremely concerned that Asian countries are attracting many of the firms now established in Mexico. This was clearly shown when Mexico tried to block China's accession to the WTO. However, the country's leaders seem to view the lack of competitiveness as a problem mostly arising from differences in labour costs, ignoring the close relationship between the country's performance and its technological capabilities (in a broad sense, including adoption, adaptation and creation). Failure to recognise this critical link will result in further loss of productivity.

Take, for instance, Mexico's export performance versus that of China.[2] In the period between the start of NAFTA and 2000, Mexico's exports to the United States (which are about 90 per cent of total Mexican exports) performed at a similar level to those of China. From 1996 to 2000, exports to the United States by both Mexico and China increased by 17 per cent. But Mexico has lost ground since 2000: from 2001 to 2003 Mexican exports to the United States increased by 2.5 per cent, while exports from China increased by 22 per cent.

Nor is this a purely cyclical phenomenon. Among the 141 products that Mexico exported to the United States in 2003, there was a reduction in export volume for 54 products, totalling $5.5 billion. For the same 54 export products, China experienced an increase in exports of $11.8 billion. For the remaining 87 products, Mexican exports increased to $8.9 billion, but $3 billion of that amount was due to oil exports. Meanwhile, for the same 87 products, China's exports to the United States increased to $15.3 billion. Mexico is losing exports for several products among its 15 largest exports (passenger cars, computer accessories, apparel and household goods). Even more indicative and concerning is that Mexico is losing exports even in products for which, due to their size or weight (for example, furniture, household appliances), it would be expected to enjoy a significant advantage.

Underlying this is the fact that the quality of the competitive environment for firms in Mexico is becoming less attractive than that of its main training partners and competitors. It is not just that Mexico's competitive position is quite low for an economy so highly integrated with the US and Canadian economies. Even more alarming is the reality that its position is weakening, whereas the competitive positions of China and South Korea are improving. Falling TFP, stagnant value added of exports, and a still unsatisfactory competitive environment all indicate that 'the flight of firms', which seems to be replacing the capital flight of the 1980s, is not merely a transitional phenomenon. Instead, it is the tip of the iceberg, signalling a need to deepen NAFTA economic openness through concerted action by the government and the private sector to dramatically improve the investment climate, and to create an environment more conducive to generating, diffusing and applying knowledge.

EMERGENCE OF MEXICAN MULTINATIONAL CORPORATIONS

The large private Mexican companies are a heritage and a result of the application of protectionist policies in the Mexican market. Those policies were established in 1940 and subsequently, and they lasted until the beginning of the 1980s. Nevertheless, the change from a protectionist model to one based on international competition has been executed at a time of big economic convulsions. Such convulsions were set off by at least two economic crises: one in 1982 and another in 1995. Moreover, there was stagnation and slow economic growth in the years 1982–88 and 2000–04.

These elements reveal an important difference between Mexico and the Asia Pacific region. Countries in the Asia Pacific region suffered only one financial crisis, in 1997. Moreover, notwithstanding the severity of the crisis, the region was able to quickly recover its high economic growth rates. Another difference is that, since the application of NAFTA in 1994, the large private Mexican companies had to adapt to competition by US companies, which had an advantage in practically every aspect. The American market was very appealing because of its huge dimensions, but at the same time it was highly competitive. Moreover, most big enterprises in Mexico had virtually no experience of exporting, unlike companies in Asia, which began to experiment with different models for exporting products and components after only a short time of import substitution.

No less important in the Asia Pacific region was the regional industrial restructuring driven by the Japanese economy since the 1960s. In a certain sense, Mexico was unable to take advantage of a 'flying geese model' in Latin America, unlike countries in Asia, for which Japan's regional industrial restructuring since the 1960s was a powerful driver of industrial change.

In sum, the most important differences between the Mexican and Asian liberalisation experiences were that in Mexico the process was faster; it was applied in the middle of several economic and financial crises; the state did not support and strategically direct the evolution of private companies; and there was no regional impact of successive industrial transformations that could have helped its development. Moreover, in Mexico linkages between small and medium-sized enterprises (SMEs) and multinationals were weak, unlike in Asia.

The liberalisation process in Mexico was not accompanied by a strategy to strengthen linkages between SMEs and multinational enterprises (MNEs). The low level of technological capacity, the lack of skilled human resources and the weak access to financing have hindered the incorporation of SMEs into multinational networks. For example, in some regions in Mexico foreign multinationals have had to import the components they require rather than buying them from local suppliers. On the other hand, Mexican multinationals, as we have mentioned, are producing goods with a low level of complexity and thus do not produce deeper linkages with SMEs. Mexico must implement and sustain a policy to strengthen the participation of SMEs in the exporting network of Mexican and foreign MNEs.

Despite these negative factors, a rising group of businesses – mainly large enterprises – that have been increasing their competitive edge could compare with world-class businesses. Mexican companies have pursued a variety of strategies that, far from stemming from a master or common plan, reflect their own conditions and wishes. In this situation, only a limited number of large Mexican companies have been able to build up their position in the national and international markets. A ranking of the 40 largest Mexican companies between 1995 and 2002, based on each company's assets, sales and profits, showed that only a select group has been able to move from crisis to a level of national and world competitiveness. Only companies in this small group have become what today are referred to as multinational regional businesses[3] with important assets. To survive in a time marked by crisis and with slow growth of the national market, the largest and most powerful Mexican companies became multinationals.

Most large Mexican companies are located in the middle-tech industry segment (Table 7.3) and most of their sales are in the domestic market. Between 1995 and 2002 only nine of the main 40 Mexican companies increased either their exports from Mexico or their sales to foreign markets by affiliates abroad. Amongst these, only five carried out more than 50 per cent of their total sales in foreign markets.[4] In contrast, products from the large foreign companies based in Mexico are mainly for the foreign market. In the automobile sector this accounts for 81 per cent of the value of sales, in the chemicals sector it is 86 per cent, and in information technology it is 51 per cent.

Large firms in the middle-tech and high-tech segments of the market became competitive at world level, and some began to invest abroad. In 2004 Mexican direct investment abroad was around $17.5 billion,[5] up from $11.9 billion in 2001 (Figure 7.1). And between 2001 and 2004, outflows increased from $122 million a year to $3.5

Table 7.3   Firms by size and industry level of technology (no. of units and share of total)

	Total	Size			
		Micro	Small	Medium	Large
Total manufacturing	328,718	306,083	16,205	3,379	3,051
Share of total (%)	100	93.1	4.9	1.0	0.9
Resource-based	53.7	51.3	1.8	0.3	0.2
Low-tech	26.2	24.2	1.5	0.3	0.2
Medium-tech	19.1	16.9	1.5	0.4	0.3
High-tech	1.0	0.6	0.2	0.1	0.1

Source: Authors' estimates based on INEGI, Censos Economicos 2004.

Figure 7.1   Mexico direct investment abroad ($ million)

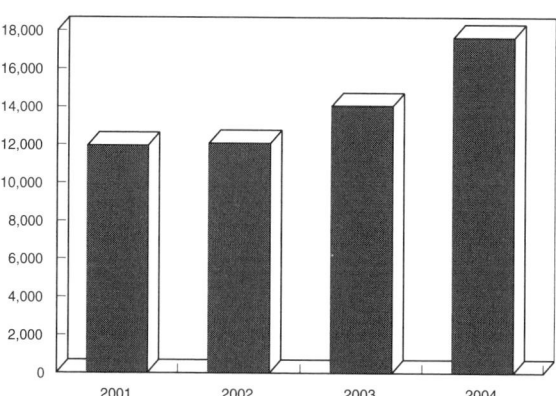

Source: Authors' calculations using data from Secretaria de Economia (2006); see <http://www.economia.gob.mx/index.jsp?P=1175>.

billion a year as Mexican companies became more competitive. There is no detailed information as to where they invest, so it is only by looking at each company that we can see which companies are involved and where.

Large businesses have taken advantage of NAFTA and other free trade agreements and have reached alliances with international and domestic businesses. Foreign companies looked for Mexican companies to get into the domestic market more easily and Mexican companies searched for partners, mainly in the United States and Latin America, to get into foreign markets. This has been reflected in the capital mix of the largest 500 firms: there is an increasing share of foreign firms in the capital of large Mexican firms. Nonetheless, from 2000 to 2005 those alliances faded out, especially in auto parts and electronic appliances. Yet new companies – for example, Braun, Daewoo and LG – entered the Mexican market in a direct way without making alliances with Mexican partners. The absence of such alliances has great implications for Mexican businesses: on the one hand, it means they are left out of the multinational production chains; on the other, it represents a missed opportunity for technology transfer (Table 7.4).

Large firms that have become multinational have concentrated in Mexico City and in Monterrey. These cities are the home of the most dynamic and modern firms in the country; some are now listed on databases such as the one collected by Forbes.

In the following sections we describe the main features of the multinationals listed in Table 7.5.

Table 7.4 Alliances of the 500 largest companies in Mexico (distribution by source of capital, per cent)

Year	National	Foreign	Mixed, with national majority	Mixed, with foreign majority
1992	63.50	12.00	21.00	3.50
1993	63.25	18.00	15.00	3.75
1994	61.39	18.23	15.88	4.50
1995	59.53	18.78	15.05	6.64
1996	67.54	18.46	9.26	4.74
1997	70.93	14.68	12.18	2.21
1998	–	–	–	–
1999	65.52	17.74	16.06	0.68
2000	–	–	–	–
2001	65.13	28.95	4.60	1.32
2002	64.80	28.95	4.60	1.65

Note: – = no data.
Source: Pozas (2005), with information from Expansión digitalised series 1994–2003 (the annual database of Expansión compares information for the two previous years, so, for example, the information for 1994 includes data from 1992 and 1993).

Table 7.5 Mexico's biggest multinational public companies ($ billion)

Rank	Name	Head-quarters location	Industry	Sales	Profits	Assets value	Market
243	Cemex	MY	Construction	15.33	2.11	26.44	23.82
300	America Telecom	MC	Telecom services	17.17	1.11	22.85	20.13
411	Carso Global Telecom	MC	Telecom services	15.36	1.05	23.81	8.36
670	Femsa	MY	Food, drink, tobacco	8.4	0.52	10.72	10.31
777	Grupo Carso	MC	Conglomerates	7.36	0.81	7.88	5.99
806	Grupo Mexico	MY	Materials	5.48	0.67	9.43	6.66
872	Grupo Financiero Banorte	MY	Banking	3.91	0.54	17.89	4.94
893	Grupo Modelo	MY	Food, drink, tobacco	4.02	0.56	6.6	11.2
939	Grupo Televisa	MC	Media	3.06	0.58	7.07	11.57
1058	Coca-Cola Femsa	MY	Food, drink, tobacco	4.18	0.49	5.9	5.62
1072	ALFA	MY	Conglomerates	6.53	0.73	5.94	3.1
1392	Grupo Bimbo	MC	Food, drink, tobacco	5.29	0.27	3.33	4.17
1416	Inbursa Financiero	MC	Banking	1.76	0.27	8.11	4.72
1828	Grupo Elektra	MY	Retailing	3	0.28	4.78	2.68
1873	Soriana	MY	Retailing	4.56	0.2	3.34	2.65
1934	Kimberly-Clark de Mexico	MC	Household and personal products	2.07	0.27	2.35	3.96

Note: MY = Monterrey; MC = Mexico City.
Source: Forbes.com section rank: 'World's biggest public companies'.

MEXICO CITY BUSINESS NETWORK: THE GLOBAL CHALLENGE

Central Mexico is the main business centre. It holds almost 20 per cent of all established businesses, with 8.9 per cent in Distrito Federal and 10.9 per cent in Estado de Mexico. Distrito Federal is home to 542 large businesses (that is, businesses with more than 500 employees) that have been the leading force of structural change in the country. They are located in all sectors. The business history of the country began in this region, but has had a continuous changing face. Trade was the initial activity of Mexico City; in the 19th and 20th centuries manufacturing changed the whole area, attracting people from the rest of the country, and Mexico City became one of the most populated cities in the world. In the late 20th century, as the agglomeration faced pollution problems, many industries were forced out of the city. Little by little the city is now becoming a service centre, attracting new investment.

One of the main challenges for firms in the regions has been to transform themselves into world-class businesses; some have been able to do so and have become global. Some of the most successful are in the telecommunication, engineering services, food industry, financial and media and entertainment sectors.

Each industry has taken a different path to global success. Success in the telecommunication industry was associated with privatisation; success in engineering services was associated with the emergence of leading professionals following educational reforms of the 1950s and 1960s; success in the media and entertainment sector was linked to government restrictions on greater competition in the sector; and banking success was associated with the privatisation policy of the 1990s. The Mexico City-based business network reaches all regions in the world (as shown in Table 7.6) and the companies involved have expansion programs to allow them to enter even more countries. Below, we describe the activities of selected companies.

Telefonos de México

The most successful Mexican multinational is Telefonos de México, which was privatised in the early 1990s. To get into the bid, Carlos Slim put in 12.9 per cent of the total value and entered a joint venture with Southwestern Bell (12.5 per cent), France Telecom (12.5 per cent) and other Mexican investors (13.1 per cent). The government deposited the remaining 49 per cent in a trust fund to be sold subsequently. During the 1990s Slim repurchased other Mexican investors' shares and the shares in the trust fund. Because of the size of the operation, Slim created a holding company, Carso Global Telecom, in 1996; today, CGT holds 74 per cent of all shares. In between, it created a spin-off – America Telecom (AMX) – to manage cellular and international investment. Both Carso Global Telecom and AMX have been listed on the New York Stock Exchange since 2001. Carso Global Telecom manages traditional telephone services, while AMX focuses on wireless communications. AMX is the largest telecommunications company in Latin America and the tenth largest in the world.

Carso Global Telecom has invested in the United States and in companies in various South American countries (Table 7.7). All this acquisition has allowed Telmex to develop economies of scale in the telecommunications business, and has provided the

Table 7.6 Largest multinational corporations in Mexico City and locations of their subsidiaries and businesses

Country	America Telecom	Carso Global	Grupo Carso	Grupo Televisa	Grupo Bimbo	Grupo Financiero Inbursa	Ingenieros Civiles Asociados
Argentina	✓				✓		✓
Bermuda	✓						
Bolivia							✓
Brazil	✓	✓	✓		✓	✓	
Chile		✓		✓	✓	✓	
China		✓	✓				
Colombia	✓			✓	✓		
Costa Rica					✓		
Czech Republic					✓		
El Salvador	✓				✓		✓
Germany		✓	✓				
Guatemala	✓	✓	✓		✓		✓
Honduras	✓				✓		
Mexico	✓	✓	✓	✓	✓	✓	✓
Nicaragua	✓	✓	✓		✓		
Peru					✓		
Spain		✓	✓	✓	✓		
Uruguay	✓						
USA		✓	✓	✓	✓	✓	✓
Venezuela	✓				✓		

Source: Annual reports of the corporations. See <www.amtelecom.com.mx>, <www.cgtelecom.com.mx>, <www.gcarso.com.mx>, <www.televisa.com.mx>, <www.gibsa.com.mx>, <www.inbursa.com.mx>, <www.kimberly-clark.com.mx>, <www.lica.com.mx>.

opportunity to get into new areas of telecommunications, which is the most dynamic area of business in Latin America.

Grupo Carso, a brother company of Carso Global Telecom, has developed businesses in different industries. Sanborns is the largest integrated store in Mexico; its business includes the largest library in Mexico, music store and restaurant services, and CD and DVD retailing (Mixup, Discoland and Feria del Disco). El Globo is a pastry business. Condumex focuses on energy, auto parts and telecommunications. Nacobre is a copper and aluminium producer. Frisco is in the chemical and mining industry. Porcelanite makes high-quality ceramic floors. And Cigatam is a cigarette retailer. The group operates in the United States, Guatemala, Nicaragua, Brazil, Germany, Spain and China, as shown in Table 7.6.

Table 7.7   Carso Global Telecom's reach

Country	Company
Brazil	Five companies, including Proveedor de Servicios de Telecommunications
Chile	Holding company with the acquired shares of ATT Telmex Corporation
Argentina	Techtel – LMDS Comunicaciones Interactivas
	Telmex Argentina, SA
	Proveedor de Servicios de Telecomunicaciones a clientes corporativos en Argentina
	Proveedor de Servicios de Datos en Argentina
Colombia	Telmex
	Proveedor de servicios de Telecomunicaciones
Peru	Telmex

Source: Annual reports of the company; see <www.cgtelecom.com.mx>.

Grupo Televisa

Another successful business is Grupo Televisa, the largest media group in the country. It began operations in the 1950s: when the government allowed private corporations to carry TV signals, the company obtained concessions for three channels. In 1972, it changed its name to Televisa SA de CV and became a media producer. To obtain finance through advertising, it got into cable television, radio and music production. In 1982 it obtained regional networks. In the early 1990s the Azcarraga family took control of the company, transforming Televisa into Grupo Televisa. The company operates in Latin America (Colombia and Chile), the United States (through Univision) and Spain. It is one of the leading producers of media programs in the world and has a large influence on the Hispanic population of the United States. Its soap operas have been quite successful in Asian countries.

Grupo Bimbo

Grupo Bimbo is one of the oldest corporations in the bakery industry in Mexico. It opened its doors in December 1945, with bread products, but has evolved to become a very diversified operation with 4,500 products. It has 73 factories in Mexico, the United States, Latin America (Guatemala, Honduras, Costa Rica, El Salvador, Nicaragua, Colombia, Peru, Argentina, Chile, Uruguay, and Venezuela) and Europe (the Czech Republic and Spain). It has been quite successful in getting into the Hispanic market in the United States, where Mexican-style bakery products are in demand; it has become the leading bakery store in the south.

ICA

Ingenieros Civiles Asociados (ICA) began its operations in 1947, when a group of engineers led by Bernardo Quintana decided to engage in civil engineering services. In the first stage (the 1950s), it carried out its activities in Mexico, gaining experience in infrastructure building and being the first to develop industrial park complexes. During the 1960s it began operations in Latin America (Guatemala, Ecuador, Honduras, Dominican Republic, Panama and Chile), developing large infrastructure projects. It built the underground system in Chile and airport runways in Panama. Its success led the company to become involved in more global operations in the 1980s and early 1990s: in dams and irrigation systems in El Salvador, in the airport in Belize, in the Neuquen Bahia Blanca gas line in Argentina, and in housing in Waterview, Florida, and the water system of Chicago in the United States. In the late 1990s the firm's prestige helped it to get contracts to build the Atacama gas line in Chile, the Chile–Argentina gas line, the Bolivia–Brazil gas line, the speed train in Puerto Rico, and the south highway network in Panama.

Hildebrando

Medium-sized businesses in Mexico are now developing a culture for transnational operations. Many high-tech businesses – for example, in the software industry – have accepted the challenge. A successful firm that started operations in the 1980s is Hildebrando, one of the largest software producers in Mexico City. In 14 years, Hildebrando has grown from a three-person project to an organisation with more than 500 employees. In February 2000, Warner-Lambert granted Hildebrando its 'Best Quality Provider' award for the fifth consecutive year. In every year since 1998, *Expansion* magazine has featured Hildebrando as one of Mexico's top 500 firms. Revenues have grown by a factor of 5.6 since 1993, reaching $14 million in 2001.

Hildebrando has opened offices in Mexico City, Guadalajara, and Monterrey, as well as in the United States (Miami) and Spain (Madrid). Its software factory, located in Mexico City, has the capacity and infrastructure to support 450 developers in a multitude of projects. According to its website,[6] Hildebrando 'strives to build strong lasting business relationships with clients'; over 60 per cent of its revenue comes from customers who have done business with the company for more than five years. The client portfolio of the company shows how it has been successful in supporting a variety of businesses in their efforts to improve management. Hildebrando has 14 years of experience in developing information systems for a variety of industries – 14 years that have allowed it to develop not only a great amount of knowledge about the technology available but also extensive 'know-how' about its application in the business environment.

Overview of companies

The above cases give us an overview of the types of multinational businesses that have developed in central Mexico. They have been pushed into modernisation not only by industry specifics, but also by the restructuring of the city. Most are in the services sector, and that is the type of specialisation that the city is likely to continue to develop.

MONTERREY: MULTINATIONALS CLOSE TO THE BORDER[7]

The northern city of Monterrey has become the second largest manufacturing network in Mexico, just after central Mexico. Monterrey is in the state of Nuevo León, 200 kilometres south of Laredo, Texas. It has a great industrial tradition: for over a century, it has hosted some of the most symbolic companies in Mexico, such as Cervecería Cuauhtémoc Moctezuma and Fundidora de Monterrey (which shut down operations in 1986). Its businesses are known as some of the most innovative and creative in the whole of Latin America, not only in Mexico. Moreover, Monterrey's industrial strength lies in an important difference between it and other industrial cities in the Mexican border zones. In these other cities, *maquilas* dominate the business spectrum; in Monterrey, industries focus on the cement, glass, petrochemical, metallurgic and food and beverage sectors. Moreover, companies in Monterrey are said to have a long-lasting tradition of being able to function in both the Mexican and US markets.

According to *Forbes* magazine (29 March 2006), seven out of the 17 Mexican companies that appear in the list of the 2,000 largest in the world are based in Monterrey: Cemex, Femsa, Banorte, Coca-Cola Femsa, Alfa, Elektra and Soriana.

After the 1982 financial crisis in Mexico, the main problems faced by Monterrey companies were debt growth and an increase in 'idle capacity' as a consequence of market contraction and a fall in investment. Most companies implemented a strategy to re-finance their debts and facilitate the entry of foreign capital. The importance of the debt in this context can be seen from the following example. In 1986, the debts of Monterrey corporations represented one-third of total private debt in Mexico.[8] The response of several companies (Cemex, Vitro, IMSA, Pulsar and Alfa) was to reorient productive effort towards foreign markets, and to invest overseas. These strategies proved to be effective and allowed the companies to resist another financial crisis in 1995.

Cemex

The story of Cemex is amazing.[9] In the past 25 years of relentless changes, it has gone from being a local company in an underdeveloped country to being the third largest cement company in the world. The name of Monterrey is, now more than ever, linked with what the company stands for. The company emerged from local capital and was consolidated under the import substitution program of the 1940s to the 1960s. To begin with, it focused on local and national needs. However, the contraction of the national market due to the 1982 financial crisis resulted in a great change in the company's operational strategy. The events that took place in the international cement sector also affected the company's perception of opportunities and threats, since the European cement groups were starting to take over many plants in the United States, Canada and South America.

Cemex was forced to adapt and become aggressive to defend its own market in Mexico. Its initial strategy was to consolidate its position in the national market; at the same time it began exporting to international markets. By 1985 Cemex had a 33 per cent share of the whole Mexican cement market. Later, the company initiated a cycle of acquisitions in the national market: it bought Anahuac in 1987 and Tolteca in 1989. Such moves gave it 67 per cent of the domestic market, and it became the sixth largest world producer. Its exports grew, and in 1987 and 1988 over 27 per cent of its production went to world markets, especially to the United States. Since 1985 its strategy has focused on conquering more space in the US market through co-ownership and exports.

In 1990 the company had to modify its strategy because of an anti-dumping lawsuit in 1989 against Mexican cement. Thus, Cemex began to acquire cement plants in the United States so that it could sell directly to its clients in that market. This situation made the company consider the option of market diversification so that it would not have to depend only or mainly on the United States. This triggered the idea of becoming a global corporation and trying to locate in emerging markets such as Spain. In 1992, Cemex bought the company Valenciana de Cementos and LACSA in Spain, paying $1.849 million for both companies.

After these first moves Cemex began to acquire companies all over the world – in Venezuela in 1994; in Panama in 1994; and in the Dominican Republic, Colombia, the Philippines, Indonesia, Chile and Costa Rica in 1995–99. It is worth highlighting that during the 1995 crisis Cemex reinforced its world strategy and added to its trading business. In that year, it exported to 54 countries on four continents. Twenty-one per cent of what the company trades in these markets was produced in plants not owned by Cemex. In 2000 Cemex bought the US giant Southdown, becoming the most important cement producer in the United States. It is important to realise the significance of what the company did during the 1990s: of all the cement companies in the world, only Cemex is based in an underdeveloped country.

Cemex has continued to acquire companies throughout the world, particularly in emerging markets, where it has absorbed competitors and taken over their market share. The acquisition of the British company RMC in 2005 is particularly important. Cemex spent $5,000 million on the acquisition, as a result of which it will have access to the European Union market, particularly to the new member countries such as Hungary and Poland. At present Cemex is focusing on key markets such as Brazil, Russia, India and China. The world market is now the main pillar of its activities, and sales abroad represent 81 per cent of its business. As well as this good news, the company benefited when the US government finally removed the anti-dumping tariff on Mexican cement sales.

IMSA

The IMSA group, a very important producer of steel and metal products, has also sold some of its operations. For example, in April 2006 it sold all its operations in the Chilean CAP SA. However, the company maintained its dynamism because the sale was accompanied by an investment plan for the Latin American region estimated at $180 million in 2006 and by a restructuring of the company's operations. The group has decided to concentrate its capacity and operations in one steel company, IMSA

Acero. This decision made IMSA Acero the biggest steel company in Mexico in terms of sales. According to the group's estimates, the restructuring process will generate savings of over $600 million. The restructure involves changes in operations, creation of value and changes to staff. For example, the company has proposed the relocation of its Richmond, California, plant to Shreveport, Louisiana. It has also invested $120 million in enlarging its Monterrey station in order to produce a new line of steel sheet. This will diversify its products and be an innovation in the sector.

IMSA Group exports its products to over 30 countries on five continents. It has distribution and manufacturing operations in Mexico, the United States, Europe, Central America and South America. The importance of its activities in the international market is illustrated by the fact that 50 per cent of its income came from abroad in 2005.

Gruma

Grupo Maseca (Gruma), which produces food products, has 80 plants in 13 countries in North and South America. It exports its products to 50 countries. Gruma has a strategy for national and international expansion. On the national level, the company increased its market share of corn flour from 65 to 75 per cent when it bought its main competitor in Nuevo León, Agroinsa, in October 2005. Internationally, Gruma has aimed to extend its distribution and production points, focusing on the creation of plants in places that already demand the product but to which the product has to be brought from other places. For example, products for China had to be supplied by Los Angeles and products for Russia had to be supplied by Italy. Gruma is now building a plant in Shanghai, and it was expected to begin construction of a Russian plant in 2006. This should reduce costs and guarantee that products are fresh. Another example of Gruma's expansion strategy is the recent acquisition of the Rosita Investments factory in Australia, which provides an annual revenue of $22 million. The establishment of plants in China, Russia and Australia are especially important for Gruma's future growth. The company is concentrating on Asia and Oceania, where it projects an investment of $1,000 million in the next five years. The goal is to reach countries such as Malaysia, Indonesia and India. The next step for Gruma would be to enter Africa, which it plans to do in 2008.

Moreover, Gruma intends to double its capacity in the United States by 2009. It already has 20 per cent of the tortilla and corn flour market in the United States. This amounts to 50 per cent of its total profits and close to 60 per cent of its total income.

Even when it has sold companies, Gruma has followed a strategy of expanding to foreign markets. An example is the sale of the Venezuelan Molinos Nacionales CA. It allowed Gruma to buy more assets in another business, Derivados de Maíz Seleccionados SA, giving it a 60 per cent share of that company.

Femsa

Another successful group is Femsa, which has the second largest Coca-Cola bottling group in the world; one of the most important brewing companies in Mexico; and one of the fastest growing businesses in the world, the Oxxo convenience-store chain.

It began as a traditional company in Monterrey, but has been able to adapt to new times and to create innovative products and services. With some of the most popular beers in the country and internationally, the company has become specialised in the beer business and is now expanding towards new markets, such as Canada and Brazil. Its main beers – Dos Equis (XX) and Sol – have been successfully introduced into Canada; in Brazil the company has bought 68 per cent of Cervejarias Kaiser, allowing it to enter this new space. Moreover, Femsa has a national expansion plan – to build a mega-distribution centre in Puebla, accompanied by a brewing plant. This will involve an investment of $46 million and is expected to generate more than 500 direct jobs and benefit 12,000 farmers. The Femsa beverages are sold in about two million sale points, satisfying more than 170 million people in nine countries. However, the main export market for these types of products is the United States, which still accounts for 90 per cent of the company's exports.

The case of Oxxo is an impressive one. It is opening stores at a faster rate in Mexico – one every 14 hours – than Starbucks is in the United States. This business has an annual growth rate of 20 per cent; the company expects to open more than 650 stores per year. Femsa's business is still confined to Mexico, but the company expected to begin its expansion into Latin America in 2006.

Vitro

Other big companies have not had the same success. Some have had to adapt their strategies – for example, by restructuring their main activities or adopting policies to attract foreign investment to balance domestic competition. Others are struggling for survival, with huge debts and low sales, and could eventually disappear.

An example is the glass company Vitro, a major participant in flat glass, glass containers and the glassware business. The company has been severely affected by large debt, estimated at around $1.3 billion in early 2006. This has forced it to concentrate its efforts on its competitive lines and on increasing its exports. Vitro has followed a divestment strategy to allow it to remain competitive in its core products. By July 2005 the company had ended seven strategic alliances with foreign partners in non-strategic sectors. In the last two years, Vitro has sold five companies in sectors such as household appliances. However, with one exception, the foreign partner has kept the plants in Mexico.

As mentioned above, some sales are due to the need to reduce the amount of debt. Examples are the sale of Crisa by Vitro and sales by Cydsa (see below) in 2005. However, other sales are due not only to the need to cut down debt but also to focus the company's production in one sector, concentrating and increasing the expansion potential of a limited number of products. An example is Vitro's sales of Vifisa (dedicated to the development of fibres), Vancan, Bosco Plastics and Química M. These sales were accompanied by an investment plan of $100 million for 2006 with the objective of reinforcing the businesses the company now sees as strategic: flat glass and glass containers, with special emphasis on the automobile industry and the food sector. In the case of the automobile industry the investment was to be around $9 million in 2006, involving the development of new production platforms, the introduction of new products and productivity improvement; such changes should result in an increase in sales of over 6 per cent. Vitro is also building up new alliances and acquisitions, mainly in its flat glass division; for example, it recently formed an association with Asahi Glass, looking for technological improvements.

For some companies, divestment and concentration have been accompanied by not only increased investment in strategic sectors inside Mexico, but also expansion to certain geographic zones possessing a great potential for growth. For example, the growing Hispanic market in the United States appears to be an opportunity for Vitro and has given the company export growth rates of over 10 per cent: in the first trimester of 2005 alone, the sale of glass containers grew by 18 per cent in comparison to 2004, while exports grew by 12 per cent.

Alfa

Alfa is a very important conglomerate that has displayed a similar strategy to the one implemented by Vitro. Its annual sales amount to about $6.3 billion. For many years the group operated in a wide range of industries such as steel and the food and canning sector. In recent years, it has focused on strengthening its most profitable businesses. This strategy led to the company selling Hylsamex (steel) to its Argentinean partner Techint. However, the strategy has favoured an expansion of some activities. An example is Nemak, which produces aluminium engine heads for automobiles in plants near Monterrey and in the Czech Republic. Nemak currently supplies 23 automobile plants in North America, Europe, South America, China and Australia. It recently acquired two aluminium casting companies in Canada and it is planning to set up operations in China and the United States.

Sigma, in the food sector, is another strategic company for Alfa, given its high profitability and its consolidated position. Finally, the petrochemical industry represents another opportunity for Alfa; in 2004 the company increased its foreign sales in this industry by 43 per cent.

Cydsa and Pulsar

There are exceptions to the success of Monterrey companies. Examples are Cydsa and Pulsar. Cydsa was born in 1945, at the beginning of the import substitution period. Specialising in chemicals, plastic and textiles, the group had 18 companies by 2000. The group began in the textile and cellulose sector, but its largest waves of expansion took place in the 1960s thanks to alliances with foreign companies such as BF Goodrich and a diversification of its products through the acquisition of chemical and water companies. This was probably one of the companies that better managed the crises of the 1980s, but after the 1995 shock sales stopped growing and began to decrease; in 2005 the company reported a major loss of $44.6 million. Today, this company has sold all its subsidiaries in order to pay its debts and has had to sell 60 per cent of its assets for foreign capital.

Grupo Pulsar, now extinct, was once one of the most important corporations in Monterrey. It began in 1981, on the eve of the Mexican economic crisis. In 1985 it acquired one of the most important tobacco companies in Mexico, Cigarrera La

Moderna, as well as an agricultural company. It also set up a construction company, Grupo Krone. In 1988, it acquired an insurance company, Seguros La Comercial, and entered the agriculture–genetic engineering sector in an attempt to produce special seeds. In the 1990s, Grupo Pulsar expanded by buying insurance and agricultural companies in Mexico. In 1995, it created Seminis, a high-tech fruit and vegetable seed producer. It continued to create companies and diversify its products in 1996. For example, it formed Bionova, a company for packing and processing fresh products; Merkafon, a teleservices company; and Omega, a real estate company. In 1997 it entered the health business sector after signing an agreement for a joint venture with the Hospital Medica Sur; it has control over the Santa Engracia Hospital in Monterrey. At its peak, the Savia holding through which all these enterprises were managed reported sales close to $3 billion and had operations in 110 countries.

The company's main focus was seeds and genetically modified products. In its best years, the company was able to gain 22 per cent of the international seed market. To finance its expansion, the company acquired a $1.3 billion debt and started to sell some of its other businesses. In 1997 it sold its tobacco company Cigarrera La Moderna for $1.7 billion to British American Tobacco. And later it sold Seguros Comercial América (an insurance company) to the Dutch company ING.

Nevertheless, Pulsar was unable to sustain all its projects and began to sell them. The main cause of Seminis's downfall was an overinvestment in seed improvement, leading to overproduction at a time when demand was contracting, particularly in the US market. Campaigns against genetically modified food by environmentalist NGOs like Greenpeace also contributed to the company's problems. Other aggravating factors were climate change and a strong Mexican currency, which acted to the detriment of Seminis exports. In 2003 Pulsar had to sell Seminis to the Fox Pain investment fund, which later ceded it to Monsanto.

SCENARIOS FOR MEXICAN FOREIGN DIRECT INVESTMENT ABROAD

As the Mexican economy has opened to global competition and companies aim to become competitive at world level, Mexican firms have accepted the challenge and are moving toward transnational businesses. More and more firms are likely to follow this trend, but it is too soon to have a clear idea of how they will evolve. To understand the behaviour of the large Mexican multinationals, we have to take into account the strong shocks suffered by the Mexican economy in the last 25 years. These include at least two financial crises, in 1982 and 1995; a very aggressive liberalisation policy; and slow or modest growth rates. A small group of Mexican companies were able to overcome the internal conditions and became multinationals. They have been very successful, mainly in areas requiring medium-tech capability.

Moreover, government policies at a local level are attempting to minimise the impact of exports as they encourage people to change from traditional manufacturing exports to other manufacturing exports. Two examples can be cited. One is in the state of Queretaro, where people are promoting the aerospace industry. Some investment has been made in this new Mexican industry to provide components to multinationals in the aerospace sector. Another example is the establishment of the so-called knowledge industries in Monterrey. Here the local government is supporting joint efforts by businesses and universities to produce goods in the information and knowledge industries as a way to break reliance on traditional manufacturing industries.

Other companies have struggled to survive amidst international competition. Outstanding debts have forced many to downsize and to consolidate in areas where they are relatively competitive. The pattern of indebtedness in Mexico has been different from that of Asian multinationals. In Mexico, increasing debt was initially a response to financial crisis and a slump of sales in the domestic market. In contrast, the debts taken on by Asian multinationals mainly served to make them more productive and to support industrial and technological change. Mexican companies have had to sell plants and non-strategic business to get fresh resources to enable them to pay their debts and finance new investments. Most have gone abroad to widen their businesses and benefit from more dynamic markets. Some have gradually disappeared in a process marked by destruction of SMEs in the Mexican private sector.[10]

The managers of big companies have pointed out that high costs and the lack of incentives in Mexico have forced them to look for better opportunities in other parts of the world. During the last five years they have invested a total of $16 billion dollars abroad. In 2005 they invested $5.2 billion. This investment is being used for foreign takeovers, but the creation of new overseas plants in the manufacturing sectors is a very important aspect of their international engagement. Nonetheless, given the low level of intra-firm trade for Mexican multinationals, their globalisation will not necessarily translate into an incentive for future Mexican economic development, which will continue to be a huge challenge.

Finally, we think that an isolated effort by a large company is not enough to encourage the development of new high-tech industries. A clear example is Pulsar's experience with its Seminis project. Successful stories reveal that success will require resolute state support and alliance between different Mexican groups to share risks and minimise the possibilities of failure. These will be decisive factors for Mexico, with the problems that it faces nowadays.

NOTES

1. Foreign-owned assembly plants.
2. The following figures are from Chami (2005).
3. See Garrido (2006).
4. This information comes from Pozas (2005).
5. As specified on the web page of Banco de México on May 2006 (<www.banxico.org.mx>).
6. See <http://www.hildebrando.com.mx/>.
7. In Monterrey there is an important group of scholars dedicated to the study of the evolution of the city's corporations and their relevance at the national and international level. We would like to particularly thank Mario Cerutti and Maria de los Angeles Pozas, who have published the results of major studies on the issue.
8. See Cerutti *et al.* (1999: 75).
9. The following information is taken mainly from a historical review of Monterrey's multinationals by Cerutti (2000, 2003). Information on the current situation of and future planning for Monterrey's multinationals was taken from local newspapers such as *El Norte* and *Milenio*.

10 According to *Reforma* (14 April 2006), 11,000 SMEs in the manufacturing sectors were shut down between 2001 and 2005, leading to a loss of 529,000 jobs. In the case of Monterrey, the share of local suppliers to *maquila* companies fell between 1994 and 2004. This led to an increased presence of foreign companies in the supplier networks (Fouquet and Moreno 2006).

REFERENCES

Cerutti, M. (2000) *Propietarios, Empresarios y Empresa en el Norte de México.[Owners, Entrepreneurs and Enterprise in the North of Mexico]*, México, Siglo XXI Editores.

Cerutti, M. (ed.) (2003) *Del Mercado Protegido al Mercado Global: Monterrey 1925–2000 [From a Protected Market to the Global Market: Monterrey 1925–2000]*, México, Trillas.

Cerutti, M., I. Ortega and L. Palacios (1999) 'Grupos economicos en el norte de México [Business groups in the north of Mexico]', in E. Gutierrez Garza, *La Globalización en Nuevo Leon [Globalization in Nuevo Leon]*, México, ediciones El Caballito.

Chami, J.B. (2005) 'Competing for the US import market: NAFTA and non-NAFTA countries', paper presented at the conference 'Free Trade in the Americas', Baylor University, 6–7 October 2005.

Fouquet, A. and R. Moreno (2006) 'Ilusiones y transformaciones en la maquiladora de exportación regiomontana [Illusions and transformations in the exporting assembly manufacturing of Monterrey]', *Comercio Exterior*, 56(4): 312–25.

Garrido, C. (2006) 'Empresas, economía nacional y sistema financiero en México. Evolución desde 1995, tendencias y desafíos [Domestic economy, businesses and financial system in Mexico. Evolution, trends and challenges since 1995]', pp. 17–69 in María de los Ángeles Pozas (ed.), *Estructura y Dinámica de la Gran Empresa en México: Cinco Estudios Sobre su Realidad Reciente [Structure and Dynamics of the Large Enterprises in Mexico: Five Studies upon its Recent Reality]*, México: El Colegio de México.

Garrido, C. (1999) 'Las multinacionales mexicanas [Mexican multinational enterprises]', in D. Chudnovsky (ed.), *Las Multinacionales Latinoamericanas: Sus Estrategias en Un Mundo Globalizado*. Buenos Aires: Fondo de Cultura Económica.

INEGI (Instituto Nacional de Estadística, Geografía e Informática [National Institute of Statistics, Geography and Informatics]) (2004) 'National Economic Census' [Censo Económico Nacional], <http://www.inegi.gob.mx>.

Pozas, M.A. (2005) 'Nuevas tendencias en la inserción de las grandes empresas en la economía mundial [New trends in the insertion of large enterprises in the world economy]', paper presented at the workshop 'El futuro del trabajo en México [The future of labour in Mexico]', AMET, Tecnológico de Monterrey, 11 October.

8 Emerging transnational corporations from East Asia: the case of mainland China

Edward K.Y. Chen and Ping Lin

INTRODUCTION

For a long time, developing countries acted only as host countries for multinational activities and never as home countries. But multinational activities are no longer monopolised by developed countries. Since the late 1960s, we have witnessed the rise of transnational corporations (TNCs) from developing countries, led by Hong Kong TNCs and those from Taiwan and South Korea, among others. We call these the first generation of TNCs from less developed countries (LDCs). Since the 1990s, more and more TNCs from developing countries have emerged; these 'second-generation' TNCs from LDCs include the Chinese TNCs such as Haier, TCL, Huawei and Lenovo that have received worldwide attention.

The emergence of developing country foreign direct investment (FDI) and TNCs can be explained by the 'flying geese hypothesis' (Akamatsu 1962; Chen 1991), which stipulates that economies in a region will undertake a subregional industrial division of labour.[1] More industrialised economies will pass on their mature industries to the next tier of economies via FDI in the face of changing comparative advantage. Japan was the first to pass on industries such as textiles and clothing and electronic and electrical products to the then newly industrialising economies of Hong Kong, Singapore, Taiwan and South Korea. Hong Kong was the first developing economy to pass on its mature industries to other developing economies, in the 1970s. Hong Kong manufacturing firms that undertook FDI in the 1970s were therefore among the first of the so-called Third World TNCs (Chen 1981, 1983). Data from the United Nations Conference on Trade and Development (UNCTAD) show that today most of the TNCs from developing economies are based in East and Southeast Asia; during the period 2001–03, Hong Kong accounted for 31 per cent of the average annual total outflows from developing economies, Singapore 25 per cent, Taiwan 15 per cent, China 11 per cent, South Korea 8 per cent, and Malaysia 3.4 per cent.[2]

In this chapter, we examine the characteristics of China's outward FDI and identify the major motives of Chinese TNCs for their investments abroad. In line with the existing literature (Behrman 1972; Dunning 1993, 1998), China's outward FDI motives can be classified as resource seeking, market seeking, efficiency seeking, and strategic asset seeking. While seeking natural resources is important, we will argue that strategic asset seeking is the dominant driving force for Chinese TNCs going abroad. This is mainly due to the fact that massive FDI inflow and the entry of the world's leading multinationals to China during the past two decades have put tremendous competitive pressure on Chinese firms in domestic markets. Such competition pressure has forced top Chinese firms to go abroad to acquire complementary assets such as established brand names, advanced technology, and a reputation from their presence in advanced economies. In other words, outward FDI is to a large extent a response to FDI inflow to China and has been used as a vehicle for the acquisition of advanced technology abroad.

The rise of LDC transnationals raises a number of interesting issues. For example, do the existing general theories of FDI by developed countries explain the role of TNCs from developing countries in the development of the host countries? In the initial stages of development, the characteristics of TNCs from developed countries are sometimes different from those from developing countries. Below, we discuss three main areas of difference.

First, ownership and control are typically different in TNCs from LDCs and TNCs from developed countries. Most LDC transnationals establish joint ventures with local partners in the host country rather than establishing wholly-owned subsidiaries there. This occurred, for example, for some South Korean TNCs. Furthermore, Lecraw (1981), using discriminant analysis in a statistical study of FDI in economies of the Association of Southeast Asian Nations (ASEAN), finds that LDC transnationals have lower foreign equity participation than developed country TNCs. The difference in ownership pattern is not a surprise because LDC transnationals usually produce mature products using standardised technology and with high price elasticity of demand. Thus, the bargaining power of LDC firms is usually weaker than their developed country counterparts and it is much more difficult for them to establish wholly-owned subsidiaries in the host countries, even if they want to. In addition, LDC transnationals are not as anxious to obtain complete control as developed country TNCs are, because they have little fear of losing control over standardised technology, while developed country TNCs are usually anxious to monopolise the relatively advanced technology that they introduce. More importantly, LDC transnationals, even when given a choice, tend to prefer joint ownership with local entrepreneurs so that they can gain knowledge of local distribution channels and local economic and political environments. In some cases, LDC transnationals go for joint ventures because this form of ownership is politically more acceptable to the host country government and because local entrepreneurs can provide the financial resources and the administrative staff. Today, LDC transnationals are less likely to enter into joint ventures than they have been in the past, as illustrated by the Chinese TNCs discussed below. Very often they now invest abroad through mergers and acquisitions (M&As) to gain majority or complete control. Technology mobility and capital mobility make it easier for LDC transnationals to compete in host countries than it has been in the past.

The second area where LDC transnationals differ from developed country TNCs is their geographical distribution. Developed country TNCs tend to establish subsidiaries worldwide, but LDC transnationals usually operate in their own region; they sometimes operate in other developing countries, but only occasionally operate in developed countries. This phenomenon can be partially explained by the product lifecycle hypothesis: LDC transnationals can best exploit their advantages in other developing countries. Another important reason is increasing regional economic cooperation and integration in the region.

In this chapter, we examine the case of China, which indicates that the path of investing abroad by today's LDC transnationals is more diverse. Unlike earlier generations of LDC transnationals, which tend to invest in developing countries within their region, many of today's LDC transnationals choose to invest in developing countries outside their region. For example, investments by Asian TNCs in Latin America have become more significant recently. Occasionally, some LDC transnationals may invest substantially in developed countries at an earlier stage of their development (as is the case with Haier in China).

The third major area of difference between TNCs from LDCs and those from developed countries concerns technology transfer and scale of production. LDC transnationals tend to transfer less advanced and less capital-intensive technologies to host countries and the scale of production is usually smaller than in their developed country counterparts. Earlier studies in both Southeast Asia and Latin America demonstrated that LDC transnationals tend to transfer to host countries technologies which have been adapted for developing country situations. In comparing the factor intensity between LDC transnationals and their developed country counterparts, it is nonetheless important to examine whether the differences in factor intensity are the result of their involvement in different industries or the result of the choice of technology in similar lines of production. It is often observed that LDC transnationals tend to operate in industries with low advertising intensity and/or low R&D intensity. Thus, the greater amount of labour-intensive technologies used by LDC transnationals may simply reflect the fact that LDC transnationals tend to operate in more labour-intensive industries. Even if the comparison of factor intensity between LDC and developed country TNCs is made with reference to a single industry, there is still the possibility that LDC transnationals tend to engage in the production of those products which are less sophisticated and less capital-intensive within the product range of the industry under consideration.

Today, the second-generation LDC transnationals often have to compete in similar products and in similar industries as domestic firms and developed country TNCs in their host countries (as in the case of Huawei to be examined in this chapter). They have to use the most recent technology and capitalise on their lower costs of production so as to survive and excel in the host country markets. Thus, the distinction between developed country TNCs and LDC transnationals in factor intensity and level of technology has eroded over time.

There are also differences between the first and second generations of LDC transnationals. In the earlier years, LDC transnationals from South Korea and Taiwan, like those from Japan, were mostly companies which were protected and even assisted by government policies before they went overseas to start operation. Those from Hong Kong were relatively small companies which invested abroad because of lower labour costs and which bypassed trade restrictions when their overseas markets were threatened. The second-generation, big LDC transnationals of today are different. They often invest abroad because of the severe competition at home imposed by both domestic and foreign firms. In such cases, the companies are often not well prepared when they begin their global businesses. They do not have strong ownership-specific advantages and their only means of survival is often very competitive prices. This competition effect reflects the fact that today's world economy is much more integrated and much freer than it was two to three decades ago, so that firms' investments abroad are influenced more by market forces than by government protection.

In the rest of this chapter, we first review the trends and patterns of China's outward FDI in recent years. Then we identify the major motivations of Chinese investors. We differentiate two types of outward FDI they undertake. One is investment by state-owned enterprises; these are mostly in natural resource industries and aim to secure an adequate supply of resources (for example, energy) for the rapidly growing Chinese economy. The other type of Chinese outward FDI is mostly market driven. It is motivated primarily by the desire to seek new markets overseas; strategic assets, such as established brands; advanced technology; or even a reputation for being able to survive and profit in domestic markets in advanced economies. We then present evidence to support the view that the motive to seek strategic assets is a direct consequence of China's opening up its own markets to foreign competition and of Chinese firms' declining market share and profit margin on their home turf. At the end of the chapter, we relate Chinese experience to the general framework of FDI and TNCs – the ownership–internalisation–location paradigm – and argue that this paradigm explains the emergence of Chinese TNCs in recent years. We present three detailed case studies of Chinese TNCs – Haier, Huawei and TCL – in Annex 8.1.

AN OVERVIEW OF CHINA'S OUTWARD FDI

Trends

China's outward FDI started when China opened up to the outside world in 1978. During 1978–85, China's outward FDI, mainly by state-owned enterprises, was guided by the central government for the purpose of trade and economic cooperation with other countries. From 1986 to 1991, restrictive policies were liberalised and non-state firms were allowed to invest abroad. From 1992 to 1998, there was a surge in offshore investment by local and provincial enterprises, often in Hong Kong (see Wong and Chan 2003; Wang 2005).

China started to formulate its 'go out' policy in the early 1990s. The policy took shape in 1997 when the former president Jiang Zemin declared that Chinese enterprises 'should better utilise both the domestic and overseas markets and resources both in and outside China' (Jiang Zemin 1997). Since then, attracting FDI inflow and 'going out' have been regarded as the 'two wheels' of China's opening-up policy. In 2000, the 'go out' policy was included in China's tenth Five-Year Plan for National Economic and Social Development in anticipation of China's accession to the World Trade Organization (WTO). Chinese outward FDI has grown considerably since the early 1990s. By the end of 2003, China's accumulated outward FDI was $37 billion, surpassing that of South Korea, with accumulated outward FDI of $34.5 billion (Table 8.1). In

Table 8.1   Outward FDI stock in selected countries ($ billion)

Country	1985	1995	2003
China	0.01	15.8	37.0
South Korea	0.5	10.2	34.5
Taiwan	0.2	25.1	65.2
Singapore	4.4	35	90.9
Malaysia	1.4	11.0	29.7
Thailand	0.0	2.3	3.3
India	0.0	0.3	5.1
Japan	44.0	238.5	335.5
United States	238.4	699.0	2,069.0
United Kingdom	100.3	304.9	1,128.60

Source: UNCTAD, FDI/TNC database, <http://www.unctad.org/fdistatistics>.

2005, China's outward FDI reached $12.26 billion in non-financial sectors, up 123 per cent from the previous year (China Ministry of Commerce 2005c).

During the past two decades, Chinese TNCs have invested in many countries, but especially in Hong Kong, the United States and, to a lesser extent, the Russian Federation and Australia (Table 8.2). Table 8.3 shows the breakdown of outward FDI by all Chinese firms that invested overseas between 1991 and 2004; about half of the total investments were in Hong Kong. Within Asia, Hong Kong is the most attractive place for Mainland China enterprises, followed by Japan, South Korea, Singapore and Macau, although more and more Chinese enterprises have gone to developing countries in Southeast Asia since the Asian financial crisis in 1997.[3] In recent years, more and more Chinese firms have invested in Russia and other former members of the Soviet Union. For instance, in 2004, 52 Chinese enterprises gained approval to invest in Russia, compared to 19 in Germany and 13 in the United Kingdom. Chinese firms have also invested in countries in Latin America and Africa (China Ministry of Commerce 2005a). Some of China's leading producers of household appliances, such as Gree and Chunlan, have invested in South America.

In terms of industry breakdown, a significant proportion of Chinese outward FDI takes place in natural resource related industries. This can be seen from Table 8.4, which shows that three of the five Chinese TNCs on the list of the top 50 TNCs from developing countries in 2003 were in the resources sector. In fact, for much of the past two decades, the Chinese government has sought to ensure the supply of domestically scarce products through outward FDI. Chinese firms have been actively investing abroad in such key sectors as minerals, petroleum, timber and fisheries. For example, the China International Trust and Investment Corp (CITIC) purchased stakes in Australian mineral companies back in the 1980s; the China National Petroleum Corporation (CNPC) recently acquired the Canadian-based company PetroKaz; and

Table 8.2 Outward FDI from China by destination country, 1979–2003[a]

Rank[b]	Country	No. of projects					1979–2003	Value of investment (1979–2003) ($ mill)
		1999	2000	2001	2002	2003		
1	Hong Kong	24	15	26	40	73	2,098	4,340.7
2	United States	21	15	19	41	83	786	947.6
3	Russian Federation	12	14	12	27	41	523	546.2
4	Australia	3	13	6	15	10	225	464.4
5	Denmark	0	0	0	0	1	3	459.7
6	Canada	1	8	4	4	11	155	443.8
7	South Korea	1	5	2	7	10	72	302.5
8	Thailand	3	6	9	5	11	245	263.8
9	Macau	3	4	6	2	9	238	214.2
10	Peru	1	1	2	0	3	23	202.1
11	Indonesia	0	1	2	6	6	65	168.1
12	Mexico	2	1	1	1	2	47	167.4
13	Cambodia	13	7	7	3	4	65	158.4
14	Bermuda	2	0	1	0	1	11	148.4
15	Zambia	4	3	3	1	0	18	134.4
16	Brazil	1	3	4	8	6	73	129.0
17	South Africa	14	17	2	3	10	108	126.5
18	Singapore	6	6	3	6	16	188	97.9
19	Vietnam	2	17	12	20	17	90	93.1
20	Japan	1	2	6	11	14	250	89.6
21	Germany	1	1	3	6	17	167	75.6
22	Mongolia	15	12	7	7	9	78	73.9
23	Myanmar	1	7	3	5	0	38	66.1
24	Mali	1	1	0	0	0	5	58.1
25	Egypt	5	3	2	3	5	32	56.3
26	Nigeria	2	1	8	9	13	62	56.0
27	United Arab Emirates	2	3	3	0	8	78	50.1
28	New Zealand	0	0	2	2	2	28	49.4
29	Papua New Guinea	0	1	0	0	0	20	44.7
30	Kazakhstan	7	5	1	3	8	59	43.1
Total[c]		220	243	232	350	510	7,470	1,1427.2

Notes:
a Projects approved by the Ministry of Commerce.
b Ranked by total value of investment during 1979–2003.
c Total of all destinations, not just the top 30.
Source: China Ministry of Commerce (2005b).

the China National Offshore Oil Corporation (CNOOC) recently bid unsuccessfully for the US-based company Unocal.[4] This pattern of investment in natural resource oriented industries by Chinese firms is not surprising, given former president Jiang Zemin's approach to markets and resources (see above).

Table 8.3   Outward FDI from China by destination region, 1991–2004 ($ million)

Year	Total no. of projects approved	Value of investment in all projects	Asia	Africa	Europe	North America	Latin America	Oceania
1991	207	367.0	55	7	80	34	16	15
1992	355	195.3	106	23	131	46	26	23
1993	293	95.9	107	28	58	48	20	32
1994	106	70.6	49	12	14	17	6	8
1995	119	106.4	61	26	7	12	10	3
1996	102	293.8	53	23	8	10	4	4
1997	128	169.3	55	41	22	1	4	5
1998	266	259.0	85	40	78	21	32	10
1999	220	590.6	86	54	34	22	21	3
2000	243	551.0	102	52	32	23	19	15
2001	232	707.5	106	45	32	23	17	9
2002	350	982.6	141	36	63	45	46	19
2003	510	2086.9	279	53	47	94	25	12
2004[a]	829	3711.8	354	77	164	115	78	41

Note:
a The figures for 2004 are for non-financial sectors only.
Source: China Ministry of Commerce (2005a, 2005b).

Types of investment

Greenfield investment (by establishing solely funded subsidiaries or joint ventures with local partners) has been a major format of China's outward FDI, particularly in the fields of home electrical appliances, electronics, and textile industries. For example, China's top electronic appliance makers – Haier, TCL and Gree – have all set up production lines outside China, and some Chinese enterprises have chosen to set up R&D centres overseas, often in developed countries. Huawei Technologies, a leading China-based high-tech enterprise in the communication equipment industry, has established eight regional R&D headquarters and 32 branches overseas. More and more Chinese firms are using cross-border M&As as a means of outward FDI. In 2005, Chinese companies channelled $9.8 billion into overseas acquisitions, up from $3.8 billion in 2004. The Ministry of Commerce forecasts that China's outward FDI will rocket by at least 22 per cent annually over the next five years, with the cumulative total projected to top $60 billion by 2010.[5] Table 8.4 contains information about some recent major cross-border M&As initiated by Chinese companies, including Lenovo's acquisition of IBM's personal computer (PC) section, which caused much attention worldwide.

Cross-border M&As by Chinese firms can be further divided into two subcategories. The first is resources exploitation. An example is CNOOC, which became the biggest

Table 8.4 Major cross-border mergers and acquisitions by Chinese manufacturers, 2002–05

Year	Acquiring firm	Target	Industry	Value ($ million)
2002	TCL	Schneider Electronics, Germany	Electronics	8.2
2002	China Netcom	Asia Global Crossing Ltd, Hong Kong	Telcommunications	270
2002	Huali Group of Shanghai	Moltech Power Systems, US	Machinery / motor	20
2002	Shanghai Automotive Industry Corp. (SAIC)	GM-Daewoo Motor alliance (equity stake), Korea	Automobile	60
2002	Haixin Group	Glenoit Crop Speciality Fabrics (sliver knit pile fabric division), US	Fabric	14
2003	BOE Technology	Hynix Semiconductor flatpanel display unit, Korea	LCD	380
2003	BOE Technology	26.4% stake in TPV (a PC monitor manufacturer, Korea	PC monitor	135
2003	TCL	Thomson (TV production business)	TV	517
2004	Lenovo	IBM PC units, US	Computers	1,750
2005	China National	PetroKazakhstan	Petroleum	4,180

Note: LCD = thin film transistor liquid crystal display
Sources: UNCTAD cross-border M&A database (<http://www.unctad.org/fdistatistics>); PriceWaterhouse Coopers (<http://www.pwchk.com>); Deng (2006); *BusinessWeek*, various issues.

offshore oil producer in Indonesia by buying off the stakes of some local companies.[6] The second is the extension of production and marketing worldwide. This is the most common activity among Chinese firms investing abroad. Examples include Shanghai Automotive and TCL. The former bought 10 per cent of the shares of GM Daewoo and the latter purchased the bankrupt Schneider, a leading German electronics company. Wanxiang Group, one of the top Chinese companies in the automotive parts industry, bought up UAI, an American automotive parts producer facing delisting in the National Association of Securities Dealers Automated Quotations (NASDAQ), at a cost of $2.8 million. This deal pulled Wanxiang's marketing cost down dramatically as UAI buys $25 million worth of brakes from Wanxiang every year.[7]

In general, Chinese TNCs have been quite flexible about what form of outward FDI they undertake. For instance, TCL's investments in Vietnam and Europe have taken the form of acquisition of local producers and/or established local brand names, whereas its investment in India takes the form of joint venture. Similarly, Haier has used M&As in its entry to Italy, and joint ventures in some Asian countries. The increasing tendency to use cross-border acquisitions is directly related to the strategic asset seeking motive mentioned above. It also reflects Chinese TNCs' strong desire to become global players quickly.

Ownership of Chinese TNCs

During the past two decades, and particularly in the 1990s, Chinese TNCs started to attract attention throughout the word. Table 8.5 shows the top Chinese TNCs that made the list of the top 50 non-financial TNCs from developing countries in 2003. Currently, most of China's top TNCs are giant state-owned companies and are in resource related industries. According to the Ministry of Commerce (2005b), 43 per cent of all outward foreign investors in 2003 that had gone through the Ministry of Commerce's approval process were state-owned. The remainder were private, limited,

Table 8.5 Chinese firms in the top 50 largest non-financial TNCs from developing economies in 2003

Corporation	Foreign asset rank	Industry	Assets ($ million)	Sales ($ million)	Employment (No. of people)
China Ocean Shipping (Group) Company	7	Transport and storage	8,547	6,076	4,600
China National Petroleum Corporation	13	Petroleum exploration, refining, distribution	4,060	5,218	22,000
China State Construction Engineering Corporation	19	Construction	3,417	2,716	17,051
China National Offshore Oil Corporation	38	Petroleum and natural gas	1,467	1,877	1,000
China Minerals Corporation	46	Metals mining and processing	1,150	1,933	973

Source: UNCTAD, World Investment Report 2005; <http://www.unctad.org/wir> or <http://www.unctad.org/fdistatistics>.

holding or collectively owned companies. When the finance sectors are included in the statistics, some state-owned banks also rank highly (Table 8.6).

The large scale of the state-owned enterprises may stem largely from such firms receiving privileged access to capital and technology and, perhaps most importantly, receiving government protection in important sectors such as resources and finance. On the other hand, the competitive strength of major global TNCs may have dampened the emergence of home-grown private TNCs in sectors that are relatively open to foreign competition and FDI. However, the most well-known Chinese TNCs (for example, Haier, Huawei, Lenovo, TCL, Galanz) have established themselves in sectors that have been the most open to foreign competition, such as the electronic and electrical industries.

MOTIVATIONS OF CHINESE TNCS

The literature on TNCs has identified four types of outward FDI:

- resource seeking FDI, which aims to secure abroad natural resources which are either unavailable or too expensive in the home country;
- market seeking FDI, which drives TNCs to expand their production and sales in overseas markets;
- efficiency seeking FDI, whereby a TNC invests in other countries in order to improve its productivity (for example, by moving its production to countries with lower labour costs); and
- strategic asset seeking FDI, whereby firms pursue long-term strategic objectives by purchasing overseas assets (for example, established brand names, advanced technologies and local capacities, including R&D and know-how) to improve their global competitiveness (Behrman 1972; Dunning 1993, 1998).

Table 8.6 Presence of Chinese TNCs in 2005 Fortune Global 500 and Asian top 50 companies

Asia 50	Global 500 rank	Company	Revenue ($ million)
7	31	Sinopec	75,076.70
9	40	China State Grid	71,290.20
10	46	China National Petroleum	67,723.80
41	212	China Life Insurance	24,980.60
45	224	China Mobile	23,957.60
49	229	Industrial & Commercial Bank of China	23,444.60

Source: Fortune Global 500, 2005.

According to Dunning (1998: 50), 'the most significant change in the motives for FDI over the last two decades has been the repaid growth of strategic asset seeking FDI'. While traditional FDI motivations were based on how to exploit or transfer firms' resources to a host country, asset seeking FDI is undertaken in order to access and gain new knowledge or acquire necessary strategic assets in a host country. Put differently, FDI is used as a means for TNCs to tap into or develop strategic resources in a foreign market – for example, market intelligence, technological know-how, management expertise, or simply reputation from being established in a prestigious market. The asset-seeking perspective emphasises that FDI is 'pulled' towards centres of innovation located in recipient countries. This backward flow of knowledge and technology from the host to investing countries is not new. Earlier studies (e.g. Lall 1983) discussed it at length with reference to South Korean and Taiwanese TNCs. Today, the second-generation LDC transnationals are motivated not just by the desire for new technologies but by the desire for other strategic assets as well.

All four types of motivation apply to Chinese TNCs, but there are some distinct features.

Resource seeking investment

As mentioned earlier, the search for resources abroad has been a major motivation for investment by some Chinese companies since the early 1980s. The Shanghai Office of the Germany-based Roland Berger Strategy Consultants recently surveyed an élite group of top 50 leading Chinese firms. They found (von Keller and Zhou 2003) that seeking natural resources is the main imperative for outward FDI for 20 per cent of the firms surveyed. Examples of such motivation are the international expansions of large state-owned companies such as CNOOC and CNPC. Another example is in the steel industry. Shanghai Baosteel has invested in six joint ventures in Australia, Brazil and South Africa to gain access to both iron-ore mining and steel marketing (Deng 2004). As China's economy grows rapidly, and with the rising demand for energy and raw materials, the motivation for overseas investment in natural resources is likely to remain strong. Most outward FDI in resource seeking is conducted by state-owned enterprises.

Market seeking investment

An important motive for TNCs to establish production lines abroad is the search for new markets. This is also true of China, despite its vast domestic market. Von Keller and Zhou (2003) found that, for 60 per cent of Chinese TNCs, the search for markets was the strongest motivation for outward investment. Examples of this type of motivation are TCL's entry into Vietnam, and its purchase of Schneider AG in Germany; Huawei's expansion in eastern Europe; and Haier's purchase of an Italian refrigerator facility. Annex 8.1 provides more details of these cases.

The market seeking motive may also be important when there are trade and/or non-trade barriers which favour local production over exporting. When such barriers exist in foreign markets, there is a 'jumping the tariff' incentive for outward FDI. For example, the Haier Group established its manufacturing facilities in the United States partially to avoid American quota restrictions and potential anti-dumping suits (Deng 2004).[8]

Strategic asset seeking investment

Some Chinese firms have invested in developed economies in both North America and Europe. They have a relative competitive disadvantage there, but also have a major motive in the possibility of obtaining advanced technology or well-known brand names. The acquisition of advanced technology and brand names can boost a Chinese TNC's reputation worldwide and enhance its competitiveness both abroad and within China's domestic markets. Von Keller and Zhou (2003) found that 16 per cent of the Chinese firms they surveyed regard the acquisition of advanced technology and brand equity as the strongest motivation for outward FDI. An interesting example of technology seeking outward FDI is Shanghai Electronic Group's buy-out of the bankrupt Akiyama Publishing Machinery Company in Japan in 2003. This was done to obtain state-of-the-art printing machine technology. Another successful example of access to proprietary technology concerns China's Bicycles Corporation of Shenzhen. The company bought an American bicycle company to learn how to produce the high specification models in the United States and then transferred the technology back to its Shenzhen plant, which now has a highly successful export market (Deng 2004).

During the 1980s and 1990s, the main form of technology acquisition by Chinese firms was piecemeal purchase of equipment and technology licensing. That approach was not satisfactory as Chinese firms were often unable to buy the most advanced technology from foreign companies. Moreover, more and more Chinese firms now realise that technology alone will not allow them to compete in international markets: they also need recognisable brand names, and these cannot be built from scratch within a short period. However, cross-border M&As can be a quick and useful means for Chinese companies to obtain brand names, sophisticated technology and/or well-established channels in one package, if they are capable of managing the combined company or the acquired entity. Lenovo's acquisition of IBM's PC division in 2004 reflected Lenovo's ambition to become an international player in the PC business by obtaining an established brand overnight.

Efficiency seeking investment

Given the abundance of labour in China, Chinese TNCs do not have a strong motive to reduce labour costs by investing abroad. However, Chinese firms may use FDI as a means to gain exposure to the outside world and to increase production volume so as to enhance learning-by-doing and/or achieve economies of scale, thereby improving efficiency. Haier's investments in Southeast Asia were motivated by such considerations, according to Liu and Li (2002).

Dancing with the wolf: the competition effect

Competitive pressure in domestic markets is another important factor that leads to second-generation LDC transnationals going abroad. Since China opened up to the outside world in the late 1970s, most Chinese industries (except a few protected sectors) have faced increasingly intense competition, due to economic reform and the entry of foreign firms as well as non-state-owned enterprises. In fact, competition is so intense that there has been significant excess production capacity in industries such as clothing, automobiles, electronics and household appliances. Competitive pressure in domestic markets has been a major driving force behind the 'going global' strategy of many Chinese TNCs. As Wu (2005) summarises:

> ... fierce economic competition and declining domestic revenues, combined with government encouragement and financial support, are pushing Chinese firms to globalize...

For example, Huawei has to compete on its home turf with such global players as Alcatel, Lucent, Motorola, Nortel, Nokia and Siemens. In some cases, contrary to the popular perception overseas of a 'local-first' market similar to Japan and South Korea, some state-owned customers in China demand a harder bargain from their countrymen than from foreign suppliers. Given the highly competitive nature of doing business in China, Huawei feels it must develop overseas.[9]

Another example concerns the case of Haier. The Chinese household appliance industry has been one of the most competitive in China. Massive foreign entry since the early 1990s has caused many domestic producers to exit the market.[10] Running with extra capacity, firms have engaged in constant price wars, which have driven profit margins down. Facing intense competition, Haier CEO Zhang Ruimin declared that the company had to 'dance with the wolves', and introduced the slogan that 'No true brand name can be created unless one goes global' (see Yan and Hu 2001).

Price wars also occurred in the PC market during the 1990s. For example, Legend (now Lenovo) had to compete with foreign competitors such as HP and Dell. As Legend's chief finance officer pointed out, 'if we just focus on China, we cannot generate returns for our shareholders'.[11] Similarly, the top television producer TCL went abroad because of fierce competition in the domestic markets. The price wars in China are 'brutal', says the chief finance officer of TCL: 'We do not want to compete this way forever.'[12]

The competition effect is related to and consistent with Huang's (2003) view on inward FDI to China. Huang (2003) argues that a main reason for China's success in attracting inward FDI, and one which was omitted in previous studies, is that Chinese domestic firms are too weak and are not capable of competing with leading TNCs. In fact, Huang argues (2003: 3–4):

> China's financial and economic institutions have worked to reduce the ability of domestic firms, especially domestic private firms, to provide some of the same benefits brought about by FDI ... FDI has come to play a substantial role in the Chinese economy because of systematic and pervasive discrimination against efficient and entrepreneurial domestic firms.

APPLICATION OF THE CONVENTIONAL TNC THEORY TO CHINA

The 'eclectic paradigm of international production' (Caves 1971; Dunning 1981) is perhaps the most accepted theoretical framework in which to analyse transnational enterprises. According to this framework, the extent, form and pattern of FDI is determined by the configuration of three types of advantages – ownership, internalisation and location. First, firms need to possess ownership advantages to be able to compete with firms in another country. The ownership advantages are the possession of intellectual property, scale economies and so on. Second, it is in the best interest of firms that if possible the possessed ownership advantages are transferred across national boundaries within the organisation itself, rather than being sold or licensed to other firms. Third, assuming that the previous two conditions are satisfied, locational advantages determine whether export from the home economy or local production in the host market will take place. The locational advantages here are the specific attractions of the host country as a site of investment ('pull factors') as well as disincentives in the home country ('push factors').

It is difficult to argue that Chinese TNCs possess strong ownership advantages in the sense discussed in the FDI literature and in the case of TNCs from developed countries. Most Chinese TNCs – for example, Haier, TCL and Huawei – were not well-recognised brand names internationally when they first invested abroad.[13] After all, these companies are very young; China has only begun to open up to the outside world in the past three decades, and many companies were created only around two years ago.

However, the Chinese TNCs possess a strong competitive advantage: they provide good-quality products and sell them at low prices. They can be considered as value-for-money products: they may not be of the best quality but they are of better value than others when price is taken into consideration. This advantage explains why TCL has become the largest television producer in the world and Galanz the largest microwave oven supplier in the world. It also explains why Huawei has become a formidable competitor of Cisco.

Chinese TNCs can achieve this value-for-money advantage because of low labour costs in China. For instance, Huawei was able to build up a large R&D team at its Shenzhen headquarters partly because the cost of top scientists and engineers in China is only about 25 per cent of that in the United States and Europe. In 2005, about 48 per cent of Huawei's staff were engaged in R&D. Despite the value-for-money advantage, Chinese TNCs may be disadvantaged if foreign markets regard Chinese products as being of inferior quality even if they are cheaper. This is now the perception of the 'made-in-China' label. This, plus cut-throat competition in the domestic market, may lead to the belief that 'Chinese companies often venture abroad not from a position of strength but of weakness' (Balfour 2005). Therefore, it is largely true that until recently Chinese TNCs have not had strong ownership advantages to exploit in other countries. Instead, their outward FDI has been motivated by the desire to seek ownership advantages in foreign markets – strategic asset seeking in particular – as mentioned earlier.[14] However, it can be argued that industrial design and technology will soon become an ownership advantage of Chinese TNCs as a result of low-cost R&D at home and the rapid seeking of strategic assets overseas. For example, Haier is developing a range of high-end electrical appliances which are probably the most sophisticated on the market, and Huawei has become a global leader in voice-over-internet protocol service and other telecommunications equipment.

The strategies of Chinese TNCs have some interesting locational features. Following the example of TNCs from South Korea and Taiwan, some Chinese TNCs started their outward FDI process from developing economies.[15] This choice was made primarily because market competition in developing countries is not as intense as that in developed countries. Moreover, Chinese TNCs considered political factors in choosing where to invest. This was in order to minimise potential risks. For instance, both TCL and Huawei put significant emphasis on investing in former socialist countries such as Vietnam and countries that used to belong to the Soviet Union. In addition, top managers from both companies explicitly addressed the importance of cooperating with countries that have good and stable relationships with China (Cheng and Liu 2003). Such examples indicate that political affinity and cultural affinity play a part in Chinese TNCs' choice of host countries.

In contrast, Haier chose a 'difficult first, then easy' strategy when it decided to undertake its first greenfield FDI in the United States in 1999, a few years after it started exporting refrigerators to the United States. Haier's philosophy is that 'once you build a brand name in developed markets, then you will face little resistance to expand business into developing countries' (Liu and Li 2002). Haier's move signals its confidence in the quality of its products, which can confer a strategic advantage in both foreign and domestic markets, despite high production costs in the United States.

Chinese TNCs also show different patterns in the time at which they undertake outward FDI. Some firms use a similar strategy (developing countries first and then developed countries) to that of South Korean and Taiwanese TNCs; some adopt the reverse sequence of moves; and others make simultaneous moves.

TCL adopted the South Korea–Taiwan pattern which some Chinese scholars call the 'countryside surrounding the city' strategy. In its early stage of the outward FDI process, TCL specifically chose Vietnam to establish its first overseas production site in the mid-1990s. This was primarily because Vietnam is near TCL headquarters in Guangdong province but perhaps also because both countries are socialist, as discussed above. TCL then expanded to other countries in Southeast Asia, the Middle East, and South America, before later on investing in developed countries (via the acquisition of the cell phone business of Alcatel in 2003 and brands of Thomson RCA in 2004).

Huawei invested first in Russia, in 1997, and subsequently in the Middle East, Africa and South America. At almost the same time, it was targeting the US and European Community markets (see Cheng and Liu 2003: Chapter 8). In 2000, it established R&D centres in the United States, in Silicon Valley and Dallas. Huawei's simultaneous-move strategy may be related to the highly dynamic nature of telecommunication equipment markets, which induces or even forces firms to expand production and sales of existing products in developing countries and at the same time search for advanced knowledge in developed markets in order to gain and sustain competitive advantages in R&D.

CHALLENGES FACING CHINESE TNCs

At present, China's TNCs seem to be able to face the challenges of investing abroad. Through carefully designed expansion strategies, top Chinese TNCs are making progress in outward FDI. Low labour costs are obviously one core advantage. Even when Chinese firms have operations in other countries (including high-cost developed countries), they can benefit from China's abundant labour force at home, especially skilled professional labour, and this can benefit Chinese TNCs' operations all over the world.

In addition, Chinese TNCs are aware of the risks underlying their expansion strategies and are doing whatever they can to survive in highly competitive international markets. For instance, unlike what Japanese firms did in the past, Chinese TNCs are quick to adopt 'localisation' strategies in human resource management. For example, the top managers in Haier's production branch come from America, and Huawei has recruited local talent in its operations in Europe and India.

However, some people are concerned about how well Chinese TNCs can fare. Perhaps the most important and natural question is how competitive the Chinese TNCs really are in the global markets *vis-à-vis* TNCs from other LDCs such as Brazil, Mexico, India, Russia, South Korea, Taiwan and Hong Kong, and TNCs from the developed countries.

Generally speaking, Chinese TNCs are still technology followers whose competitive advantage rests largely on low production costs. In contrast, Japan's strongest companies succeeded internationally by offering new products such as Sony's creative consumer electronics and Toyota's 'just-in-time' production method. Japan's innovation capability was based on a long period during the 1950s and 1960s when firms imported foreign advanced technology and successfully learned from it. This led to Japanese firms being able to substantially upgrade their innovative capability. Chinese firms have been less significant and successful in absorbing imported technology, despite the fact that the Chinese government has had a policy of 'swap the market for technology' since the early 1980s which requires foreign investors to transfer advanced technology to China as a condition for entering China's markets.[16] While top Chinese TNCs have increased their R&D expenditures and been able to produce much patented technology and many products,[17] their R&D scales are still lower than leading multinational companies in the world.

Government support for Chinese TNCs – both real and perceived – may not have been as instrumental and effective as in the case of, say, South Korea's TNCs (such as LG and Samsung). Within the WTO framework, Chinese TNCs cannot enjoy the benefits of industrial policies in the way that South Korean TNCs did prior to the mid-1990s or that Japanese companies did through the Ministry of International Trade and Industry in the 1960s to the 1980s. In fact, government links with Chinese TNCs may hurt them abroad. For instance, the provincial electrical appliance maker Sichuan Changhong Electric Co. last year saw its US colour television sales dwindle to almost nothing after it was hit with anti-dumping duties of 25 per cent – not necessarily because it was actually selling its goods below cost but because its government ownership made it appear to have an unfair advantage over privately owned rivals.

Furthermore, as newcomers to the global economy, Chinese TNCs still have a lot to learn about global business strategies, foreign cultures and how to run a truly transnational company. They lack knowledge about and skills in cross-border investments, as reflected in recent acquisitions of international brands by Chinese

TNCs. An example is Lenovo's acquisition of IBM's PC division: some people have raised doubts about whether Lenovo is able to manage a big foreign business and retain IBM's customers and employees. A previously loyal IBM user commented[18] that 'it feels uncomfortable; international IBM has become Lenovo'. To curb these risks, Lenovo has appointed a senior IBM vice-president as its chief executive, transferred its head office to New York, and chosen to retain IBM as the preferred supplier of after-sale service outside China. Another example is TCL's acquisition of France's Thomson: TCL was criticised for having purchased a loss-making business with a severely faded television brand (RCA). Moreover, major differences in culture and corporate practice have created greater management problems than expected, especially over issues such as pay levels and communication across two languages, in both Lenovo–IBM and TCL–Thomson transactions.[19]

CONCLUSIONS

The recent emergence of Chinese TNCs provides an interesting case study of the second generation of LDC transnationals, not only because these TNCs are from the largest and fastest-growing developing economy in the world, but also because their emergence is closely related to the massive and persistent inward FDI that China has been receiving during the past two decades, particularly FDI by developed country TNCs. What can we learn from the emergence of Chinese TNCs in relation to the development of TNCs and their impacts on the global economy?

First, does the experience of Chinese TNCs conform to the conventional theory of FDI? As newcomers in the era of rapid globalisation, it is no surprise that emerging TNCs from China have adopted strategies that are different from those used by leading TNCs from advanced economies. For instance, the strategic asset seeking motive seems to be a dominating determinant for outward FDI by Chinese TNCs. This motive stems from two inter-related aspects: (a) intense competition in domestic markets, where the Chinese TNCs have to compete with giant global TNCs, and (b) Chinese TNCs' desire to seek strategic assets to complement their low-cost advantages in manufacturing and enhance their competitiveness in both the domestic and international markets. In other words, Chinese TNCs' outward FDI has served as a vehicle for the importation of advanced technology, often from advanced economies.

Backward flow of technology is not an entirely new phenomenon. It was certainly an important motive for South Korean and Taiwanese firms to invest in developed countries in the 1970s and 1980s, often supported by government policies for enhancing technology at both the firm and national levels. The difference is that Chinese TNCs seek strategic assets abroad because of severe competition and declining market shares in domestic markets. Though relatively weak, the ownership advantages of today's LDC transnationals are more identifiable than those of LDC transnationals in the past. It is clear that Chinese TNCs possess ownership advantages in production costs resulting from lower labour and R&D personnel costs (for example, Haier, TCL and Huawei). In this sense, the conventional ownership–locational–internalisation framework in FDI theory is still useful in explaining outward FDI by developing country firms, at least those from China.

Second, what impacts have the LDC transnationals' FDI had on the host countries and/or the world economy? It may be too early to assess their impacts systematically, because the LDC transnationals – especially the second-generation ones – are still at an early stage of development.[20] However, it is useful to emphasise that the focus of interest is different now and has a new dimension. In the past, studies of impacts of TNCs on host countries focused on transfer of appropriate technology and the resulting effects on employment and income generation. Today, many LDC transnationals, whether they are operating in LDCs or developed countries, strive to become global players. Assessment of the impacts of LDC transnationals should naturally include their impacts on the global economy.

For host countries and other markets, today's LDC transnationals produce value-for-money products benefiting consumers and producers. For the well-established developed country TNCs, the emergence of LDC transnationals constitutes a potential threat in the global markets. Developed country TNCs could respond by launching head-on competition with LDC transnationals by capitalising and improving on their ownership advantages, in particular technological advancement. Alternatively, developed country TNCs could further improve their competitive advantages by investing more in LDCs such as China, in order to make use of the lowest costs of production and R&D there. This is indeed happening, albeit in selected industries. For example, partly in response to the emergence of Huawei and its low-cost strategy in the international markets, global telecommunications suppliers are moving more of their activities to China.[21] In general, the emergence of Chinese and other LDC transnationals has created a new competitive environment for global business players. While LDC transnationals face some difficulties in this formidable period of their development, developed country TNCs are also encountering great challenges in retaining their predominance in global businesses.

NOTES

1. The original paper of Akamatsu (1962) only describes the import–export cycle of a country in the process of development. The concept was later extended to describe FDI flows and the resulting subregional division of labour in industrial production.
2. The relative importance of Latin American TNCs seems to have declined over time. On the other hand, India's outward FDI has increased rapidly in recent years, accounting for 3.3 per cent of average annual total outflows from developing countries in 2001–03. Not revealed by these aggregate data is the emergence of global corporations in countries such as Brazil, Mexico, Egypt, Russia and South Africa, whose aggregate outward FDI may not be significant (*BusinessWeek*, 31 July 2006). One should note that fluctuations of outward FDI statistics are significantly affected by cross-border mergers and acquisitions in particular years.
3. In 2003, for instance, of the 510 Chinese firms that got approval to invest outside Mainland China, 73 chose Hong Kong, 16 chose Singapore, 17 chose Vietnam, 14 went to Japan, and 10 went to South Korea (*China Commerce Statistical Yearbook* 2004).
4. In a recent empirical study, Buckley *et al.* (2006) found that China's outward FDI was positively related to the level of natural resource endowment of the host country during the period 1984–2001.

5   'Behind the Chinese M&A surge', *BusinessWeek*, 26 July 2006.
6   'The struggle of the champions', *The Economist*, 8 January 2005.
7   'A survey of China's overseas investments', *People's Daily*, 26 February 2004. See <http://english1.peopledaily.com.cn/200402/26/print20040226_135898.html>.
8   In an interview with a reporter, Haier CEO Zhang Ruimin said that one of the two main reasons for Haier establishing its factory in South Carolina was to avoid US non-tariff trade barriers such as environmental protection standards with regard to packaging materials for refrigerators. A more important reason for Haier's FDI in the United States, according to Zhang, was to establish a reputation for being able to enter and compete in the US market. See Yan and Hu (2001: 398).
9   See 'Huawei and ZTE: dragons on the wing', 1 May 2005, <http://www.bdachina.com/EN/features/AnalysisInfo.aspx?id=24>.
10 Other companies were sold because they were suffering losses. For example, domestic refrigerator firms such as Wanbao, Yangtze and Snowflake were sold to foreign companies around 1994.
11 'Chinese companies abroad: the dragon tucks in', *The Economist*, 30 June 2005.
12 'Bursting out of China', *BusinessWeek*, 17 November 2003. The occurrence of the Asian financial crisis which resulted in a big reduction in TCL's sales in South East Asia in 1998 was another reason for TCL to expand abroad according to Wang *et al.* (2005).
13 For example, TCL had a slow start in Vietnam when it first invested there in 1996, simply because few people in Vietnam had heard of the brand name. Haier has been trying very hard to establish its brand name in the United States.
14 Lack of ownership advantages does not necessarily contradict the fact that these Chinese TNCs have undertaken outward FDI already. From the viewpoint of industrial organisation, weak competitors may still be able to survive in oligopoly markets dominated by more efficient firms as long as the market is big enough. In other words, possession of ownership advantages may be a sufficient (rather than necessary) condition for outward FDI.
15 Outward FDI from South Korea and Taiwan can be divided into two waves. The first wave occurred during the 1960s and 1970s when South Korea and Taiwan FDI mostly targeted adjacent countries in Asia; the second wave took place in the 1980s and 1990s and was directed at the more developed regions of the world (Hoesel 1999). As South Korean and Taiwanese firms became more sophisticated, and their international network broadened and intensified, the need for both to exploit the markets in more advanced economies and tap into their intellectual assets became more important.
16 The overdependence of foreign technology and the lack of incentive and capability of Chinese firms to innovate on their own is the main reason that the central government of China recently introduced the nationwide champion of 'independent innovation' as stipulated in China's new Ten-Year Program for Science and Technology.
17 In 2004, Haier spent about 4 per cent of its total revenue on R&D; TCL was planning to increase its R&D expenditure to 3 per cent of sales in 2004 and to 5 per cent by 2005. See *BusinessWeek,* 8 November 2004.
18 'IBM's brand loyalty holds key for Lenovo', *Financial Times*, 9 December 2004; 'Lenovo buys IBM's PC Unit for $1.75bn', *Financial Times*, 9 December 2004.
19 'Business: champ or chump?', *The Economist*, 11 December 2004.
20 For some of the first generation of LDC transnationals, such as Hong Kong, there is enough information to evaluate the effect of their outward FDI on the host economies. For example, Chen (2004) contains detailed discussions of the impacts of Hong Kong's FDI on the export capability and productivity changes of firms in Mainland China.
21 'The challenger from China: why Huawei is making the telecom world take notice', *Financial Times*, 11 January 2005.

REFERENCES

Akamatsu, K. (1962) 'A historical pattern of economic growth in developing countries', *Developing Economies,* 1 (Preliminary issue): 1–23.
Balfour, F. (2005) 'The age of Chinese MNCs is here', *BusinessWeek*, 15 September.
Behrman, J.N. (1972) *The Role of International Companies in Latin America: Autos and Petrochemicals*, Lexington MA: Lexington Books.
Buckley, P., J. Clegg, A. Cross, X. Lui, H. Voss and P. Zheng (2006) 'Host country determinants of Chinese outward FDI', mimeo, University of Leeds.
Caves, R. E. (1971) 'International corporations: the industrial economics of foreign investment', *Economica*, 38(1): 1–27.
Chen, E.K.Y. (1981) 'Hong Kong multinationals in Asia: characteristics and objectives', pp. 79–99 in K. Kumar and M.G. McLeod (eds), *Multinationals from Developing Countries*, Lexington MA: D.C. Heath.
—— (1983) *Multinational Corporations, Employment and Technology,* London: Macmillan.
—— (1991) 'Economic restructuring and industrial development in the Asia-Pacific: competition or complementarity?', *Business and the Contemporary World*, 5(2):67–88.
—— (2004) 'Hong Kong as a source of FDI: experience and significance', mimeo, Lingnan University.
Cheng, Dong-sheng and Li-li Liu (2003) *The Truth of Huawei* [in Chinese], Beijing: Contemporary China Press.
China Ministry of Commerce (2004) *China Commerce Yearbook 2004*, Beijing: China Commerce Press.
—— (2005a) *China Commerce Yearbook 2005*, Beijing: China Commerce Press.
—— (2005b) 'Chinese outward foreign direct investment', mimeo.
—— (2005c) 'Statistical bulletin of China's outward foreign direct investment', <http://hzs.mofcom.gov.cn/aarticle/date/200609/20060903095437.html>.
Deng, Ping (2004) 'Outward investment by Chinese MNCs: motivations and implications', *Business Horizon*, 47(3): 8–16.
—— (2006) 'Investing for strategic resources and its rationale: the case of outward FDI from Chinese companies', mimeo, Maryville University of St Louis.
Dunning, J.H. (1981) *International Production and the Multinational Enterprises*, London: Allen and Unwin.
—— (1993) *Multinational Enterprises and the Global Economy*, Wokingham: Addison-Wesley.
—— (1998) 'Location and the multinational enterprises: a neglected factor?', *Journal of International Business Studies*, 29(1): 45–86.
Hoesel, R. van (1999) *New Enterprises from Korea and Taiwan: Beyond Export-led Growth,* London: Routledge.
Huang, Y. (2003) *Selling China: Foreign Direct Investment during the Reform Era*, Cambridge: Cambridge University Press.
Jiang, Zemin (1997) 'Advancing the task of establishing the socialist market economy with Chinese characteristics into the twenty first century', speech at the Fifteenth National Meeting of the Chinese Communist Party, 1997, Beijing.
Lall, S. (ed.) (1983) *The New Multinationals: The spread of Third World Enterprise*, London: John Wiley.
Lecraw, D. (1981) 'The internationalization of firms from LDCs: evidence from the ASEAN region', pp. 37–51 in K. Kumar and M.G. McLeod (eds) *Multinationals from Developing Countries*, Lexington MA: D.C. Heath.
Liu, H. and Kequan Li (2002) 'Strategic implications of emerging Chinese multinationals: the Haier case study', *European Management Journal*, 20(6), 699–706.
von Keller, E. and W. Zhou (2003) 'From middle kingdom to global market: expansion strategies and success factors for China's emerging multinationals', Munich: Roland Berger Strategy Consultants.

Wang, Yu-liang (2005) 'China go global [in Chinese]', Beijing: China Finance and Economics Publishing House.

Wang, Zengtao, Zhuang Guijun and Siufeng Fan (2005) 'The determinants and analytical framework of Chinese TNCs going global: the case of TCL [in Chinese]', *Nankai Management Review*, 8(3): 88–94.

Wong J. and S. Chan (2003) 'China's outward direct investment: expanding worldwide', *China: An International Journal*, 1(2): 273–301.

Wu, F. (2005) *The globalization of corporate China*, Seattle WA: National Bureau of Asian Research.

Yan, Jianjun and Hu Yong (2001) *Haier: Made in China*, Beijing: Hainan Press.

ANNEX 8.1 CHINESE TNCS: CASE STUDIES

Haier Group

Founded in 1984, Haier Group is the world's fourth largest white goods manufacturer and one of China's top 100 electronics and information technology companies. In each year since 2002, Haier has been ranked first among China's most valuable brands for the manufacture of 15 products, including refrigerators, airconditioners, washing machines, televisions, water heaters, personal computers, mobile phones and kitchen integrations. Haier was ranked first of China's top ten global brands by the China State Bureau of Quality and Technical Supervision (CSBTS) for refrigerators and washing machines. On 30 August 2005, Haier was ranked first of China's top ten global brands by the *Financial Times*. In 2005, Haier had 240 subsidiary companies and 30 design centres, plants and trade companies and more than 50,000 employees throughout the world. Haier's 2005 global revenue was RMB103.9 billion ($12.8 billion).

The origin of the Haier brand

Haier initially introduced its entire production technology facility from Germany's Liebherr in 1984. Before 1992 Haier's refrigerators were sold under the brand name of QINDAO LIEBHERR. In 1992, when its initial agreement with Liebherr expired, Haier started using QINDAO Haier; in 1993 the brand name was switched to Haier (Yan and Hu 2001: 231–233).

In 1984 the Qingdao General Refrigerator Factory was an ailing township enterprise that owed RMB1.47 million ($178,000), manufactured shoddy products and had a surly workforce. In 1984, the local government appointed Zhang Ruimin and his colleagues to the enterprise. Zhang Ruimin had to borrow money from nearby farmers to pay salaries to employees before the Spring Festival. Over the past two decades, Haier has gone through three stages of development.

Branding stage (refrigerators, 1984–96)

In 1984–96, Haier limited its manufacturing to refrigerators, aiming to establish a quality product. Through various quality control measures and creative management by Zhang Ruimin, Haier refrigerators gradually became a leading brand in China. In 1993, the Haier brand was officially recognised as a famous brand; in 2005 it was valued at RMB70.2 billion. Focusing on refrigerators, Haier explored and gathered experience in corporate management to lay a solid foundation for its later expansion.

Diversifying stage

In 1997 Haier began to produce colour televisions, indicating initial success in the brown goods sector following its cross-sector restructure as the No. 1 white goods supplier in China since its origin in 1984 and marking a significant advance of Haier Group towards an international conglomerate. In subsequent years, Haier expanded its manufacturing activities to the businesses of airconditioners, washing machines, water heaters, personal computers, and mobile phones. One advantage of this diversification strategy among closely related goods is that Haier can economise on promotion costs because these products are often displayed in the same areas in retailing stores. In addition, Haier has enjoyed beneficial spillover effects from transferring its established refrigerator brand image to newly introduced household appliances.

Internationalisation stage

Unlike other Chinese MNCs, Haier adopted a 'difficult first, then easy' strategy. Its first overseas greenfield investment was in a refrigerator production line in South Carolina in the United States in 1999. Haier's philosophy is that 'once you build a brand name in developed markets, then you will face little resistance to expand business into developing countries'. Haier's 'difficult first, then-easy' strategy in its internationalisation stage was similar to the strategy it had previously used domestically, when it first obtained brand name and dominance in big cities such as Beijing and Shanghai, and then expanded to smaller cities and rural areas (Yan and Hu 2001). It had also invested in some Southeast Asian developing countries (though not in the form of greenfield investment), in order to build volume and acquire international experience (Liu and Li 2002).

When entering the US market, Haier adopted a product-focused strategy. It initially focused on marketing refrigerators only. Once refrigerators secured a market position, the company introduced washing machines. The promotion of subsequent products was much cheaper because of the firm's established reputation as a high-quality producer of refrigerators.

Huawei Technology

Established in 1988, Huawei Technology Co. Ltd is a telecommunications equipment manufacturer based in Shenzhen, Guangdong Province of China. It specialises in R&D, production and marketing of communications equipment, and provides customised network solutions for telecommunications carriers in different countries. In 2005, Huawei's contracted sales reached $8.2 billion, an increase of 47 per cent from the previous year, of which 60 per cent came from international sales. Currently Huawei provides products and solutions for over 270 operators worldwide, and 22 of the world's top 50 operators use Huawei's products and solutions. Its products are deployed in over 70 countries, including the United States, Germany, France, the United Kingdom, Spain, the Netherlands, Russia, Brazil, Thailand, Singapore, Egypt, Nigeria, and Venezuela.

In order to support its global operations, Huawei has set up 55 branch offices and eight regional headquarters worldwide. It has R&D centres in Dallas, Silicon Valley, Bangalore, Stockholm, Moscow, Beijing and Shanghai. Ten per cent of its 34,000 employees are non-Chinese.

Huawei has now become a leading vendor in the industry. In terms of market share, Huawei is currently No. 1 in digital switches and the next generation network and No. 2 in both asymmetric digital subscriber line (ADSL) broadband and the optical network. Huawei has also become one of the few vendors in the world to provide end-to-end 3G solutions.

Huawei's internationalisation process started in 1996 when it won its first overseas contract from Hong Kong's Hutchison–Whampoa to provide fixed-line network products. In 1997, Huawei entered the Russian market, and it subsequently entered the Middle East, Africa (in 2002) and South America. Almost simultaneously, Huawei was targeting the US and European Community markets (see Cheng and Liu 2003: Chapter 8). In 2000, it established R&D centres in Silicon Valley and Dallas in the United States. In 2005, British Telecom elected Huawei as a preferred 21 Century Network ('21CN') supplier to provide multi-service network access components and transmission equipment for the British Telecom 21CN network.

As a newcomer battling against the perception that Chinese companies produce cheap, unreliable goods, Huawei has used aggressive strategies to win contracts.

High intensity of R&D

China-based, cost-effective R&D is one of Huawei's advantages. From its inception, even in the information technology recession period in the early 2000s, Huawei invested over 10 per cent of its revenue in R&D. This is comparable to leading transnational corporations in the world. Huawei set up its first R&D centre in 1995, only seven years after the birth of the company and at a time when most Chinese companies did not even realise the importance of R&D and intellectual property rights. In addition to independent R&D, Huawei has consistently cooperated with the world's leading players such as TI, Motorola, Qualcomm, IBM, Infineon, Intel, Agere, ADI, ALTERA, SUN, Microsoft, Oracle and NEC. This speeds up its responses to the changing market, and helps it to gain advanced technology and management experience from a global perspective. In 2005, about 48 per cent of Huawei's staff engaged in R&D.

Low-pricing strategy

Huawei's emphasis on R&D, along with the very low costs of R&D staff in China (the salary of industrial scientists and engineers in China is one-fifth to one-quarter of that in developed countries), has given Huawei a great advantage in international markets. In fact, Huawei's prices can be 30 per cent lower than those of established suppliers (*Financial Times*, 11 January 2005).

Service competition

In the early days of its development, Huawei realised that it might not be able to compete head to head with leading multinational companies such as Cisco in the international market. It adopted the strategy of competing in services and costs. Huawei has developed a reputation for its eagerness to tailor technologies to specific needs of its customers, and for doing so much more quickly than its competitors. To provide speedy and tailor-made services, Huawei has opened overseas offices in Europe and sometimes outsources locally in these countries.

TCL Group

TCL is now the largest television producer in the world, with annual sales of 18 million sets and 10 per cent of the global market. Founded in 1981, TCL began as a manufacturer of magnetic tapes. It developed rapidly during the 1990s to become one of China's fastest growing companies; it has had an average growth rate of 42.65 per cent for the past 12 years. The company was successfully restructured from a state-owned enterprise in 2002.

TCL's internationalisation started in 1996 when it first established a production facility in Vietnam. It then expanded to other countries, including India, the Philippines, Russia, Singapore, Indonesia, India, Thailand, Mexico, the Middle East and Australia. In 2003, TCL acquired the cell phone business of Alcatel, becoming the first large-scale cross-border merger and acquisition by a Chinese multinational corporation. In 2004, TCL set up a joint venture with France's Thomson Group, creating TTE Corporation, obtaining control of the RCA brand. At the time, TCL was hailed as the first Chinese company to compete on the international stage with large international corporations. TCL now has three core TV brands: TCL, Thomson and RCA. TCL is a leading brand in China and some emerging markets, and the Thomson and RCA brands provide TCL with a foothold in the European and North American markets. At the beginning of 2006, TCL had ten overseas manufacturing facilities.

9 Multinational production networks and the new geo-economic division of labour in Pacific Rim countries

Prema-chandra Athukorala

International fragmentation of production (involving the splitting of the production process into discrete activities which are then allocated across countries) has been an increasingly important facet of economic globalisation over the past three decades. With a modest start in electronics and clothing industries in the late 1960s, multinational production networks have gradually evolved and spread into many industries such as sport footwear, automobiles, televisions and radio receivers, sewing machines, office equipment, power and machine tools, cameras and watches, and printing and publishing. At the formative stage, the process involved locating small fragments of the production process in a low-cost country and reimporting the assembled components to be incorporated in the final product. Subsequently, production networks began to encompass many countries engaged in the assembly process at different stages, resulting in multiple border crossings by product fragments before they are incorporated in the final product. Recently two other important developments in the process have set the stage for rapid expansion in the share of fragmentation-based trade in world trade. First, some fragments of the production process in certain industries have become 'standard fragments' which can be effectively used in a number of products.[1] Second, as international networks of parts and comments supply have become firmly established, producers in advanced countries have begun to move the final assembly of an increasing range of consumer durables (for example, computers, cameras, TV sets and motor cars) to overseas locations in order to be physically closer to their final users and/or take advantage of cheap labour.

The expansion of fragmentation-based international exchange has been underpinned by three mutually reinforcing developments. First, rapid advancements in production technology have enabled the industry to slice the value chain into finer, 'portable', components. Second, technological innovations in communication and transportation have shrunk the distance that once separated the world's nations, and improved the speed, efficiency and economy of coordinating geographically dispersed production processes. This has facilitated the establishment of 'services links' to combine various fragments of the production process in a timely and cost-effective manner. Third, liberalisation policy reforms in both home and host countries have considerably removed barriers to trade and investment (Jones 2000; Jones and Kierzkowski 2001).

Conventionally, international fragmentation of production took the form of a multinational enterprise (MNE) building a subsidiary abroad to perform some of the functions that it once did at home. Thus there was a close relationship between foreign direct investment (FDI) and trade in parts and components (henceforth referred to as fragmentation-based trade) within vertically integrated manufacturing industries (Helleiner 1989). However, in recent years, fragmentation practices have begun to spread beyond the domain of MNEs. As production operations in host countries have become firmly established, MNE subsidiaries have begun to subcontract some activities to local (host-country) firms to which they provide detailed specifications and even fragments of their own technology. At the same time, many firms which are not part of MNE networks have begun to procure components globally through arm's-length trade. Moreover, many MNEs in electronics and related industries have begun to rely increasingly on independent contract manufacturers for the operation of their global-scale production networks – a process that has been facilitated by the standardisation of some components and by advances in modular technology (Sturgeon 2003; Brown and Linden 2006). These new developments suggest that an increase in fragmentation-based trade may or may not be accompanied by an increase in the host-country stock of FDI (Brown *et al.* 2004: 305).

A sizeable literature points to the growing importance of fragmentation-based specialisation for economic growth and structural transformation in countries on the Pacific Rim.[2] It is clear that, while growth in fragmentation-based trade is now a global phenomenon, such trade is far more important in Pacific Rim countries, particularly those in East Asia, than elsewhere in the world – and it is growing rapidly. However, as yet no one has systematically examined this new form of international specialisation or tried to identify what implications it might have for economic transformation for individual countries in the region and for regional economic integration. The literature on the issues is by and large based on the traditional notion of horizontal specialisation in which countries trade goods that are produced, from start to finish, in just one country. In a context where fragmentation-based trade is growing rapidly, this conventional approach can lead to misleading inferences as to the nature and extent of trade integration among countries. There are two reasons for this. First, the total amount of recorded trade could be a multiple of the actual value of final goods, because goods in process cross multiple international borders before being embodied in the final product. Second, and perhaps more importantly, intra-regional patterns of fragmentation-based trade and trade in related final goods ('final trade') are unlikely to follow the same geographic patterns as extra-regional ones, so trade shares calculated using reported data can lead to wrong inferences as to the relative importance of the region and the rest of the world for growth in a given country or region.

The purpose of this chapter is to examine the extent, trends and patterns of international production fragmentation and its implications for trade patterns in Pacific Rim countries, with special emphasis on the regional and global integration of countries in East Asia. I place particular emphasis on the implications of China's evolving role in the process of international fragmentation of production for trade patterns in the region. The analysis is based on a systematic separation of fragmentation-based trade from total trade flows using a new dataset extracted from the United Nations (UN) trade database. I examine the Pacific Rim experience in the wider global context, focusing specifically on the comparative experiences of the North American Free Trade Agreement (NAFTA) and the European Union (EU).

The chapter is organised as follows. First, I discuss the procedure I used in extracting data from the UN trade data tapes and discuss data quality. Then I examine the nature and extent of 'fragmentation-based trade' and the role of Pacific Rim countries in this new global division of labour. I subsequently deal in turn with the growing importance of fragmentation-based specialisation for intra-regional trade and for the creation of new supply-side complementarities among countries in the region, with emphasis on the emerging role of China in regional production networks; the implications of the rapid expansion of fragmentation-based trade for intra-regional versus extra-regional trade patterns; and challenges posed by the fragmentation-based international division of labour for the conventional changing comparative advantage ('flying geese') approach to the analysis of growth patterns in the region. The final section presents the key policy inferences.

DATA

The data for this chapter are compiled from the UN Comtrade database, based on Revision 3 of the Standard International Trade Classification (SITC, Rev. 3). They cover the period from 1992 to 2004. The year 1992 was selected as the starting point because by this time countries accounting for over 95 per cent of total world manufacturing trade had adopted the revised data reporting system. The analysis ends in 2004, the most recent year for which data are available for all reporting countries.

In its original form (SITC, Rev. 1), the UN trade data reporting system did not provide for the separation of parts and components from final manufactured goods. The version introduced in the late 1970s (SITC, Rev. 2, which was fully implemented by most countries only in the early 1980s) adopted a more detailed commodity classification which provided for the separation of parts and components within the machinery and transport sector (SITC 7). However, considerable overlap between some advanced-stage assembly activities and related final goods within the sector made it difficult to separate fragmentation-based trade from total trade (Ng and Yeats 2001).[3] Revision 3, introduced in the mid-1980s, marked a significant improvement over Revision 2. In addition to redressing the issue of overlaps within SITC 7, it provided for the separation of parts and components trade in the miscellaneous goods sector (SITC 8). These two sectors together accounted for around 70 per cent of total world manufacturing trade (defined as goods belonging to SITC 5 through 8 less SITC 68 (non-ferrous metals)) during the period under study. The list of parts and components identified at the five-digit level for these two sectors provides the basis of my empirical analysis. There are 225 five-digit products (168 belonging to SITC 7 and 57 belonging to SITC 8).[4]

Despite its significant improvement over the previous version, SITC Revision 3 does not provide for the construction of data series covering the entire range of fragmentation-based trade. Data reported under SITC 7 provide a comprehensive coverage of fragmentation-based trade, but data for SITC 8 do not seem to fully capture fragmentation-based trade within that commodity category. For instance, for some products – such as clothing, furniture and leather products – in which outsourcing is prevalent (and perhaps has been increasing), some related components (for example, pieces of textiles, parts of furniture, parts of leather soles) are presumably recorded under other SITC categories. Moreover, there is evidence that production fragmentation has been spreading beyond SITC 7 and 8 to other product categories such as pharmaceutical and chemical products (falling under SITC 5) and machine tools and various metal products (SITC 6). Assembly activities in software trade, too, have recorded impressive expansion in recent years. These are lumped together with 'special transactions' under SITC 9. As a result, my tabulations of the magnitude of fragmentation-based trade are downward biased. However, the magnitude of the bias is unlikely to be substantial because fragmentation-based international specialisation is predominantly concentrated in the machinery and transport equipment category (SITC 7) (Yeats 2001; Feenstra 1998).

As regards the country coverage and classification, I use the term 'Pacific Rim' to refer to the member countries of the Asia-Pacific Economic Cooperation (APEC) group. These include countries in East Asia, countries party to NAFTA, Australia, New Zealand, Peru and Chile.[5] East Asia is defined to include Japan, the newly industrialised economies (NIEs) in North Asia (South Korea, Taiwan and Hong Kong), China and members of the Association of Southeast Asian Nations (ASEAN) Free Trade Area (AFTA). Among the AFTA member countries, only the six largest economies – Indonesia, Malaysia, the Philippines, Thailand, Singapore and Vietnam – are covered; Brunei, Cambodia, Laos and Myanmar are ignored because of lack of data.

The data are tabulated using importer records, which are considered to be more appropriate for analysing trade patterns than are the corresponding exporter records. The reasons for this are discussed by Ng and Yeats (2003: Appendix 1) and Feenstra *et al.* (1999, 2005). Data from importer records are less susceptible to double counting and erroneous identification of the source/destination country in the presence of entrepôt trade than are data based on reporting country records (for example, China's trade through Hong Kong and Indonesia's trade through Singapore). Also, some countries fail to properly report goods shipped from their own export-processing zones; they simply lump these exports into one highly aggregated category of 'special transactions' under SITC 9. There is no fully satisfactory solution for these problems, but it is generally believed that data compiled from importer records are less susceptible to recording errors and reveal the origins and composition of trade more accurately than other records, because there are normally important legal penalties for incorrectly specifying this information on customs declarations. Among the countries I cover in this chapter, Taiwan is not covered in the UN data system; Vietnam has not yet begun to make data available using the standard UN format; and Singapore did not report data on its bilateral trade with Indonesia, for political reasons.[6] In these cases, I filled the data gaps using the corresponding trading partner records.

PRODUCT FRAGMENTATION: TRENDS AND PATTERNS

Table 9.1 shows the growing importance of trade in parts and components[7] in world manufacturing trade. The value of total world component trade increased from about $404 billion in 1992 to $1,258 in 2004. This is a compound annual growth rate of 13.6 per cent, compared with 12.4 per cent growth in total manufacturing exports. The share of components in total world manufacturing exports increased from 21 per cent to over 26 per cent between 1992 and 2004. Components accounted for over one-third of the total increment in world manufacturing exports between 1992 and 2004.

Pacific Rim countries account for the bulk of world trade in components. Their share in total world exports of components increased from 52.9 per cent in 1992 to 62.3 per cent in 2004 (Table 9.1). The share of East Asia (including Japan) increased even faster, from 29.6 per cent to 43.6 per cent between 1992 and 2004. This was in spite of a notable decline in the share of Japan, the dominant economy in the region. The share of developing East Asian countries (East Asia excluding Japan) increased from 14.0 per cent to 31.9 per cent. Within that group, all reported countries recorded increases in world market shares. Interestingly, the significant increase in the relative importance of East Asia in fragmentation-based trade took place against the backdrop of a notable decline in share by NAFTA and EU countries.

For component trade, East Asian countries as a group show a much higher degree of dependence on fragmentation-based trade than any other region in the world. In 2004, components accounted for 33.5 per cent of the total manufacturing exports of East Asian countries, compared with 20.9 per cent for EU countries, 30.7 per cent for NAFTA countries and a world average of 26.3 per cent. Within East Asia, AFTA countries – in particular Malaysia, the Philippines, Singapore and Thailand – stand out for their heavy dependence on product fragmentation for export dynamism. In 2004, components accounted for 47.8 per cent of total manufacturing exports in AFTA countries, up from 31.9 per cent in 1992. The growing importance of China in component trade is particularly noteworthy. Its share in total world exports increased from 1.0 per cent in 1992 to 8.3 per cent in 2004. Between 1992 and 2004, China's share of components in manufacturing exports increased from 4.8 per cent to 18.8 per cent; on the import side, the increase was from 21.6 per cent to 42.1 per cent. At the same time, the share of Hong Kong in world component trade has eroded as a result of the dramatic relocation of manufacturing ventures to mainland China.

Some observers (USITC 1999; Kierzkowski 2001; Kaminski and Ng 2005) predicted that the formation of NAFTA and the integration of some new countries emerging from the former Soviet Union with the rest of Europe would adversely affect the relative position of developing East Asian countries in world assembly activities. They suggested that significant tariff reduction, proximity to industrial countries and relatively low wages by regional standards (though not compared to some East Asian countries) would confer important advantages on Mexico (in penetrating the US market) and countries on the European periphery (in penetrating the EU). However, this prediction does not seem to have materialised. For developing East Asian countries, the world

Table 9.1 World trade in parts and components, 1992–2004 (per cent)

Country/region	Exports				Imports			
	Country/regional composition		Share in total manufacturing exports		Country/regional composition		Share in total manufacturing imports	
	1992	2004	1992	2004	1992	2004	1992	2004
APEC	52.9	62.3	25.8	32.5	43.2	57.2	25.9	33.0
East Asia	29.6	43.6	23.3	33.5	18.9	35.3	25.2	39.7
Japan	15.6	11.7	28.9	37.5	3.8	3.9	21.1	28.7
Developing East Asia	14.0	31.9	19.1	32.2	15.1	31.5	26.5	41.7
China	1.0	8.3	4.8	18.8	2.5	9.8	21.6	42.1
Hong Kong SAR	2.1	1.1	21.1	32.9	2.2	5.5	14.9	38.6
Taiwan	3.2	6.2	22.2	46.3	2.0	3.2	32.6	38.8
South Korea	1.9	4.9	19.7	35.6	1.4	3.0	27.0	36.3
AFTA	5.9	11.6	31.9	47.8	7.1	10.0	36.2	46.4
Indonesia	0.1	0.3	2.6	14.2	0.5	0.6	20.0	28.1
Philippines	0.5	2.3	34.1	74.8	0.5	1.4	33.0	55.9
Malaysia	2.0	4.3	38.3	58.1	1.6	3.0	42.8	58.1
Singapore	2.6	3.1	43.9	53.2	3.4	3.3	43.6	48.3
Thailand	0.7	1.5	21.5	32.6	1.0	1.6	28.3	40.0
Vietnam	0.0	0.1	1.0	6.0	0.0	0.2	7.7	17.8
Oceania	0.2	0.3	13.3	16.5	1.2	0.9	20.1	18.0
Australia	0.2	0.2	14.7	18.3	1.0	0.8	20.3	18.5
New Zealand	0.0	0.0	9.1	11.7	0.2	0.1	19.1	15.6
NAFTA	22.9	18.3	30.4	30.7	22.6	20.8	26.9	26.3
United States	17.4	13.4	30.7	32.3	13.0	14.0	23.2	24.4
Canada	3.6	2.3	28.5	23.9	6.0	3.7	32.4	27.9
Mexico	1.8	2.5	31.2	30.7	3.6	3.2	37.5	36.8
Other APEC countries	0.0	0.0	5.6	3.8	0.3	0.2	17.0	15.4
Chile	0.0	0.0	7.2	4.5	0.2	0.1	16.6	15.5
Peru	0.0	0.0	2.2	1.9	0.1	0.1	18.3	15.1
European Union 15	41.1	29.0	18.8	20.9	16.0	13.7	7.7	10.2
Other	6.0	8.7	12.4	17.3	40.8	28.8	47.1	38.9
World (%)	100.0	100.0	21.2	26.3	100.0	100.0	21.7	26.2
World ($ billion)[a]	4,03.8	1,257.8			386.4	1,241.7		

Notes: AFTA = ASEAN Free Trade Area; APEC = Asia Pacific Economic Cooperation; NAFTA = North American Free Trade Area; SAR = Special Administrative Region.

a By definition, percentage shares in exports and imports for a given year should be identical. The minor differences seem to reflect recording errors and differences in measurement arising from the use of the CIF (cost, insurance, freight) price for reporting imports and f.o.b. (free on board) price for most reporting of exports.

Source: Compiled from the UN Comtrade database.

market share in fragmentation-based trade has increased at a much faster rate than that of either NAFTA or EU countries.

The explanation for the continued pre-eminence of East Asia in component trade seems to lie in four powerful supply-side factors.

First, despite rapid growth, manufacturing wages in China and other latecomers to export-oriented industrialisation in East Asia (Malaysia, Thailand, Vietnam and the Philippines) remain lower than or comparable to those in countries on the European periphery and Mexico.[8] Moreover, significant differences in wages among countries in the East Asia region have provided the basis for rapid expansion of intra-regional product sharing systems, giving rise to increased cross-border trade in components.

Second, the relative factor cost advantage has been supplemented by relatively more favourable trade and investment policy regimes and by better port and communication systems that facilitate trade by reducing the cost of maintaining 'services links' (Baldwin 2006; Jones et al. 2004; Athukorala and Yamashita 2005).

Third, for over three decades there has been rapid economic expansion in several countries in the region, and this seems to have brought about 'market thickness' (referring to the diversification of the composition of traded goods of a country as an outcome of rapid growth and structural transformation), with a positive impact on the location of outsourcing activity (Grossman and Helpman 2005).

Finally, economic history seems to have played a part: from the start, MNEs often chose the region (firstly Singapore and subsequently Malaysia and other countries) as a location of outsourcing activities. There is a general tendency for MNE affiliates to become increasingly embedded in host countries the longer they are present there and the more conducive the overall investment climate of the host country becomes over time (Rangan and Lawrence 1999). Also, as first comers in this area of international specialisation, countries in East Asia (particularly Singapore, South Korea, Taiwan and Malaysia) offer considerable agglomeration advantages for companies that are already located there. When selecting new sites, MNEs operating in assembly activities are strongly influenced by the presence of other key market players in a given country or neighbouring countries. With a long period of successful operation in the region, many MNEs (particularly those based in the United States) have significantly upgraded technical activities in their regional production networks in East Asia and assigned global production responsibilities to affiliates located in more mature countries (in particular Singapore and Taiwan, and also Malaysia in recent years) (Borrus 1997; McKendrick et al. 2000).

PRODUCTION NETWORKS

The discussion in this section is based on data on regional bilateral trade flows reported in Tables 9.2, 9.3 and 9.4. Tables 9.2 and 9.3 give data on the geographic profile of manufacturing trade and trade in parts and components respectively. Table 9.4 reports percentage shares of parts and components in bilateral flows of manufacturing trade. The data reported in these tables vividly show the growing importance of component trade in intra-regional trade flows in Pacific Rim countries, particularly among countries in East Asia. Intra-regional trade accounts for a much larger share in component exports and imports in East Asia than in total exports and imports. Moreover, the share of components in total intra-regional imports is much larger than in exports,

Table 9.2 Direction of manufacturing trade: total manufacturing, 1992–2004 (per cent)

Exporter		Exports									Imports								
		APEC	EA	Japan	DEA	CH	AFTA6	NAFTA	EU	Other	APEC	EA	Japan	DEA	China	AFTA	NAFTA	EU	Other
APEC	1992	69.0	32.6	3.9	28.7	9.8	11.9	36.4	18.0	13.1	80.3	50.0	26.9	23.1	6.5	8.7	30.3	16.8	2.9
	2004	75.7	44.4	5.5	38.9	18.6	12.7	31.3	13.9	10.4	83.4	57.0	17.3	39.7	13.7	13.4	26.4	13.8	2.9
East Asia (EA)	1992	70.3	41.7	3.0	38.7	14.5	15.7	28.6	17.2	12.5	80.5	60.7	30.7	30.0	9.9	11.1	19.8	16.5	2.9
	2004	76.1	56.3	6.2	50.1	25.6	15.5	19.8	13.9	10.0	85.7	71.2	21.0	50.2	15.3	18.4	14.4	12.4	2.0
Japan	1992	66.1	35.5	–	35.5	9.2	14.2	30.7	19.4	14.5	74.8	31.7	–	31.7	4.6	13.2	43.1	21.9	3.3
	2004	74.0	49.8	–	49.8	20.7	15.3	24.3	15.0	11.0	87.1	62.8	–	62.8	23.6	20.5	24.3	12.5	0.4
Developing East Asia (DEA)	1992	75.2	49.1	6.5	42.5	20.7	17.5	26.1	14.6	10.2	81.3	64.7	34.9	29.8	10.7	10.8	16.6	15.8	2.9
	2004	76.9	58.8	8.6	50.2	27.5	15.6	18.0	13.5	9.6	85.5	72.4	24.0	48.4	14.2	18.1	13.1	12.3	2.2
China (CH)	1992	79.3	63.1	3.3	59.9	45.0	9.2	16.2	11.9	8.8	81.5	71.7	28.6	43.1	24.2	6.2	9.8	15.1	3.4
	2004	76.4	57.5	8.2	49.3	33.9	8.7	18.9	14.3	9.3	83.7	76.2	23.0	53.2	16.2	14.7	7.4	13.5	2.8
AFTA6	1992	77.0	47.6	8.4	39.3	7.3	26.8	29.4	15.5	7.5	80.9	63.4	34.3	29.2	3.8	16.7	17.5	16.7	2.4
	2004	80.0	63.8	10.2	53.6	15.8	27.9	16.2	12.9	7.1	87.1	69.5	21.5	48.0	11.4	24.2	17.6	11.8	1.1
EU	1992	18.1	7.9	1.3	6.5	2.2	2.8	10.2	62.5	19.5	26.4	15.3	9.6	5.6	1.3	2.1	11.2	67.3	6.3
	2004	21.5	10.0	1.3	8.6	4.2	2.8	11.5	51.6	26.9	31.8	21.1	6.5	14.6	6.3	4.2	10.6	58.9	9.3
NAFTA	1992	66.9	18.5	5.2	13.3	2.6	5.9	48.4	19.1	14.0	80.1	39.7	23.3	16.4	3.1	6.5	40.5	17.0	2.9
	2004	75.0	20.3	4.1	16.2	4.4	6.9	54.7	13.9	11.1	80.5	38.9	12.5	26.4	11.5	7.0	41.6	15.5	4.0
World	1992	44.4	20.3	2.6	17.7	5.8	7.4	24.1	38.7	16.9	52.9	31.3	17.5	13.9	3.7	5.1	21.5	42.2	5.0
	2004	51.4	28.2	3.5	24.7	11.4	8.2	23.2	30.7	17.9	59.8	40.0	12.0	28.0	10.3	8.7	19.8	32.0	8.2

Note: – = not applicable; AFTA = ASEAN Free Trade Area; APEC = Asia-Pacific Economic Cooperation; EU = European Union; NAFTA = North American Free Trade Area.

Source: Compiled from the UN Comtrade database.

Table 9.3 Direction of manufacturing trade: parts and components, 1992–2004 (per cent)

Exporter	Year	Exports									Imports								
		APEC	EA	Japan	DEA	GCH	AFTA	NAFTA	EU	Other	APEC	EA	Japan	DEA	CH	AFTA	NAFTA	EU	Other
APEC	1992	74.5	36.1	4.9	31.1	8.3	14.3	38.4	16.9	8.6	84.4	51.2	25.8	25.4	5.6	11.1	33.2	13.3	2.3
	2004	81.2	54.4	6.1	48.3	22.9	16.1	26.9	12.1	6.7	86.3	61.5	17.5	44.0	11.2	18.0	24.8	11.1	2.6
East Asia (EA)	1992	79.6	48.0	4.1	43.9	12.9	19.8	31.6	15.2	5.1	86.1	62.7	28.8	33.9	9.2	15.0	23.3	12.3	1.6
	2004	83.9	67.4	6.8	60.6	31.1	18.8	16.5	11.2	4.8	88.9	73.6	19.7	53.9	13.1	22.6	15.3	9.5	1.6
Japan	1992	77.8	40.3	–	40.3	6.9	17.2	37.5	17.0	5.2	83.0	33.4	–	33.4	4.0	13.8	49.6	14.7	2.3
	2004	83.3	58.5	–	58.5	24.3	19.3	24.8	12.9	3.8	90.1	66.4	–	66.4	19.0	22.1	23.6	9.5	0.4
Developing East Asia (DEA)	1992	81.3	55.1	7.8	47.3	18.5	22.2	26.2	13.6	5.0	86.5	67.0	33.0	34.0	9.9	15.1	19.5	12.0	1.5
	2004	84.1	70.2	9.0	61.2	33.3	18.6	13.9	10.7	5.2	88.8	74.5	22.1	52.3	12.3	22.7	14.3	9.5	1.8
China	1992	86.4	74.2	4.2	70.0	45.4	13.3	12.1	7.9	5.7	85.0	72.0	25.1	46.8	22.4	9.5	13.1	13.2	1.7
	2004	86.0	74.4	7.8	66.6	47.3	10.4	11.6	8.8	5.2	88.4	81.0	22.5	58.6	13.6	20.0	7.3	9.3	2.3
AFTA6	1992	81.5	53.1	9.1	44.0	7.2	30.1	28.4	13.7	4.8	85.9	65.5	31.1	34.3	4.0	21.5	20.4	12.5	1.6
	2004	82.8	68.2	9.5	58.7	17.9	29.1	14.5	12.5	4.7	88.5	68.6	20.1	48.6	10.2	26.6	19.9	10.3	1.1
EU	1992	17.3	7.5	1.3	6.2	2.0	2.9	9.8	66.1	16.7	25.5	13.3	7.5	5.8	0.7	2.5	12.2	69.0	5.5
	2004	22.4	11.5	1.5	10.1	4.4	3.9	10.9	53.0	24.6	31.6	19.8	5.6	14.2	4.4	5.8	11.8	60.0	7.8
NAFTA	1992	68.2	21.5	6.0	15.5	2.7	7.5	46.6	19.0	12.9	82.7	39.5	22.8	16.7	1.9	7.3	43.2	14.3	3.1
	2004	75.5	26.4	4.5	21.9	5.3	10.2	49.1	13.9	10.6	81.7	39.8	13.5	26.3	8.0	9.7	41.9	14.0	4.3
World	1992	48.8	22.9	3.3	19.6	5.1	9.1	25.9	38.5	12.7	55.1	31.0	15.7	15.3	3.0	6.5	24.1	40.7	4.2
	2004	58.9	37.2	4.1	33.1	14.9	11.4	21.7	27.8	13.3	64.4	44.2	12.5	31.7	8.5	12.5	20.2	28.8	6.8

Notes: – = not applicable; AFTA = ASEAN Free Trade Area; APEC = Asia-Pacific Economic Cooperation; EU = European Union; NAFTA = North American Free Trade Area.

Source: Compiled from the UN Comtrade database.

Table 9.4 Share of parts and components in bilateral trade flows, 1992–2004 (per cent)

Exporter	Year	Exports									Imports								
		APEC	EA	Japan	DEA	GCH	AFTA6	NAFTA	EU	Other	APEC	EA	Japan	DEA	GCH	AFTA6	NAFTA	EU	Other
APEC	1992	49.1	52.2	39.8	55.9	34.9	79.5	47.0	38.6	31.5	52.1	48.2	58.1	39.6	19.9	67.9	57.7	35.4	29.7
	2004	57.6	80.5	52.1	87.4	81.3	103.4	39.4	44.1	32.9	63.0	63.5	74.6	59.5	36.3	82.9	62.1	41.5	37.9
East Asia (EA)	1992	51.4	53.2	39.2	55.4	34.1	83.9	49.3	35.1	18.8	54.6	52.5	65.2	44.4	24.5	83.1	60.3	34.6	17.8
	2004	68.2	83.9	55.8	89.4	84.5	87.3	40.5	45.4	24.2	70.7	70.1	80.2	67.0	42.2	81.2	73.3	46.4	44.0
Japan	1992	44.8	46.6	–	46.6	28.8	57.8	43.4	30.9	30.1	65.5	47.7	–	47.7	17.3	74.2	82.2	27.5	36.6
	2004	57.8	70.1	–	70.1	67.3	80.7	42.4	42.6	34.4	63.8	62.4	–	62.4	36.7	89.4	67.2	30.2	70.6
Developing East Asia (DEA)	1992	58.4	63.1	51.0	65.9	41.9	65.2	50.5	35.9	22.3	52.4	50.5	59.2	43.7	24.6	85.7	59.6	39.3	17.7
	2004	72.3	89.6	59.1	98.0	91.0	75.3	37.7	46.0	27.4	72.0	70.8	73.2	69.6	45.4	87.3	77.4	51.1	34.8
China	1992	43.7	47.2	51.7	46.9	40.5	58.1	30.1	26.7	25.9	42.6	41.0	35.9	44.3	37.8	62.6	54.3	35.7	20.7
	2004	59.8	68.7	50.8	71.7	74.2	63.6	32.6	32.8	29.5	67.2	67.6	62.1	70.0	53.2	86.7	62.6	44.0	51.1
AFTA6	1992	69.3	75.4	60.0	80.3	58.7	89.1	61.1	40.8	38.5	58.6	59.2	55.5	63.6	41.9	75.3	56.9	36.7	30.9
	2004	82.1	84.6	70.4	86.2	71.2	92.3	53.0	66.1	58.0	76.8	73.9	71.7	75.1	60.1	84.4	86.8	58.2	63.2
EU	1992	47.0	50.5	40.1	57.3	38.3	71.1	45.8	41.2	38.4	50.5	44.5	53.6	33.8	12.4	54.0	56.8	35.8	32.7
	2004	45.2	68.8	45.2	79.1	60.4	98.2	38.9	42.3	41.0	53.9	50.5	64.5	44.5	26.9	76.5	57.2	37.3	36.2
NAFTA	1992	61.4	60.2	35.0	72.5	66.6	83.2	62.2	53.7	56.7	53.1	44.5	54.3	33.2	12.6	58.6	64.9	47.3	34.8
	2004	61.4	82.0	45.7	94.4	87.6	96.1	49.2	53.7	55.2	55.2	53.3	60.6	50.4	31.8	86.0	58.3	46.9	38.5
World	1992	56.0	56.4	41.9	60.5	38.8	85.0	55.7	39.9	40.9	54.8	49.8	58.5	41.7	21.0	70.5	61.8	40.9	31.8
	2004	64.0	86.8	55.2	65.2	86.5	78.2	45.6	41.6	41.3	62.0	64.4	73.2	60.8	36.7	99.6	58.0	41.7	43.1

Note: – = not applicable; AFTA = ASEAN Free Trade Area; APEC = Asia-Pacific Economic Cooperation; EU = European Union; GCH = Greater China; NAFTA = North American Free Trade Area.

Source: Compiled from the UN Comtrade database.

and has increased at a faster rate; this reflects the fact that the region relies more on the rest of the world as a market for final goods than as a market for components.

Within East Asia, AFTA countries stand out for the high share of components in their intra-regional trade flows.[9] The share of components in total intra-regional exports in AFTA countries increased from 89.1 per cent in 1992 to 92.3 per cent in 2004 (Table 9.4). On the import side, the increase was from 75.3 per cent to 84.4 per cent. According to country-level data (not reported here, for brevity), the share of components in manufacturing exports and imports amounted to over four-fifths in Singapore, Malaysia and the Philippines and over two-thirds in Thailand. South Korea and Taiwan are also involved in sizeable trade in components with the other countries in the region. The share of components in total intra-regional trade of East Asia (both in exports and imports) of all East Asian countries has increased at a much faster rate (from 48.0 per cent to 67.4 per cent in exports and from 62.7 per cent to 73.6 per cent in imports) compared to that in trade with any other region (Table 9.3). The intra-regional share of component trade (both in exports and imports) is also much larger in Pacific Rim countries than in EU countries, because of the heavy concentration of component trade within East Asia.

As already noted, China was a late entrant in the fragmentation-based global division of labour, but it has already begun to replicate the overall regional patterns.[10] The share of Chinese imports of total manufacturing coming from East Asia increased from 64.3 per cent in 1992 to 76.2 per cent in 2004 (Table 9.5). This increase was dominated by components. The regional share of total Chinese imports of components increased from 37.6 per cent to 77.7 per cent between 1992 and 2004. Components accounted for over 90 per cent of the total increment in Chinese intra-regional manufacturing imports between 1992 and 2004. Japan continues to remain the major regional source country, but there was a notable diversification of source country composition between 1992 and 2004. The most notable development was the rapid growth of the combined share of AFTA countries, from a mere 0.9 per cent in 1992 to 19.3 per cent in 2004. Within AFTA countries, the import shares of Malaysia and the Philippines increased faster than that of Singapore. By 2004, Malaysia's share in total Chinese imports of components stood at 7.9 per cent, compared to Singapore's share of 3.5 per cent. The import shares of Taiwan and South Korea also increased persistently. However, the share of Hong Kong declined as many of the manufacturing activities carried out by Hong Kong businesses relocated to Mainland China. Overall, the data clearly suggest that China's trade integration through fragmentation-based trade is not predominantly limited to Greater China. The procurement network has rapidly expanded to cover other countries in the region.

On the export side, China's aggregate intra-regional share has declined persistently in both total manufacturing and component exports. Overall, China's evolving export patterns exhibit a clear and increasing extra-regional bias, in contrast to greater regional integration on the import side. This difference reflects the increasingly important role of China as a final product assembler for advanced-country markets using middle products procured from the region. Since about the mid-1990s, China's net imports from countries in developing East Asia have increasingly exceeded its exports to those countries (Athukorala 2005). The main reason for this trade deficit has been China's

Table 9.5 Direction of China's manufacturing trade, 1992, 1996 and 2004 (per cent)

	Exports			Imports		
	1992	1996	2004	1992	1996	2004
(a) Total manufacturing						
Japan	9.2	18.2	12.7	20.5	28.7	26.6
Hong Kong	53.1	23.7	18.5	27.9	8.4	4.3
Taiwan	0.6	1.6	2	9.9	17	17.3
South Korea	1.4	3.5	3.7	3.1	12.1	14.6
AFTA6	3.2	5.7	6.2	2.6	5.0	12.5
Indonesia	0.4	0.7	0.8	1.1	0.7	1.0
Malaysia	0.5	0.9	1.4	0.4	1.3	3.9
Philippines	0.2	0.5	0.6	0.1	0.1	2.1
Singapore	1.4	2.4	2.0	0.6	2.0	3.1
Thailand	0.6	0.7	0.8	0.2	0.9	2.3
Vietnam	0.1	0.5	0.5	...	...	0.1
Total East Asia	67.6	52.7	43.0	64.3	71.8	76.2
Total world trade	100	100	100	100	100	100
(b) Parts and components						
Japan	8.6	18.8	11.1	24.2	35.0	25.3
Hong Kong	61.0	22.9	27.0	5.3	8.6	4.2
Taiwan	1.7	3.7	3.6	5.3	10.4	16.9
South Korea	1.5	5.4	4.3	1.9	7.6	12.2
AFTA6	4.8	10.8	11.5	0.9	7.5	19.3
Indonesia	0.7	1.4	0.8	0.0	0.1	0.5
Malaysia	1.0	2.4	3.8	0.1	1.7	7.9
Philippines	0.3	0.7	1.1	0.0	0.3	4.7
Singapore	2.4	5.2	3.9	0.7	4.2	3.5
Thailand	0.5	0.8	1.6	0.1	1.3	2.7
Vietnam	0.1	0.3	0.3	...	...	...
Total East Asia	77.6	61.1	57.2	37.6	69.1	77.7
Total world trade	100	100	100	100	100	100

Note: ... = zero or negligible.
Source: Compiled from the UN Comtrade database.

increasing reliance on countries in the region for parts and components for its booming domestic final-goods assembly activities. Net trade in parts and components with other countries in the region increased from about $2 billion in 1997 to over $50 billion in 2004.

PRODUCTION FRAGMENTATION AND REGIONAL VERSUS GLOBAL ECONOMIC INTEGRATION

So far I have examined the growing importance of fragmentation-based trade for emerging economic interdependence among countries of the Pacific Rim, East Asia and other subregions. I now examine the implications of this new form of international specialisation for the relative importance of intra-regional versus global economic integration and the way in which latecomers in the region are catching up in the growth process through economic globalisation. These two issues are central to the contemporary debate on growth dynamism and the process of intra-regional versus inter-regional economic integration in East Asia.

There is a vast literature on standard trade data analysis (essentially based on the traditional notion of horizontal specialisation, in which trade is an exchange of goods that are produced from start to finish in just one country). This literature unequivocally points to a persistent increase in intra-regional trade in East Asia (whether Japan is included or not) from about the early 1980s (see, for example, Kwan 2001; Drysdale and Garnaut 1997; Frankel and Wei 1997; Petri 1993; Pearson 1994; Ng and Yeats 2003). This evidence figures prominently in the current regional debate on forming regional trading arrangements covering some or all countries in East Asia. In particular, the proponents of the proposal to expand AFTA to encompass Japan, China and South Korea (the ASEAN+3 proposal) often refer to deepening economic interdependence reflected in intra-regional trade among these countries as evidence of its likely success (Ng and Yeats 2003; Baldwin 2006). Increasing trade integration is also cited as an indicator of the potential benefits of monetary integration in the region (Kwan 2001).

However, the above discussion on the emerging patterns of intra-regional component trade casts doubts on the validity of these inferences. I have noted two important peculiarities of trade patterns in East Asia compared to total global trade and trade patterns for EU and NAFTA countries. First, component trade has played a much more important role in trade expansion in East Asia relative to the overall global experience and the experiences of countries in other major regions. Second, trade in components accounts for a much larger share in intra-regional trade than in trade with the rest of the world. Given these two peculiarities, trade flow analysis based on reported trade data is bound to yield a misleading picture as to the relative importance of intra-regional trade relations (as against global trade) for growth in East Asia (and AFTA and other subregional groupings therein). This is because growth based on assembly activities eventually depends on demand for final goods, which depends increasingly on extra-regional growth.

Alternative estimates of intra-regional trade shares reported in Table 9.6 help to illustrate this argument. Panels A and B show the inter-regional trade shares estimated using data on total (reported) trade and trade in components; the figures come from Tables 9.2 and 9.3. Intra-regional shares of 'net trade' (that is, total trade minus components) are reported in panel C.

There is no notable difference between the intra-regional trade shares of Pacific Rim countries calculated on the basis of data on 'total trade' (that is, total manufacturing trade as reported in standard trade statistics) and 'final trade' (reported manufacturing trade net of parts and components). However, the two alternative estimates are vastly different for East Asia, particularly for developing Asia and AFTA countries: both the level in the two given years and the change over time of intra-regional trade shares are significantly lower in terms of estimates based on final trade. For instance, the intra-

Table 9.6 Intra-regional trade shares: total manufacturing, parts and components, and final trade, 1992 and 2004 (per cent)

		APEC	East Asia[a]	Developing East Asia[b]	AFTA6	NAFTA	EU
A Total manufacturing							
Exports	1992	69.0	41.7	42.5	26.8	48.4	62.5
	2004	75.7	56.3	50.2	27.9	54.7	51.6
Imports	1992	80.3	60.7	29.8	16.7	40.5	67.3
	2004	83.4	71.2	48.4	24.2	41.6	58.9
Trade (exports + imports)	1992	74.2	49.4	35.3	20.6	44.3	64.8
	2004	79.4	62.8	49.4	26.1	47.5	52.7
B Parts and components							
Exports	1992	74.5	48.0	47.3	30.1	46.6	66.1
	2004	81.2	67.4	61.2	29.1	49.1	53.0
Imports	1992	84.4	62.7	34.0	21.5	43.2	69.0
	2004	86.3	73.6	52.3	26.6	41.9	60.0
Trade (exports + imports)	1992	79.0	54.4	39.8	25.1	44.5	67.5
	2004	83.7	70.3	56.8	27.9	45.4	58.2
C Final goods[c]							
Exports	1992	63.8	36.7	37.8	22.2	50.6	59.6
	2004	68.2	40.4	32.3	24.1	61.8	53.6
Imports	1992	76.6	58.7	25.8	11.6	38.0	65.8
	2004	79.4	56.6	40.4	17.6	41.4	56.4
Trade (exports + imports)	1992	69.7	45.2	30.9	15.3	43.5	62.6
	2004	73.5	45.2	35.9	20.8	49.7	54.4

Notes: AFTA = ASEAN Free Trade Area; APEC = Asia-Pacific Economic Cooperation; EU = European Union; NAFTA = North American Free Trade Area.
a Including Japan.
b Including AFTA countries
c Total manufacturing net of parts and components (A − B)
Source: Compiled from the UN Comtrade database.

regional share of total manufacturing trade in developing East Asia increased from 35.3 per cent in 1992 to 49.4 per cent in 2004. However, in terms of estimates based on final trade, the share increased from 31 per cent to 36 per cent. While the difference between intra-regional shares of final and total trade is observable for both exports and imports, the magnitude of the difference is much larger on the export side. In 2004 only 32 per cent of final goods exported from developing East Asia found markets within the region, compared to 50 per cent in total exports. Moreover, for all East Asian countries Japan is a much smaller market than NAFTA or EU countries for final goods exports. It is also interesting to note that, unlike in the case of East

Asia (or developing East Asia and AFTA), the estimated intra-regional trade share for NAFTA, EU and other regional groupings are remarkably resilient to the inclusion or exclusion of component trade.

In sum, the estimates presented in this section support the hypothesis that, where fragmentation-based trade is expanding rapidly, the standard trade flow analysis can lead to misleading inferences regarding the ongoing process of economic integration through trade. When data on assembly trade are excluded from trade flows, my estimates suggest that extra-regional trade is much more important than intra-regional trade for continued growth in East Asia, whether or not Japan is included. Thus, the ongoing process of product fragmentation seems to have strengthened the case for a global approach to trade and investment policymaking rather than a regional one.

PRODUCTION FRAGMENTATION AND GROWTH PATTERNS: PRELIMINARY OBSERVATIONS

The received view on growth patterns in countries in the Asia Pacific region stipulates a dynamic process of changing comparative advantage, a process in which each country rapidly shifts its output from raw materials to manufactures, and within manufactures shifts from labour-intensive to more capital- and technology-intensive sectors. The Japanese economists Akamatsu (1961) and Kojima (2000) described this sequential growth pattern as the flying geese pattern of development; it is consistent with the Hecksher–Ohlin explanations of how trade patterns are likely to change with the accumulation of human and physical capital (Balassa 1979).

A large number of studies carried out in the 1980s and early 1990s have shown that the flying geese pattern of growth holds remarkably well in East Asia.[11] Specifically, authors such as Petri (1993) have found that Japan began to compete with the United States in technologically sophisticated products from about the early 1980s, that NIEs followed the Japanese export structure with a lag of 15–20 years, that the economies in Southeast Asia are ten years further behind, and that China trails the Southeast Asian countries by another few years. This view of orderly, sequential economic transformation has profound implications for trade and industrial policy. The rapidly changing structure of exports implies that competitive pressure is experienced by countries at lower levels on the ladder, but it also means that there are new export opportunities for newcomers, as countries on higher rungs vacate export markets. For importing countries, according to this view, the source of competitive pressure in traditional labour-intensive products is expected to shift; however, to the extent that imports from one country merely displace imports from another, no new domestic resource adjustment costs arise. For instance, at the top levels of the ladder the United States and Japan find themselves in direct competition in technologically sophisticated products, but the competitive pressure is tolerable because most of these products create their own markets.

Has this sequential process of economic transformation been disturbed by the ongoing process of production fragmentation? The flying geese growth paradigm is based on the conventional (product-based) division of labour among economies. It assumes a competitive relationship among countries in the growth process, rather than a complementary one. This permits countries to climb the growth ladder on the basis of their own competitiveness achieved through policy reforms. Fragmentation-based international specialisation permits firms to relocate at each stage of the production process to places where production can be conducted at the lowest cost. This process could well disturb the sequential process of economic transformation. It permits firms in countries on the upper rungs of the growth ladder to remain internationally competitive in some segments of the production process (such as in product/component design, production of skill- and technology-intensive components, and various headquarter functions) even when rising incomes and related domestic cost pressures begin to erode their competitiveness in integrated production of the whole product at home. This, in turn, could constrain the growth process of countries on the middle rungs of the ladder, while countries on the lower rungs still benefit from their relative labour cost advantages. In other words, in the face of rapid expansion of fragmentation-based specialisation in the world economy, countries at the middle levels are confronted with the increasingly challenging task of finding ways to 'tech up' and enter the global knowledge economy, so as to escape the trap of having to dumb down to compete in standardised manufacturing (and, increasingly, standardised services) (Garrett 2004).

The growing complementarity of production processes across countries resulting from production fragmentation has implications for latecomers wishing to catch up in the growth process. This is an important subject for further research. Lall and Albaladejo (2004), Rodrik (2006) and Schott (2006) have done some useful ground-clearing work in this direction. Their studies focus on the implications of China's rise as a major trading nation for the global economy, but their findings have important general implications for the subject at hand.

Lall and Albaladejo (2004) examine changing the technological sophistication of Chinese exports from a comparative regional perspective by disaggregating export data on the basis of a commodity classification that reflects factor intensity properties of end products. Rodrik (2006) undertakes a comparative analysis of the sophistication of the export profile of China relative to its income level based on a newly constructed index that measures the productivity level associated with a country's export basket. Schott (2006) examines the relative sophistication of China's exports to the United States by comparing China's export bundle and prices (unit values) within broader product categories to those of the relatively skill- and capital-abundant members of Organisation for Economic Co-operation and Development (OECD) countries as well as to similarly endowed US trading partners.

The findings of Rodrik (2006) and Lall and Albaladejo (2004) suggest that, within about 1½ decades, China has ended up with an export basket that is significantly more sophisticated than what would be normally anticipated for a country at its income level. Put differently, taken at face value these results seem to suggest that the complementarity in specialisation patterns dictated by the ongoing process of product-fragmentation-based specialisation does not seem to have created an unsurmountable constraint to China's economic transition. The authors combine their findings with some (selective) impressionistic accounts of China's industrial policy to suggest that

China's activist policy has played a pivotal role in China's export success by nurturing domestic capabilities in consumer electronics and other advanced product lines.

The findings of these studies, however, need to be treated with caution because the authors have failed to take the ongoing process of product fragmentation into account in the analysis. This is a serious limitation because, although the end products of electronics, electrical items, automobile and other related products belonging to medium-tech and high-tech product categories are obviously capital/technology-intensive, assembly activities within the production process (both component assembly and final assembly) are generally low-tech and highly labour intensive. In other words, the mere fact that a given country is exporting final goods (end products) in a highly fragmented high-tech industry does not necessarily imply the domestic production of those goods. Therefore the classification of final commodities by factor intensity is not the same as the classification of the production process occurring in these countries by factor intensity. Put simply, any analysis of the technology structure of exports (as in Lall and Albaladejo 2004) or the technological sophistication of products (Rodrik 2006) based on the readily available data on total (reported) trade data is likely to come up with an exaggerated picture of the technological sophistication of China's exports.

Over the past ten years, China's export composition has undergone a dramatic shift away from conventional labour-intensive product lines and towards more sophisticated ones (Table 9.7). For instance, between 1994–95 and 2003–04, the share of miscellaneous manufactured products (SITC 8) (consisting predominantly of clothing, footwear, toys and sporting goods, and other labour-intensive products) declined from 55.6 per cent to 37.4 per cent. Conversely, there was an increase in the share of machinery and transport equipment (SITC 7) (consisting predominantly of various capital- and technology-intensive products) from 24.7 per cent to 46.3 per cent. This increase was underpinned by China's highly publicised export success in a wide range of electronics and electrical products (falling under SITC categories 75, 76 and 77). However, data on the relative importance of parts and components in machinery and transport equipment trade (reported in panels B, C and D of Table 9.7) clearly suggest that the role of Chinese firms (most of which are subsidiaries of MNEs) in the global production chain of these products is mostly limited to final assembly.

China's total imports of machinery and transport equipment are dominated by parts and components. The share of parts and components accounted for 62.5 per cent of total imports of this product category in 2003–04, up from 40.3 per cent in 1994–95. By contrast final goods (total exports minus parts and components) still account for about two-thirds of total exports in 2003–04. Trade balance in machinery and transport equipment increased from –9.7 per cent of exports to over 35 per cent in 2003–04, as the outcome of a dramatic increase in the trade surplus in final goods. However, the trade deficit in parts and components widened, from –8.3 per cent to –15.1 per cent. Given the fact that the production of parts and components is generally more capital- and technology-intensive than final assembly, these figures suggest that by and large China's export success has so far been underpinned by its comparative advantage in international production arising from labour abundance rather than by the increased sophistication of the export mix.[12]

Table 9.7 Product fragmentation and the structure of manufacturing exports from China, 1994–2004 (per cent)

SITC code	Commodity category	1994–95[a]	1999–2000[a]	2003–04[a]
A	*Export composition*			
5	Chemicals and related products	4.1	3.5	3.5
6	Manufactured goods classified by material[b]	15.6	13.1	12.8
7	Machinery and transport equipment	24.7	35.0	46.3
71	Power generating machinery	1.1	1.3	1.0
72	Special industrial machinery	0.5	0.5	0.8
73	Metalworking machinery	0.2	0.2	0.2
74	General industrial machinery	1.7	2.1	2.9
75	Office machines	4.1	9.3	15.5
76	Telecomm. and sound recording equipment	9.3	9.5	12.7
77	Electrical machinery and parts	6.8	10.7	11.7
78	Road vehicles	0.9	1.2	1.3
79	Other transport equipment	0.2	0.2	0.2
8	Miscellaneous manufactured goods	55.6	48.4	37.4
84	Clothing and accessories	20.2	15.4	11.5
85	Footwear	8.6	6.2	4.1
894	Toys, games etc.	9.5	9.4	6.7
	Total	100	100	100
B	*Share of parts and components in machinery and transport equipment exports*			
71	Power generating machinery	15.0	27.9	32.2
72	Special industrial machinery	23.4	27.5	26.9
73	Metalworking machinery	19.7	29.2	38.1
74	General industrial machinery	27.5	35.5	35.8
75	Office machines	44.3	42.6	35.4
76	Telecomm. and sound recording equipment	17.4	23.9	22.5
77	Electrical machinery and parts	30.4	38.7	47.0
78	Road vehicles	34.6	38.3	51.6
79	Other transport equipment	16.4	18.4	19.4
7	Total	26.8	34.7	35.0
C	*Share of parts and components in machinery and transport equipment imports*			
71	Power generating machinery	58.7	69.7	68.1
72	Special industrial machinery	16.9	22.2	20.5
73	Metalworking machinery	19.2	23.4	23.0
74	General industrial machinery	26.1	38.9	40.0
75	Office machines	64.0	63.6	65.3
76	Telecomm. and sound recording equipment	54.9	72.4	76.5
77	Electrical machinery and parts	68.6	80.7	84.6
78	Road vehicles	32.1	55.1	53.1
79	Other transport equipment	8.0	13.4	13.3
7	Total	40.3	59.9	62.5
D	*Trade balance in machinery and transport equipment*			
	Total trade	–9.7	35.8	35.6
	Trade in parts and components	–8.3	–10.7	–15.1
	Trade in final products	2.4	60.6	62.9

Notes:
a Two-year averages.
b SITC 6 net of SITC 68 (non-ferrous metals).

Source: Compiled from the UN Comtrade database.

This inference is consistent with the findings of Schott (2006), who examined the relative 'sophistication' of China's exports to the United States in 1972–2001. By comparing China's export bundle to that of the relatively skill- and capital-abundant members of the OECD as well as to that of similarly endowed US trading partners, Schott (2006) found that China's export bundle increasingly overlaps with that of more developed countries, rendering it more sophisticated than that of the other countries with similar factor endowments. By contrast, his comparison of prices (unit values) within product categories reveals that China's exports 'sell at a substantial discount relative to its level of GDP and the exports of the OECD countries' (Schott 2006: 15). Schott stops short of probing this rather puzzling contrast between the observed product sophistication and price trends, but it is certainly consistent with the nature of China's participation in fragmentation-based specialisation in global manufacturing trade. China is engaged in the labour-intensive stages of production (mostly final assembly) in otherwise advanced industries.

CONCLUDING REMARKS

There is clear evidence that fragmentation-based specialisation has become an integral part of the economic landscape of East Asia. Trade in components has been expanding more rapidly than that of conventional final-goods trade. The degree of dependence on this new form of international specialisation is proportionately larger in East Asia than in North America or Europe. It seems to be the outcome of the relatively more favourable policy setting for international production, agglomeration benefits arising from the early entry into this new form of specialisation, and considerable inter-country wage differentials in the region.

A notable recent development in the international fragmentation of production in the region has been the rapid integration of China into the regional production networks. This development is an important counterpoint to the popular belief that China's global integration will crowd out other countries' opportunities for international specialisation. My estimates support the hypothesis that, where fragmentation-based trade is expanding rapidly, the standard trade flow analysis can lead to an understatement of the trading significance of China in the process of economic integration through trade. China's imports of components from East Asia have grown rapidly, in line with the rapid expansion of manufacturing exports, mostly to North American and EU countries.

Production fragmentation has certainly played a pivotal role in the continuing dynamism of the East Asian economies and increasing intra-regional economic interdependence. This does not, however, mean that the process has contributed to lessening the region's dependence on the global economy. The high intra-regional trade shares reported in recent studies largely reflect rapidly expanding intra-regional trade in components. There is no evidence of rapid intra-regional trade integration in final products. In fact, the region's growth based on vertical specialisation depends inexorably on its extra-regional trade in final goods, and this dependence has *increased* over the years. The growing importance of China as both a regional exporter and a regional importer has begun to change the picture in recent years, but extra-regional trade is likely to remain the engine of growth of the region in the foreseeable future.

Put simply, growing trade in components has made the East Asian region increasingly reliant on extra-regional trade for its growth. In this context, East Asian countries would be better off if they upheld universal principles of economic openness.

Finally, what are the implications of these findings for the contemporary policy debate on regional economic cooperation? In particular, is the newfound fondness of countries in the region for free trade agreements consistent with the objective of maximising gains from the ongoing process of international product fragmentation?

Trade in components and final assembly is postulated to be relatively more sensitive to tariff changes than is final trade (or total trade as captured in published trade data) (Yi 2003). Normally a tariff is incurred each time a good-in-process crosses a border. Consequently, a one percentage point reduction in tariff leads to a decline in the cost of production of a vertically integrated good by a multiple of this initial reduction, in contrast to a 1 per cent decline in the cost of a regular traded good. Tariff reduction may also make it more profitable for goods that were previously produced entirely in one country to become vertically specialised. Consequently, in theory, the trade-stimulating effect of free trade agreements would be higher for trade in parts and components than for normal trade, other things remaining unchanged. However, in reality, much would depend on the nature of rules of origin built into free trade agreements (Garnaut 2003). Trade-distorting effects of rules of origin are presumably more detrimental to fragmentation-based trade than to conventional final-goods trade, because of the inherent difficulties in defining the 'product' for duty exemption and because of the transaction costs associated with the bureaucratic supervision of the amount of value added in production coming from various sources. Moreover, maintaining barriers to trade against non-members (while allowing free trade among members) can thwart 'natural' expansion of fragmentation-based trade across countries.

To benefit from the new opportunities for trade expansion through the fragmentation-based division of labour, the best policy choice appears to be multilateral liberalisation through the World Trade Organization process; the ongoing process of product fragmentation seems to have strengthened the case for a global, rather than a regional, approach to trade and investment policymaking. The APEC-wide approach to regional trade liberalisation, with a firm commitment to open regionalism, remains only a second best strategy. Baldwin (2006) put forward a case for a 'New East Asia regional management effort' with a reinforced ASEAN+3, with a view to ensuring smooth functioning of the process of fragmentation-based specialisation (which he dubs 'Factory Asia'). My findings do not lend support to his case. Baldwin has correctly identified the importance of fragmentation-based specialisation for economic growth in these countries, but unfortunately he has completely overlooked the important fact that the growth dynamism based on this new form of specialisation depends on extra-regional trade in final goods, and this dependence has in fact increased over the years.

NOTES

1   Examples include long-lasting cellular batteries originally developed by computer producers and now widely used in cellular phones and electronic organisers; transmitters which are used not only in radios (as originally designed) but also in personal computers and missiles;

and electronic chips, the use of which has spread beyond the computer industry into consumer electronics, motor vehicle production and many other product sectors (Jones 2000; Jones and Kierzkowski 2001; Brown *et al.* 2004).

2   Key contributions to this literature include Borrus (1997), Naughton (1999), McKendrick *et al.* (2000), Ng and Yeats (2001, 2003) and Dobson and Chia (1997).

3   For instance 'television tubes' were not separable from 'TVs' and 'computer processors' were lumped together with 'computers'.

4   The list is available in Athukorala (2003), Appendix A-5.

5   The terms 'Pacific Rim countries' and 'APEC countries' are used interchangeably in the remainder of the chapter.

6   In 2005 Singapore started releasing data on trade with Indonesia, after the Indonesian government had pressured it for decades to do so.

7   Henceforth I use the term 'components' in place of 'parts and components', for brevity.

8   The average annual compensation (salary/wage plus other remuneration) per worker in selected countries in the years indicated was as follows: China $1,835 (2001); Indonesia $880 (2000); Philippines $2,965 (2000); Thailand $3,345 (1994); Malaysia $4,380 (2000); Vietnam $650 (2000); Taiwan $14,420 (1997); South Korea $15,780 (2000); Singapore $20,440 (2000); Poland $2,502 (2000); Hungary $2,898 (2000); Czech Republic $4,150 (1998); Mexico $8,050 (2000). These figures are from Nicita and Olarreaga (2006: Statistical Appendix) except for China, where they are from China Statistical Press (2003) (average wage for Beijing, Tianjin, Shanhai, Zhejiang, Liaoning and Guangdon), and Vietnam, where they are from Vietnam General Statistical Office (2000).

9   Rapid growth of intra-regional fragmentation-based trade in AFTA countries clearly pre-dates the formation of AFTA in 1994. Whether the formation of AFTA would have provided further impetus for the expansion of this trade remains an unresolved issue that warrants further study. From its inception in the early 1960s, this form of international exchange in these countries took place under virtual free trade conditions as part of the policy emphasis on export-led industrialisation. Trade liberalisation under AFTA may have simply substituted for the existing tariff concessions rather that generating new incentives (Athukorala and Yamashita 2006).

10 It is important to note that cross-border production networks in East Asia were already well established when China's rapid penetration in world manufacturing trade began in the early 1990s. This new form of division of labour could have been sustained even without China's entry.

11 See Petri (1993), Pearson (1994) and the works cited therein.

12 The data reported in Table 9.7 (Panel B) point to a modest increase in the share of parts and components in exports. This share in the total export of machinery and transport equipment increased from 26.8 per cent in 1994–95 to 35.0 per cent in 2000–04. The increase is particularly notable for electrical machinery and parts (from 30.4 per cent to 47.0 per cent) and road vehicles (from 34.6 per cent to 51.6 per cent). However, it is not possible to interpret these increases as an indication of an increase in production sophistication (a shift from labour-intensive final assembly to capital- and technology-intensive component production) because parts and components in export records include both domestically 'designed and produced' components and components that are simply 'assembled and/or tested'. The available evidence on global production chains in electronics components suggest that activities undertaken in China are still largely (if not totally) confined to simple assembly and testing (see Brown and Linden 2006 and the works cited therein). Further research into the extent to which China's involvement in fragmentation-based specialisation has evolved from mere assembly to local production of intermediate skill- and technology-intensive products is certainly warranted.

REFERENCES

Akamatsu, K. (1961) 'A theory of unbalanced growth in the world economy', *Weltwirtschaftliches Archiv*, 86: 196–217.
Athukorala, Prema-chandra (2003) 'Product fragmentation and trade patterns in East Asia', Trade and Development Discussion Paper 2003/21, Division of Economics, Research School of Pacific and Asian Studies, Australian National University, Canberra.
—— (2005) 'Component trade and China's regional economic integration', pp. 139–163 in R. Garnaut and L. Song (eds.), *The China Boom and its Discontents*, Canberra: Asia Pacific Press.
Athukorala, Prema-chandra and Nobuaki Yamashita (2006) 'Production fragmentation and trade integration: East Asia in a global context', *North American Journal of Economics and Finance*, 17(4): 233–256.
Baldwin, R. (2006) 'Managing the noodle bowl: the fragility of East Asian regionalism', Centre for Policy Research (CEPR) Discussion Paper 5561, London: CEPR.
Balassa, B. (1979) 'Changing patterns of comparative advantage in manufactured goods', *Review of Economics and Statistics*, 61(2): 259–266.
Borrus, M. (1997) 'Left for dead: Asian production networks and the revival of US electronics', pp. 215–239 in B. Naughton (ed.), *The China Circle: Economics and Technology in the PRC, Taiwan and Hong Kong*, Canberra: Brookings Institution Press.
Brown, C. and G. Linden (2006) 'Offshoring in the semiconductor industry: a historical perspective', pp. 279–333 in L. Brainard and S.M. Collins (eds), *Brookings Trade Forum 2005: Offshoring White-Collar Work: The Issues and the Implications*, Washington DC: Brookings Institution Press.
Brown, D.K., A.V. Deardorff and R.M. Stern (2004) 'The effect of multinational production on wages and working conditions in developing countries', pp. 279–332 in R.E. Baldwin and L.A. Winters (eds), *Challenges of Globalization: Analyzing the Economics*, Chicago: University of Chicago Press.
China Statistical Press (2003) *China Statistical Yearbook*, Beijing: China Statistical Press.
Dobson, W. and Chia, S. Yeu (1997) *Multinationals and East Asian Integration*, Singapore: Institute of Southeast Asian Studies.
Drysdale, P. and R. Garnaut (1997) 'The Pacific: an application of a general theory of economic integration', pp. 183–224 in C.F. Bergsten and M. Noland (eds), *Pacific Dynamism and the International Economic System*, Washington DC: Institute for International Economics.
Feenstra, R. (1998) 'Integration of trade and disintegration of production in the global economy', *Journal of Economic Perspectives*, 14(4): 31–50.
Feenstra, R.C., Wen Hai, Wing T. Woo and Shuni Uao (1999) 'Discrepancies in international trade data: an application to China–Hong Kong entrepôt trade', *American Economic Review*, 89(2): 338–343.
Feenstra, R.C., R.E. Lipsey, Haiyan Deng, Alyson C. Ma and Hengyong Mo (2005) 'World trade flows, 1962–2000', National Bureau of Economic Research (NBER) Working Paper 11040, Cambridge MA: NBER (<http://www.nber.org/chapters/w11040>).
Frankel, J.A. and Shang-Jin Wei (1997) 'The new regionalism and Asia: impact and policy options', pp. 83–130 in A. Panagariya, M.G. Quibria and N. Rao (eds), *The Global Trading System and Developing Asia*, Oxford: Oxford University Press.
Garnaut, R. (2003) 'Australia and Japan: time to be important to each other again', address to the Australia-Japan Business Cooperation Committee conference, Kyoto, 5 October 2003, Division of Economics, Research School of Pacific and Asian Studies, Australian National University (mimeo).
Garrett, G. (2004) 'Globalization's missing middle', *Foreign Affairs*, 83(6): 1–6.
Grossman, G.M. and E. Helpman (2005) 'Outsourcing in a global economy', *Review of Economic Studies*, 72 (1): 135–159.

Helleiner, G.K. (1989) 'Transnational corporations and direct foreign investment', pp. 1142–1480 in H. Chenery and T.N. Srinivasan (eds), *Handbook of Development Economics, Volume 2*, Amsterdam: North Holland Press.

Jones, R.W. (2000) *Globalization and the Theory of Input Trade*, Cambridge MA: MIT Press.

Jones, R.W. and H. Kierzkowski (2001) 'Globalization and the consequences of international fragmentation', pp. 365–381 in R. Dornbusch, G. Calvo and M. Obstfeld (eds), *Money, Factor Mobility and Trade: Festschrift in Honor of Robert A. Mundell*, Cambridge MA: MIT Press.

Jones, R.W., H. Kierzkowski and C. Lurong, C. (2004) 'What does the evidence tell us about fragmentation and outsourcing', *International Review of Economics and Finance*, 14 (3): 305–316.

Kaminski, B. and F. Ng (2005) 'Production disintegration and integration of Central Europe into global markets', *International Review of Economics and Finance*, 14: 377–390.

Kierzkowski, H. (2001) 'Joining the global economy: experience and prospects of the transition economies', pp. 231–253 in S.W. Arndt and H. Kierzkowski (eds), *Fragmentation: New Production Patterns in the World Economy*, Oxford: Oxford University Press.

Kojima, Kiyoshi (2000) 'The "flying geese" model of Asian economic development: origin, theoretical extensions, and regional policy implications', *Journal of Asian Economics*, 11(4): 375–401.

Kwan, C.H. (2001) *Yen Bloc: Toward Economic Integration in Asia*, Washington DC: Brookings Institution Press.

Lall, S. and M. Albaladejo (2004) 'China's competitive performance: a threat to East Asian manufactured exports?', *World Development*, 32(9): 1441–1466.

McKendrick, D.G., R.F. Doner and S. Haggard (2000) *From Silicon Valley to Singapore: Location and Competitive Advantage in the Hard Disk Drive Industry*, Stanford CA: Stanford University Press.

Naughton, B. (ed.) (1999) *The China Circle: Economics and Technology in the PRC, Taiwan and Hong Kong*, Washington DC: Brookings Institution Press.

Ng, F. and A. Yeats (2001) 'Production sharing in East Asia: who does what for whom, and why?', pp. 63–109 in L.K. Cheng and H. Kierzkowski (eds), *Global Production and Trade in East Asia*, Boston MA: Kluwer Academic Publishers.

—— (2003) 'Major trade trends in East Asia: what are their implications for regional cooperation and growth?', Policy Research Working Paper 3084, Washington DC: World Bank.

Nicita, A. and M. Olarreaga (2006) 'Trade, production and protection 1976–2004', Washington DC: World Bank (see <www.worldbank.org>).

Pearson, C.S. (1994) 'The Asian export ladder', pp. 35–52 in Shu-Chin Yang (ed.), *Manufactured Exports of Asian Industrializing Economies: Possible Regional Cooperation*, New York: M.E. Sharpe.

Petri, P. (1993) 'The East Asian trading bloc: an analytical history', pp. 21–48 in J.A. Frankel and M. Kahler (eds), *Regionalism and Rivalry: Japan and the United States in Pacific Asia*, Chicago: Chicago University Press.

Rangan, S. and R. Lawrence (1999) *A Prism on Globalization*, Washington DC: Brookings Institution Press.

Rodrik, D. (2006) 'What's so special about China's exports?', National Bureau of Economic Research (NBER) Working Paper 11947, Cambridge MA: NBER.

Schott, P.K. (2006) 'The relative sophistication of Chinese exports', National Bureau of Economic Research (NBER) Working Paper 12173, Cambridge, MA: NBER (see <http://www.nber.org/papers/w12173>).

Sturgeon, T.J. (2003) 'What really goes on in Silicon Valley? Spatial clustering and dispersal in modular production networks', *Journal of Economic Geography*, 3: 199–225.

USITC (United States International Trade Commission) (1999) *Production Sharing: Use of U.S. Components and Material in Foreign Assembly Operations, 1995–1998*, Washington DC: USITC Publication 3265.

Vietnam General Statistical Office (2000) *Analysing the Results of the Industrial Survey of Vietnam – 1999*, Hanoi: Statistical Publishing House.

Yeats, Alexander (2001) 'Just how big is global production sharing?', pp. 108–143 in S. Arndt and H. Kierzkowski (eds), *Fragmentation: New Production Patterns in the World Economy*, New York: Oxford University Press,.
Yi, Kei-Mu (2003) 'Can vertical specialization explain the growth of world trade', *Journal of Political Economy*, 111(1): 52–102.

10 Multinational corporations and Pacific regionalism

Philippa Dee

INTRODUCTION

Time was that investment was investment, and trade was trade, and the contribution of each to economic development was examined separately. Foreign direct investment (FDI) was to be encouraged by having a good investment climate, because investment added to the stock of resources for economic development. Trade was to be encouraged by having an open trading regime, because trade provided the discipline of competition, ensuring the most efficient use of the resources available.

Now it is recognised that FDI and trade respond jointly to the complex forces of economic geography. Both phenomena reflect 'a tug of war between forces that tend to promote geographical concentration and those that tend to oppose it – between "centripetal" and "centrifugal" forces' (Krugman 1998: 8). And the key players making the balancing decisions that determine the resulting trade and investment flows are multinational corporations.

Centripetal forces tend to ensure that economic activity is concentrated. Centripetal forces include large local markets (which create both backward and forward linkages), thick labour markets, and pure external economies (such as information spillovers). In an international context, an important centripetal force is plant-level economies of scale. These provide an incentive to concentrate production in a particular location and serve other markets via international trade.

Centrifugal forces tend to ensure that economic activity is dispersed. Centrifugal forces include immobile factors (for example, skilled labour, land) whose shortage may bid up factor prices and restrict further concentration, and purely external diseconomies (for example, congestion). In an international context, two important centrifugal forces are transport costs (both trade barriers and shipping costs) that make it relatively expensive to serve a market via trade, and differences in factor endowments, which may make it expensive to concentrate all stages of production at home. A final important factor is firm-level economies of scale, which mean that even if economic activity is geographically dispersed, it is still carried out by the same firm, hence promoting FDI.

Early models of multinational behaviour that reflected a balancing of these forces were models of horizontal and vertical FDI. Horizontal FDI was 'market seeking'. It reflected a desire to place economic activity close to markets, so as to avoid trade costs. Vertical FDI was 'factor seeking'. It reflected a desire to carry out the unskilled labour-intensive parts of production in locations with relatively abundant unskilled labour.

Early examples of literature that explained the behaviour of multinationals in these terms included Markusen (1984) and Helpman (1984). These models forced FDI to take one or the other of these forms. More recent studies have integrated the two motivations for FDI, particularly in the 'knowledge capital' model of FDI by Markusen (1997, 2002).

But anecdotal evidence suggests that these characterisations of multinational behaviour may be too simplistic. For example, Victor Fung, a Hong Kong clothing and textile executive, no longer describes himself as being in the textile and clothing business, but rather describes himself as being in the supply chain management business. He describes how his company may divide the production process for a particular clothing order into six or more steps in different countries throughout the East Asian region, and will re-optimise the supply chain for each new order. He describes this process as the 'democratisation' of the global production system, where every economy has a place (Fung 2005). Further, firms such as his may invest in some countries and deal at arm's length in others. This behaviour is better described in network terms, rather than as simple horizontal or vertical FDI. Other chapters in this volume describe similar behaviour (see Boyson and Han, Chapter 2, and Chen and Lin, Chapter 8). Athukorala (Chapter 9) shows that such product fragmentation has made East Asia increasingly reliant on extra-regional trade, strengthening the case for a global rather than a regional approach to trade and investment policymaking.

This chapter has two aims. The first is to determine empirically whether there is a unique regional model of FDI ('somewhere') in the Asia Pacific region, driven by such 'network' behaviour. This question is examined by estimating a theoretical model of FDI that can account for such behaviour, and seeing whether it fits FDI patterns in the Asian region better than elsewhere. The second purpose is to determine empirically whether the investment provisions of preferential trade agreements (PTAs) have had any influence on this regional investment behaviour. This question is examined by including measures of the extent of investment provisions in the estimated model of FDI. The results suggest that the answer to the first question is affirmative and the answer to the second is negative. By comparing this investment behaviour to that in other regions, the chapter draws conclusions about fruitful directions for future regional integration initiatives.

THEORETICAL MODELS OF FDI

Some recent empirical studies of the determinants of FDI have used a gravity model specification of investment (e.g. Stein and Daude 2001; Yeyati *et al.* 2003; Bevin and Estrin 2004; Egger and Pfaffermayr 2004a; Dee and Gali 2005). According to this model, investment is driven by the sizes of the sending and receiving countries and by the distance between them, where the latter is a proxy for total transport costs. The justification is a loose one – since models of trade in differentiated products provide theoretical backing for a gravity model specification of *trade*, and since such models also explain FDI, they therefore provide backing for a gravity model specification of *investment*. The arguments recognise that trade and investment are linked, and can be either substitutes or complements, but the arguments are largely informal.

More recently, 'post-gravity' empirical specifications of the determinants of FDI have been drawn from formal analytical models in which decisions to trade or invest are made endogenously, based on such factors as economies of scale and transport costs. Seminal studies in this vein are Carr *et al.* (2001); Markusen and Maskus (2002); Blonigen and Davies (2000); Blonigen *et al.* (2003); Blonigen and Davies (2004); and Carr *et al.* (2003). Simulations of the formal analytical models provide testable hypotheses that are then tested econometrically using real world data. Blonigen and Davies (2000) do a head-to-head comparison of the Markusen and Maskus specification with a gravity model and find that the Markusen and Maskus model consistently fits the data better.[1]

Most models of either form find that the investment provisions of PTAs boost FDI activity.[2] However, most 'post-gravity' specifications are based on a relatively simple, single-stage representation of production in a two-country framework, ruling out the possibility of the network pattern described by Victor Fung (2005). Their findings of a positive effect of the FDI provisions of PTAs could be the result of mis-specification of the underlying investment behaviour or, alternatively, a naïve specification of the investment provisions of PTAs. Further, most tests of the post-gravity specifications have been made using datasets that describe FDI into and out of the United States. This is because the United States is one of the few countries to collect systematic data on the activities of foreign affiliates. However, the behaviour of US multinationals investing abroad, or of other multinationals investing in the United States, need not be representative of multinational activity in the region more generally.

Very recently, a new class of analytical models has allowed for more 'complex' patterns of trade and investment (Ekholm *et al.* 2003; Grossman *et al.* 2003; Yeaple 2003; Egger *et al.* 2004; Baltagi *et al.* 2005). These could provide a richer specification of the determinants of FDI, taking account of its network characteristics and its interactions with trade flows. Of these specifications, Baltagi *et al.* (2005) is the most promising, because it allows for two-stage production in a three-country framework. It therefore makes provision analytically for a network pattern of trade and investment, and so is less likely to suffer mis-specification bias.

In this model, four types of 'complex' FDI are possible, depending on the combinations of relative factor endowments, transport costs, and economies of scale. Taking d as the parent country, i as the host country and j as the third country, the investment patterns of the parent country can be:

- horizontal – plants in d and i, with exports from d to j
- export platform (complex horizontal) – plants in d and i, with exports from i to j
- vertical – plants in i and j, with exports from i to d
- complex vertical – plants in i and j, with exports from j to d.

Baltagi and his colleagues make clear that the complex vertical pattern is also underpinned by exports from i to j, so this pattern corresponds closely to that described by Victor Fung. If export platform FDI was accompanied by exports from j to d it could also correspond to a network pattern, differing only from complex vertical FDI in that the interaction between d and j was arm's length via trade rather than via FDI. However, other motivations may be present in the Asia Pacific region.

One of the strengths of this framework is that it shows how the incentives for parent d to invest in host i depend not just on the characteristics of the particular host i, but also on the characteristics of other countries in the network j. Indeed, the so-called third-country effects play an important role in being able to infer which type of investment is taking place between d and i.

Using simulations of their analytical model, Baltagi and his colleagues show that all four types of bilateral FDI between d and i should be expected to increase with bilateral total size, with the parent-to-host capital endowment ratio (K_d/K_i) and with the parent-to-host skilled labour ratio (H_d/H_i), and to decrease with the unskilled labour ratio (L_d/L_i). The effects of similarity in size between d and i are mixed.[3]

Thus far there are no clear predictions about the mathematical signs of particular determinants that can be used to distinguish which type of FDI is taking place. However, two interaction terms are important. The first is between the d-to-i capital endowment ratio and bilateral size. This captures the fact that d's capital abundance is more in favour of bilateral FDI at larger bilateral size. The second interaction term is the product of log differences in relative factor endowments and log transport costs. This accounts for the fact that an increase in transport costs would lead to more horizontal-type investment (simple or complex) and less vertical-type investment.

The third-country effects also help to distinguish which type of investment is occurring between d and i. In general terms, the third-country effects reflect a trade-off between demand and supply effects. The bigger j is, the more it is likely to appeal as an alternative base for investment, so as to serve the local market directly. However, such relocation also depends on supply factors – on j's factor endowments relative to i, but also on j's supply of exports to d and i. The pattern of expected third-country effects is reported, along with own-country effects, in Table 10.1. As noted, the signs of the third-country effects are useful ways to distinguish which type of bilateral FDI is occurring between d and i.

For estimation purposes, the framework of Baltagi *et al.* (2005) has been extended in two ways. The first is to include distance as an explicit additional determinant of bilateral FDI, as was done in Egger and Pfaffermayr (2004b). Greater distance between d and i would increase the cost of serving i's market via exports (thus promoting FDI), but it may also increase the set-up costs of establishing a branch in i (thus reducing FDI). Hence the sign of this variable is ambiguous, irrespective of the type of FDI taking place. However, its inclusion will reduce the risk of mis-specification, and hence reduce the risk of mis-attributing the potential effects of PTAs.

Finally, the framework has been expanded to include index measures of the investment provisions of any PTAs between d and i (own-country effects) and d and j (third-country effects). In estimating their framework, Baltagi *et al.* (2005) made provision for spatial correlation in error terms. One obvious source of such spatial

Table 10.1 Expected signs of determinants of complex FDI from parent country to host country

	Mode of FDI			
Explanatory variable	Horizontal	Export	Vertical platform	Complex vertical
Bilateral changes[a]				
dis = distance between d and i	+/-	+/-	+/-	+/-
G = bilateral size of d plus i	+	+	+	+
S = similarity in size of d and i	+/-	+	-/+	+/-
k = $\ln(K_d/K_i)$	+	+	+	+
h = $\ln(H_d/H_i)$	+	+	+	+
l = $\ln(L_d/L_i)$	-	-	-	-
gamma = G*k	+	+	+	-
phi = $\ln(dis)*(k-l)$	+	+	-	+/-
risk rating of i	+	+	+	+
FTA liberalisation between d and i:				
Cross-border trade	+/-	+/-	+/-	+/-
Investment	+	+	+	+
Movement of people	+/-	+/-	+/-	+/-
Third-country changes[b]				
wG = bilateral size of d and j	+	+	+	+
wS = similarity in size of d and j	+	+	+/-	+/-
wk = $\ln(K_d/K_j)$	-	+	+	-
wh = $\ln(H_d/H_j)$	+	+	-	-
wl = $\ln(L_d/L_j)$	+	-	+	-
wgamma = wG*wk	+	+	-	+
wphi = $\ln(dis_{dj})*(wk-wl)$	+	+	+/-	+
wrisk = risk rating of j	-	-	-	+/-
FTA liberalisation between d and j:				
Cross-border trade	+/-	+/-	+/-	+/-
Investment	-	-	-	+/-
Movement of people	+/-	+/-	+/-	+/-

Notes: FDI = foreign direct investment; FTA = free trade agreement
a d is parent, i is host and j is third country; see text for an explanation of other variables.
b   Predicted signs of wG to wphi are based on reasonably low values of transport costs.
Source: Based on Baltagi et al. (2005).

correlation is the existence of PTAs. Hence, in the current specification, this effect has been incorporated deterministically, using index measures of the provisions of PTAs.

Thus the full specification used for estimation purposes is as follows:

$$F_t = \beta_0 + \beta_1 dis + \beta_2 G_t + \beta_3 S_t + \beta_4 k_t + \beta_5 h_t + \beta_6 l_t + \beta_7 gamma_t + \beta_8 phi_t + \beta_9 risk +$$
$$\beta_{10} P_t + \beta_{11} wG_t + \beta_{12} wS_t + \beta_{13} wk_t + \beta_{14} wh_t + \beta_{15} wl_t + \beta_{16} wgamma_t + \beta_{17} wphi_t$$
$$+ \beta_{18} wrisk + \beta_{19} wP_t + u_t$$

where

F_t is the log of the bilateral stock of outward FDI from parent d to host i in year t

dis is the distance between d and i

$G_t = \ln(GDP_d + GDP_i)$ is a measure of absolute bilateral country size in year t

$S_t = (1 - s_d^2 - s_i^2)$ where $s_d = GDP_d/(GDP_d + GDP_i)$ and $s_i = GDP_i/(GDP_d + GDP_i)$ is a measure of similarity in country size in year t

$k_t = \ln(K_d/K_i)$; $\quad h_t = \ln(H_d/H_i)$; $\quad l_t = \ln(L_d/L_i)$

$gamma_t = G_t k_t \quad phi_t = \ln(dis)(k_t - l_t)$

$risk$ is a measure of country investment risk in host i

P_t is one or more index variables measuring the strength of the investment provisions of any PTA in place between d and i in year t.

The remaining variables, prefixed with w, measure third-country effects. These are measured as the inverse distance-weighted averages of the corresponding variables between the same parent d and all of its other third-country hosts j in year t. Thus, for example, wG_t is a weighted average of $\ln(GDP_d + GDP_j)$ over all of d's other host countries j, where the weights are the inverse of distance between d and j. This is based on the idea that the strength of third-country effects is likely to decay with distance, as found in Egger and Pfaffermayr (2004b). And as in Baltagi et al. (2005), the specification includes a measure of host-country investment risk.

This specification is estimated on a panel of annual data covering up to 32 parent countries and up to 109 hosts over the period 1988–97. Not all parents or hosts are present in the sample in all years, so the panel is highly unbalanced. But when a parent country appears in a given year, its hosts in that year are reasonably representative. Hence the measures of third-country effects are also representative. The entire dataset has 5,826 observations. The data sources and countries are listed in Annex 10.1.

The real-world data on which the specification is estimated clearly violate the analytical model of Baltagi et al. (2005) in several key respects. Their model predicts that multinationals will only arise in countries that are well endowed with capital and skilled labour. Yet in the real world, countries such as Malaysia and Thailand invest non-trivial amounts in locations like the United States, despite having an absolute disadvantage in both capital and skilled labour. How to treat this issue seems to be at the heart of the debate between Blonigen et al. (2003) and Carr et al. (2003) about whether relative endowments should be measured as simple or absolute differences. The approach here is to note that even in the simple Heckscher–Ohlin framework, notions of relative factor abundance become slippery 'on-average' concepts once the model is extended beyond two goods and two factors. However, it is reasonable to suppose that countries such as Malaysia and Thailand will invest more in the United States as their absolute disadvantage in capital or skilled labour lessens. This is consistent with the empirical specification used by Baltagi *et al.* (2005) and shown above, where relative endowments are measured using simple rather than absolute differences.

The first research task is to estimate the above specification on various country groupings, to see if particular patterns of FDI can be discerned for that grouping, on the basis that the signs of the coefficients for that grouping follow one or more of the patterns identified in Table 10.1. The second research task is to see whether the measures **P** or **wP** have any significance.

THE EXPECTED EFFECTS OF INVESTMENT PROVISIONS OF PTAs

If **P** is significant, it means that the bilateral FDI between parent d and host i is significantly affected by the investment provisions of PTAs signed between d and i. Potentially, then, this variable can measure gross 'investment creation' between the parties to a PTA, although, as shall be seen shortly, whether 'creation' or 'destruction' is expected depends on the type of provision.

If **wP** is significant, it means that the bilateral FDI between parent d and host i is significantly affected by the investment provisions of PTAs signed between d and its other investment partners j. Potentially, then, this variable can measure 'investment diversion', although, once again, the expected sign depends on the type of provisions.

How should we characterise the investment provisions of PTAs? This is not straightforward, because of the variety of ways in which investment provisions are incorporated in PTAs. Firstly, there are (at least) two broad types of agreements.

- GATS-style agreements follow the architecture of the General Agreement on Trade in Services under the World Trade Organization. Investment provisions typically only cover FDI in services; this is because commercial presence is one of the modes by which services are traded. Further, GATS-style agreements are typically positive-list agreements, so only the particular services sectors that are nominated by a member country are bound by the provisions of the agreement.

- NAFTA-style agreements follow the architecture of the North American Free Trade Agreement between Canada, Mexico and the United States. These agreements typically have one chapter covering cross-border trade in services and a separate chapter covering investment in all sectors. Further, NAFTA-style agreements are typically negative-list agreements, so all sectors are automatically covered by the provisions of an agreement unless a member indicates otherwise in an annex of reservations and exclusions.

In addition to these (and a host of other) architectural issues governing the *form* of an agreement, there are issues of *content*. A negative-list architecture may appear to guarantee a relatively liberal agreement, but this need not be the case in practice if the participants append lengthy lists of reservations and exclusions.

For the current exercise, the services and investment provisions of PTAs have been 'mapped' using the templates outlined in Tables 10.2–10.4. Table 10.2 covers the provisions governing the cross-border trade in services (modes 1 and 2 in GATS terminology); Table 10.3 covers the provisions governing investment (GATS mode 3); and Table 10.4 covers the provisions governing the movement of natural persons (GATS mode 4). Within each table, there has been a relatively comprehensive mapping of the *form* of an agreement, while a few broad indicators have been selected to gauge the *content*. Each PTA agreement is then assigned a numerical score between 0 and 1 against each particular characteristic of form or content, with higher values indicating a more liberal agreement. These scores are of ordinal rather than cardinal importance.

The various services provisions covering cross-border trade and the movement of natural persons have been scored, along with the investment provisions, in order to account for possible substitution between the different modes of services delivery. If an agreement is particularly generous in opening up cross-border trade, for example, this could promote cross-border trade at the expense of delivery via commercial presence, and hence at the expense of FDI. The provisions governing the movement of natural persons affect the movement of individual service providers (particularly in the professions) who operate on their own account. But they also affect the longer-term movement of expatriate employees of foreign multinationals. Hence more generous provisions on the movement of natural persons could boost or reduce FDI, depending on the relative importance of mode 3 versus mode 4 delivery, and on the possibility of substituting between them.

The expected signs of the PTA variables shown in Table 10.1 reflect the expectation that more liberal bilateral investment provisions should boost bilateral FDI, while more liberal third-country investment provisions could reduce FDI. The signs of the provisions governing cross-border trade and the movement of natural persons are ambiguous, since it is unclear whether these modes of delivery are general equilibrium substitutes for or complements to FDI. While the FDI data cover FDI in all sectors, not just in services, it is widely thought that services account for at least half of all FDI. So substitution among modes of service delivery could be expected to show up in the aggregate FDI data.

The scoring has been applied to all the major agreements in force between countries in the econometric sample in the years leading up to 1997. These agreements are listed in Table 10.5. This table also shows the simple average of the scores against all possible services and investment characteristics for these agreements. The average scores suggest that among the most liberal agreements are NAFTA and its Latin American clones (particularly the agreement between Colombia, Mexico and Venezuela), the Australia New Zealand Closer Economic Relations Trade Agreement, and the agreements among European nations (European Union, European Free Trade Association and the European Economic Area). The Mercosur agreement among four Latin American countries and the ASEAN Framework Agreement on Services are also relatively liberal in their architecture, although their sectoral coverage is very limited.[4]

240 *Philippa Dee*

Table 10.2 Template for scoring cross-border trade in services

	Category	Score
FORM OF AGREEMENT		
Scope	Covers everything	1
	Excludes only air passenger transport or government services	0.8
	Excludes air passenger transport and government services (same as GATS)	0.75
	Excludes a little more than GATS (e.g. financial services)	0.5
	Excludes a lot more than GATS	0.25
	Endeavours with unspecified scope (cooperation or no detailed provisions)	0.2
	No services provisions	0
MFN	Negative list bindings	1
	Positive list bindings	0.75
	Best endeavours	0.25
	No commitment	0
MFN exemptions	None	1
	None for new bilateral agreements	0.5
	Some for new bilateral agreements	0.25
	For all existing and new bilateral agreements or no commitment on MFN	0
National treatment	Negative list bindings	1
	Negative list bindings – some sectors	0.75
	Positive list bindings	0.5
	Best endeavours	0.25
	No commitment	0
Market access (i.e. prohibition on QRs as in GATS)	Negative list bindings	1
	Negative list bindings – some sectors	0.75
	Positive list bindings	0.5
	Best endeavours	0.25
	No commitment	0
Local presence not required (right of non-establishment)	Has this provision	1
	Has this provision, but with some exemptions	0.5
	Does not have this provision	0
Domestic regulation	General provisions as in GATS plus necessity test (or equivalent)	1
	General provisions as in GATS (transparency, not a disguised restriction)	0.75
	Measures in a reasonable and impartial manner	0.4
	Provisions for specific sectors (e.g. professions)	0.25
	No provisions	0
Transparency (scores additive)	Prior comment	0.3
	Publish (as in GATS)	0.4
	National inquiry point (as in GATS)	0.3
Recognition	General provisions as in GATS (non-discrimination, based in international standards) plus provisions for all sectors	1

Table 10.2 (cont.)

	Category	Score
	General provisions as in GATS (non-discrimination, based in international standards) plus provisions for specific sectors	0.75
	General provisions as in GATS (non-discrimination, based in international standards)	0.5
	Provisions for specific sectors (e.g. legal, engineering)	0.25
	Encouragement	0.2
	No provisions	0
Monopolies and exclusive services providers	Stronger than general provisions in GATS	1
	General provisions as in GATS (requirement not to act inconsistently with commitments, not anti-competitive in other markets)	0.75
	General provisions as in GATS plus some exceptions	0.6
	Provisions for specific sectors (e.g. telecommunications)	0.5
	No provisions	0
Business practices	Stronger than GATS	1
	General provisions as in GATS (consult with a view to eliminating)	0.75
	Provisions for specific sectors	0.5
	No provisions	0
Transfers and payments	No restrictions except to safeguard balance of payments	1
	Restrictions in other prescribed circumstances	0.5
	No provisions	0
Denial of benefits (i.e. rules of origin)	Denial only to persons that do not conduct substantial (or any) business operations in other party	1
	Tougher treatment to specific sectors	0.75
	Tougher treatment to all sectors	0.5
	Total denial if owned by third party, or no provisions to prevent denial	0
Safeguards	General provisions	0
	Provisions for particular sectors	0.25
	Future negotiations	0.5
	No provisions or banned	1
Subsidies (may be in separate subsidies chapter but covers services)	Provisions limiting their use	1
	Consultation	0.5
	Future negotiations to limit their use	0.25
	No provisions	0
Government procurement in services (could be in separate GP chapter)	Provisions on non-discriminatory access	1
	Provisions for access in some sectors	0.75
	Future negotiations	0.5
	No provisions	0
Ratchet mechanism	All subsequent unilateral liberalisation to be bound	1
	Sectoral exceptions to ratchet mechanism	0.75
	No mechanism	0
Telecommunications (scores additive)	Interconnection (access to and use of PSTN and services by service suppliers of other party)	0.5

Table 10.2 (cont.)

	Category	Score
	Unbundling	0.1
	Particular services (e.g. leased circuits, resale, number portability)	0.1
	Competitive safeguards	0.1
	Universal service obligations	0.1
	Allocation of scarce resources (e.g. spectrum)	0.1
Financial services (scores additive)	Prudential carve out	0.4
	Provision for recognition of prudential measures	0.2
	NT for access to payments and clearing systems	0.1
	New financial services	0.1
	Privacy	0.1
	Data transfer	0.1
CONTENT OF AGREEMENT	For negative list agreements, look at non-conforming measures	
	For positive list agreements, look at specific, horizontal and MFN commitments	
General reservations or exceptions – modes	No modes excluded by one or more parties	1
	One mode excluded by one or more parties (e.g. mode 4)	0.5
	Two or more modes excluded by one or more parties, or no provisions	0
General reservations or exceptions – measures	No measures (MFN, NT, MA) excluded by one or more parties	1
	One measure (e.g. MA) excluded by one or more parties	0.5
	More than one measure excluded by one or more parties, or no provisions	0
Sectoral exclusions (out of 46 substantive sectors) (least generous treatment among members of FTA)	No sectors excluded by one or more parties	1
	1–10 sectors excluded by one or more parties (e.g. maritime, audiovisual)	0.8
	11–20 sectors excluded by one or more parties (e.g. maritime, audiovisual)	0.6
	21–30 sectors excluded by one or more parties	0.4
	31–40 sectors excluded by one or more parties	0.2
	More than 40 sectors excluded by one or more parties, or no provisions on services trade	0
Sub-national exclusions	No measures at sub-national (state or provincial) level excluded	1
	Measures at local level excluded by one or more parties	0.7
	Measures at state level excluded by one or more parties	0.4
	Measures at all sub-national levels excluded by one or more parties, or no provisions on services trade	0
Other general exclusions	No other general exclusions	1
	One other exclusion (e.g. for minorities, land purchases) by at least one party	0.5
	Two or more other exclusions (e.g. for minorities, land purchases) by at least one party	0

Notes: FTA = free trade agreement; GATS = General Agreement on Trade in Services; GP = government procurement; MA = market access; MFN = most favoured nation; NT = national treatment; PSTN = public switched telephone network; QRs = quantitative restrictions.

Source: Compiled by author.

Table 10.3 Template for scoring investment

Category		Score
FORM OF AGREEMENT		
Sectoral coverage	Beyond services (in separate chapter)	1
	Services only (mode 3 in services chapter)	0.5
	Based on bilateral treaties	0.4
	Endeavours without specified scope	0.25
	None	0
Scope of MFN, NT etc. provisions (scores additive)	Establishment (i.e. greenfield)	0.3
	Acquisition (i.e. merger)	0.2
	Post-establishment operation	0.3
	Resale (i.e. free movement of capital)	0.2
MFN	Negative list bindings	1
	Positive list bindings	0.75
	Best endeavours	0.25
	No commitment	0
MFN exemptions	None	1
	None for new bilateral agreements	0.5
	Some for new bilateral agreements	0.25
	For all existing and new bilateral agreements, or no provisions to prevent exemptions	0
National treatment	Negative list bindings – all sectors	1
	Negative list bindings – some sectors	0.75
	Positive list bindings – all sectors	0.5
	Best endeavours	0.25
	No commitment	0
Nationality (residency) of management and board of directors (including exceptions)	Cannot restrict either	1
	Cannot restrict either, with sectoral exceptions	0.75
	Can partially restrict board of directors	0.5
	Can partially restrict management or both. Alternatively, sectoral promises to liberalise, but no general promise	0.25
	No provisions limiting restrictions	0
Performance requirements	No local content, trade or other specified requirements (e.g. on tech transfer, or where to sell)	1
	No local content or trade requirements (i.e. as in TRIMS)	0.75
	Provisions more limited than TRIMS	0.5
	No provisions	0
Transparency (in services or investment chapter) (scores additive)	Prior comment	0.3
	Publish (as in GATS)	0.4
	National inquiry point (as in GATS)	0.3

Table 10.3 (cont.)

Category		Score
Denial of benefits (i.e. rules of origin)	Denial only to persons that do not conduct substantial (or any) business operations in other party	1
	Tougher treatment for specific sectors	0.75
	Tougher treatment for all sectors	0.5
	Total denial if owned by third party, or no provisions	0
Expropriation etc. (scores additive)	Minimum standard of treatment	0.2
	Treatment in case of strife	0.4
	Expropriation and compensation	0.4
Transfers and payments	No restrictions except to safeguard balance of payments	1
	Restrictions in other prescribed circumstances	0.5
	No provisions	0
Investor-state dispute settlement	Yes	1
	No	0
Safeguards	General provisions	0
	Provisions for particular sectors	0.25
	Future negotiations	0.5
	No provisions	1
Subsidies (may be in separate subsidies chapter but covers investment)	Provisions limiting their use	1
	Consultation	0.5
	Future negotiations	0.25
	No provisions	0
Government procurement (could be in separate GP chapter)	Provisions on non-discriminatory access	1
	Provisions for access in some sectors	0.75
	Future negotiations	0.5
	No provisions	0
Ratchet mechanism	All subsequent unilateral liberalisation to be bound	1
	Sectoral exceptions to ratchet mechanism	0.75
	No mechanism	0

CONTENT OF AGREEMENT

Category		Score
General reservations or exceptions	No measures (MFN, NT, MA) excluded by one or more parties	1
	One measure (e.g. MA) excluded by one or more parties	0.5
	More than one measure excluded by one or more parties, or no provisions	0
Sectoral exclusions (out of 46 substantive sectors)	No sectors excluded by one or more parties	1
	1–10 sectors excluded by one or more parties (e.g. maritime, audiovisual)	0.8
	11–20 sectors excluded by one or more parties (e.g. maritime, audiovisual)	0.6
	21–30 sectors excluded by one or more parties	0.4

Table 10.3 (cont.)

	Category	Score
	31–40 sectors excluded by one or more parties	0.2
	More than 40 sectors excluded by one or more parties, or no provisions on investment	0
Sub-national exclusions	No measures at sub-national level excluded	1
	Measures at local level excluded by one or more parties	0.7
	Measures at state level excluded by one or more parties	0.4
	Measures at all sub-national levels excluded by one or more parties, or no provisions on investment	0
Other general exclusions	No other general exclusions	1
	No other general exclusions, but some exclusions for some sectors	0.75
	One other exclusion (e.g. for minorities, land purchases) by at least one party	0.5
	Two other exclusions (e.g. for minorities, land purchases) by at least one party, or no provisions on investment	0

Notes: GATS = General Agreement on Trade in Services; GP = government procurement; MA = market access ; MFN = most favoured nation; NT = national treatment ; TRIMS = Agreement on Trade Related Investment Measures.
Source: Compiled by author.

A simple average of liberalisation scores gives equal weight to each and every characteristic. This is most probably inappropriate, and the simple overall average has not been entered into the econometric specification. Ideally, the score for each characteristic should be entered separately; the econometric estimates of the coefficients would then indicate which (if any) characteristics are significant. At a practical level, the high degree of multi-collinearity between many individual characteristics means that most of the individual PTA variables drop out, making it hard to draw any conclusions at all. As an alternative, factor analysis is used to identify linear combinations of individual characteristics that are not collinear with each other, but that jointly reproduce most of the variation in the original characteristics data. This is done separately for the provisions governing cross-border trade, investment and the movement of natural persons (since the expected signs of these differ) and for provisions on form and content, leading to $3 \times 2 = 6$ sets of factors. But even here, at least some factors drop out. In the final specification, the PTA variables are simple averages across these six sets of characteristics – the form and content (respectively) of the provisions governing cross-border trade, investment and movement of natural persons. This ensures that most PTA variables stay in the specification, so that lack of significance does not simply reflect lack of independent in-sample variation.

246 *Philippa Dee*

Table 10.4 Template for scoring movement of natural persons

Category		Score
FORM OF AGREEMENT		
Sectoral coverage	Beyond services and investment (separate chapter)	1
	Services and investment (in both services and investment chapters)	0.75
	Services only (mode 4 in services)	0.5
	Endeavours	0.25
	None	0
Scope	Allows permanent immigration	1
	Includes access to labour market	0.75
	Temporary movement only	0.5
	No clear scope	0.25
	None	0
Immigration	Requires changes to immigration procedures (e.g. visa quotas or eligibility criteria)	1
	Subject to existing immigration laws and procedures, or no provisions	0
MFN for mode 4 delivery	Negative list bindings	1
	Positive list bindings	0.75
	Best endeavours	0.25
	No commitment	0
MFN exemptions	None	1
	None for new bilateral agreements	0.5
	Some for new bilateral agreements	0.25
	For all existing and new bilateral agreements or no commitment on MFN	0
National treatment for mode 4 delivery	Negative list bindings	1
	Negative list bindings – some sectors	0.75
	Positive list bindings	0.5
	Best endeavours	0.25
	No commitment	0
Market access (i.e. prohibition on QRs as in GATS)	Negative list bindings	1
	Negative list bindings – some sectors	0.75
	Positive list bindings	0.5
	Best endeavours	0.25
	No commitment	0
Domestic regulation	General provisions as in GATS plus necessity test (or equivalent)	1
	General provisions as in GATS (transparency, not a disguised restriction)	0.75
	Measures in a reasonable and impartial manner	0.4

Table 10.4 (cont.)

	Category	Score
	Provisions for specific sectors (e.g. professions)	0.25
	No provisions	0
Transparency for mode 4 delivery (scores additive)	Prior comment	0.3
	Publish (as in GATS)	0.4
	National inquiry point (as in GATS)	0.3
Transparency for temporary movement of people (scores additive)	Expedite procedures	0.3
	Publish	0.4
	Answer queries or comments	0.3
Recognition	General provisions as in GATS (non-discrimination, based in international standards) plus provisions for all sectors	1
	General provisions as in GATS (non-discrimination, based in international standards) plus provisions for specific sectors	0.75
	General provisions as in GATS (non-discrimination, based in international standards)	0.5
	Provisions for specific sectors (e.g. legal, engineering)	0.25
	Endeavours	0.2
	No provisions	0
Denial of benefits (i.e. rules of origin)	Denial only to persons that do not conduct substantial (or any) business operations in other party	1
	Tougher treatment for specific sectors	0.75
	Tougher treatment for all sectors	0.5
	Total denial if owned by third party or no provisions	0
Ratchet mechanism	All subsequent unilateral liberalisation to be bound	1
	Sectoral exceptions to ratchet mechanism	0.75
	No mechanism	0

CONTENT OF AGREEMENT: SERVICE DELIVERY

	Category	Score
General reservations or exceptions	No measures (MFN, NT, MA) excluded by one or more parties	1
	One measure (e.g. MA) excluded by one or more parties	0.5
	More than one measure excluded by one or more parties, or no provisions on movement of people	0
Sectoral exclusions (out of 46 substantive sectors)	No sectors excluded by one or more parties	1
	1–10 sectors excluded by one or more parties (e.g. maritime, audiovisual)	0.8
	11–20 sectors excluded by one or more parties (e.g. maritime, audiovisual)	0.6
	21–30 sectors excluded by one or more parties	0.4
	31–40 sectors excluded by one or more parties	0.2
	More than 40 sectors excluded by one or more parties, or no provisions on movement of people	0

Table 10.4 (cont.)

Category		Score
Sub-national exclusions	No measures at sub-national level excluded	1
	Measures at local level excluded by one or more parties	0.7
	Measures at state level excluded by one or more parties	0.4
	Measures at all sub-national levels excluded by one or more parties, or no provisions on movement of people	0
Other general exclusions	No other general exclusions	1
	One other exclusion (e.g. for minorities, land purchases) by at least one party	0.5
	Two other exclusions (e.g. for minorities, land purchases) by at least one party, or no provisions on movement of people	0

CONTENT OF AGREEMENT: FACILITATION OF MOBILITY

Category		Score
Skill coverage (least generous treatment among members of FTA)	All groups (including unskilled)	1
	All business persons, traders and investors, intracorporate transferees, and professionals	0.5
	A subset of the above (e.g. specialists, managers and intracorporate transferees)	0.25
	No groups	0
Short term entry (least generous treatment among members of FTA)	Over 90 days or no time limit mentioned	1
	Up to 90 days	0.75
	Up to 60 days	0.5
	Up to 30 days	0.25
	Unspecified	0.1
	No short-term entry, or non-binding service provisions (e.g. endeavours)	0
Long-term entry (least generous treatment among members of FTA)	5 years or more or no time limit mentioned	1
	Up to 4 years	0.8
	Up to 3 years	0.6
	Up to 2 years	0.4
	Up to 1 year	0.2
	Unspecified	0.1
	No long-term entry, or non-binding service provisions (e.g. endeavours)	0
Quotas on numbers of entrants	No (or not mentioned)	1
	Yes, or non-binding service provisions (e.g. endeavours)	0
Local labour market testing or other criteria	All such tests prohibited or not required	1
	Some such tests prohibited or not required	0.5
	No prohibitions (or not mentioned or in non-binding service provisions (e.g. endeavours))	0

Notes: FTA = free trade agreement; GATS = General Agreement on Trade in Services; MA = market access; MFN = most favoured nation; NT = national treatment; QR = quantitative restrictions.
Source: Compiled by author.

Table 10.5 Preferential trade agreements and average liberalisation scores[a]

Agreement	Date	Membership dynamics	Score (0–1)
EEC/EU	1958	Austria (joined 1995), Belgium-Luxembourg, Denmark (joined 1973), Finland (joined 1995), France, Germany, Greece (joined 1981), Hungary (joined 2004), Ireland (joined 1973), Italy, Netherlands, Poland (joined 2004), Portugal (joined 1986), Spain (joined 1986), Sweden (joined 1995), United Kingdom (joined 1973)	0.54
EFTA	1960	Austria (left 1995), Denmark (left 1972), Finland (joined 1961, left 1995), Iceland (joined 1970), Norway, Portugal (left 1985), Sweden (left 1985), Switzerland, United Kingdom (left 1972)	0.53
CACM	1961	Costa Rica (joined 1962), El Salvador, Honduras, Nicaragua	0.03
EC–Switzerland	1973	EU membership, Switzerland	0.03
EC–Iceland	1973	EU membership, Iceland	0.03
EC–Norway	1973	EU membership, Norway	0.03
Bangkok agreement	1976	Bangladesh, China (joined 2001), India, Korea, Lao PDR, Sri Lanka	0.03
LAIA	1981	Argentina, Bolivia, Brazil, Chile, Colombia, Ecuador, Mexico, Paraguay, Peru, Uruguay, Venezuela	0.03
Sparteca	1981	Australia, Fiji, New Zealand, Papua New Guinea, Solomon Islands	0.03
US–Israel	1985	Israel, United States	0.03
CER	1989	Australia, New Zealand	0.63
Mercosur	1991	Argentina, Brazil, Paraguay, Uruguay	0.47
EFTA–Turkey	1992	EFTA membership, Turkey	0.03
CARICOM–Venezuela	1992	Dominican Republic, Venezuela	0.04
Chile–Colombia	1993	Chile, Colombia	0.04
EFTA–Israel	1993	EFTA membership, Israel	0.04
CEFTA	1993	Hungary, Poland	0.03
EFTA–Romania	1993	EFTA membership, Romania	0.04
Chile–Bolivia[b]	1993	Bolivia, Chile	0.08
EEA	1994	EU membership, Iceland, Norway	0.57
NAFTA	1994	Canada (joined precursor in 1988), Mexico, United States (joined precursor in 1988)	0.60
COMESA	1994	Egypt (joined 1998), Madagascar, Mauritius,	0.08
EC–Romania	1995	EC membership, Romania	0.38
SAPTA	1995	Bangladesh, India, Nepal, Pakistan, Sri Lanka	0.03
Bolivia–Mexico	1995	Bolivia, Mexico	0.62
Costa Rica–Mexico	1995	Costa Rica, Mexico	0.59
Colombia–Mexico–Venezuela	1995	Colombia, Mexico, Venezuela	0.67
CARICOM–Colombia	1995	Colombia, Dominican Republic	0.03
ASEAN Framework Agreement on Services	1995	Indonesia, Lao PDR (joined 1997), Malaysia, Philippines, Singapore, Thailand	0.44

250 *Philippa Dee*

Table 10.5 (cont.)

EC–Turkey	1996	EU membership, Turkey	0.04
Chile–Mercosur[b]	1996	Mercosur membership, Chile	0.05
Canada–Israel	1997	Canada, Israel	0.03
Israel–Turkey	1997	Israel, Turkey	0.52
Canada–Chile	1997	Canada, Chile	0.62
Bolivia–Mercosur[b]	1997	Mercosur membership, Bolivia	0.04

Notes: ASEAN = Association of Southeast Asian Nations; CACM = Central American Common Market; CARICOM = Caribbean Community; CEFTA = Central European Free Trade Agreement; CER = Closer Economic Relations (of Australia and New Zealand); COMESA = Common Market for Eastern and Southern Africa; EC = European Community; EEA = European Economic Area; EEC = European Economic Community; EFTA = European Free Trade Association; EU = European Union; LAIA = Latin American Integration Association; NAFTA = North American Free Trade Agreement; PDR = People's Democratic Republic; SAPTA = South Asian Association for Regional Cooperation (SAARC) Preferential Trading Arrangement

a The table covers all major agreements in force between countries in the econometric sample in the years leading up to 1997, except the Andean agreement, which is not included because decision 439 was not signed until 1998.
b Not notified to the World Trade Organization.

Source: Compiled by author.

The in-sample variation in the PTA variables comes from two sources. Firstly, some agreements are more liberal than others, and so have higher scores. Second, new agreements were formed and some existing agreements experienced changes in membership during the 1988–97 estimation period. So some pairs of countries have a positive value for their bilateral PTA variables in the years after forming or joining their agreement, but zero values for the years before. The use of such dynamic PTA dummies has been shown to be important for properly identifying the effects of PTAs (Dee and Gali 2005).

IS THERE A REGIONAL MODEL OF FDI IN THE ASIA PACIFIC REGION?

A key question is where to look – what is the appropriate definition of 'the region'? Figures 10.1–10.3 present recent data on FDI into various country groupings. Since the theoretical framework shows that host characteristics play a critical role in FDI, the groupings are of hosts, and for consistency the host countries are restricted to those that are also represented in the econometric sample. The inward FDI is from all sources, not just the sources represented in the econometric sample.

Figure 10.1 compares the inward FDI stocks in two broad country groupings, Europe and the Asia Pacific Economic Cooperation (APEC) region. Europe and APEC show a similar pattern, although the growth of FDI stocks into the APEC region was slightly higher than into Europe. FDI stocks into APEC slightly more than tripled over the 1990–2000 period, while those into Europe slightly less than tripled.

Figure 10.2 compares FDI stocks into socioeconomic groupings of countries (where the lower income, lower middle income and upper middle income groupings follow the World Bank definitions of these groups). Between 1990 and 2000, FDI into the

Figure 10.1 Inward FDI stocks into broad geographic regions (US$ billion)

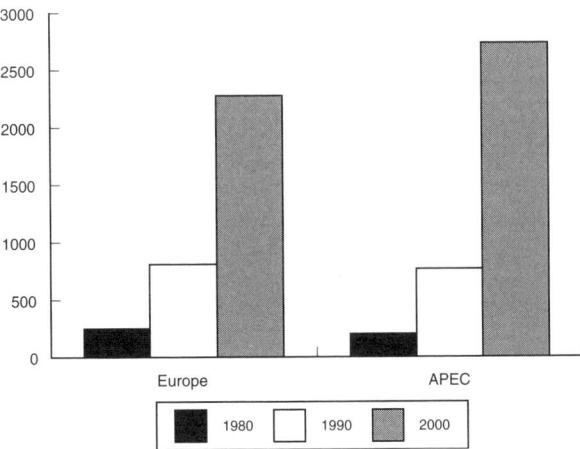

Source: UNCTAD, <http://www.unctad.org/Templates/Page.asp?intItemID=3199&lang=1>.

Figure 10.2 Inward FDI stocks into socioeconomic groupings of regions (US$ billion)

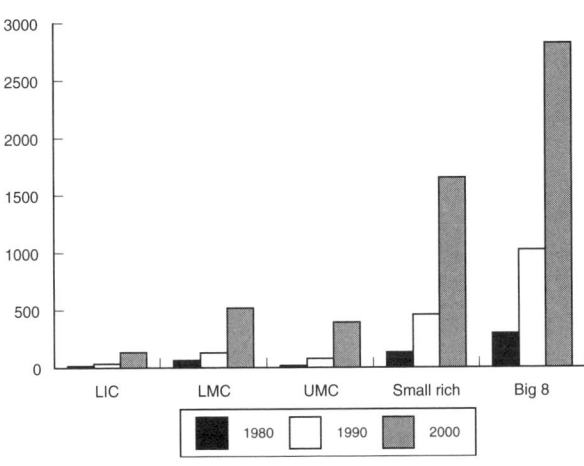

Notes: LIC = lower income, LMC = lower middle income, UMC = upper middle income; see text for explanation of 'small rich' countries and 'Big 8' (big eight).

Source: UNCTAD, <http://www.unctad.org/Templates/Page.asp?intItemID-3199&lang=1>.

two lowest income groupings roughly quadrupled, while it increased fivefold into the upper middle income group. In all cases, this growth was from a very low base. At the other end of the spectrum, the FDI into the 'big eight' FDI countries grew by about the same rate as into Europe. These countries – Canada, France, Germany, Japan, the Netherlands, Switzerland, the United Kingdom and the United States – dominate as the main sources of accumulated FDI stocks. Figure 10.2 confirms that they also dominate as destinations of FDI. However, FDI stocks into the 'small rich' countries (developed countries other than the big eight) grew faster than those into the big eight over 1990–2000. They grew slightly faster than into the APEC region as a whole.

Figure 10.3 compares FDI stocks into smaller 'geographic' groupings. FDI stocks in the Middle East and North African (MENA) countries, sub-Saharan Africa and South Asia are still relatively small, although over 1990–2000 stocks into sub-Saharan Africa almost quadrupled, while those into South Asia grew sixfold. FDI stocks into Latin American countries were much more significant, and quadrupled over the 1990–2000 period. However, FDI into 'Asia' dominated in absolute terms, and grew almost sevenfold over 1990–2000. Here, 'Asia' is defined as ASEAN+4 – the ASEAN countries plus China, Hong Kong, Japan and South Korea.

The figures suggest that in terms of volumes and growth rates, there is nothing special about the broad APEC region, although there might be something special about the Asian grouping of ASEAN+4.

Figure 10.3 Inward FDI stocks into 'geographic' groupings of regions (US$ billion)

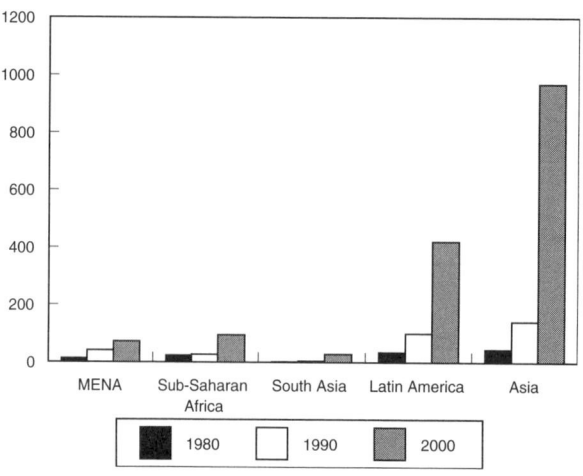

Notes: 'Asia' = ASEAN+4; MENA = Middle East and North Africa.
Source: UNCTAD, <http://www.unctad.org/Templates/Page.asp?intItemID=3199&lang=1>.

Tables 10.6–10.8 present the results of estimating the above specification of the determinants of FDI separately for each of the same socioeconomic or geographic country groupings of host countries. All estimating equations also included three types of fixed effects – time dummies, parent dummies and host dummies – although for brevity the coefficients on these variables are not reported. The triple indexing approach to fixed effects is advocated by Matyas (1997, 1998). Hausman tests strongly rejected the alternative, random effects specification of both parent and host effects. The specifications fit the data far better than a gravity specification estimated on similar data (Dee and Gali 2005).

In the remainder of this section, I examine the signs of the coefficients on the bilateral and third-country determinants to see if FDI into any of these regions corresponds closely to one or more of the archetypes of simple or complex horizontal or vertical FDI, as summarised in Table 10.1. The next section examines the significance of the variables describing the investment provisions of PTAs, to see if there is any evidence of investment being 'created' or 'diverted' by these provisions.

Over the whole sample, distance has a significant negative effect on FDI, as it does for most host groupings. This suggests that the effect of distance in adding to trade costs, thus boosting FDI as an alternative way of serving the market, is outweighed by the effect of distance in adding to the set-up costs of establishing a foreign affiliate.

Over the whole sample, bilateral country size is insignificant, as it is for many host groupings, despite a strong prediction from the analytical model that it should be positively associated with FDI, no matter what the motivation for the FDI. Over the whole sample, relative bilateral factor endowments do not play a particularly strong role: relative capital stocks matter but, somewhat surprisingly, relative stocks of unskilled labour do not.

The critical interaction and third-country variables suggest that, over the whole sample, the motivations for FDI are mixed. The signs of the own-country interaction variables are consistent with complex vertical FDI, but the third-country endowment variables suggest an export platform motivation, while the third-country interaction variables are consistent with simple vertical FDI. This mixed finding, and lack of significance of some key variables, motivates the search for a clearer picture among smaller groupings of host countries.[5]

A clearer picture fails to emerge when looking at Europe or the broad Asia Pacific region (Table 10.6). Using the signs of the coefficients that are significant, both regions appear to have the same mix of motivations as the whole sample. In Europe, perversely, FDI increases with the relative unskilled labour abundance of the parent country, and decreases as the host becomes less risky (measured as a higher value of the risk variable). In the Asia Pacific region, FDI reduces as bilateral size increases, also contrary to the theoretical framework. This suggests possible mis-specification of the motivations explaining FDI into Europe and the broad Asia Pacific region.

When looking at the big eight investors (Table 10.7), the signs of the significant coefficients are consistent with FDI into the region being driven by vertical or complex vertical motivations, although this region has the same perverse signs as Europe for unskilled labour and country risk. It also has a perverse sign on bilateral country size,

Table 10.6 Econometric results for bilateral FDI stocks into broad regions[a]

Variable	All hosts	Europe	APEC

Dependent variable: log of outstock from source country; time period 1988–97; unbalanced panel; fixed effects estimation

Motives for FDI
Bilateral

Variable	All hosts	Europe	APEC
dis = distance between d and i	–0.00018***	–0.00096***	–0.00013***
G = bilateral size of d plus i	0.05	0.11	–0.28*
S = similarity in size of d and i	1.08***	0.70	0.43
k = $\ln(K_d/K_i)$	1.09***	2.36***	–0.22
h = $\ln(H_d/H_i)$	0.20	0.04	0.39*
l = $\ln(L_d/L_i)$	–0.05	3.94***	–2.01***
gamma = G*k	–0.03**	–0.22***	0.04
phi = $\ln(dis)*(k-l)$	–0.07***	0.04	–0.08**
risk	0.39***	–0.72***	0.10

Third country

Variable	All hosts	Europe	APEC
wG = bilateral size of d and j	1.04***	1.18*	2.08***
wS = similarity in size of d and j	–0.31	1.41	7.52***
wk = $\ln(K_d/K_j)$	5.36***	2.97	5.68***
wh = $\ln(H_d/H_j)$	0.44*	1.05***	–0.12
wl = $\ln(L_d/L_j)$	–8.26***	–6.67***	–5.18***
wgamma = wG*wk	0.10	0.11	–0.03
wphi = $\ln(dis_{dj})*(wk-wl)$	–0.93***	–0.68**	–0.77***
wrisk	0.04	–0.01	–0.18**

FTA variables[b]
Bilateral

Variable	All hosts	Europe	APEC
cb_f_ave	–1.74*	0.50	Dropped
cb_c_ave	3.61***	–2.44	–10.42***
i_f_ave	5.35***	0.20	16.22***
i_c_ave	2.20*	1.84	25.29***
mp_f_ave	–4.98***	–2.33	9.61***
mp_c_ave	–4.63***	2.14	–31.88***

Third country

Variable	All hosts	Europe	APEC
wcb_f_ave	11.01***	5.44	7.48**
wcb_c_ave	7.12*	12.64**	4.05
wi_f_ave	–17.20***	–11.58	–15.18**
wi_c_ave	–10.12**	–15.20**	–5.22
wmp_f_ave	10.38*	5.18	7.28
wmp_c_ave	0.62	2.70	1.10
Status of FTA variables	Stable	Unstable	Unstable
R squared	0.82	0.86	0.83
Reset test – F value	39.99***	58.13***	21.29***

Notes

a Fixed effects not reported. Estimated using robust standard errors. *** = significant at the 1% level; ** = significant at the 5% level; * = significant at the 10% level. See text for explanation of other variables. Reset test Ho: model has no omitted variables.

b cb = cross-border trade, i = investment, mp = movement of natural persons, f = form, c = content, ave = average.

Source: Estimated by author.

Table 10.7 Econometric results for bilateral FDI stocks into socioeconomic groupings[a]

Variable	Big eight	Small rich	Upper middle income	Lower middle income	Lower income
Dependent variable: log of outstock from source country, time period 1988–97, unbalanced panel, fixed effects estimation					
Motives for FDI					
Bilateral					
dis = distance between d and i	–0.00009***	–0.00021***	–0.00011***	–0.00018***	–0.00002
G = bilateral size of d plus i	–0.85**	–0.64*	0.23	1.31***	0.89
S = similarity in size of d and i	–0.64	0.52	1.55*	2.17***	0.90
k = $\ln(K_d/K_i)$	2.88**	0.39	4.16***	2.55**	5.16***
h = $\ln(H_d/H_i)$	0.01	–0.07	0.71**	–0.24	0.38
l = $\ln(L_d/L_i)$	1.52**	1.48**	2.70**	–2.81**	0.43
gamma = G*k	–0.11**	–0.05	–0.13**	–0.11**	–0.14
phi = $\ln(dis)*(k–l)$	0.19***	–0.01	–0.26***	–0.16***	–0.43***
risk	–1.02***	0.17	0.46***	–0.60	1.31**
Third country					
wG = bilateral size of d and j	–0.80	1.00*	0.85	3.06**	–0.61
wS = similarity in size of d and j	9.14***	–2.25	–24.26***	0.73	8.84
wk = $\ln(K_d/K_j)$	3.49	7.24***	5.04	11.39***	13.00***
wh = $\ln(H_d/H_j)$	0.09	1.27***	1.76**	–0.41	–0.67
wl = $\ln(L_d/L_j)$	–7.18***	–9.20***	–2.42	–6.25*	–12.28***
wgamma = wG*wk	0.22	–0.03	–0.49	–0.39	–0.06
wphi = $\ln(dis_{dj})*(wk–wl)$	–0.92***	–0.72***	0.20	–0.88**	–1.02***
wrisk	–0.13	0.27**	0.51**	–0.13	0.70***
FTA variables[b]					
Bilateral					
cb_f_ave	5.84***	–5.76***	Dropped	766.12***	Dropped
cb_c_ave	10.96***	8.12***	–3.60	–0.94	–4.29
i_f_ave	12.60***	11.87***	–28.93**	639.30***	10.13
i_c_ave	12.21***	–3.18	Dropped	Dropped	Dropped
mp_f_ave	Dropped	–13.19***	8.63	–42.77***	Dropped
mp_c_ave	–33.05***	–0.60	23.11	90.32***	Dropped
Third country					
wcb_f_ave	2.61	13.65***	30.13***	3.62	–4.41
wcb_c_ave	11.54**	5.30	–33.15**	–8.72	23.93**
wi_f_ave	1.33	–13.75*	–81.28***	–12.36	–0.14
wi_c_ave	–3.58	–7.07	18.71	26.59**	14.42
wmp_f_ave	–10.47	6.03	76.21***	22.28	–22.34
wmp_c_ave	–5.71	–1.62	–0.55	–27.79***	–30.33**
Status of FTA variables	Stable	Stable	Unstable	Unstable	Unstable
R squared	0.89	0.83	0.79	0.81	0.91
Reset test – F value	27.87***	29.48***	4.09***	3.22**	0.55

Notes

a Fixed effects not reported. Estimated using robust standard errors. *** = significant at the 1% level; ** = significant at the 5% level; * = significant at the 10% level. See text for explanation of other variables. Reset test Ho: model has no omitted variables.

b cb = cross–border trade, i = investment, mp = movement of natural persons, f = form, c = content, ave = average.

Source: Estimated by author.

Table 10.8 Econometric results for bilateral FDI stocks into 'geographic' groupings[a]

Variable	MENA	Sub-Saharan Africa	South Asia	Latin America	Asia
\multicolumn{6}{l}{Dependent variable: Log of outstock from source country, time period 1988–97, unbalanced panel, fixed effects estimation}					
Motives for FDI					
Bilateral					
dis = distance between d and i	0.00047***	−0.00037***	−0.00045*	−0.00018***	−0.00008***
G = bilateral size of d plus i	−5.01	4.13***	−0.79	–	0.64	0.64*
S = similarity in size of d and i	3.52	2.68	−2.68	−0.52	2.38***
k = $\ln(K_d/K_i)$	17.58***	−3.49	6.87	−1.29	3.05***
h = $\ln(H_d/H_i)$	0.47	0.34	0.84	−0.06	0.52**
l = $\ln(L_d/L_i)$	−18.98***	9.67***	−1.25	1.18	−3.86***
gamma = G*k	−0.18	−0.22*	−0.15	0.03	−0.15***
phi = $\ln(\text{dis})$*(k−l)	−1.65***	0.80***	0.05	0.06	−0.17***
risk	−0.11	−0.11	1.53	−0.04	0.08
Third country					
wG = bilateral size of d and j	8.01**	−0.61	−5.18**	1.35	2.58***
wS = similarity in size of d and j	4.21	54.53***	−0.83	11.64	9.07***
wk = $\ln(K_d/K_j)$	−5.01	6.12	3.58	9.89	5.71**
wh = $\ln(H_d/H_j)$	−0.06	3.04**	−1.00	0.64	−0.18
wl = $\ln(L_d/L_j)$	1.92	−14.06*	−20.23***	−6.38	−5.63***
wgamma = wG*wk	0.15	0.59	1.14***	−0.24	−0.02
wphi = $\ln(\text{dis}_{dj})$*(wk−wl)	0.48	−1.59	−2.30***	−0.47	−0.86***
wrisk	0.03	0.47	0.21	0.59***	−0.27***
FTA variables[b]					
Bilateral					
cb_f_ave	Dropped	Dropped	Dropped	Dropped	Dropped
cb_c_ave	Dropped	Dropped	Dropped	0.11	8.87
i_f_ave	Dropped	Dropped	10.15	−36.21***	−17.79
i_c_ave	Dropped	Dropped	Dropped	Dropped	Dropped
mp_f_ave	Dropped	Dropped	Dropped	Dropped	Dropped
mp_c_ave	Dropped	Dropped	Dropped	32.49**	Dropped
Third country					
wcb_f_ave	−2.83	2.76	−37.66***	7.63	−5.02
wcb_c_ave	−18.95	2.08	30.94*	−13.92	−8.72
wi_f_ave	36.20	24.95	65.34**	−18.74	10.36
wi_c_ave	18.48	−13.90	18.06	22.34	34.94***
wmp_f_ave	−27.43	−46.27	−66.42	22.06	−7.10
wmp_c_ave	−0.43	26.64	−34.48	−16.70	−29.00***
Status of FTA variables	Stable	Stable	Unstable	Stable	Stable
R squared	0.87	0.92	0.96	0.87	0.83
Reset test – F value	4.59***	3.29**	5.63***	6.30***	13.08***

Notes:
a Fixed effects not reported. Estimated using robust standard errors. *** = significant at the 1% level; ** = significant at the 5% level; * = significant at the 10% level. See text for explanation of other variables. Reset test Ho: model has no omitted variables.
b cb = cross-border trade, i = investment, mp = movement of natural persons, f = form, c = content, ave = average.

Source: Estimated by author.

suggesting that smaller countries that 'return-invest' into the big eight sources of FDI 'are not driven by the desire to defray set-up costs in a big market. Their motivation is more likely to be related to marketing activity. In the small rich countries, there is little in the bilateral variables to distinguish the motivation for FDI, although the third-country variables are consistent with a mix of export platform and vertical motivations. Again, there is a perverse sign on bilateral country size.

In the three lower socioeconomic groupings, it is only in the lower middle income group that FDI appears to be attracted by the unskilled labour abundance of the host country. Interestingly, this country grouping includes China. The other variables suggest a mix of motivations for FDI into the lower middle and lower income groups. They suggest a complex vertical motivation for FDI into the upper middle income group, although the lack of significance of third-country effects means that this evidence is weak.

Turning to smaller 'geographic' groupings (Table 10.8), there is similar weak evidence of a complex vertical motivation for FDI into MENA and sub-Saharan African countries, although the latter group has a perverse sign on the unskilled labour endowment variable. No clear motivation for FDI into South Asia is discernible from the third-country interaction variables.

For the Latin American group, there seems little in the new economic geography to explain FDI into the region. Distance, risk, and unexplained heterogeneity (via the fixed effects) appear to carry all the explanatory power.

By contrast, FDI into the Asian group appears to fit the new economic geography explanation best. The interaction and third-country variables still suggest a mix of motivations – complex vertical, simple vertical and export platform. But most of the other variables are also significant, and none has a perverse sign. In particular, relative endowments of capital, skilled and unskilled labour all play a role, consistent with fine divisions of comparative advantage implicit in the network pattern of production and trade described in the introduction.

Thus it appears that there could be a pattern of FDI unique to the Asian region. This is not because FDI into the region falls neatly into one of the archetypes of complex FDI identified by Baltagi *et al.* (2005). Rather, it is that FDI in the region responds relatively clearly to the forces of economic geography that are present in their model, unimpeded by other considerations. While comparative advantage is an important driving force, it is mitigated by considerations of economies of scale and transport costs. The resulting patterns of FDI (and trade) reflect complex horizontal and vertical motivations. This pattern emerges most clearly for the Asian grouping of ASEAN+4, not for APEC as a whole.

DO THE INVESTMENT PROVISIONS OF PTAs PLAY A ROLE?

The influence of PTAs is assessed not just by looking at the formal statistical significance of the PTA variables. The variables are also subject to considerations of model mis-specification. Although the empirical specifications include all variables suggested by the formal analytical model, the Reset tests suggest that with one exception (the lower income group), there are omitted variables. Furthermore, the formal tests of significance are made using robust standard errors, which correct for heteroskedasticity (especially in the variable measuring bilateral size). But calculating robust standard errors using residuals that include the influence of omitted variables could mean that the PTA variables appear to be significant, when in reality they are proxying for omitted variables. Indeed, in several of the specifications, PTA variables appear significant using robust standard errors, but are insignificant when normal standard errors are used. Because of their dummy variable nature, the PTA variables are susceptible to this instability in a way that the other variables are not. Accordingly, Tables 10.6–10.8 also report the status of the PTA variables as being stable or unstable, according to whether the significance changes when normal rather than robust standard errors are used.

On this basis, attention is paid to the PTA variables for the big eight and small rich country hosts, and for the developing countries divided along geographic rather than socioeconomic lines. These are the specifications in which the significance of the PTA variables is insensitive to the choice of standard errors. The PTA variables have quite different patterns of significance across these different groupings.

FDI into the big eight is positively related to the investment provisions of the PTA agreements that the big eight sign with the source countries, and is not deflected by the investment provisions of PTAs that those source countries might sign with third parties. Both the form and the content of the investment provisions matter.[6]

Furthermore, FDI into the big eight is positively related to the provisions covering cross-border trade in services in the agreements with source countries, suggesting that cross-border trade in services and FDI are general equilibrium complements rather than substitutes for those source countries. This may not be surprising. Cross-border trade is an important mode of delivery for services such as insurance, and insurance is a necessary adjunct activity to many others, including FDI in both services and manufacturing. Finally, FDI into the big eight is negatively related to the content of the provisions covering the movement of natural persons in the agreements with source countries. This suggests that the movement of natural persons and FDI are general equilibrium substitutes for those source countries, in terms of accessing the markets of the big eight. FDI into the big eight is also boosted by the provisions governing cross-border trade that the source countries sign with third parties. This probably reflects the headquarters role of the big eight.

FDI into the small rich countries is positively related to the form of the investment provisions of agreements that they sign with source countries, and inversely related to the form of provisions governing cross-border trade and the movement of natural persons, though positively related to the content of the cross-border provisions. The FDI into small rich countries is deflected by the form of the cross-border or investment provisions that the source countries sign with third parties. In the case of the investment provisions, this means that the FDI into the small rich countries is reduced. The relative magnitudes of the coefficients mean that if the source countries sign agreements with all third parties that are equally as generous in the form of their investment provisions as the agreements they sign with each small rich country, then each small rich country will on average suffer investment diversion that slightly exceeds investment creation.

FDI into MENA countries and sub-Saharan Africa appears to be unaffected by the services or investment provisions of PTAs. This is largely because the provisions signed by these countries to date have been minimal – as reflected by all the bilateral PTA variables being dropped. By the same token, FDI into these countries is not deflected by the services and investment provisions of PTAs that source countries might sign elsewhere. The results are similar for South Asia, although South Asia is somewhat affected by PTAs that its source countries sign with third parties. However, not all these latter results are robust.

As noted in a previous section, the Latin American countries have signed PTAs that have some of the most liberal services and investment provisions. Despite this, the form of those investment provisions seems to deflect rather than attract FDI. The specifications that use more disaggregated measures of PTA provisions give some small insight into this result. The negative impact does *not* come from the provisions governing nationality requirements, performance requirements, transparency, denial of benefits (that is, rules of origin, which are typically very liberal for investment), expropriation, investor-state dispute settlement, government procurement, or the incorporation of a ratchet mechanism. These are provisions that are given a heavy weight in the second two factors from factor analysis, whereas it is the first factor (which gives heavy weight to all other provisions governing form) that is responsible for the negative impact on FDI. However, lack of in-sample variation in the individual PTA characteristics precludes verifying which particular characteristic is responsible for this effect.

Finally, FDI into the ASEAN+4 group is not significantly affected by the services or investment provisions of the PTAs that these countries sign with the source countries. It is positively affected by the investment provisions of the PTAs that the source countries sign with third countries. This is further evidence that FDI into the Asian grouping has network characteristics. If the PTAs that the source countries sign with third countries facilitate investment linkages within a network, they can also boost rather than deflect bilateral investment. And FDI into the Asian grouping is negatively affected by the provisions that source countries sign with third parties governing the movement of natural persons. This is consistent with the movement of natural persons being a general equilibrium substitute for FDI (as found elsewhere), in the Asian context in which FDI with third parties is a complement to bilateral FDI within the network.

The estimated effects of the services and investment provisions of PTAs on FDI within the whole sample can be seen to be dominated by the effects on the FDI into the big eight and the small rich countries. This is not surprising. What is more revealing from a policy perspective is how the services and investment provisions of PTAs interact with host country characteristics across the different regional groupings. I deal with this in the concluding section.

CONCLUSIONS

The first aim of this chapter was to determine empirically whether there was a unique regional model of FDI (somewhere) in the Asia Pacific region, driven by complex 'network' behaviour of multinational corporations. There does appear to be a pattern of FDI unique to the region. This is not because FDI in the region falls neatly into a single archetype pattern, but rather because FDI responds relatively clearly to the forces of economic geography, unimpeded by other considerations. While comparative advantage is an important driving force, it is mitigated by considerations of economies of scale and transport costs. The resulting patterns of FDI (and trade) reflect complex horizontal and vertical motivations. This pattern emerges most clearly for the Asian grouping of ASEAN+4, not for APEC as a whole.

The second aim of this chapter was to determine empirically whether the investment provisions of PTAs have had any influence on regional investment behaviour.

In terms of attracting FDI, the clear winners from the investment and services provisions of PTAs appear to be the big eight – the countries that are also the main sources of accumulated FDI. The big eight do not suffer from investment diversion.

The small rich countries have been able to attract FDI by signing investment provisions into PTAs with source countries, although this effect can be offset by provisions in the same agreements that boost forms of service delivery that substitute for FDI. More importantly, the small rich countries have suffered investment diversion when the source countries have included investment provisions in PTAs with third countries.

The African and South Asian groupings of developing countries have not been major players in signing PTAs over the estimation period, but they have been largely insulated from any investment diversion when their source countries sign PTAs with third parties. And although many countries in the Latin American group have signed NAFTA-style PTAs with strong investment provisions, this appears not to have attracted FDI into the region.

Finally, the phenomenal growth of FDI into the Asian region appears not to have been driven by the investment or services provisions of PTAs signed with their bilateral source countries. But the network nature of regional investment among the ASEAN+4 means that individual members have been insulated from any investment diversion when their source countries have signed PTAs with third parties. This is because the investment that the sources make in third countries can be a general equilibrium complement to bilateral investment within the overall Asian network.

This last finding is particularly striking. It means that when FDI and trade are sufficiently driven by fundamentals, in a way that takes advantage of fine divisions of comparative advantage, but subject to considerations of economies of scale and transport costs, the resulting network patterns of investment do not need to be boosted by investment provisions of PTAs. Further, the network patterns can be sufficiently strong to insulate a country from investment diversion when the FDI source countries play the PTA game elsewhere. This is in strong contrast with the findings for Latin America. When FDI and trade are not sufficiently driven by fundamentals, the investment provisions of PTAs signed with source countries have little real effect.

Thus the investment provisions of PTAs pose neither a threat nor a promise to FDI in the Asian region. But a very real threat may come from the trade provisions of PTAs. In contrast to investment provisions, the trade provisions do not have generous rules of origin. PTAs that require 'substantial transformation' or 40 per cent value added to ensure that an exporter is eligible for preferential treatment in the importing country are inimical to fine divisions of comparative advantage. On this issue, the last word belongs to Victor Fung (2005):

> From a business standpoint, the supply chain should be structured not just to qualify for favourable 'rule of origin' treatment, but in the optimal way to create a product, namely the most cost-effective way for the final consumer. Why should I worry about where the point of 'substantive transformation' is? Why should I worry about it occurring in any particular location in order to qualify for duty-free treatment? The whole world should trade on the basis of economics. If the future world trading regime is to mirror economic reality and to allow the use of modern business strategies, we need a single, over-arching framework for trade.

NOTES

I thank Ryo Ochiai for exceptional research assistance.

1. Blonigen (2005) gives a comprehensive review of the empirical literature on FDI determinants.
2. The findings on the effects of host country *trade* restrictions on FDI have been more variable. This is not surprising, since theory suggests that the impact of host trade restrictions on inward FDI is ambiguous.
3. Export platform FDI from d to i would increase with similarity, while horizontal and complex vertical FDI would increase with the size of d relative to i. However, vertical FDI would decrease with the d to i size ratio.
4. Content has been scored so that it reflects current commitments for all years in which an agreement is in force, even if (as in the case of the ASEAN Framework Agreement on Services and the European Union agreement) commitments have become more generous over time. Indeed, the first sectoral commitments under the ASEAN Framework Agreement on Services were not made until 1997, two years after the architecture of the agreement was signed. But even on current commitments, the ASEAN Framework Agreement on Services scores very poorly on content, so this feature of the scoring is not expected to influence the results.
5. Note that splitting the sample by source countries gave the same mixed and indeterminate results as for the sample as a whole.
6. Although Japan is a member of the big eight, it is largely exempt from this assessment because it had signed no PTAs over the period.

REFERENCES

Baltagi. B., P. Egger and M. Pfaffermayr (2005) 'Estimating models of complex FDI: are there third-country effects?', Centre for Policy Research Working Paper No. 73, New York: Syracuse University.

Bevin, A.A. and S. Estrin (2004) 'The determinants of foreign direct investment into European transition economies', *Journal of Comparative Economics*, 32: 775–87.

Blonigen, B. (2005) 'A review of the empirical literature on FDI determinants', *Atlantic Economic Journal*, 33: 383–403.

Blonigen. B. and R. Davies (2000) 'The effects of bilateral tax treaties on US FDI activity', NBER Working Paper No. 7929.

Blonigen, B. and R. Davies (2004) 'The effects of bilateral tax treaties on US FDI activity', *International Tax and Public Finance*, 11: 601–22.

Blonigen. B., R. Davies and K. Head (2003) 'Estimating the knowledge-capital model of the multination enterprise: comment', *American Economic Review*, 93(3): 980–94.

Boisso, D. and M. Ferrantino (1997) 'Economic distance, cultural distance, and openness in international trade: empirical puzzles', *Journal of Economic Integration*, 12(4): 456–84.

Carr, D., J. Markusen and K. Maskus (2001) 'Estimating the knowledge-capital model of the multinational enterprise', *American Economic Review*, 91(3): 693–708.

—— (2003) 'Estimating the knowledge-capital model of the multinational enterprise: reply', *American Economic Review*, 93(3): 995–1001.

Dee, P. and J. Gali (2005) 'The trade and investment effects of preferential trading arrangements', pp. 133–75 in T. Ito and A. Rose (eds), *International Trade in East Asia*, Chicago and London: University of Chicago Press.

Egger, P. and M. Pfaffermayr (2004a) 'The impact of bilateral investment treaties on foreign direct investment', *Journal of Comparative Economics*, 32: 788–804.

—— (2004b) 'Distance, trade and FDI: A Hausman–Taylor SUR approach', *Journal of Applied Econometrics*, 19: 227–46.

Egger, P., M. Larch and M. Pfaffermayr (2004), 'Multilateral trade and investment liberalization: effects on welfare and GDP per capita convergence', *Economics Letters*, 84: 133–40.

Ekholm, K., R. Forslid and J. Markusen (2003) 'Export platform foreign direct investment', NBER Working Paper No. 9517.

Fung, V. (2005) 'Business perceptions and expectations regarding the WTO Doha negotiations', *APEC Economies Newsletter*, 9(12), December.

Grossman, G., E. Helpman and A. Szeidl (2003) 'Optimal integration strategies for the multinational firm', NBER Working Paper No. 10189.

Haveman, J. (2000) *International Trade Data*, <http://www.macalester.edu/research/economics/PAGE/HAVEMAN/Trade.Resources/TradeData.html>, accessed 31 August 2001.

Helpman, E. (1984) 'A simple theory of international trade with multinational corporations', *Journal of Political Economy*, 92(3): 451–71.

IMF (International Monetary Fund) (2001) *The World Economic Outlook (WEO) Database May 2001*, <http://www.imf.org/external/pubs/ft/weo/2001/01/data/index.htm>, accessed 18 June 2002.

Krugman, P. (1998) 'What's new about the new economic geography', *Oxford Review of Economic Policy*, 14(2): 7–17.

Markusen, J. (1984) 'Multinationals, multi-plant economies, and the gains from trade', *Journal of International Economics*, 16(3–4): 205–26.

—— (1997) 'Trade versus investment liberalization', NBER Working Paper No. 6231.

—— (2002) *Multinational Firms and the Theory of International Trade*, Cambridge MA: MIT Press.

Markusen, J. and K. Maskus (2002) 'Discriminating among alternative theories of the multinational enterprise', *Review of International Economics*, 10(4): 694–707.

Matyas, L. (1997) 'Proper econometric specification of the gravity model', *World Economy*, 20(3): 363–68.

—— (1998) 'The gravity model: some econometric considerations', *World Economy*, 21(3): 397–401.

OECD (Organisation for Economic Co-operation and Development) (2001) *International Direct Investment Statistics Year Book: 1980–2000*, Edition 2001, Paris.

Stein, E. and C. Daude (2001), 'Institutions, integration and the location of foreign direct investment', paper prepared for the 2001 Annual Meeting of the Boards of Governors, Inter-American Bank and Inter-American Investment Corporation, Santiago de Chile.

UNCTAD (United Nations Conference on Trade and Development) (1992a) *World Investment Directory. Foreign Direct Investment, Legal Framework and Corporate Data, Volume 1: Asia and the Pacific*, New York: United Nations.

—— (United Nations Conference on Trade and Development) (1992b) *World Investment Directory. Foreign Direct Investment, Legal Framework and Corporate Data, Volume 2: Central and Eastern Europe*, New York: United Nations.

—— (United Nations Conference on Trade and Development) (1993) *World Investment Directory. Foreign Direct Investment, Legal Framework and Corporate Data, Volume 3: Developed Economies*, New York: United Nations.

—— (United Nations Conference on Trade and Development) (1994) *World Investment Directory. Foreign Direct Investment, Legal Framework and Corporate Data, Volume 4: Latin America and the Caribbean*, New York: United Nations.

—— (United Nations Conference on Trade and Development) (1997a) *World Investment Directory. Foreign Direct Investment, Legal Framework and Corporate Data, Volume 5: Africa*, New York: United Nations.

—— (United Nations Conference on Trade and Development) (1997b), *World Investment Directory. Foreign Direct Investment, Legal Framework and Corporate Data, Volume 6: West Asia*, New York: United Nations.

—— (United Nations Conference on Trade and Development) (2000), *World Investment Directory. Foreign Direct Investment and Corporate Data, Volume 7: Asia and the Pacific, 2 parts*, New York: United Nations.

World Bank (2001), *World Development Indicators Database on CD-ROM*, Washington DC: World Bank.

Yeaple, S. (2003) 'The complex integration strategies of multinationals and cross country dependencies in the structure of foreign direct investment', *Journal of International Economics*, 60: 293–314.

Yeyati, E., E. Stein, and C. Daude (2003) 'The FTAA and the location of FDI', paper presented to the Pacific Economic Cooperation Council (PECC) Trade Forum, Washington DC, 22–23 April.

ANNEX 10.1 DATA SOURCES

The foreign direct investment (FDI) data were the same as used by Dee and Gali (2005). The data came from two sources. The main source was the United Nations Conference on Trade and Development (UNCTAD). It publishes bilateral investment data for various continents in a series of volumes.

- Volume 1: Asia and the Pacific (UNCTAD 1992a). Country tables provide data on FDI flows and stocks for 21 countries during the 1980s.
- Volume 2: Central and Eastern Europe (UNCTAD 1992b). Country tables provide data on FDI flows and stocks for 26 countries during the 1980s.
- Volume 3: Developed economies (UNCTAD 1993). Country tables provide data on FDI flows and stocks for 22 countries during the 1980s.
- Volume 4: Latin America and the Caribbean (UNCTAD 1994). Country tables provide data on FDI flows and stocks for 24 countries during the 1980s.
- Volume 5: Africa (UNCTAD 1997a). Country tables provide data on FDI flows and stocks for 53 countries during the late 1980s and early 1990s.
- Volume 6: West Asia (UNCTAD 1997b). Country tables provide data on FDI flows and stocks for 15 countries during the late 1980s and early 1990s.
- Volume 7: Asia and the Pacific (UNCTAD 2000). Country tables provide data on FDI flows and stocks for 23 countries during the 1990s.

The second source was the Organisation for Economic Co-operation and Development (OECD), which collects FDI data for OECD reporter countries and a number of OECD and non-OECD partner countries. For many developed countries, the OECD data were used to extend the UNCTAD bilateral data which ended at 1991. The OECD data are available electronically. The above UNCTAD investment directories are not available electronically, although two subsequent ones are. UNCTAD use a country-specific definition of FDI and the OECD uses a semi-standardised definition of FDI – the OECD benchmark definition. Not all OECD countries comply with the OECD benchmark definition, which requires 10 per cent or more of the ordinary shares or voting power for investment to be 'direct'. The OECD uses the 'fully consolidated' system; that is, the subsidiary of a subsidiary is automatically a subsidiary.

The bilateral FDI data have a number of limitations.

- There is little consistency in the attribution of nationality to transit investment (that is, FDI undertaken by a regional headquarters rather than a parent company).
- The coverage is limited, even in developed countries. For example, the UK statistics exclude oil and the financial sector in most years. Given the importance of the United Kingdom as a financial centre of the world and as an oil trading country, this leads to a serious underestimation of the United Kingdom's foreign investment.
- The data are sporadic for developing and underdeveloped countries.
- Stock data are imputed from flows data by simple cumulative addition, with no allowance for depreciation.

The GDP data measure GDP at purchasing power parity (PPP). Most of the GDP data were sourced from the World Bank's World Development Indicators (WDI) (World Bank 2001). Insufficient data were available for some economies and some years, and data were supplemented from the International Monetary Fund and the OECD (IMF 2001; OECD 2001).

The GDP data were converted to current international dollars using PPP conversion factors from the WDI. The data were insufficient for some economies and years. In these cases, PPP conversion factors were estimated by extrapolating the data backwards. GDP at PPP was then calculated by dividing GDP in local currency units by the PPP conversion factors.

The primary source of the distance data was Boisso and Ferrantino (1997), who calculate the distance between the two largest cities. Distance is measured in kilometres and is the great circle distance or 'as the crow flies'. Data were not available for a number of smaller economies, and data for the missing economies were taken from Haveman (2000), who measures the distance between capital cities.

The remaining data came from essentially the same sources as Baltagi *et al.* (2005). Capital stock data were estimated using the same perpetual inventory method from data on real gross fixed capital formation taken from the WDI. Skilled and unskilled labour forces were computed by applying skilled and unskilled labour proportions to total labour force data, where the latter also came from the WDI. Unlike Baltagi and his colleagues, I took the skilled and unskilled labour proportions from the Barro and Lee dataset (available at <http://www.cid.harvard.edu/ciddata/ciddata.html>), since this had better coverage of developing countries than WDI did. Skilled labour was defined as those with 'higher school attained' (rather than 'higher school complete'). Country investment risk data came from the International Country Risk Guide (available at <http://www.prsgroup.com/icrg/icrg.html>).

FDI source countries: Australia, Austria, Belgium–Luxembourg, Brazil, Canada, Chile, China, Colombia, Denmark, Finland, France, Germany, Iceland, India, Italy, Japan, Korea, Malaysia, Netherlands, New Zealand, Norway, Pakistan, Poland, Portugal, Romania, Singapore, Spain, Sweden, Switzerland, Thailand, United Kingdom, United States.

FDI destination countries: Algeria, Angola, Argentina, Australia, Austria, Bahamas, Bahrain, Bangladesh, Barbados, Belgium–Luxembourg, Belize, Bolivia, Brazil, Burundi, Cameroon, Canada, Central African Republic, Chile, China, Colombia, Congo (Republic), Costa Rica, Côte d'Ivoire, Cyprus, Denmark, Dominican Republic, Ecuador, Egypt, El Salvador, Ethiopia, Fiji, Finland, France, Gabon, Germany, Ghana, Greece, Guatemala, Guinea, Guyana, Honduras, Hong Kong, Hungary, Iceland, India, Indonesia, Iran, Ireland, Israel, Italy, Jamaica, Japan, Jordan, Kenya, Korea, Kuwait, Lao People's Democratic Republic, Madagascar, Malawi, Malaysia, Mali, Malta, Mauritania, Mauritius, Mexico, Morocco, Mozambique, Nepal, Netherlands, New Zealand, Nicaragua, Nigeria, Norway, Pakistan, Panama, Papua New Guinea, Paraguay, Peru, Philippines, Poland, Portugal, Romania, Rwanda, Saudi Arabia, Senegal, Sierra

Leone, Singapore, Solomon Islands, South Africa, Spain, Sri Lanka, Suriname, Sweden, Switzerland, Syrian Republic, Tanzania, Thailand, Togo, Trinidad and Tobago, Tunisia, Turkey, Uganda, United Arab Emirates, United Kingdom, United States, Uruguay, Venezuela, Zambia, Zimbabwe.

11 Governing multinational corporations in the Pacific

Robert Scollay

INTRODUCTION

The increasing prominence of multinationals is a well-known feature of today's increasingly globalised international economy. The forces of globalisation accentuating the role of multinationals have operated especially powerfully in the Asia Pacific region, characterised by market-driven integration based on intense trade and investment linkages. These linkages have facilitated the fragmentation of regional production in a number of sectors through the development of extensive production networks and integrated value chains.

Governments of the region have endeavoured to reinforce the market-driven integration of the region through cooperative activity in the Asia-Pacific Economic Cooperation (APEC) process, and more recently and more controversially through a proliferation of preferential trading arrangements (PTAs), but have largely refrained from the establishment of supranational institutions to undertake economic governance functions on behalf of national governments. The region in fact exhibits a wide diversity in political systems and economic governance institutions, reflecting wide differences in levels of development as well as a range of historical, cultural and economic factors. These factors have also led to the evolution of several distinct models of multinational structure and operation. North American multinationals, Japanese multinationals, multinationals owned by overseas Chinese, and mainland Chinese multinationals each have their own distinctive features. These and other features of the Asia Pacific region create a distinctive policy context for economic governance issues raised by multinationals, but perhaps also help to explain why an analysis of these issues adapted to the specifics of the Asia Pacific regional context has been slow to emerge.

The economic governance issues relating to multinationals are complex and many-sided. In illustration of this point this chapter will focus on four areas of economic governance where the role of multinationals has particular importance: competition policy, taxation, investment agreements and corporate social responsibility (CSR). It will review policy issues raised by multinationals in each of these areas, and discuss how distinctive features of the Asia Pacific region affect the ways in which these issues are addressed. It will endeavour to highlight some of the differences in disciplinary perspectives toward analysis of these issues, as well as differences in perspective between theorists and practitioners.

The extended discussion of competition policy in the next section is the principal focus of the chapter. This is followed by shorter sections on investment agreements, CSR and taxation. A final section discusses the outlook for disciplines on the governance of multinational corporations in the region.

COMPETITION POLICY

One consequence of the growing importance of multinationals is to accentuate the importance of addressing anti-competitive practices that are cross-border in their operation and/or effects, of which international cartels are perhaps the exemplar with the highest profile in recent times. Another is an increasing need to consider competition issues in the context of foreign direct investment (FDI), particularly in the case of mergers and acquisitions. There is both a national and an international dimension to action on cross-border competition issues. National governments need to have the capacity to protect themselves against anti-competitive practices originating beyond their borders. There is also a growing understanding of the role that international cooperation can play in enhancing the effectiveness of action in such cases.

A wave of successful prosecutions of international cartels by the US Department of Justice in the late 1990s drew attention to the potentially enormous scale of the international cartel problem. Klawiter (1999) lists 18 corporations that pleaded guilty and were fined in international cartel cases between 1996 and 1999, with a further 30 active investigations under way. Connor (2002) identifies 31 international food-and-feed-ingredient cartels and 14 non-agricultural cartels that were discovered between 1996 and 2002, leading to 'overcharging' of customers estimated at over $200 billion. Evidence from these investigations contradicted arguments that cartels are generally unstable and as a result largely ineffectual. US Assistant Attorney General Joel Klein noted that these cartels are 'by no means transient or unstable'. He said: 'They are powerful and sophisticated and, without intervention by antitrust authorities, will often go on indefinitely' (Klein 1999a). Klein (1999b) also notes that ongoing discovery of new cartels indicates that the full scale of the problem has not yet been fully revealed.

In the majority of cases to date the US antitrust authorities have prosecuted international cartel members on the grounds of damage to US interests. Klawiter (1999) notes that the majority of companies prosecuted were foreign, including companies from Japan, Germany, Switzerland, the Netherlands and Belgium. Klein (1999b) emphasises the effectiveness of US anti-cartel enforcement as the principal factor behind the successful prosecutions, but notes also that 'many of our international cartel cases would have been much less successful if we had not had the assistance of foreign law enforcement agencies'. The European Union and Canada have also been increasingly taking successful action against international cartels.

While action against international cartels has been largely limited to a handful of countries concerned with damage inflicted within their own borders, the damage caused by international cartels almost certainly spreads across the entire global economy. Klein (1999b) notes that international cartels:

... don't just hurt consumers in the U.S. or any other single country. Almost by definition, they hurt consumers worldwide.

This implies that all Asia Pacific economies have an interest in effective anti-cartel enforcement. This is reflected in the ongoing spread through the region of formal antitrust legislation and anti-cartel enforcement, including extra-territorial enforcement, noted by Paul (2006).

There is also likely to be an Asia Pacific dimension to some, if not many, international cartels. One example is the lysine cartel, led by US firm Archer Daniels Midland and Japanese firm Ajinomoto, with two Korean firms as junior partners. Cooperation in anti-cartel enforcement has however been slow to spread among Asia Pacific economies, although Paul (2006) notes that Australian and Japanese antitrust authorities have now demonstrated a willingness to cooperate in international cartel investigations. Further indication of a growing trend for the involvement of Asia Pacific economies in international cooperation efforts comes from recent reports of investigations by US and European regulators into a possible international cartel of manufacturers of liquid crystal display monitors, in which probes by Japanese and Korean authorities have apparently played an important role, with support also sought from authorities in Taiwan (Anon. 2006).

The extent of international cooperation in international anti-cartel enforcement should not however be overstated. Jenny (2002) concludes that international cooperation against cartels 'remains quite limited' and is 'the exception rather than the norm', even though competition authorities have found cooperation useful in cases where it has been used. It appears that most cooperation is of an informal nature, and that limitations on the exchange of confidential information are an important constraint.

Jenny (2002) does note that international cooperation has been more extensive in the area of mergers. Once again, however, cooperation has been developed furthest between the United States and the European Union, where it has been facilitated by an increasing degree of convergence in approaches to merger issues, and where cooperation nevertheless remains primarily informal. Cooperation across the Asia Pacific region is again much less in evidence.

The apparent preference of competition authorities for informal rather than formal cooperation is one factor suggesting that the establishment of formal international frameworks, especially multilateral frameworks, for competition law enforcement is unlikely to occur in the near future. There are other important practical obstacles to the development of a global or even regional approach to competition law enforcement. Several factors contribute to the considerable difficulty of reaching agreement on a common approach to some key issues. They include significant differences in legal traditions, both in general and in relation to competition law; different weightings given to the competing considerations underlying the competition policy approach to mergers; and different weightings to be given to related issues for vertical restraints outside the 'hard core' cases. Differences may also exist in the value traditionally attached to competition and competitive markets. Lall (1997) points out that approaches to competition policy have been developed mainly within Western traditions. In many

Asian economies on the other hand there has traditionally been rather a fear of 'destructive competition', which is only slowly giving way to convictions on the over-riding benefits of competitive markets. Aghion *et al.* (1997) introduce a further differentiation, based on firm behaviour rather than culture and tradition. Focusing on effects on technology adoption, their model shows that effective competition policy will reduce the incentive of profit-maximising firms to adopt new technology, while having the opposite effect on 'conservative' or 'satisficing' firms characterised by considerable organisational slack.

Wijckmans (2003) points out further that many developing economies lack the capacity to implement and enforce competition law. He makes the obvious point that competition law is of little or no value in the absence of the ability and willingness to enforce it. This point is of course fundamental to efforts at international cooperation, since the effectiveness of any arrangements for international cooperation, whether formal or informal, binding or non-binding, must depend on enforcement at the national level. Evenett *et al.* (2002) also emphasise the importance of capacity across the full spectrum of competition policy. They note, for example, that 'if aggressive prosecution of cartels [is not] complemented by vigilance in other areas of competition policy, ... firms will respond to the enhanced deterrents to cartelisation by merging or taking other measures that lessen competitive pressures'.

In the face of these many obstacles, it is perhaps no surprise that the most ambitious attempt to date at establishing a multilateral framework, the proposal to introduce competition policy into the World Trade Organization (WTO) agenda and rules, as one of the so-called 'Singapore issues', had to be abandoned in the face of widespread opposition from WTO members, especially among developing countries.

Consensus on competition issues within national jurisdictions has also at times been problematic, even in developed countries. Jenny (2002) notes that when privatisation and regulatory reform movements swept through Europe and elsewhere, competition officials found themselves facing a fierce and often losing battle 'to retain jurisdiction over the regulation of competitive relationships in markets newly opened to competition'. To cite another example, the WTO negotiations on competition policy tended to highlight a cleavage between competition authorities and trade officials, with the former manifesting a deep-seated resistance to the intrusion of the latter into international competition policy matters.

The factors militating against the evolution of a common international approach to competition law are very much in play in the Asia Pacific region, with its wide differences in legal traditions, capacities and business cultures. Recognition of this led the Pacific Economic Cooperation Council (PECC) to propose an alternative 'principles-based' approach in its 'Competition Principles' (PECC 1999), later picked up in a modified form by APEC in its 'Principles to Enhance Competition and Regulatory Reform' (APEC 1999).

PECC noted that APEC economies are 'at different stages along the economic development and policy spectrums', with 'different levels of institutional capacity, different access to policy instruments, and different views with respect to optimum policy sequencing' that 'cannot be ignored'. In addition to providing flexibility to allow for these differences, the PECC Principles are noted for their strong advocacy of a move away from approaches such as the so-called 'efficiency approach, based on a welfare calculus', in favour of an approach to promote the competitive process itself, rather than the 'welfare of competitors'. This emphasis on the competitive process is based in turn on an underlying conviction of the value of well-functioning competitive markets in contributing to the achievement of economic efficiency and rising living standards.

PECC highlighted four 'first level core' principles as fundamental to promotion of the competitive process: comprehensiveness (in the sense of ensuring a competition dimension for all economic policies with impacts on globalising markets), transparency, accountability, and non-discrimination (in the sense of assuring 'competitive neutrality in respect of the different modes of domestic and international supply'). These principles are argued to offer appropriate guidance for the way in which all APEC economies approach competition, regardless of level of development and perspective on competition law and policy issues.

In the meantime, competition agencies have been following an approach to the international dimensions of competition policy that is perhaps more pragmatic than, but not necessarily incompatible with, the principles-based approach. With competition policy now off the WTO agenda for the foreseeable future, interested competition agencies have formed an International Competition Network (ICN)[1] of competition authorities (Monti 2004). The ICN is a vehicle for sharing views and experiences on the improvement of the interface between competition policy and international commerce, possibly leading, for example, to consideration of more efficient procedures for parallel investigations by authorities of different economies into international mergers. Efforts such as these to improve efficiency in process, using international cooperation to eliminate unnecessary costs and delays, cohere strongly with the views of Wijckmans (2003), who argues that they are much more important and useful than any effort to achieve harmonisation of approaches to merger control, which he sees as problematic and possibly doomed to failure. In the area of vertical restraints, Wijckmans argues that the greatest gains will come from improvements in information sharing, taking care at the same time to give due weight to legitimate business interests in protecting their business secrets. The ICN is in fact taking steps to strengthen inter-agency cooperation against international cartels.

The clearest convergence between the ICN- and principles-based approaches is seen in the ICN project to develop sets of 'Guiding Principles' and 'Recommended Practices' for control of multi-jurisdictional mergers. Monti (2004) foresees the gradual emergence of a 'collection of authoritative best practices'.

In addition to the practical issues discussed above, the analytical literature provides some warnings against too readily assuming an easy coincidence of interests between countries in competition matters. In competition policy frameworks where both consumer and producer interests enter into assessment of the effects of anti-competitive practices, especially in frameworks based on the so-called 'efficiency' criterion, it cannot be assumed that conclusions reached in relation to impacts on the domestic market will coincide with assessments of impact on the global market. For example, in the case of mergers that lead to both lower costs and higher prices, the assessment of the overall impact will depend on the relative weight of consumer and producer interests in the market being assessed. It is possible that a merger that would be approved in a jurisdiction covering a relatively small proportion of the world's consumers would be rejected in a jurisdiction covering a larger share of the world's consumers. Head and Ries (1997) cite the example of the proposed acquisition of the Canadian firm de Havilland by a consortium led by French and Italian firms, which was favoured by the Canadian, French and Italian governments but was rejected by the European Commission, representing a larger proportion of the world's consumers. Conversely, as Head and Ries show, it is possible that a jurisdiction covering a relatively small share of the world's consumers might approve a merger that reduces global welfare. This obviously raises the possibility of a strategic use of competition policy, designed to maximise domestic welfare gains at the expense of partner economies. Ironically, in the analysis by Head and Ries the risks of such an outcome are likely to be highest in competition decisions by jurisdictions in small economies with powerful producer interests but a relatively small share of the world's consumers.

The possibility of divergence between domestic and global welfare outcomes is a general point not limited to the case of mergers. Zweifel and Zach (2003) show that vertical restraints practised by multinationals are likely to have more unambiguously adverse effects in foreign markets than in the multinationals' home market. This again raises the possibility that practices that reduce global welfare might be approved by the domestic jurisdiction of a multinational.

A recent article by Tay and Willman (2005) highlights a further dimension of these issues. They model cross-border mergers in a way that once again assumes that global and domestic welfare effects do not coincide. The relative impact of domestic competition policy on domestic and global markets depends on the proportion of consumers in each market. Tay and Willman examine first the case of non-cooperation between competition authorities, both in the case of 'territoriality', where authorities make decisions only on mergers that are under their jurisdiction, and in the case of 'extra-territoriality', where they can also take decisions on mergers taking place outside their jurisdiction. Under territoriality, the resulting global competition policy regime is too lax, in the sense that too few mergers are blocked to maximise global welfare, while under extra-territoriality the regime is too strict, in the sense that too many mergers are blocked.

For present purposes the most interesting results in the Tay and Willman paper are those derived when they analyse the outcome of a cooperative approach where a global competition authority is established to make decisions on merger proposals on the basis of their impact on global welfare. The economies comprising the global economy are assumed to be of equal size and power. The global welfare gain under this scenario exceeds that under the two non-cooperative scenarios. The global authority internalises the trans-border externalities and achieves a 'first-best global competition policy'. This case is then contrasted, however, with an 'asymmetric regime', where the global economy is divided between one country that exercises extra-territorial powers and a 'fringe of smaller countries' that are unable to do so in their own right. Thus the powerful country can block every merger that harms its interests, while the 'powerless' can block only those mergers under their own jurisdiction. It is therefore no surprise that the outcome for the powerful country dominates the outcome for the powerless, and more particularly that the outcome for the powerful country in this asymmetric case dominates the outcome it can expect in the cooperative case of the global competition authority. In theory the powerless could induce the powerful country to adopt the cooperative approach with the global competition authority by making side-payments, but Tay and Willman regard this, no doubt correctly, as unrealistic.

Tay and Willman suggest that their conclusion provides one possible explanation for the current situation, where the major players in the global authority, notably the United States and the European Union, clearly 'prefer bilateral cooperation over a truly global arrangement'. In the Tay and Willman model, the United States and European Union have no incentive to move from the current situation to the global arrangement, because such a move would harm their economic interests. 'Benign neglect' is harmful to the interests of small and powerless countries, while serving the interests of the major players.

This discussion of competition policy issues leads in the end to some uncomfortable questions. Abuses such as cartelisation and anti-competitive mergers have potentially damaging effects throughout the global economy, including in the Asia Pacific region. The increasingly cross-border character of these abuses means that countries are vulnerable to these damaging effects regardless of where the perpetrators of the abuses are located. Yet the ability to effectively combat these abuses is confined, both globally and in the Asia Pacific region, to a relatively small group of countries, and these are in general the same countries that have been able to develop modalities for cooperation, primarily informal, in addressing the cross-border dimensions of the abuses. There is little incentive for this group of countries to extend cooperation to the 'fringe' of less well-equipped and generally smaller countries outside their 'inner circle'. The theoretical analysis of Tay and Willman suggests one reason for this. At a more practical level, Jenny (2002) points out that cooperation between the two groups of countries would tend to be a 'one-way street', since it is much more likely that 'fringe' countries will want to investigate large international firms from the 'inner circle' operating in their territories, where they may well have achieved a degree of market dominance, than that large countries in the 'inner circle' will want to investigate firms from the 'fringe countries' operating in the 'inner circle', which are much less likely to have a dominant market position. Cooperation between countries in the two groups would thus be likely to result in the fringe countries making extensive requests for assistance from those in the 'inner circle', which would have very little to gain from the process.

In these circumstances some 'fringe countries' may be left with little effective defence against anti-competitive abuses, especially those originating outside their borders. It is possible that in some cases effective enforcement in the 'inner circle' countries may, as a side-effect, counteract the effects of abuses in the 'fringe countries' as well, but these side-effects are likely to be accidental rather than systematic.

Jenny (2002) asks whether this situation is sustainable: in his words, 'whether international co-operation on anti-trust can remain largely an informal process initiated on a selective basis by a small group of competition authorities for their own benefit or for the benefit of firms in their jurisdiction'. He concludes that change is probably inevitable, for several reasons. First, the incidence of cross-border anti-competitive practices is likely to increase in parallel with the progress of globalisation. Second, the number of countries seeking to combat these practices through their own effective competition regimes and through cooperation with other countries will continue to increase. Third, and as a consequence of the first two reasons, informal cooperation at a bilateral and even regional level will increasingly be seen as inefficient and unnecessarily cumbersome. Fourth, a situation where many developing countries are effectively excluded from the benefits of competition policy and are unable to enforce their own competition laws against foreign firms will increasingly be seen as unfair and unacceptable. Fifth, increasing understanding of the scale of international cartels and their damaging effects will fuel a growing demand for effective action against this form of abuse at both the regional and global levels.

It may perhaps be reasonable to conclude that the outlook for the Asia Pacific region is for the gradual evolution of a region-wide approach to competition policy, facilitated by the implementation of effective competition regimes by those economies currently lacking them, and featuring a steady growth of international cooperation in terms of both the intensity of cooperation and also the number of economies participating. In the immediate future it is likely that this evolution will continue through informal contacts among the region's competition agencies, facilitated by networks such as the ICN. At some point, however, a demand may crystallise for more systematic or even more formal cooperation efforts. If and when that occurs, APEC appears ready-made as a suitable vehicle for these developments.

INVESTMENT AGREEMENTS

The development of international investment agreements has a long and chequered history. An attempt from within the Organisation for Economic Co-operation and Development (OECD) to establish a Multilateral Agreement in Investment was famously stillborn, and more recently investment had to be dropped from the agenda of the WTO's Doha Development Agenda as part of an effort to remove blockages to progress in the negotiations. Provisions on investment remain scattered piecemeal through the existing WTO agreements, including the Agreement on Trade Related Investment Measures and the General Agreement on Trade in Services.

Meantime there has been a proliferation of bilateral investment treaties (BITs) and there is also a growing trend for investment chapters to be included in the PTAs that have been proliferating in recent years, driven in no small part by competition, among developing countries in particular, to attract FDI. There is of course an extensive literature on the effects and effectiveness of international investment agreements, reviewed for example in Banga (2003). Here however the focus is on their possible role as instruments for the governance of multinational corporations.

An inspection of the typical content of these arrangements shows that in practice they are primarily concerned with the removal of restrictions on FDI, through provisions on non-discrimination and national treatment, and with protection of the rights of investors, through provisions requiring transparency of laws, regulations and administrative guidelines as well as adherence to agreed fair and minimum standards of treatment that stipulate the availability of full repatriation and convertibility of funds relating to investment, restrain host economies from practising direct or indirect expropriation, and require the availability of an enforceable investor–state dispute settlement process. In many cases there are also provisions designed to discourage, if not proscribe, the use of incentives.

All of these measures are important for fostering an environment in which investment can move freely across international borders and thus contribute to the efficient allocation of the world's capital. Measures to protect the rights of investors are particularly important for developing countries engaged in fierce competition to attract FDI. Recognising the relevance of these considerations to its Bogor goals, APEC sought in its Non-Binding Investment Principles, adopted in 1994, to promote the inclusion in the investment regimes of its members each of the types of provisions enumerated in the above paragraph.[2]

These typical provisions of a BIT or the investment chapter of a PTA stop short of imposing standards of conduct on the foreign investors. On this issue APEC's Non-Binding Investment Principles merely state that 'acceptance of foreign investment is facilitated when foreign investors abide by the host economy's laws, regulations, administrative guidelines and policies, just as domestic investors should'. The not unreasonable presumption is that regulation of foreign investor behaviour is a matter for the domestic legislation of the host economy and, where relevant and appropriate, of the home economy.

Nevertheless the upsurge of interest in CSR, discussed further in the next section of this chapter (and in Chapter 12 in this volume by Djisman Simanjuntak) has been reflected in proposals that CSR provisions should be included in bilateral investment agreements. For example, the International Institute for Sustainable Development (IISD) has incorporated obligations relating to CSR in the draft investment agreement that it is promoting as a suitable model for BITs between developed and developing countries (Mann *et al.* 2005).

Proposals for the inclusion of CSR obligations in international investment agreements have been contentious. On the one hand, if they are to be enforceable, it could be argued that they will be perceived as onerous by potential investors and thus act to discourage FDI, in contradiction to the purpose of the agreement. On the other hand, if they are to be included only on a 'best efforts' basis, and thus non-enforceable, as is the case with most of the provisions in the draft agreement proposed by Mann *et al.* (2005), they may be criticised for lacking any real practical effect. In any event, while provisions such as those in the draft of Mann *et al.* (2005) are known to have been proposed in some bilateral negotiations, they do not so far appear to have met with ready acceptance, particularly by home country governments.

CORPORATE SOCIAL RESPONSIBILITY

The expanding role of multinationals has coincided with a rapid growth of interest in and concern about CSR. One index of the extent to which CSR has penetrated the policy debates surrounding multinationals is that the World Bank now contains its own Corporate Social Responsibility Practice.

CSR is defined by one member of that practice as 'socially minded behaviour such as respecting human rights, refusing to pay bribes, caring for local communities, and adhering to environmental standards'. Its proponents generally see it as filling a vacuum resulting from the inability of formal international institutions to keep pace with the global economy by developing enforceable rules dealing with these issues. Where enforceable rules do not exist, CSR advocates seek to secure voluntary adherence to codes of conduct or standards that reflect acceptable or desirable practice. These codes and standards are typically voluntary in practice, but they could in principle be incorporated into mandatory instruments. The inclusion of CSR obligations in the draft investment agreement proposed by Mann *et al.* (2005), discussed in the preceding section, is one example of this.

Companies can, and in some cases no doubt do, adopt and implement CSR standards in the absence of any form of coercion. They may do so because they value social responsibility objectives for their own sake, or because it is profitable, for example if it leads to improvements in their energy efficiency. However CSR is most often discussed in the context of concerted campaigns by non-government organisations (NGOs), trade unions and others to pressurise multinationals to behave according to desired standards or principles. When pressure has to be exerted in this way, the incentives for multinationals to comply are essentially reputational; the firms are encouraged to conclude that compliance will elicit a favourable response from customers, suppliers, employees and other stakeholders, including even governments, and that this is turn will have a positive effect on profitability.

The term 'civil regulation' has been applied to the techniques used to encourage firms to practise CSR. Newell (2001) provides an extensive discussion of civil regulation and gives many examples of its various manifestations. One side of civil regulation involves the techniques for exerting pressure on the multinationals. Consumer boycotts and the dissemination of adverse publicity are the techniques that have received the greatest amount of publicity. Shareholder activism, where activists purchase shares in order to gain access to company meetings, at which they seek to embarrass the company and its directors, has also been used in a number of countries. Some NGOs have engaged in litigation to seek judgments requiring the target firm to modify its behaviour. The other side of civil regulation involves the instruments used to formalise any bargain that may be struck. Codes of conducts have been popular instruments for this purpose, and some NGOs have also established 'stewardship regimes' with their multinational adversaries/partners.

Klein and Harford (2004) discuss the condition in which pro-CSR campaigns are likely to be effective. First and foremost the target firms must operate on a long time horizon; otherwise the reputational incentive will not be strong. Second, the pressure must be relatively easy to apply. For example, boycotts are likely to be easiest to implement when the target firm operates in competitive consumer markets where the customers can easily switch to alternative products, but will be more difficult to operate against firms that produce intermediate goods. Third, the offenders must be easily identified, so that firms can be reasonably sure that their adversaries will be aware whenever they 'step out of line'. Finally, the cost of compliance should be light compared to the cost of the reputational damage that can be inflicted on the company. Voluntary standards will often be appropriate on these grounds, since a firm will generally try to satisfy its critics in ways that are not excessively expensive. If the cost of compliance is too high, on the other hand, the firm will obviously have an incentive for non-compliance.

There may well be questions as to the quality of the outcome of CSR campaigns. As Klein and Harford (2004) point out, targets may be chosen for their high profile or because they are relatively easy to get at, rather than because they are the worst offenders. In that case the worst abuses will go uncorrected. The choice of issue may also be problematic. Generally the issues chosen will be high profile and with a high emotive content, since support is easier to mobilise in such cases. These issues may not necessarily, however, correspond to the direct areas of need, whether the objective be poverty reduction or environmental protection. Social groups or issues with the most urgent need for action may be bypassed if they do not appeal to the activists that mount the CSR campaigns. A mismatch between action and need may be especially a risk when the activists are rich NGOs in developed countries while the intended beneficiaries are marginalised people in poor developing countries. If the objective of the campaign is not carefully and appropriately established, unintended results may follow, the classic case being campaigns to eradicate child labour that may have led to increases in child prostitution. Inserting CSR obligations into investment agreements also needs careful consideration. If the effect is to increase the perceived costs of investing in the country concerned, investment may be diverted to other more hospitable destinations. On the other hand there is anecdotal evidence, for example in Cambodia, of investment being attracted precisely because of the existence of acceptable labour standards or the willingness to institute them. Presumably the reputational considerations underlying this choice would reflect the success of past campaigns.

Ward (2004) argues that in developing countries there is a role for the public sector in building capacities and institutions that can help to ensure that CSR demands are generated within those countries as much as or more than from stakeholders in rich countries. It is obviously desirable that CSR is promoted in a way that reflects priorities in the recipient communities. On the other hand it must also be conceded that public policymaking in developing countries, including the development of policies toward trade and investment promotion, can at times fail to give adequate regard to those priorities. Likewise there can be no doubt that good governance in the public sector is a very desirable, if not essential, complement to CSR in the private sector, and in many developing countries there is much to do in this area. Corruption in the private sector is generally closely connected to corruption in the public sector, for example, and it is much easier for private firms to be environmentally responsible if the public sector is pursuing sound environmental policies.

TAXATION

Taxation of multinationals is a highly complex and technical subject, with an extensive literature, a full survey of which is beyond the scope of this paper. Here I provide a brief discussion of recent contributions to an issue that has perhaps drawn more attention than any other issue relating to the taxation of multinationals, namely the choice of taxation strategies to combat transfer pricing by multinationals. It is interesting to note that the issue of the potentially competing interests of governments, which appeared in the earlier discussion of competition policy, also features prominently in this literature.

Transfer pricing is a well-known stratagem whereby multinationals adjust the prices at which intra-firm trade takes place, so as to distribute their profits between the various countries in which they operate in the way that minimises their overall tax burden. The ability of multinationals to take advantage of transfer pricing is naturally of concern to governments because of its potential impact on their tax base. If the use of transfer pricing is unconstrained, governments become powerless to sustain independently set tax rates, and a 'race to the bottom' in tax rates ensues. This is consistent with the well-known finding on the consequences of capital mobility

In the case of transfer pricing however there is a defence available to governments. In order to combat this profit-shifting behaviour by multinationals governments can endeavour to monitor transfer-pricing behaviour so that they can assess the appropriateness of the prices used, and adjust where necessary for their impact on the multinationals' tax payments, or even impose penalties where transfer pricing for the purpose of tax avoidance is detected. The typical rule against which the appropriateness of transfer prices has been assessed is based on the 'arm's-length' approach, whereby the transfer prices used are compared with the price that would be agreed by two completely independent units. Significant differences between the arm's-length price and the transfer price actually used would be corrected by the tax authorities so as to cancel out the effect of the transfer pricing in reducing the firm's tax liability. This arm's-length approach is endorsed by the OECD.

Governments, however, became increasingly sceptical about the effectiveness of the arm's-length technique, and began to switch from this price-oriented approach to a profit-oriented approach whereby the profits declared by companies may be adjusted for tax purposes in cases where the firm's profitability is shown to be significantly lower than the profitability of comparable firms in the same situation over a defined time period. The comparable profit method (CPM) introduced by the United States in the 1990s is an example of a profit-oriented approach. It seeks to align the profits for tax purposes of multinational subsidiaries operating in the United States with the average profits for tax purposes of comparable US firms. It was aimed especially at Japanese multinationals operating in the United States.

An interesting paper by Eden *et al.* (2005) endeavours to assess the effectiveness of penalties for inappropriate transfer-pricing behaviour by estimating the effects of US penalties for transfer price manipulation on the stock market valuation of Japanese companies with US subsidiaries. They find that the penalties appeared to result in a very substantial drop in the cumulative market valuation of the companies concerned, indicating that the penalties are indeed very effective. They note that tax authorities of other governments have been following the United States' lead, and portray multinationals as 'caught in the middle, facing penalties at home and abroad' as governments 'strive to retain what they see as their fair share of corporate profits'.

This leads to an obvious question as to whether cooperation between governments might produce a more favourable outcome. Papers by Raimondos-Møller and Scharf (2002) and Mansori and Weichenrieder (2001) address the issue. Raimondos-Møller and Scharf note that when governments intervene with regulation to curb profit-shifting by means of transfer pricing, the 'race to the bottom' is likely to be replaced by a 'race to the top', resulting in reduced production and trade. This result is also obtained by Mansori and Weichenrieder who find that tax revenue is also depressed. Both papers suggest that cooperation could deliver a more favourable outcome. Raimondos-Møller and Scharf demonstrate the existence of cooperative solutions whereby harmonisation of transfer pricing rules leads to a Pareto improvement, but find also that harmonisation based on the arm's-length principle may not in fact be Pareto-improving. Raimondos-Møller and Scharf do not however address the question of whether governments have an incentive to cooperate in this way.

Schjelderup and Weichenrieder (1999) note a possible downside of the search for more effective ways to curb profit-shifting behaviour. They develop a model in which switching from the price-oriented approach to the profit-oriented approach to curbing transfer pricing will reduce imports, although it may not change transfer prices. This leads them to suggest that a shift to the profit-oriented approach such as CPM may be supported by protectionist interests as a possible instrument for protection and strategic trade policy.

Transfer pricing is not the only activity that can give rise to concerns over the international distribution of tax revenue. In the Asia Pacific region there has recently been considerable controversy over profit realisations from asset sales by foreign private equity funds, for example in Korea and Japan. Whether tax on such profits accrues to the host or home governments has important implications for the welfare effects of the investments concerned.

OUTLOOK FOR DISCIPLINES ON GOVERNANCE OF MULTINATIONALS IN THE ASIA PACIFIC REGION

The economic governance issues relating to multinationals are complex and multi-dimensional. While cooperation can lead to improved outcomes it is not always clear that compelling incentives for cooperation exist. In some cases there appears to be a clear incentive for key economies not to behave cooperatively, as in the Tay and Willman analysis of competition policy.

Trade policy faces analogous problems of non-cooperative behaviour. In this case however the WTO provides a payoff to cooperation in the form of a multilateral institutional framework for the operation and enforcement of rules for the conduct of international trade. No comparable framework yet exists for competition policy, investment and taxation, and the analysis of Tay and Willman suggests that large, powerful countries may in fact have incentives to block the establishment of such a framework on a global or even regional basis.

There is also little prospect of a comprehensive regulatory framework being established for these issues at the regional level in the near future. While many of the region's new PTAs include provisions on competition policy and investment, their membership structure is for the most part bilateral or at best plurilateral, and many studies have highlighted the obstacles standing in the way of establishing broader regional groupings. Furthermore, as highlighted for example by Trewin and Scollay (2006), the provisions of the region's PTAs on issues like competition policy and investment vary greatly in the extent to which they impose substantive enforceable obligations, and in most of them the obligations tend toward the 'soft', non-enforceable end of the spectrum, especially in the case of competition policy. Provisions on investment often appear to be carefully designed to avoid any requirement for policy change on the part of member governments. Development of an institutional capability to regulate the behaviour of multinationals at the regional level would require deep integration of a kind that to date has been achieved only by the European Union; Asia Pacific economies are still very far from contemplating, let alone having the capacity to implement, this degree of integration at the region-wide level.

The conclusion is inescapable that for the foreseeable future the formal regulation of multinationals in the region will depend on the maintenance and enforcement of the standards, rules, norms and regulations for corporate governance at the national level in their home and host countries.

Nevertheless scope exists for cooperation at a level below formal regulation to make a significant contribution to the improvement of corporate governance arrangements in the region. Regular consultations based on the sharing of information, experiences and ideas, and the development of 'best practice' guidelines can work to gradually lift national standards region-wide, and can also lead to useful cooperative initiatives between agencies of the region's governments. Some of these consultations occur within institutions centred outside the region that involve subsets of the region's economies, such as the OECD and the ICN, and some take place in a subregional context, for example within the frameworks of the Association of Southeast Asian Nations, the North American Free Trade Agreement or the Australia New Zealand Closer Economic Relations Trade Agreement. At the region-wide level APEC provides the obvious institutional framework for consultative activity of this kind.

Investment and competition policy are already included within APEC's trade and investment agenda, while taxation in principle lies within the competence of APEC finance ministers. APEC's principles on investment and competition policy, adopted respectively in 1994 and 1999, were high points of APEC's work in these areas, and a concerted effort would be required to recover momentum, as well as to develop a work program on taxation issues. Some adaptations to APEC's structure might need to be made as well. Competition policy and taxation in particular tend to be the jealously guarded territory of their own bureaucracies, and it is likely that a process independent of trade officials and ministers would need to be established if these subjects are to be pursued energetically and effectively within APEC. A formal regulatory role for APEC will however be precluded as long as APEC members are unwilling to move in the direction of binding, enforceable commitments at the APEC-wide level.

There are also other institutions that play an important role in disciplining multinationals, in particular the region's financial and capital markets. As these markets become more efficient and more integrated, so does the probability increase that poor standards of corporate behaviour and governance will be punished while sound behaviour and governance are rewarded. The need to establish and maintain sound reputations among the investors in these markets leads to pressure for improved quality of domestic corporate regulation and improved transparency in corporate governance, including through the adoption of best-practice accounting standards, and other indicators of sound corporate practice such as accreditation with the International Organization for Standardization (ISO).

Disciplining of multinationals in areas of CSR remains largely outside the domain of financial markets, despite the development of concepts such as triple bottom line accounting. In this area the 'watchdog' role of NGOs is more important, along with competition in product markets characterised by increasing consumer awareness associated with rising levels of education.

In summary, for the foreseeable future formal regulation of multinationals in the Asia Pacific region is likely to remain largely the province of the governments of home and host countries, with processes of international consultation and cooperation providing both a stimulus and support for improving the quality of domestic regulation. Competition in international financial and capital markets generates pressure on both governments and the multinationals themselves for improved standards of governance, while multinationals can also expect growing pressure for improved governance from both product market competition and NGO activity.

NOTES

This paper has benefited in numerous places from insightful comments on an earlier version by Hugh Patrick, Juan Palacios, Hadi Soesastro, Chia Siow Yue, Kyung-tae Lee and Peter Drysdale. All errors and other deficiencies remain the sole responsibility of the author.

1. Membership of the ICN is by agencies, not by economies. Included among the members of the ICN are agencies from all APEC economies except Brunei Darussalam, China, Hong Kong China, Papua New Guinea, Russia and Vietnam.
2. As with competition policy, PECC provided the antecedent to APEC's investment principles, in this case with their proposed Pacific Investment Code. After finalisation of the investment principles APEC's agenda focused more on investment promotion than on investment liberalisation or regulation. Recently there has been an effort within APEC to revitalise its investment liberalisation agenda.

REFERENCES

Aghion, P., M. Dewatripoint and P. Rey (1997) 'Corporate governance, competition policy and industrial policy', *European Economic Review*, 41: 797–805.

Anon. (2006) 'Probe into possible LCD cartel', *Sydney Morning Herald*, 13 December.

APEC (Asia-Pacific Economic Cooperation) (1994), *APEC Non-Binding Investment Principles*, Jakarta: APEC.

Anon. (2006) 'Probe into possible LCD cartel', *Sydney Morning Herald*, 13 December.

APEC (Asia-Pacific Economic Cooperation) (1999) *APEC Principles to Enhance Competition and Regulatory Reform* (annexed to the 1999 Declaration of APEC Economic Leaders).
Banga, R. (2003) 'Impact of government policies and investment agreements on FDI inflows to developing countries: an empirical evidence', New Delhi: Indian Council for Research on International Economic Relations.
Connor, J.M. (2002) 'International price fixing: resurgence and deterrence', paper presented at the American Agricultural Law Association annual meeting, Indianapolis, 26 October.
Eden, L., L. Juarez and D. Li (2005) 'Talk softly but carry a big stick: transfer pricing penalties and the market valuation of Japanese multinationals in the United States', *Journal of International Business Studies*, 36(4): 398–423.
Evenett, S.J., M.C. Levenstein and V.Y. Suslow (2002) '*International cartel enforcement: lessons from the 1990s*, World Bank Policy Research Working Paper No. 2680, Washington DC: World Bank.
Head, K. and J. Ries (1997) 'International mergers and welfare under decentralized competition policy', *Canadian Journal of Economics*, 30(4b): 1104–1123.
Jenny, F. (2002) 'International cooperation on competition: myth, reality and perspective', paper presented at the University of Minnesota Law School Conference on Global Antitrust Law and Policy, Minneapolis, 20–21 September.
Klawiter, D.C. (1999) 'International cartel enforcement in the 1990s: antitrust comes to the global market', paper presented at the ABA Annual Meeting 1999, Section of Antitrust Law, 10 August.
Klein, J.I. (1999a) 'Statement of Assistant Attorney General Joel I. Klein', US Department of Justice, 20 May.
—— (1999b) 'The war against international cartels: lessons from the battlefront', paper presented at the Fordham Corporate Law Institute 26th Annual Conference on International Antitrust Law and Policy, New York, 14 October.
Klein, M. and T. Harford (2004) *Corporate Responsibility: When Will Voluntary Reputation Building Improve Standards?*, Washington DC: World Bank.
Lall, A. (1997) 'ASEAN approaches to competition policy', in F. Flatters and D. Gillen, *Competition and Regulation*, Kingston: Queens University.
Mann, H., K. von Moltke, L. Peterson and A. Cosbey (2005) *IISD Model International Agreement on Investment for Sustainable Development*, Winnipeg: International Institute for Sustainable Development.
Mansori, K. and A. Weichenrieder (2001) 'Tax competition and transfer pricing disputes', *Finanz Archiv*, 58(1): 1–11.
Monti, M. (2004) 'Competition policy in a global economy', *International Finance*, 7(3): 495–504.
Newell, P. (2001) 'Managing multinationals: the governance of investment for the environment', *Journal of International Development*, 13: 907–919.
Paul, G.L. (2006) 'Asia-Pacific cartel enforcement: a survey of recent developments and relevant legislation', Washington DC: White & Case.
PECC (Pacific Economic Cooperation Council) (1999), *Competition Principles*, Singapore: PECC.
Raimondos-Møller, P. and K. Scharf, (2002) 'Transfer pricing rules and competing governments', *Oxford Economic Papers*, 54: 230–246.
Schjelderup, G. and A. Weichenrieder (1999) 'Trade, multinationals and transfer pricing regulations', *Canadian Journal of Economics*, 32(3): 817–834.
Tay, A. and G. Willman (2005) 'Why (no) global competition policy is a tough choice', *Quarterly Review of Economics and Finance*, 45: 312–324.
Trewin, R. and R. Scollay, (2006) 'Australia and New Zealand CEPs/FTAs with the ASEAN countries and their implication on the AANZFTA', report for the ASEAN Secretariat.
Ward, H. (2004) *Public Sector Roles in Strengthening Corporate Social Responsibility: Taking Stock*, Washington DC: World Bank.
Wijckmans, F. (2003) 'Internationalization of competition policy observations from a European practitioner's perspective', *The Antitrust Bulletin*, Winter.
Zweifel, P. and R. Zach (2003) 'Vertical restraints: the case of multinationals', *The Antitrust Bulletin*, Spring.

12 Corporate social responsibility and capital accumulation

Djisman S. Simanjuntak

INTRODUCTION

In the last 25 years or so, businesses have been faced with a new environment – one where the borders of the firm have become blurred and, as a consequence, owners and management have been obliged to address a much more complex set of issues than in the past. In particular, they must now carefully weigh the need to maximise profit against other bottom lines.

One reason for this increasing complexity is that the lives of modern humans have become more knowledge-intensive. Dependence on existing information may not be new, but the current situation appears to be unprecedented. One reason is that increasing digitisation has allowed the various streams of science and technology to combine more easily, resulting in more complex scientific and technological advances. Moreover, the new technologies unleash the forces of globalisation that push movements of people, goods, services, capital and information across national and regional borders with an ever-growing magnitude and at an accelerating pace. In response to the new technologies, governments around the globe reduce or even remove many barriers to regional and global flows of people, goods, services, capital and information; one consequence is that more and more markets can be serviced by multinational corporations (MNCs) from fewer locations.

Another reason for increasing business complexity is that the interface between firms and people's daily lives occurs at more and more points. The single most important force behind this is growth in the importance of the firm in capitalist economies. However, the redefinition of the division of labour between the state and business has also been a factor. In the past – as early as the 1970s – many technologies were considered indivisible in the sense that existing demand could be met by a single plant. This was thought to justify state monopolies in areas such as electricity generation, the provision of drinking water, highways, telecommunications, railway transportation, airlines and postal services. As technologies are increasingly divisible, lean structures become a realistic option even in the fortresses of state monopolies. A result is that the last 30 years have been a period of 'marketisation' and privatisation. In particular, governments have often sought to sell state-owned enterprises (SOEs) to private owners. Many of the SOEs were very large and used privatisation as a way of getting to achieve best-practice management. They carried out privatisation through global share offerings, giving additional impetus to cross-border mergers and acquisitions (M&As) (Evenett 2003).

Even without such cross-border operation, the new world economy would have become more complex. For example, with integration deepening in the wake of new technologies and heavily reduced border barriers, firms must deal with many complex issues. The world at large is confronted with myriad environmental issues ranging from greenhouse gas emissions to over-fishing. Major conservation and environmental protection initiatives will be required if the human quest for better standards of living is to be sustained. Decades ago, multinational businesses were tainted by allegations of abuse of labour rights and corruption. When poor people cannot afford the fruits of science and technology, issues of philanthropy necessarily arise – for example, in the pharmaceutical industry. With the deepening of globalisation in the last 30 years or so, the issues have become increasingly complex, involving the lives of more and more people, spread all over the world, in more and more cultural milieus in more and more countries. In these new circumstances, a decision by a few people occupying a small board of a particular MNC can affect billions of people. Corporations in general, and MNCs in particular, are having to reinvent themselves in order to harmonise their interests and those of their stakeholders. They are having to address the issue that has become known as corporate social responsibility (CSR).

In this chapter, I analyse the issue of CSR in the context of Pacific economies. I begin by discussing capital accumulation as the core responsibility of the firm. In fact, I see capital accumulation as perhaps even more socially responsible than corporate philanthropy, which in many cases appears to be merely cosmetic. Next I deal with elements of social responsibility other than capital accumulation. I then deal with the impacts of CSR and possible mechanisms to implement CSR, taking into account the fact that CSR has long ceased to become a purely national issue. I argue that for many corporations CSR has become a global issue and for many more a regional issue. I note that identifying good CSR is a lot easier than translating it into reality. In particular, it is easier to pass laws on CSR than to force firms to comply with them. The repertoire of instruments is limited. Given the nature of the open and high-speed world economy, meaningful progress in CSR requires a complex web of coalitions, including regional and global ones. Finally, I discuss the importance of the principles of CSR for corporations that are active in the Pacific region.

THE CHARACTERISTICS OF CSR

CSR is not a newly invented concept. Back in the 1970s when developing countries were struggling to establish a 'new international economic order', a code on restrictive practices of MNCs was made an important part of the proposed new order. Long before the current wave of debates on CSR, the Organisation for Economic Cooperation and Development (OECD) had already come up with its 'Guidelines for Multinational Enterprises', which included guidelines on disclosure, employment and industrial relations, environment, combating bribery, customer interests, science and technology, competition and taxation (OECD 2001). In its widest sense, CSR is an inherent part of the firm's nature as a team production or a network of inter-related chains of value-creating elements. CSR has been evolving since the day humans invented the firm (Anderson 1989).

Three features of CSR evolution stand out. First, the CSR concept has tended to cover an increasingly wide area, with the rising complexity of business. Second, people have demanded that corporations take greater social responsibility, and show a greater commitment to it, going beyond merely cosmetic actions. Third, the geographical reach of CSR has widened as firms' sourcing and distribution activities have become more global.

Given the complexity of the issues covered, definitions of CSR are widely open to contention.

- Wikipedia[1] defines CSR as 'a company's obligation to be sensitive to the needs of all of the stakeholders in its business operations'. Stakeholders in this sense include employees, customers, suppliers, community organisations, subsidiaries and affiliates, joint ventures, local neighbourhoods, investors, and shareholders (or a sole owner).
- The World Business Council for Sustainable Development defines CSR as 'the continuing commitment by business to behave ethically and contribute to economic development while improving the quality of life of the workforce and their families as well as of the local community and society at large'.[2]
- Lisa Whitehouse (2005: 161) draws attention to the growing public power of corporations and looks at CSR as a way of legitimising the exercise of such public power.
- Some other authors underline the need to go beyond what the law or regulation prescribes. For example, Maximiano (2006) notes that the public expect a 'compliance-plus' attitude in respect of CSR.
- Heal (2005) refers to CSR as the entirety of corporate actions which reduce the extent of externalised costs or avoid distributional conflicts.

Despite differing definitions, the meaning of CSR is clear: a corporation is responsible for its actions or inactions not only to its shareholders but also to a very wide range of stakeholders, who are in turn scattered around the globe, articulating extremely diverse interests from diverse walks of life. People use terms like 'triple bottom line', 'multiple bottom line', 'enlightened self-interest' and 'warm glow' to express such a responsible way of doing business. They stress that the way in which a company gets to profit is as important as the profit *per se*.

The quest for responsible business is given impetus through initiatives that seek to spread the practices of responsible business by promoting certain conduct. The United Nations (UN) Global Compact is one such initiative. It has attracted adherents around the globe (Ruggie 2002).

CSR is not the antithesis of profit. The human quest for longer survival is staged in an increasingly difficult landscape. It is increasingly difficult and more expensive to find new natural resources and knowledge. As corporations become more important in the search for solutions to human needs, profit as the source of additional capital stock is increasingly indispensable. In the absence of adequate profit, corporations may be cornered in a situation where they behave irresponsibly.

I consider profit making or capital accumulation to be the pivotal responsibility of the corporation, the one around which other elements of CSR rotate. To harmonise profit making with all other elements of CSR as far as possible, the market structure in which profit making occurs needs to be as free as possible from imperfections or elements of monopoly power. Governments and societies can do a lot to reduce such imperfections. Yet imperfections are inherent in life at large and in business in particular. A knowledge economy makes no exception. Whether one talks about information and communication industries or food production, knowledge and skills are dispersed unequally among participants. The unequal dispersion of knowledge and skills results in monopoly profit, which is the positive difference between unit price and unit cost, in favour of the firm, which enjoys a larger share of knowledge and skills. It is a kind of constant in business as a whole, though monopoly profit is ephemeral in the history of individual companies. That is because it sows its own demise in that it attracts newcomers who will then take care that the difference between unit price and marginal cost is eroded asymptotically. However, to get to such profit a corporation has to plough back a larger fraction of its profit into a continuous search for newer solutions as reflected in the rising expenditure on R&D as a fraction of sales in knowledge-intensive businesses in all sectors.

The race for competitiveness through greater R&D endeavours is likely to remain an important feature of global business. Through such endeavours, even ageing businesses in developed economies may be reinvented.

CAPITAL

Capital can be understood as the present value of future streams of income out of natural capital, produced capital and intangible capital (Corrado *et al.* 2005). Its composition changes over time. The recent shift in favour of intangible capital is of particular relevance to CSR, because intangible capital consists mainly of organisational capital, which largely resides within corporations. Before turning to a more detailed discussion of intangible capital, I shall discuss natural capital and produced capital in the context of CSR.

Natural capital includes space, time, climate, weather, mineral resources, biodiversity, and flora and fauna resources. Physically, natural capital is scarce in absolute terms. Its use by humans will always be subject to the laws of physics and chemistry. However, we can and should continuously seek the best possible way to deploy scarce resources. The way in which natural capital is used depends very strongly on the firm as the key player. In particular, the use of natural capital through a corporation-centred model appears to be more efficient than the use of natural capital through communal mechanisms where rights are ill defined. Nevertheless, there is a lot to learn and there is potential for greater efficiency. In particular, the corporation-centred mode of operation is largely orientated to gluttony, leading to a rapid depletion of natural capital. Wars have often been a result of struggles for scarce resources. We are currently spending enormous human and financial resources to gain a better understanding of how the corporation-centred mode of natural capital use produces undesirable impacts and on finding better ways to cope with the costs that arise as a result (UNEP 2006). There is a new culture of parsimony where the scarcity of natural capital is recognised as a core element. Corporations are searching for ways to integrate such a culture into corporate governance and management as part of their endeavours to become socially responsible.

Produced capital is a first derivative of natural capital. It takes the form of infrastructure such as roads, ports, telecommunications, electricity and freshwater facilities and a wide range of corporate and household physical assets such as plant and machinery, office machines, and vehicles. In the past, most people thought that the infrastructure part of capital was best dealt with by SOEs. Moreover, technologies, especially infrastructure technologies, were seen as indivisible. As a result, people thought that, if private firms were allowed to control infrastructure, there would be a risk that consumers would be exploited recklessly.

As a result of these perceptions, state control of infrastructure was almost universally adhered to in the past, even among capitalist economies. After World War II, it became the dominant mode of infrastructure provision in countries that emerged as independent states. In the case of developing economies, state ownership of infrastructure is justified partly on the basis that the private sector is not capable of pioneering, managing and funding large-scale projects.

However, technologies do change, and they do so at a rapid pace. Since the end of World War II, technologies have become more complex, making competition in infrastructure initially a real possibility and later a reality. This occurred almost indiscriminately across sectors and spaces. The precise legal status of firms seems to be no longer relevant to participation in the infrastructure business. Private companies, including MNCs, have even become major players in infrastructure provision and maintenance. As a result, there is hardly a sector left where people can avoid private companies while seeking to satisfy their needs. Our daily lives now greatly depend on how good corporate directors are in exercising their power, including the discretionary part of power which is virtually beyond the reach of the law. Thus, irresponsible corporate decisions and acts can leave millions of people spatially stranded or virtually isolated.

Competition through the involvement of private companies is not necessarily inferior to state control in dealing with the complex issues of infrastructure. Experience in the last 30 years or so suggests that competition has worked well in producing some infrastructure at relatively low prices. Yet people continue to oppose such competition. Whenever one of the Bretton Woods institutions holds a major meeting, such opposition is particularly noticeable, constantly reminding the shareholders and managers of large corporations that they must consider the needs of diverse stakeholders when conducting their corporate governance and management functions. As intangible capital, notably reputation, becomes increasingly important, CSR will continue to gain importance as a factor in sustainable success for a growing number of corporations.

The third type of capital is intangible capital. This is the greatest part of the total capital available to modern humans and their corporations. There are several reasons for this. One concerns accounting methods. It is easier to account for the value of steel used in producing a car than it is to account for the value of a patent, industrial design, trademark, copyright, trade secret or other form of intellectual property. Given these imperfections in accounting methods, intangible capital is more likely to be a source of monopoly power than the other forms of capital. Furthermore, intangible capital is treated as 'residual', capturing the parts of value that are not attributable to natural capital or produced capital.

However, the large share of intangible capital is by no means a mere accounting trick. Its increasing importance has something to do with the fact that human-made things are getting 'smarter' every day. Proponents of new growth theory[3] say that today's capital is smarter than yesterday's capital but will be less smart than tomorrow's capital. They say that, if capital does get 'smarter' every day, ceaseless growth is a possibility.

Two of the most consistent trends in the evolution of human production methods are the increasing intellectual contribution to human-made things and the process of aiding human-made things with computational and sensory devices that allow certain things to look intelligent. Perhaps we can even define progress as the increase in the intellectual content of human-made things. Some people argue that the increase in intellectual content is occurring at an increasing speed. In particular, some people say that private companies are increasingly overtaking governments and formal learning institutions as major sites of intellectual advances. They are able to do this through trial and error, learning by doing, imitation, scientific research, and tapping into public global knowledge. Meanwhile, entrepreneurs and corporate professionals have developed ingenious methods to make it possible for people to reduce the severity of scarcity in some areas, to choose from a wider range of options and to pay a declining unit price while seeking to experience more from life. However, a blessing is always incomplete. If the increasing intellectual content in human-made things is driven by corporations, there is a risk that more and more human-made things will fall into corporate ownership. In this way, public goods can become private. For example, audio and visual recordings can turn hitherto unprotected folklore into privately owned recorded performances.

What is more, corporations are playing an increasingly dominant role in the accumulation and deployment of intangible capital. There is a risk that the proliferating protection of intellectual property rights (IPRs) will get out of hand, making more and more goods and services increasingly difficult to access and making the search for new ones increasingly difficult and costly.

'Organisational capital' is one of the most important elements of intangible capital. It consists of workforce training, employee 'voice' and work design (Black and Lynch 2005). It is the organisational capital that makes a company distinct within a population of companies. Building architecture, raw materials, plant and office machinery, logistic facilities and networks are more or less generic in nature, being increasingly available in the market. However, the knowledge and skills of the workforce require constant nurturing and are unique to a firm. The extent to which a firm is able to benefit from an employee's competencies depends a great deal on the prevailing governance and management. In some archaic structures, employees are expected only to obey orders; the greatest part of the human potential is thereby left dormant. A system that encourages employees to raise their voices can now make a difference between winners and losers. The existence of mechanisms for employee participation is an important element of CSR. It is not new. However, with rising knowledge intensity in business, effective employee participation can be an important source of productivity improvement.

The firm can be seen as the engine of capital accumulation. Its foremost responsibility is to keep the engine of accumulation running. People today need a greater amount of capital to satisfy a given unit of need than they have in the past. More capital is undoubtedly needed as more and more people achieve a higher standard of living.

CAPITAL ACCUMULATION

In the popular sense of the word, 'social responsibility' covers all elements other than profit maximisation, wealth maximisation or the maximisation of shareholder value – in short, the bottom line. However, this view is fallacious. In reality the firm is never completely uncoupled from its stakeholders. It buys inputs from numerous providers who are scattered around the globe and it sells output to diverse buyers who are also scattered around the globe. In doing so the firm must do something that goes beyond the mere bottom line, whether this is due to legal obligations or ethical considerations.

However, firms face a dilemma when they are confronted with the difficult choice of giving benefits to extra-firm stakeholders at the cost of the bottom line or raising their wealth at the cost of extra-firm stakeholders. At issue are corporate egotism, corporate philanthropy, corporate altruism and other forms of social responsibility.

Selfishness and egotism are rooted in basic human instincts; philanthropy, altruism and other forms of responsible behaviour are the product of painstaking nurturing. People who sit in leading positions in corporate organisations are not immune from such behavioural principles. In spite of nurturing, selfishness and egotism occasionally afflict corporate leaders when they face dilemmas, and such behaviour may put the survival of the firm at stake. Such situations are often expressed as zero-sum games, but selfishness and egotism are indispensable for survival. A firm that fails to add to its stock of capital relative to that of competitors will be selected out sooner or later. It is therefore important to remember that the bottom line is a necessary part of CSR because it is essential to the firm's survival and growth.

The concept of the firm

It is difficult to identify the origin of the idea of the firm. Initially firms were multi-purpose institutions where religious interests, political interests, territorial interests and wealth accumulation were mixed – for example, the House of the Medici, the British East India Company, the Dutch East India Company and the Dutch West India Company. Over time, firms increasingly focused on capital accumulation, largely spinning off their other functions. There was a social impact as the division of labour between different elements of society deepened with this increasing focus on wealth or capital accumulation.

There are competing and complementary views as to why firms exist. Some people view the firm as a vehicle to reduce uncertainties and simultaneously reduce transaction costs. Others see it as a bundle of contracts which are doomed to remain incomplete, or as a team production in which one party possesses an information advantage over the other. If management abuses its information advantage at the cost of the shareholders, such a system can lead to problems; in numerous cases such problems have even proved deadly to the firm. In any case, as with any artificial construct, the theory of the firm is imperfect. For example, it is difficult to explain entrepreneurship by reference to the theory of firms. Moreover, prescriptions drawn from the theory are not a panacea: agency problems persist in modern corporations.

In seeking to accumulate wealth, firms try to find new or better solutions for existing human needs, or solutions for new needs, that please users around the world. Through such searches, firms are able to offer users a lower price for existing products or services and a wider range of choices. In the process, formerly expensive products and services are made affordable to even the poor. In such circumstances, the corporate self-interest in capital accumulation closely matches the interests of the public at large. As long experience shows, the ability to make things that originally were consumed exclusively by the privileged few affordable to the underprivileged mass is a wonder of capitalism.

In the CSR context, it is useful to look at the firm as a 'search engine'. In today's terms, firms are faced with the challenge of accumulating capital continuously by tapping into new discoveries such as stem cell technology, hydrogen fuel, smart materials or smart robots, to mention just a few frontier industries, while seeking to satisfy human needs for healthier and longer lives, energy, information and leisure. Needless to say, some new searches are highly controversial issues, particularly in relation to ethics, labour rights and the environment. It is becoming more and more important that firms deal with such controversies. Such issues require us to look at the firm as an engine of capital accumulation in a more holistic way.

The firm's search for new solutions occurs in an imperfect environment. There are barriers to entry and exit in virtually all businesses. Sometimes one firm has a formidably strong reputation that deters others from daring to enter a contest. At other times, government regulations are a problem. More importantly, protected IPRs are substantial entry barriers in a growing number of industries.

Information is never perfect. The same information can mean different things to different people, including people in the corporate hierarchy. Asymmetry is inherent in life, including that of the firm. Monopoly power exists at different levels in virtually all industries.

Smart firms invent unique products – however vague the term 'unique' may be – even in businesses where products are physically homogeneous. The power of firms with unique products is prone to abuse: the greater the power, the more irresistible is abusive practice. In other words, firms can act socially irresponsibly by seeking to set a price at a level that is higher than the lowest unit cost. Yet monopoly power sows the seeds of its own erosion. Stimulated partly by the monopoly profits of incumbents, competitors search for substitutes, helping to reduce monopoly power.

The protection of IPRs is designed to be temporary, though it appears excessively durable in some cases. As borders are relaxed, monopoly power is exposed to international competition. Competition tends to become tougher over time, making the penalty against abusive practices increasingly high. In the longer term, reduced imperfections will allow a firm to increasingly harmonise its corporate self-interest with the interests of users. However, there will always be some imperfections because firms will find ways of preventing their monopoly power from disappearing totally. For instance, through advertisement and peripheral differentiation, firms are able to maintain a certain level of perceived uniqueness that is valued by a number of loyal buyers who in turn find it in their interests to differentiate from one another in terms of goods and services consumed. In other words, loyal buyers are willing to pay a higher price for a product that they perceive to be unique.

The social costs of failed capital accumulation are more apparent than the social benefits associated with successful capital accumulation. Failure to accumulate capital will eventually lead to layoff, imposing costs on workers, who may number tens of thousands in the case of very large corporations. It may also deprive a whole town of its source of daily bread, because a whole town often depends on a single large employer – for example, a mining company or plantation owner. In the case of financial services, the social costs may be even greater. The failure of a major institution can trigger an industry-wide crisis, which in turn may push an entire economy to the brink of collapse. People in Indonesia, South Korea and Thailand understand well the enormous social costs of a financial crisis. And the financial costs are eventually passed on to taxpayers.

In short, a firm that can successfully accumulate capital in a sustainable way is acting socially responsibly in many ways.

ACTIVITIES OTHER THAN CAPITAL ACCUMULATION

A firm is intricately linked with a very extensive network of stakeholders. Some links are easily inferred from the firm's financial reports – for example, links with workers and suppliers. Other links are more obscure. In some cases they are the subject of legislation and regulation. In others they remain subject to discretionary decisions.

There is no way in which firms can avoid dealing with CSR. Time or market pressure may force a firm to treat workers better than is legally required. Merely complying with legally binding standards is unlikely to attract superior talents to a firm. Externally the firm engages in extensive interactions with factor providers, buyers, local communities, civil societies, governments and even international organisations, including international NGOs. The interactions are rarely idyllic, though their nature differs from one industry to another. Crafting a mutually beneficial peaceful relationship with diverse stakeholders is a necessary condition for a sustaining corporate success.

As indicated earlier, CSR is as old as the firm itself. Policymakers and researchers pay more or less attention to it at different times. When cases of flagrant irresponsibility are spotted in the corporate world – for example, the Bhopal or *Exxon Valdez* cases –

debate on corporate responsibility intensifies. Good governance and management minimise the occurrence of such cases. However, a firm may be afflicted with symptoms of irresponsibility even if managers are fully committed to CSR.

In theory, globalisation does not increase the chance of irresponsibility. In fact, it can reduce the probability of a firm acting in a socially irresponsible way, because it encourages the diffusion of best CSR practices to all corners of the globe. However, two important footnotes are in order. First, in some respects antisocial corporate behaviour has remained an important feature of the business world. Secondly, news about such behaviour now spreads instantly around the world, helping to revive strong interest in CSR.

There are strong indications that corporate managers, investors, governments and NGOs are taking CSR seriously, as indicated by the following literature and some rough tests I have carried out:

- A Google search returned more than 64 million counts for CSR. This is much more than the count of 35 million for 'good corporate governance'.
- A search for 'CSR' on the Social Science Research Network returned 62 matches compared to nine for 'good corporate governance'.
- Amazon.com listed 1,048 books on CSR compared to 251 on good corporate governance and 679 on the theory of the firm.
- By 2005, 52 per cent of the Fortune Global 250 largest firms already produced CSR reports separate from their annual financial reports (Davis *et al.* 2005).

In other words, CSR actions may be imperfect, but they are likely to persist and even increase as people become familiar with the increasing evidence that CSR can even improve financial performance.

CSR has been close to people's hearts since firms have become more important, particularly as they have evolved into major institutions. What is new is the greater attention paid to CSR in recent years. There are six main reasons for this. First of all, the world of the firm, particularly that of the large firm, has become much more transparent since the information and communication technology (ICT) revolution.

Secondly, people increasingly interact with large firms in their daily lives. This is not only because more and more people work for large firms, but also because many people are affected by the global production system in which value creation in one location depends greatly on value creation in another location and vice versa. In this environment, any irresponsible act is hot news that spreads very rapidly across the globe.

Thirdly, firms are becoming larger and more globalised. A very visible outcome of globalisation in recent years has been the wave of mega-M&As of the 1990s. In this environment, some companies became truly colossal. On the other hand, some companies have rationalised their business portfolio, spinning off peripheral businesses that later outsourced their production. Furthermore, in the course of privatisation, governments have transferred ownership of utilities and other services to dominant private firms. This has occurred particularly with telecommunication services, transportation services, ports, and electricity generation. A consequence has been that people who are critical of globalisation are particularly critical of the 'omnipresence' of some MNCs.

Fourthly, involvement in frontier industries necessarily puts large firms in the limelight. While searching for fossil energy in remote jungles, energy companies are likely to trigger heated debates on environmental issues. And ventures into stem-cell technology unleash widespread debates on the ethics of such ventures.

Fifthly, the fall of dictatorships and authoritarianism has cleared the road for a more lively debate on the behaviour of large firms.

Finally, CSR seems to have a lifecycle of its own. The cycle seems to be approaching its peak in the early years of the 21st century.

The scope of CSR

The scope of CSR is by no means clear, so the topic must be approached in a pragmatic way. There is little theory about CSR, and the topic is very difficult because it involves such extensive coverage of a wide range of issues. However, people do see CSR as having a very wide and growing scope and have a strong propensity to look at CSR in practical terms while waiting for a more solid theoretical foundation.

One way of considering the scope of CSR is to look at the Domini 400 Social Index.[4] This index is compiled by an investment firm that specialises in socially and environmentally responsible investment and that monitors the performance of various relevant US corporations. It includes eight domains with associated strengths and concerns as shown in Table 12.1.

There are other indices of CSR. Kotler and Lee (2005) listed the 25 best practices of CSR. Anderson (1989) divided CSR into categories such as business and government, business and environment, business and consumers, business and community, employer–employee relations and business and moral practices. In the current proliferating culture of rating and certification, CSR has become an important component.

Opinions differ on the appropriateness of the criteria used in each of the ratings. Vogel (2005) draws attention to many flaws in the criteria, stressing the problems that arise from the fact that what is good for one group of stakeholders may not be equally good for others and that what is good in one place is not necessarily so elsewhere. What responsibility connotes can change over time, across locations or even across firms domiciled in the same location and existing at the same time.

Four examples illustrate the complexity surrounding CSR. The first concerns a firm that engages in nuclear power technology. Such a firm may appear irresponsible to someone who considers such a capacity to be an ingredient in nuclear weapon proliferation, but responsible to someone who is interested in reducing the burning of fossil fuels because of climate change. The second example concerns the employment of child labour. From the perspective of labour rights, it is socially irresponsible to employ child labour – and child labour is even legally prohibited in most countries except under certain circumstances. Yet in many poor places many children drop out of school and roam around seeking informal jobs where they are

Table 12.1 KLD ratings and indicators for the Domini Social 400 Index

Domain	Strengths	Concerns
Community relations	Charitable giving (in US and elsewhere)	Investment controversies
	Innovative giving	Negative economic impacts
	Support for housing	
	Support for education	
	Other contributions	Other concerns
Corporate governance	Compensation to senior executives	Compensation to senior executives
	Ownership	Ownership
	Other strengths	Other concerns
Diversity	CEO, board of directors	Controversies
	Promotion	
	Work/life benefits	Non-representation
	Women/minority contracting	Other
	Employment of disabled	
	Gay and lesbian policies	
Employee relations	Cash profit sharing	Union relations
	Employee involvement	Health and safety concerns
	Health and safety	Workforce reductions
	Retirement benefits	Retirement benefit concerns
	Other	Other
Environment	Beneficial products and services	Hazardous waste
	Clean energy	Regulatory problems
	Communications	Ozone-depleting chemicals
	Pollution prevention	Substantial emissions
	Recycling	Agricultural chemicals
	Other	Climate change
		Other
Human rights	Relations with indigenous people	Burma concerns
	Labour rights	Labour rights concerns
	Other	Relations with indigenous people
		Other
Product quality and safety	R&D/innovation	Marketing/contracting controversies
	Benefits to the economically disadvantaged	Antitrust activities
	Other	Other
Controversial business issues		Concerns about alcohol, firearms, gambling, military involvement, nuclear power and tobacco

Source: KLD, <http://www.kld.com/research/socrates/indicators.html>.

even less protected than they would be in formal employment. The third example is the production of cigarettes. The cigarette industry produces hazards to human health that particularly hit poor people; on these counts, cigarette production may be seen as socially irresponsible. Yet the cigarette industry may be the source of income for thousands of low-wage people – for instance, in a few Indonesian towns. The final example concerns political considerations. From the perspective of political rights, it is socially responsible to avoid operating in dictatorships, but people may face a dilemma when they consider the perspective of the right to employment. Such examples show that most businesses have mixed impacts on human life.

It is difficult to define CSR in a way that allows it to be integrated with business operations, particularly when the responsibility involves actions going beyond legal requirements. Consider CSR in the environmental context. Every oil super-tanker on a busy route faces the possibility of an accident that may cause major environmental damage. A responsible super-tanker company minimises the probability of an accident by complying with all relevant standards. Yet accidents may happen. A socially responsible company studies all risks associated with such an accident, estimates the expected costs involved and puts in place a set of instruments that will enable the company to bear the costs if the accident occurs. The reasoning sounds simple, but it is very difficult to translate it into action.

Similar difficulties afflict companies that attempt to translate community-related CSR into action. For example, a large mine in a remote location may require people to be resettled prior to exploitation. Problems may begin when the mining company tries to identify who has the legitimate right to represent the community. If the company chooses to deal with one group of representatives, it may unintentionally antagonise other groups.

Having settled anew, people may be afflicted unexpectedly with ecological problems arising from the mining operation (for example, the loss of fresh water due to siltation resulting from the mine's activities). Defining CSR in such situations is a Herculean task. If the firm rushes in, the community is likely to be non-compliant; if the firm proceeds too cautiously, it may miss the train, to the advantage of competitors in other parts of the world.

Moreover, the company can compensate the community in different ways. It may provide good infrastructure in the settlement; provide compensation for the expected lost future income of displaced people; be actively involved in being a good neighbour in the community; provide health, education and vocational training services that will eventually allow indigenous people from around the mine to occupy a leading position in the company; and provide philanthropic support to religious groups. Most large mining companies that interact with indigenous communities include all these measures in their CSR menus. However, it is difficult to implement the measures in a way that secures a peaceful relationship with the community. The arrival of a large company in a remote place usually sows seeds of conflict in the surrounding community.

And dealing with labour rights is not a simple task. In a resource-based sector, scarcity rent may allow a company to offer a generous package to workers, who in turn may be in short supply in the particular location. Labour issues may be simpler in industries and services that are knowledge intensive. When a company chooses a particular location because it offers the possibility of low wages, it is likely to be painstaking in dealing with labour issues unless rights are compromised under an authoritarian government. Industries may move from an increasingly demanding location to a less demanding one if they are unable to strike a compromise between compliance with labour standards and international competitiveness. Corporate leaders and managers tend to have a more appreciative attitude toward labour rights than they used to; however, confronted with a heightened risk of competitive disadvantage, they often look for locations where governments tolerate substandard compliance with labour rights.

Philanthropy is perhaps the most colourful element of CSR (Smith 2003). Corporate gifts benefit religions, underprivileged children, students at all levels and in all streams, universities, researchers, refugees, hungry people, victims of natural disasters, endangered tribes, humanity at large through sponsored research on pandemics, endangered animal and plant species and historical sites. The beneficiaries may have links with the donor firm – for example, when coffee growers benefit from the philanthropy of a global café chain. In other cases the donor and recipient may have no relationship – for example, in the case of the massive donations by many corporations following the Indian Ocean tsunami of December 2004.

Resources for corporate philanthropy can come from the donor firm, its shareholders and its customers and suppliers, and from other sources, including the public at large. Some firms contribute to social causes through voluntary service by their employees. Firms find it easier to make donations when tax benefits apply. When there are no tax benefits it is more difficult for firms to decide how to determine the magnitude of any philanthropy, the kinds of assistance to be provided, and the target recipients.

Protecting the rights of minorities is another important element of CSR. Some firms reserve a seat on the board of directors for ethnic minorities, women, gay people, handicapped citizens, religious minorities or other minorities. A board with members coming from diverse backgrounds is likely to be more creative than a monolithic board, but the formation and effective management of a diverse board are more difficult than they appear at first glance. In particular, how does one define minorities in a country or region with multiple minority groups?

Finally, CSR extends to controversial issues. Two of the most prominent are bribery and a relationship with a regime that cares very little about human rights. Proponents of CSR are inclined to argue that socially responsible corporations should refuse to bribe even if it may mean they lose a business opportunity to competitors. They also expect socially responsible corporations to stay away from dictatorships. The idea of keeping a company out of controversial issues is a noble one. However, putting such an idea into practice can be problematic. In particular, when a lot is at stake, firms are more willing to compromise their corporate basic values in order to get a share in the big cake.

I now turn to the role of corporations in encouraging scientific discoveries and technological progress. This is seldom counted as an element of CSR in spite of its far-reaching implications for the future of the firm and the people connected with it. Corporations play a pivotal role in sustaining new discoveries and technological progress. This can be seen as an issue of capital accumulation. However, it deserves to be singled out as an area of CSR.

There are several reasons for this. First, technological changes are central to the human quest for sustainable development. To a great extent, the history of civilisation is the history of technological changes over hundreds of millennia. Like other production activities, technologies evolve in a way that is increasingly difficult to disentangle. Nevertheless, technology changes seem to obey a general law of increasing intellectual input.

Some technologies of the 21st century may use the same raw materials as those of earlier times, but they differ a great deal in terms of the intelligence that is used to create them. An example is petroleum products. The products that people burn in the 21st century come from the same crude oil that people of ancient times used to fuel lamps. However, they require much more scientific input. The same reasoning applies to hydrogen fuel, nuclear power, solar energy and wind energy, all of which will require much more scientific input than the products of fossil fuels have needed.

Another example is the ICT industry. The ICT transfer of the last 25 years is much more 'intelligent' than Incan couriers or Indian smoke signals. In particular, ICT connection requires digital literacy. Unfortunately, digital literacy is spread very unevenly across economies. Likewise, biotechnology solutions of the 21st century differ from plant and animal domestication thousands of years ago in requiring a much higher scientific and intellectual input. Genetic modification, organ farming and stem-cell technology are all science-driven technologies that harness advances in different branches of science. Accessing them requires digital literacy and scientific literacy. Only time will tell how long such technologies will remain benevolent. However, there are some reasons to be concerned about the current features of technology changes, and about the scientific discoveries that serve increasingly as the driver for technology changes. Thus, I suggest that support for appropriate scientific discoveries and technology changes should be considered to be an important element of CSR.

Scientific discoveries add to human knowledge and can be transmitted at costs that are increasingly affordable even to poor people in least developed economies. They therefore should have served as a strong force for convergence in economic development. In reality, market imperfections in science-driven industries and services appear to be worse than they are in other industries. In particular, market power seems to be greater and stickier in science-driven industries than in other industries. Corporations seem to have found ways to prolong monopoly power in science-intensive industries beyond what is generally possible in other industries. The adoption of scientific methods is, therefore, an important feature of business in the 21st century. Many businesses are being reinvented with a view to making them as scientific as possible. If IPRs are continuously protected, science-intensive businesses can sustain monopoly profit for a long time and can invest an increasing fraction of their profits in searches for new products and processes.

The positive contribution of IPRs to successful R&D is widely recognised. Governments have enacted IPR legislation even in countries where R&D resources are extremely limited and even when they have a limited capacity to enforce the legislation. However, large corporations, notably MNCs, tend to engage in excessive patenting, and IPR offices tend to issue patents too easily. In particular, patents may be granted for products or processes that are not rigorously defined, prompting competitors to successfully oppose the patents. More than two-thirds of the patents granted by the European Patent Office in recent years were opposed by the grantee's competitors; roughly half of the opposed patents were revoked and in the other cases protection was diluted or attenuated (Harhoff 2006). While the explicit costs associated with opposition are not very high, the implicit costs can be very high. Moreover, challenging a granted patent requires mastery of the patent technicalities. Companies from developing economies are disadvantaged in staging such opposition.

Another worrisome development in the world of IPRs relates to the privatisation of science and technology commons, or science and technology stock, which is already public and freely accessible to all interested citizens but which can be made private through mechanisation that in turn earns the stock IPR protection. Digitisation can even lead to private ownership of folklore, because the electronic recording of folklore creates property whose circulation may no longer occur freely. The same applies to plant varieties and even segments of DNA. Such tendencies for excessive patenting put less literate countries in a disadvantaged position and can hinder future scientific research (Maskus and Reichman 2005; Nelson 2006).

Persistent imperfections in science-driven industries have long been a contentious issue in international relations. Back in the 1970s and 1980s, the UN issued codes on MNCs that also cover the abusive exercise of IPRs. Unfortunately, the codes led nowhere, partly because of the highly confrontational mood in which they were stipulated. Instead, adherence to the Paris convention on industrial properties, the Berne convention on copyright and the Washington treaty on the layout design of integrated circuits are conditions of membership in the World Trade Organization (WTO). The trade-related aspects of intellectual property rights agreement of the WTO seeks to increase IPR protection, but does not cover abusive exercises of IPRs. Where the adoption and worldwide diffusion of R&D output are critical to the sustainability of economic development, it is in the interests of all economies to strike a balance between protecting IPRs and providing disincentives to the abusive exercise of IPRs.

It is somewhat puzzling that governments have been hesitant to legislate for CSR in spite of a widely shared recognition that it is a logical consequence of business evolution, especially in the last 30 years. Governments are even divided on the Kyoto protocol. Perhaps government officials have not engaged in CSR debates sufficiently. Perhaps CSR debates are yet to reach a stage where they can provide useful guidance for policymaking. Perhaps too few politicians have come across CSR to be able to champion its inclusion on the political agenda. Or perhaps there are simply not enough CSR proponents in competing firms for their views to be able to prevail. Voluntary observance is not a bad thing. Indeed, it is through such observance that firms build their 'routines' over time. However, voluntary observance leaves much room for avoidance. Cheating is easier in the absence of legally binding rules. If CSR is to become a mainstream issue in the conduct of global business, it appears to be essential that it is translated into legally binding laws and regulations. Admittedly, in many countries there is a wide gap between legislation and enforcement, and the proponents of corporate governance reform have become frustrated. However, legislating for CSR can at least help to widen its constituency, increasing the probability that firms will increasingly observe CSR.

IMPACTS AND MECHANISMS

Researchers and consultants tend to associate CSR with improvements in the bottom line (Vogel 2005). Some note a positive relation between CSR observance and corporate financial performance. In a universe of socially responsible corporations, greater responsibility may lead to a better bottom line. However, the outcome is less certain in a universe where CSR-observant corporations compete with CSR-phobic ones. Indeed, some researchers have found no positive relation between CSR observance and corporate financial performance. They believe that the fact that companies which publicly commit to CSR perform well financially within a certain period is due to factors that are partly unrelated to CSR. Moreover, companies that are committed to CSR are not immune to business failure, as demonstrated in the case of Chiquita.[5] In other words, it is hard to draw conclusions about any systematic relationship between the observance of CSR and financial success. The latter is dependent on too many factors to allow the impacts of CSR to be detectable unambiguously. Had there been a clear and durable positive relation between CSR and financial performance, companies would already have shown a strong propensity to adhere to CSR principles. The most one can say about the relationship between CSR and financial performance is that CSR is likely to improve performance but will not necessarily do so.

Perhaps the attempt to relate CSR and better profitability is misplaced. The primary reason for elevating CSR in the corporate agenda lies outside the issue of profitability. After all, being socially responsible implies in some way less appetite for risks, especially social risks, which in turn leads to lower returns. On the other hand, a weaker appetite for risks is likely to reduce the amplitude of fluctuations in financial performance, reducing the probability of a company losing its focus or going out of business. A high CSR score is very likely to result in greater financial stability. Company directors who opt for a degree of moderate risk-taking are likely to enjoy a stable moderate financial performance; those who opt for a high degree of risk-taking are likely to enjoy exceedingly strong performance in one episode only to fall into an existence-threatening 'bust' in later episodes. Corporate boards that are interested in long-term investors are, therefore, well advised to champion CSR. In a world where capital is increasingly pooled in funds with a long-term orientation, it appears to be sensible to join the champions of CSR.

But even the stability of financial performance does not seem to be the ultimate test for the merits of CSR. Given that CSR is designed to protect the interests of all stakeholders, it should be judged on the extent to which the intended protection is delivered by the firm. A large mining MNC should be accorded a high CSR rating if the communities living around its mining projects consider the MNC's presence to be welfare-enhancing; if it rehabilitates the natural environment after exploitation; if the company's workforce is satisfied with labour compensation, the working environment, freedom of association and the treatment given to minority workers; and if the company avoids publicity for involvement in controversial issues such as bribery and bowing to an authoritarian regime. By serving stakeholders in the best way possible, the firm is put in a favourable environment where it can seek to profit as much as possible. CSR observance can be seen as bait for better financial performance.

To what extent will shareholders continue to support a board which champions CSR more than competitors do? In a world where observance of CSR is rewarded positively and non-observance is penalised, championing CSR serves as a source of competitiveness. If a cheater escapes punishment, the benefits of CSR are less clear.

Firms do not seem to evolve completely randomly. As time goes by, the number of firms in an industry increases. Competition toughens. Each firm will seek to win and maintain market share by delivering features that buyers and other stakeholders consider desirable. Individually and as groups, stakeholders learn to appreciate CSR elements and are willing to incur the costs arising from the observance of CSR. In other words, the 'discovery' of CSR appears to be inherent in evolution. However, without political intervention, firms are likely to take much longer to adopt CSR practices; the costs of the irresponsible exercise of corporate power may rise to a level where business is not sustainable.

Legislation and law enforcement are critical for progress in CSR. Where CSR legislation is lacking or existing laws are not enforced adequately, firms are less likely to adopt CSR practices. CSR legislation has been an important feature of business in the last 50 years. There has been a proliferation of labour rights, minority rights, ecology, community interests and taxation provisions in relation to philanthropy laws and regulations. With the globalisation of business, many are anchored in regional and international conventions. However, CSR legislation has remained partial in nature. What is more, the enforcement of laws and regulations leaves a great deal to be desired. The less developed an economy is, the wider the gap tends to be between a legal text and its enforcement. Of the many development paradoxes, this inverse relationship between law enforcement and stage of development is one of the most saddening. By default, backwardness is more chaotic than the state of being advanced. The chaotic state is exacerbated by non-enforcement of laws. As a result the costs of information signalling, channelling and decoding are higher in backward economies than they are in developed ones.

Where laws on CSR are inadequate and enforcement of existing ones is weak, corporations will seek to weave an informal network of protection *vis-à-vis* stakeholders. Under such circumstances, the probability of governments racing to the bottom is much greater than it is under an established legal tradition. Unfortunately, the process of nurturing a legal tradition is largely an enigma. Singapore accomplished the process in one generation, but most of its neighbours suffer from a Sisyphean type of development where progress in one episode is nullified by setbacks in another.

Ingredients of the Singapore success appear to include a benevolent authoritarian leader who managed to spread the fear of law among politicians, bureaucrats, business people and the public at large, in return for very tangible improvements in living standards. The extent to which the democratic path that other countries of Southeast Asia such as the Philippines and Indonesia have opted for will also arrive at a strong legal tradition remains to be seen. Experience so far suggests that crafting a legal tradition is a much more arduous process than the dispersion of political power among the various institutions of democracy, including local governments.

Because the legal approach to CSR is unlikely to cover all CSR elements and because the enforcement of CSR legislation is often difficult, we need to develop alternative mechanisms for encouraging CSR. One is socially responsible investing (SRI). Businesses around the globe have evolved in favour of a wider shareholding. Among shareholders, in turn, managed funds have become more important. Aware of the risks involved in irresponsible acts and of the potential benefits associated with CSR, people have woven a wide network of SRI in major financial markets. Socially responsible investors put large funds together to be invested exclusively in corporations with good CSR performance. And rating agencies have extended their criteria to CSR performance. In doing so, they perform an important role in creating CSR transparency, especially because CSR is not observable directly (Johnston 2005).

More informally, activists of various kinds can apply pressure for CSR. NGOs form an extensive network of such activists. They are spread across all walks of life. Some cooperate closely with CSR-friendly companies. The UN Global Compact is one example of an activist network. Other activists make the life of CSR-phobic companies difficult through boycotts and by publicising irresponsible acts. For their part, corporations have forged various coalitions in favour of CSR – for example, the global compact coalition and the 'equator banks', which require compliance with CSR legislation and observance of informal CSR standards related to CSR in their project finance (Wright and Rwabizombuga 2006).

Whether or not CSR is associated with superior financial performance, various indicators suggest that there has been a diffusion of CSR among a rising number of corporations across national and regional boundaries as well as across industries. The idea of CSR has spread very widely around the world, although in policy terms governments have focused more attention on governance issues than on other CSR issues.

Emphasis may differ from one economy to another. R&D, for instance, is considered to be an essential element of CSR among Japanese firms (Taketani 2006) On the more practical side, listing on the Dow Jones Sustainability Index has included some companies from emerging economies (OECD 2005). More than half of the Fortune Global 250 largest firms already produce separate CSR reports and annual financial reports. And, as indicated earlier, corporations attach great importance to listing on the Domini 400 Social Index. Some companies may react to external pressure by adopting a more positive attitude towards CSR. Lee (2006) suggests that this has been the case among South Korean electronic companies.

In addition, commitment to CSR may have looked shallow in many cases. Human and financial resources devoted to CSR may have remained small compared to the resources dedicated to the bottom line of profit and wealth accumulation. Nevertheless, CSR has strongly gained in momentum, especially in the established markets of the United States and Europe.

CSR IN THE PACIFIC

The two sides of the Pacific seem to have generally taken different approaches to CSR. Countries on the eastern side, notably the United States, seem to have focused much more on the issue than have countries on the western side, including Japan. Admittedly, since the financial crises of the late 1990s, governments in western Pacific countries have done a great deal to push forward the concept of CSR in general. However, the crisis-driven reform has centred largely on good corporate governance, with less attention being paid to labour rights, the protection of community interests, corporate philanthropy or involvement in controversial issues. Perhaps the apparent disparity between the eastern and western Pacific countries' adoption of CSR initiatives arises only because companies in western Pacific countries have not publicised their initiatives as widely as have those in the United States. Moreover, Asian firms may have chosen to take a low profile in regard to CSR actions. Nevertheless, the issue of how the two sides of the Pacific can engage in joint endeavours in advancing CSR is an important one. After all, the Pacific economies are deeply dependent on each other, so much of the cost that arises from failures in CSR is likely to be felt on both sides of the Pacific.

How can Pacific countries best advance CSR?

First, informal initiatives can be important. Researchers from around the Pacific can collaborate more closely on CSR issues. They could begin by identifying how well different Pacific economies comply with CSR laws and how well they meet informal CSR norms. Such research would help to strengthen research networks in the region; such networks are essential if we are to achieve a seamlessly integrated knowledge economy for the Pacific. And a good understanding of CSR issues in the region will promote activities to solve regional CSR problems.

More formally, business communities from the region can be encouraged to integrate CSR issues into their agendas for cooperation. Chambers of commerce, industry of all types and industry associations can play an important role in promoting CSR by agreeing on voluntary regional CSR codes.

Needless to say, government CSR initiatives are also critical. Government policies constitute a major element of the overall environment in which firms operate locally, regionally and globally. Governments can accelerate progress in socially responsible business by integrating CSR elements in international agreements such as regional trade agreements (RTAs) and bilateral agreements. Given the enormous wave of RTAs in recent times, a greater emphasis on CSR-friendly provisions would have given a tremendous impetus to socially responsible business. The inclusion of CSR elements in RTAs is not new. Some agreements – for example, the North American Free Trade Agreement – have provisions on labour and environmental issues. The Association of Southeast Asian Nations (ASEAN) and the many RTAs that are being formed around it can play a pioneering role by developing a receptive attitude toward CSR. Japan can also do so by inserting CSR elements into the numerous partnership agreements with other countries, including ASEAN countries.

It may not be realistic to expect that all CSR elements will be taken up simultaneously. Initially, countries and corporations may give priority to a few issues, such as environmental issues with cross-regional impacts; compliance with basic labour rights; protection of community interests in mining, forestry and fisheries activities; and guidelines on corrupt practices. Progress in addressing such priority CSR issues is bound to benefit all Pacific economies by making this large region more attractive as a business location.

In the specific contexts that prevail in some Pacific economies, CSR may look unrealistic. However, progress often starts with an idea that serves to harness limited resources toward the attainment of a goal that derives from such an idea (Stewart 2006). Even under seemingly hopeless initial conditions, the floating of CSR issues in public debates can serve as a 'strange attractor' around which interesting constituents will later assemble.

CONCLUSION

The re-emergence of CSR as a priority issue in corporate agendas is more than a mere fashion. One reason is that governments have transferred enormous assets, including infrastructure, to corporations. As a result, corporate responsibility now stretches far beyond the bottom line of profit making. Another reason is that many corporate operations have become globalised, so any major decision by an MNC is bound to have worldwide ripples.

Unless corporations and governments take CSR seriously, many economies may experience 'globalisation immiserizing', the term used by Bhagwati (1958) for economic growth that makes a country worse off. Various mechanisms to encourage CSR should be deployed simultaneously. Governments should identify important CSR elements and integrate them into laws and regulations even if enforcement is difficult. They should do so unilaterally, regionally and globally. Business associations, the investor community, the press and NGOs can contribute by developing incentives for companies to voluntarily observe the principles of CSR. They have already done this in a multitude of ways (for example, Starbucks has committed to pay above-market prices for its coffee beans) and they can amplify their contribution by agreeing on regional CSR initiatives.

NOTES

1. See <http://en.wikipedia.org/wiki/Corporate_social_responsibility>.
2. See <http://www.wbcd.org/DocRoot/RGk8004998ErwmWXIwtF/CSRmeeting.pdf>.
3. See, for example, <http://www.freeworldacademy.com/globalleader/ecodev.htm>.
4. See <http://www.domini.com/about-domini/index.htm>.
5. Chiquita International leads the world in banana plantation and distribution activities. In 2001, it was forced to file for bankruptcy in the United States in spite of its perceived championship of CSR.

REFERENCES

Anderson, J.W. Jr (1989) *Corporate Responsibility: Guidelines for Top Management*, Connecticut: Quorum Books.
Bhagwati, J. (1958) 'Immiserizing growth: a geometrical note', *Review of Economic Studies*, 25(June): 201–205.
Black, S.E. and L.M. Lynch (2005) 'Measuring organizational capital in the new economy', pp. 205–234 in C. Corrado, J. Haltiwanger and D. Sichel (eds), *Measuring Capital in the New Economy*, Chicago and London: Chicago University Press (NBER Studies in Income and Wealth No. 65).
Corrado, C., C. Hulten and D. Sichel (2005) 'Measuring capital and technology: an expanded framework', pp. 11–45 in C. Corrado, J. Haltiwanger and D. Sichel (eds), *Measuring Capital in the New Economy*, Chicago and London: Chicago University Press (NBER Studies in Income and Wealth No. 65).
Davis, G.F., M. v. N. Whitman and M.N. Zald (2005) 'The responsibility paradox: multinational firms and global corporate responsibility', Ross School of Business Working Paper Series No. 1031.
Evenett, S.J. (2003) 'The cross border mergers and acquisitions wave of the late 1990s', NBER Working Paper Series No. 9655.
Harhoff, D. (2006) 'The battle for patent rights', pp. 21–39 in C. Peters and B. van Pottelsberghe de la Potterie (eds), *Economic and Management Perspectives in Intellectual Property Rights*, New York: Palgrave Macmillan.
Heal, G. (2005) 'Corporate social responsibility: an economic and financial framework, *Geneva Papers*, 30(3): 1–23.
Johnston, J.S. (2005) 'Signaling social responsibility: on the law and economics of market incentives for corporate environmental performance', University of Pennsylvania Law School Institute for Law and Economics Research Paper No. 05-16.
Kotler, P. and N. Lee (2005) *Corporate Social Responsibility: Doing the Most Good for Your Company and Your Cause*, Hoboken NJ: John Wiley and Sons.
Lee, K.H. (2006) 'Strategic CSR as stakeholder management: CSR in Korean electronics industry', paper presented at the International Centre for Corporate Social Responsibility and University of Nottingham conference 'CSR: Agendas for Asia', 13–14 April 2006, Kuala Lumpur.
Maskus, K.E. and J. Reichman (2005) 'The globalization of private knowledge goods and the privatization of global public goods', pp. 3–45 in K.E. Maskus and J.H. Reichman (eds.), *International Public Goods and Transfer of Technology Under a Globalized Intellectual Property Regime*, Cambridge MA: Cambridge University Press.
Maximiano, J.M.B. (2006) 'Value based leadership (VBL): going beyond regulatory approach to institutionalizing CSR', paper presented at a conference on corporate social responsibility, International Centre for Corporate Social Responsibility, University of Nottingham, 13–14 April 2006, <http://www.nottingham.ac.uk/business/ICCSR/AsiaConf06/acceptedpapers.htm>, accessed 23 November 2006.
Nelson, R.R. (2006) 'Linkages between the market economy and the scientific commons', pp. 121–138 in C. Peters and B. van Pottelsberghe de la Potterie (eds), *Economic and Management Perspectives in Intellectual Property Rights*, New York: Palgrave Macmillan.
OECD (Organisation for Economic Co-operation and Development) (2001) 'The OECD guidelines for multinational enterprises', *Policy Brief*, June: 1–8.
—— (2005) 'Corporate responsibility practices of emerging market companies: a fact finding study', Working Papers on International Investment No. 2005/3.
Ruggie, J.G. (2002) 'The theory and practice of learning networks: corporate social responsibility and the global compact', *Journal of Corporate Citizenship*, 5(Spring): 27–36.
Smith, C. (2003) 'The new corporate philanthropy', pp. 157–187 in C.K. Prahalad and M.E. Porter, *Harvard Business Review on Corporate Responsibility*, Cambridge MA: Harvard Business School Press.

Stewart, J. (2006) 'Management by morals, chapter 14 in *Evolution's Arrow: The Direction of Evolution and the Future of Humanity*, <http://users.tpg.com.au/users/jes999/14.htm>.

Taketani, K. (2006) 'Corporate social responsibility, governance and economic performance in Japanese context', paper presented at the International Centre for Corporate Social Responsibility and University of Nottingham conference 'CSR: Agendas for Asia', 13–14 April 2006, Kuala Lumpur.

UNEP (United Nations Environment Programme) (2006) *Geo Yearbook*, Nairobi: UNEP.

Vogel, D. (2005) *The Market for Virtue: The Potential and Limits of Corporate Social Responsibility*, Washington DC: The Brookings Institution.

Whitehouse, L. (2005) 'Corporate social responsibility as regulation: the argument from democracy', pp. 141–161 in J. O'Brien (ed.), *Governing the Corporation: Regulation and Corporate Governance in an Age of Scandal and Global Markets*, New Jersey: John Wiley and Sons.

Wright, C. and A. Rwabizombuga (2006) 'Institutional pressures, corporate reputation, and voluntary codes of conduct: an examination of the equator principles', *Business and Society Review*, 111(1): 89–117.

Index

Note: page references are differentiated: tables and boxes are in *italic;* figures are in **bold;** notes are indicated by 'n' between page and note numbers. For abbreviations *see* p.xvi.

Aberdeen Group, 38, 49
Accenture, 47
Acer, 91
acquisitions *see* mergers and acquisitions
activists, 180, 276
adverse publicity, 276, 301
Aegis InterWorld, 43
aerospace sector, 180
Africa, 29, 37, 119, 177, 187, 193, 197, 206, 252, 257, 259–60
AFTA, 211–13, 215–22, 228n9
ageing populations, 75
Aghion, P., 270
Agreement on Trade Related Investment Measures (WTO), 274
agricultural sector, 53, 118, 180
Agroinsa, 177
Ajinomoto, 269
Akamatsu, Kaname, 7–8, 14, 21, 22n6, 183, 200n1
Akiyama Publishing Machinery Company, 194
Albaladejo, M., 223–4
Alcatel, 195, 197
Alfa Group, 179
Alstyne, M. van, 30, 32–3
America Telecom, 171
Anderson, J.W. Jr, 293
Ann Taylor, 43
anti-dumping suits, 176, 194, 198
antitrust authorities, 268–9, 274
APEC, 18, 20, 211, 250–1, **251**, 252, 260, 267, 269–71, 274–5, 280
Apple, 91, 104
Archer Daniels Midland, 269

ARM Ltd, 67
'arm's-length' pricing, 18, 209, 278–9
Asahi Glass, 179
ASEAN, 17, 119, 133, 184, 220, 227, 252, 257, 259–60, 280, 302–3
   Framework Agreement on Services, 239
   see also AFTA
Asia, 10–17, 45, 49–54, 91, *128–31,* 145, 185, 187, 191, 302
   government policies, 269–70, 274, 279
   innovation offshoring, 58–64, 68–9, 72, 74–82
   and Mexico, 165–7, 173, 177, 181
   regional production networks, 116, 118, *122–5,* 126–7, 136
   and virtualisation, 32, 37, 40
   see also East Asia; South Asia; Southeast Asia; *individual countries*
Asian Development Bank, 6
Asian top 50 companies, *192*
assembly lines, 27
asymmetry, 109, 272–3, 290
Athukorala, Prema-chandra, 51, 233
augmenting overseas R&D, 69–70
Australia, 16, 29, 177, 179, 187, 193, 207, 211, 269
Australia New Zealand Closer Economic Relations Trade Agreement, 239, 280
automation, 33, 67–8, 92, 96, 99–102, 105, 109
automobile industry, 27–35, *34,* 41–2, 44–5, 53, 168, 178–9, 190
   see also individual firms

balanced sourcing, 49
Baldwin, R., 227
Baltagi, B., 234–5, 237–8, 257
Banga, R., 274
Bangladesh, 40
Bank, Joseph A., 43
Bank of America, 47
barriers to trade, 78, 193, 208, 227, 290
Bayh-Dole Act (US 1980), 81
best practice standards, 16, 38, 40, 42, 49, 60, 82, 271, 280–1, 284, 293
BF Goodrich, 179
Bhagwati, J., 303
Bicycles Corporation, 194
big eight investors, 253, 257–8, 260
bilateral cooperation, 273–4
bilateral FDI, 239, 253, *254–6*, 257
bilateral investment treaties (BIT), 18, 45, 274–5, 293
Bionova, 180
Blomstrom, M., 143
Blonigen, A.B., 142–3, 234, 237
boycotts, 276–7, 301
brand names, 191, 194, 196, 198–9, 204–5, 207
Braun, 169
Brazil, 29, 42, 164, 172, 176, 178, 193
Bretton Woods, 287
Brimble, P., 51, 136
British American Tobacco, 180
Brown, J.S., 49
bubble economy, Japan, 115–16
Buckley, P., 200n4
build to stock/order, 105
Burns, K., 77

Cable and Wireless, 47
Cambodia, 277
capital accumulation and CSR, 283–4, 286–91, 297, 299–300
Carr, D., 237
Carso Global Telecom, 171–2, *173*
cartels, 268–71, 273–4
cell phone industry, 41, 207
Cemex, 175–6
centrifugal/centripetal forces, 69–70, 232

chaebol, 62, 139
channel separation, 37–8
charitable donations and tax benefits, 296
Chen, E.K.Y., 51
child labour, 293
China, 8, 11–17, 20–1, 26–9, 31, 43, 47, 50–4, 69, 164–6
  division of labour, 212, 214, 218–19, *219, 225,* 228n12
  electronics industry, 60–1, 77, 103, 224
  FDI, 51, 102, 140, 145–6, **148,** 153, 156, 159, 186–200, *187–90*
  government policies, 79, 102–3
  innovation networks, 59–64, 67–9, 74–81, 84n19; 21
  mergers and acquisitions, 184, 187, *190,* 194, 198–9, 207
  PC industry *see separate entry*
  research and development, 62–4, 74, 77
  and South Korea, 140, 145–6, **148,** 153, 156, 159
  transnational corporations, 14–15, 183–6, *191–2,* 195–9, 204–7
  and US, 53–4, 187, 193–4, 197, 205, 223, 226
China International Trust and Investment Corp (CITIC), 187
China Ministry of Commerce, 191
China Ministry of Science and Technology, 103
China National Offshore Oil Corporation (CNOOC), 188–9, 193
China National Petroleum Corporation (CNPC), 187, 193
chip design, 66–7, 69, 79
Cigarrera La Moderna, 179–80
Cigatam, 172
CIO Insight survey (2004), 48
Cisco, 196
civil regulation, 276
Clausing, A.K., 143
clustering, 108–9
  knowledge workers, 58, 62, 65, 69–71, 76, 79
Coca-Cola, 177

College of Management, Georgia Institute of Technology, 48
command and control, 29, 43–51, 79
community-related CSR, 295, 300
Compaq, 102
comparable profit taxation, 278–9
competition, 71, 115, 159, 300
  anti-competitive practices, 268–74
  and China, 140, 164, 166, 184–6, 194–5, 199
  for FDI, 102, 171, 175, 178, 195, 257–9, 274–5
  for knowledge workers, 75, 136–7
  vs complementarity, 222–3, 258
competition policy, 268–74, 279–81
'Competition Principles' (PECC), 270
complementarity *vs* competition, 222–3
complementary outsourcing, 42, 66, 73, 79
complex FDI, 234–8, *236*
components and final goods, 209, 214–19, *215–17, 219*
components trade, 167, 178–80, 208–9, 212, *213, 216–17,* 218–22, *219, 221,* 224, 226–7, 228n12
Condumex, 172
Connor, J.M., 268
consolidation, 176, 178–9, 181
consumer boycotts, 276–7, 301
consumer interests, 271–2, 290–1
continuity planning, 48–50
contractual conflict, 110
control and command *see* command and control
core competencies, 3, 10, 27, 44, 89
corporate evolution, 1–4, 9–10, 26–7, *28,* 289–91
corporate social responsibility (CSR), 17–20, 267–8, 275–7, 281, 291–3
  and business complexity, 283–4
  and capital accumulation, 286–91
  characteristics of, 284–6
  impacts and mechanisms, 299–302
  in the Pacific region, 302–3
  scope of, 293–9
corruption, 277, 284, 296
cost-cutting, 107

Council of Supply Chain Management Professionals, 35
crisis management, 75
cross-border production, 51, 53, 209, 227
  see also global production networks (GPN); supply chains
cross-border trade, 238–9, *240–2,* 245, 258
customer demand, 36, 38, 89, 98, 107
customer relations, 63, 100
customs clearance, 53–4, 102–3, 214
Cydsa, 179

Daewoo, 169, 190
Datang Telecom, 62–3
de Havilland, 272
debt, 175, 179, 181
Del Monte, 36
Dell, 43–7, *46,* 91–2, 98, 195
Deloitte, 42, 47
Desai, A.M., 143–4, 151–2
developing countries *see* less developed countries (LDC); newly industrialised economies (NIE)
digital networks, 27, 54, 89, 92–4, 96–103
distance and FDI, 253
diversification, 176–7, 179–80
diversity of legal and political systems, 267, 269–70
divestment strategy, 178–81
division of labour, 3, 7–8, 126, 209, 224, 283
  China, 212, 214, 218–19, *219, 225,* 228n12
  East Asia, 211–14, 218–22, 226–7
  South Korea, 214, 218, 220
  see also fragmented production
Doha Development Agenda (WTO), 274
domestic markets, 168, 181
  competition in, 184–6, 194–5, 199
Domini 400 Social Index, 293, *294,* 301
dot.com crash, 38
Dow Jones Sustainability Index, 301
Dowling, Kurt, 38
downsizing, 75, 139, 165, 181
Dunning, J.H., 193

Index 309

East Asia, 8, 11–13, 16, 79, *134–5*, 163–4, 183, 209–10, *221*, 233
  division of labour, 211–14, 218–22, 226–7
  regional production networks, 114–16, 119–21, 126–37
  see also individual countries
eclectic paradigm, 195
ecological issues, 295
Economic Census, Mexico, 164
economic crises, 61, 139–40, 163, 167, 175, 179–80, 187, 302
economic geography, 250–7
economic integration, 7, 58, 226–7
  regional *vs* global, 219–22
Eden, L., 268
EDI applications, 92, 96, 98–100, 109
education, 63, 75, 80–2, 171, 181
efficiency criterion, 270–1
efficiency seeking FDI, 42, 192, 194
Egger, P., 235, 237
El Globo, 172
Electronics and Telecommunications Research Institute, 62
electronics industry, 45–7, 103
  China, 189–90, 192, 195–6, 198, 204–5
  division of labour, 209, 224
  innovation offshoring, 60–4, 66–7, 69–72, 74, 76–7, 79, 81–2
Electronics Supply Chain Association, 45
employee participation, 289
employment, 72, 75–6, 143, 153–6, *155*, 159–60, 165
enforcability of regulations, 270, 275, 280
environmental issues, 180, 284, 295
epistemic communities, 70–1
ERP systems, 92, 96–100, *101*, 105
European Commission, 272
European Economic Area, 239
European Free Trade Association, 239
European Union, 30, 176, 191, 193–4, 210, 212–13, 218–22, 226, 239
  and FDI, 250, **251**
  and governance of MNCs, 268–9, 273
  Japanese MNCs, 116, 119
Evenett, S.J., 270

export platform FDI, 234–5, 257
Export-Import Bank of Korea, 150
exports, 141–3, *152*, 164, 222–6
external integration, 92

fabless design houses, 67, 69
FedEx, 43, 49
Feenstra, R.C., 211
Feldstein, M., 143
Femsa group, 177–8
final assembly, 208, 218–19, 224, 226–7
final goods trade, 220–2, *221*, 224, 226–7
Fiscal Policy Research Institute, 42
flagships model, 66, 71, 140
Flaig, L.S., 31, 42, 47
Flextronics, 61, 67
flying geese model, 8, 167, 183, 222
food industry, 173, 177–9
Ford Motor Company, 4, 6, 9, 27–33, *28*, 33–5, 38–40, 43–5
foreign direct investment (FDI), 70, 115–18, 183–6, *187*, 209, **252**, 253, 264–6, 268–73
  bilateral, 239, 253, *254–6*, 257
  China, 51, 102, 185–200, *187–90*
  competition for inward, 102, 171, 175, 178, 195, 257–9, 268, 274–5
  complex, 234–8, *236*
  Europe, 250, **251**
  horizontal/vertical, 141, 143, 156, 232–5, 257
  Japan, 114–19, *115, 117*, 136, 153, 159
  Latin America, 257, 259–60
  Malaysia, 237–8
  Mexico, 168–9, **169**, 180–1
  motivation for outward, 141–2, 156–7, 186, 192–4, 196, 253
  and PTAs, 238–50, 257–61, 274–5
  Taiwan, 102, 201n15
  Thailand, 237–8
  theoretical models, 233–8, *236*, 257
  US, 234, 237–8
  see also Pacific regionalism and FDI; South Korean outward FDI
Fortune Global, *192*, 292, 301
Foxconn, 67

fragmented production, 4, 19–20, 65, 74, 119, 126, 142, 208–14, *213*, 219–27, 233
  see also division of labour
France Telecom, 171
free trade agreements/areas, 8, 15–17, 126, 164–9, 210–22, 227, 228n9, 238–9
Freeman, R.B., 63
Frisco, 172
Fujitsu, 91
Fung, Victor, 17, 233–5, 261

Galanz, 192, 196
Garcia, D.L., 77
garment industry, 40, 43
Gateway, 91
General Agreement on Trade in Services (GATS), 238, 274
General Electric, 6
General Motors, 29–30, 35, 42
genetic engineering, 180
geo-economic division of labour *see* division of labour
Geus, Aart de, 45
Girma, S., 160n4
Global Compact, 285, 301
global factory model, 59–61, 78
global innovation networks (GIN), 58–61, 63–8, 73–4, 78–9
global production networks (GPN), 3, 5–7, 60, 65–8, 101, 198, 214
globalisation, enterprise
  government policy responses, 51–4
  investment distribution, 50–1
  and revitalised command, 43–50
  and vertical integration, 27–31
  and virtualisation, 31–43
Good, D.H., 157
governance/government policies, 18, 49, 51–4, *52*, 77–82, 163–4, 180, 198, 214, 227
  Asia, 60–2, 94, 101–3, 108, 136–7, 267, 269–71, 274–5, 277, 279
  competition policy, 268–74, 279–81
  Europe, 268–9, 273
  investment agreements, 274–5, 279–81

Latin America, 53, 163
  taxation, 278–81
  US, 53, 75, 268–9, 273, 278–9
gravity model of FDI, 233–4
Gree, 189
greenfield investment, 189, 197
Greenpeace, 180
growth dynamism, 220
growth patterns, 222–6
Grupo Bimbo, 173
Grupo Carso, 172
Grupo Krone, 180
Grupo Maseca (Gruma), 177
Grupo Televisa, 173
guanxi, 11, 90, 96, 104, 110, 110n2, 111n10
'Guidelines for Multinational Enterprises' (OECD), 284

Hagel, J., 49
Haier, 183, 185, 189, 192–9, 201n8, 204–5
Hammond, J., 53
Hanson, G.H., 142
Harmonised System (HS), 150
Haveman, J., 265
Head, K., 141, 143, 272
Heal, G., 285
health sector, 180
Hejazi, W., 143
Helper, Susan, 29–30, 33–4
Helpman, E., 141–2, 233
Hendricks, Kevin, 48–9
high-tech industries, 146, 165, 168, 174, 180–1, 189
Hildebrando, 174
Hobday, M., 44
Hollon, J., 41–2
home and host governments, 275, 279–81
Home Depot, 37–8
Hong Kong, 7, 51, 54, 62, 183, 185, 187, 205, 212
horizontal FDI, 141, 143, 156, 232, 234–5
horizontal intra-firm trade, 127–32

horizontal specialisation, 209, 220
Hospital Medica Sur, 180
HP, 91–2, 102, 195
Huang, Y., 195
Huawei, 76, 183, 185, 189, 192–3, 195–7, 199–200, 205–6
human resources management, 75, 198
Hutchison-Whampoa, 205
Hylsamex, 179

Iansiti, M., 73
IBM, 42, 47, 66–7, 69, 71, 92, 102, 189, 194, 199
ICA (Ingenieros Civiles Asociados), 174
idle capacity, 175, 195
import substitution, 179
importer records, 211
IMSA group, 176–7
India, 8, 26, 41–3, 50, 59–60, 62–4, 68–9, 75–6, 176–7, 191, 198, 200n2
Indonesia, 190
Industrial Research Institute study (2003), 77
industrial restructuring, 167
informal international cooperation, 269, 273–4
information and communications technology (ICT), 4–5, 11–12, 71, 89–94, *95,* 96–102, *98, 100, 102,* 105, 109–10, 297
  see also information technology (IT)
information flows, 92, 103
information technology (IT)
  industry, 3, 9, 12, 42–3, 47–8, *48,* 72, 80, 126–7
  use in industry, 26, 35–6, *36,* 71, *100*
infrastructure, 53–4, 62, 174, 287
innovation capabilities, 61, 69, 73–4, 79, 198
innovation clusters, 58, 62, 65, 69–71, 76, 79
innovation networks, 76
  China, 59–64, 67–9, 74–81, 84n19; 21
  global (GIN), 58–9, 64–5, 67, 73–4, 78–9

innovation offshoring, 10–11
  Asia, 58–64, 68–9, 72, 74–82
  electronics industry, 60–4, 66–7, 69–72, 74, 76–7, 79, 81–2
  mobility, 64–77
innovation outsourcing, 58–9
insourcing, 44–50
Institute of Developing Economies, Tokyo, 132
intangible assets, 2, 32, 142, 166, 201n15, 286–8
Intel, 66–7, *68,* 68–9, 107
intellectual content in products, 288
intellectual property rights, 61, 73–4, 78–81, 196, 288, 290–1, 297–8
Inter American Development Bank, 6
inter-firm integration, 92
inter-firm trade, 127
international cartels, 268–71, 273–4
International Competition Network (ICN), 271, 274, 280, 281n1
International Electronics Forum (2005), 45
International Institute for Sustainable Development (IISD), 275
International Monetary Fund, 6
International Organization for Standardization (ISO), 281
international specialisation, 209, 214, 223
International Telecommunications Union, 62
InterWorld Holdings, 43
intra-firm trade, 127, *128–31, 133,* 277
intra-regional production networks, 51, 126, 132–6, 209, 214–20, *215–17, 219,* 226–7
inventory pools, 38, 98
investment, 50–1, 143–4, 160, 175, 233–4, *243–5,* 279–81, 301
  BIT, 18, 45, 274–5, 293
  provisions in PTAs, 238–50, 257–61, 274–5
investors' rights, 275
Ireland, 30
Italy, 191, 193

Japan, 7–8, 43, 49, 53, 183, 185, 195, 198, 220, 222, 301, 303
  automobile industry, 29, 33, 35
  components trade, 212, 218
  FDI, 114–19, *115, 117,* 136, 153, 159
  governance/government policies, 136–7, 269, 279
  small/medium-size firms, 116–18
  see also Japanese MNCs
Japanese External Trade Organisation, 50
Japanese MNCs, 12–13, 114–16, 119, 278
  input/output networks, 121–7
  and Latin America, 114, 116, 118, *122–5,* 126–7, *128–31*
  outward FDI, *115,* 115–18, *117*
  production/distribution networks, 127–36
  sales/procurement patterns, 118–21, *119–25, 128–31*
Jenny, F., 269–70, 273–4
Jiang, Zemin, 186, 188
Johnson Controls, 44
joint ventures, 184, 191, 193
JP Morgan Chase, 47

keiretsu, 127
Keller, E. von, 193–4
Klawiter, D.C., 268
Klein, J., 268
Klein, M., 276–7
knowledge economy, 4–5, 7, 61, 66, 141–2, 146, 180–1, 223, 283, 286, 296, 302
  sourcing, 59, 62, 69–71, 73, 78, 80
  workers, 58, 64, 69–71, 74–6, 196, 288
Kojima, Kiyoshi, 222
Korea Institute for Industrial Economics and Trade (KIET), 156
Korean National Statistical Office annual reports, 150
Korean Standard Industry Classification (KSIC), 150
Kotler, P., 293
Kraakman, R., 2
KT Group, 62

Kvaerner Pulping Inc., 43
Kyoto protocol, 298

labour costs, 194
labour rights, 284, 291, 295–6
labour-intensive production, 141–2, 151, 185, 222, 226
LACSA Group, 176
Lall, S., 195, 223–4, 269
Latin America, 114, 116, 118, *122–5,* 126–7, *128–31,* 185, 200n2, 239, 257, 259–60
  see also Mexico
Lear Corporation, 44
Lecraw, D., 184
Lee, H., 53
Lee, K.H., 301
Lee, N., 293
Legend, 195
Leng, Tse-Kang, 111n12
Lenovo, 76, 91–2, 104, 183, 189, 192, 194–5, 199
less developed countries (LDC), 13–17, 59, 143, 183–6, *187,* 193–4, 199–200, 270, 274–5, 277, 300
  see also newly industrialised economies (NIE); *individual countries*
LG Group, 62, 169
Li & Fung, 40, 49
Li, Kequan, 194
liberalisation, 70–1, 78, 126, 144, 164, 167, 180, 186, 208, 227, 259
  and PTAs, 238–9, 245, *249–50*
licensing of technology, 73
Lipsey, R.E., 143, 161n6
Liu, H., 194
livestock industry, 53
'local first' markets, 195
local markets, 121, 152
local networks, 101–3
'localisation' strategies, 198
'Logistics City,' China, 51–3
logistics platforms, sustainable, 54
logisticstoday.com, 45
low-cost labour, 42, 50, 115, 156, 159, 165, 185, 198–9, 208, 214, 223, 296

innovation offshoring, 59, 63–4, 71–2
knowledge workers, 58, 64, 69, 76, 196
LTD Management Group, 42
Lucent, 195
Lynn, Barry, 49
lysine cartel, 269

machinery sector, 118, 126, 133–6, *134–5,* 224
Malaysia, 8, 16, 54, 69, 177, 183, 218
  and components trade, 211–14
  electronic industry, 59–60, 79, 81–2
  FDI, 69, 237–8
Mann, C.L., 275–6
Mann, H., 275–6
Mansori, K., 279
maquiladoras, 165, 175
market seeking FDI, 175–7, 181, 192–4
Markusen, J., 233–4
Maskus, K.E., 298
Massachusetts Institute of Technology, 75
Matsushita Electric Industrial Co., 45
Matyas, L., 253
Maximiano, J.M.B., 285
McKinsey report (2005), 63–4
media industry, 173
medium-tech industries, 165, 168, 180
MENA countries, 259
Menlo Logistics, 40–1
Mercosur arrangements, 126, 239
mergers and acquisitions, 10, 14, 50, 79, 176–81, 268–73, 284, 292
  and Chinese transnational corporations, 184, 187, 189–91, *190,* 194, 198–9, 207
Merkafon, 180
Mexico, 15–16, 40, 53
  economic background, *163,* 163–7, *165,* 167–70, *168, 170*
  economic crises, 163, 167, 175, 179–80
  and FDI, 168–9, **169,** 180–1
  Mexico City MNCs, 171–5, *172*
  Monterrey MNCs, 175–80
  and US, 126–7, 212
micro production networks, 92, 94, 103, 110n1

Microsoft, 107
Mining and Manufacturing Survey (KNSO), 150
Ministry of Economy, Trade and Industry (Japan) reports (2005), 114
Ministry of Information Industry Research Institute, 62
minority rights, 296
Mitsubishi, 8
mobility, 5, 64–77
modernisation, 174
modular technology, 209
Moffat, Bob, 42
money flows, 103
monopoly power, 184, 283, 288, 290–1, 297
Monti, M., 271
motivation for FDI, 141–2, 156, 186, 192–5, 253, 257
Motorola, 195
movement of natural persons, 239, *246–8,* 258
Multilateral Agreement in Investment (OECD), 274

Nacobre, 172
NAFTA, 15, 17, 126, 164–7, 169, 210, 212, 220, 222, 238–9, 280, 302
Nankai Logistics Institute, 43
National Association of Securities Dealers Automated Quotations (NASDAQ), 191
National Bureau of Economic Research, 63
national innovation systems, 59, 79, 81
National Outsourcing Association (NOA) survey (2006), 47
National Science Board, 63
National Science Foundation, 75
National Semiconductor, 40–1
natural capital, 286–7
Nemak, 179
network model, 4–5, 7–9, 31–5, 233–4, 259–60
neural networks, 89–90, 103, 106
new technology-based firms (NTBF), 139

Newell, P., 276
newly industrialised economies (NIE), 119, 133, 211, 222–3
Newview, 40
Ng, F., 211
9/11 aftermath, 48–50
Nissan Motor Company, 41
Nokia, 62, 195
Non-Binding Investment Principles (APEC), 275
non-government organisations (NGO), 18–19, 180, 276–7, 281, 291–2, 301, 303
Nortel, 195
North America, 114, 116, 118–19, *122–5,* 127, *128–31,* 194
notebook industry *see* PC industry
nuclear power, 293

OECD, 18–19, 50, 54, 143, 145, 159, 166, 223, 226, 264, 274, 277–8, 280, 284
offshoring, 2–5
  see also innovation offshoring
Okidata, 43
oligopolistic rivalry, 5
Omega, 180
opportunism, 31–2
organisational capital, 288
original design manufacture (ODM), 11, 62, 96–8, *97, 102,* 104–6, 109
  ICT use, *98,* 98–100, 103–10
  Taiwan, 62, 69, 89, 91–2
Osangthammanont, Anantachoke, 42
outsourcing, 2–5, 37, 40–3, 50, 66, 73–4, 89, *91,* 97–8, 139, 214
  complementary, 42, 66, 73, 79
  innovation, 58–9
  problems of, 44–5, 47–9, *48*
overproduction, 180
Overseas Direct Investment Statistics Yearbook (E-IBK), 150
ownership advantages, 19, 22n1, 30–2, *32,* 47, 50, 164, 191, 196, 199–200, 201n14
Oxxo stores, 177–8

Pacific Asia, 8–21, 27, 53–4, 60–2, 167, 222, 267, 269–70, 273–4, 279–81
  see also Pacific regionalism and FDI
Pacific Economic Cooperation Council (PECC), 270–1, 281n2
Pacific regionalism and FDI, 17, 232–3
  and PTAs, 238–50, 257–61
  regional model, 250–7
  theoretical models, 233–8
PAFTAD, 50
Palmisano, S.J., 1–2, 10
Paranijpe, Girsh, 41
Pareto improvement, 279
Parra, Ro, 47
parts and components trade, 30, 65, 104, 114, 132–6, *134*
patents, 62, 64–5, 80
Paul, G.L., 269
PC industry, 11–12, 60, 69, 72, 89, 110, 111n11, 195
  digital networks, 92–4, *93–8,* 96–103, *102*
  market, 189, 194–5, 199
  social networks, 94–6, 103–9
  value networks, *90,* 90–2
penalties, 176, 278–9, 291
personal relationships, 89–90, 94, 101, 103–10
Petri, P., 222
petrochemical industry, 179, 297
PetroKaz, 187
Pfaffermayr, M., 235, 237
pharmaceutical industry, 30, 284
philanthropy, 284, 289, 296
Philippines, 212, 218
Philips, 62
Plan A/B program, 94, 102–3
Plaza Accord (1985), 115
political and cultural affinity, 197
political rights, 295
Porcelanite, 172
port systems, 53–4, 214
post-gravity model of FDI, 234
pragmatism, 293
preferential trade agreements (PTA), 17–18, 233–7, 253, 267, 280

investment provisions, 238–50, 257–61, 274–5
price wars, 195
'Principles to Enhance Competition and Regulatory Reform' (APEC), 270
principles-based approach to governance of MNCs, 270–1
privatisation, 171, 173, 270, 283–4, 292, 298
pro-CSR campaigns, 276–7
Procter & Gamble, 38, *39*
produced capital, 287
product development, 59, 61, 63, 66, 70–1
production networks, 11–13, 16–17, 35–40, 49, 90–109, 142, 214–22, 267
cross-border, 6–7, 13, 20–1, 228n10
see also global production networks (GPN); regional production networks
productivity, 141–2, 151, *158*
see also total factor productivity
'Professional Marketplace' database, 42
profit maximisation and CSR, 283–4, 286–91, 297, 299–300
profit-shifting, 277, 279
prosecutions of cartels, 268, 270
protectionism, 167, 171, 185–6, 192, 279
Prudential, 47
public sector, 51–3, 164, 277
Puerto Rico, 30
Pulsar, 179–81

Qualcomm CDMA standard, 62
quality control, 63
quality reduction, 107
Quanta, 111n12

Raimondos-Moller, P., 279
RCA, 197, 199, 207
real-time technology, 35–40, *36–7, 39*
recession, Japan, 116
recruitment strategies, 75–6, 137
reform movements, 270
regional economic integration, 184–5, 209, 219–22, 267, 280–1
regional networks, 114–18, 121–7, 132–6

regional production networks, 12, 16, 51, 118–21, 137, 210, 214–19, 226
regional trade agreements, 126, 302
regression analyses, 150–9
Reichman, J., 298
reputational incentives, 276–7, 281, 287
research and development (R&D), 10–13, 29
China, 62, 64, 74, 77, 185, 189, 196–200, 205–6
and CSR, 286, 298, 301
innovation offshoring, 58–9, 61–6, *68,* 68–82
South Korea, 64, 136–41, 146
resource management, 63
resource seeking FDI, 192–3
resources sector, 187–8
restructuring, 176–8
retail sector, 172, 177
revitalised command, 27, 43–51
Ries, J., 141, 143, 272
risk management, 27, 48–50, 106, 299
RMC, 176
Rodrik, S., 223
Roland Berger Strategy Consultants, 193
RosettaNet, 92, 94–6, 98–100, 103, 109, 111n9
Rosita Investments, 177
Russia, 187, 197, 205

Safarian, A.E., 143
Sainsbury (UK), 47
salaries, 72, 136–7, 228n8
Samsung, 62
Sanborns, 172
SAP-F, 98
SARS epidemic, 27, 49
Scharf, K., 279
Schjelderup, G., 279
Schneider, 190, 193
Schott, P.K., 223, 226
science and engineering, 10, 26, 29, 40, 42, 44–5, 196, 296–7
and innovation offshoring, 38, 62–3, 65–6, 70, 73, 75–6, 82
Mexico, 164–5, 171, 174, 180

Scollay, R., 280
security, concern with, 105
Seguros La Comercial, 180
self-interest, 290
semiconductor industry, 45, 60–1, 67
Seminis, 180
Shanghai Automotive, 190
Shanghai Baosteel, 193
Shanghai Electronic Group, 194
shareholders, 276, 290
Sichuan Changhong Electric, 198
Siemens, 62, 195
Sigma, 179
Silicon Valley, 64, 69, 75, 197, 206
Singapore, 7, 54, 59, 62, 64, 69, 183, 212, 218, 300–1
'Singapore issues,' 270
Singhal, Vinod, 48–9
SK Telecom, 62
skill development, 81–2, 167
Slim, Carlos, 171
small rich countries, 258, 260
small/medium-size firms, 3, 80, 92, 94, 116–18, 139–40, 156, 159, 167, 181
social networks, 94–6, 103–9
Sony, 45, 91, 104, 198
sourcing, 29–30, 38, 49, 53–4
  knowledge, 59, 62, 69–71, 73, 78, 80
South Asia, 252, 257, 259–60
South Korea, 7, 13–17, 21, 31, 40, 132, 139–41, 166
  and innovation offshoring, 59–64, 69, 79, 81
South Korean outward FDI, **144–9,** 183–7, 193, 195, 197–9, 201n15
  and division of labour, 214, 218, 220
  and domestic investment, 143–4, 160
  and employment, 153–6, *155,* 159–60
  governance, 269, 279
  and productivity, 141–2, 151, 156–60, *158*
  and trade, 141–3, 150–9, *152*
Southdown, 176
Southeast Asia, 21, 183–5, 187, 194, 197, 205, 222, 301
Southwestern Bell, 171

stakeholders, 276, 284–5, 287, 289, 291, 300
Standard International Trade Classification (SITC), 150, 210–12, 224
standardisation of components, 184, 208–9, 223
Standish Group, 43
start-up companies, 72, 75, 80
state-owned enterprises, 62, 186, 191–3, 195, 198, 206, 283, 287
steel industry, 176–7, 193
Stevenson-Yang, Anne, 103
'stewardship regimes' of NGOs, 276
STMicroelectronics, 62
strategic alliances, 31, 169, *170,* 178–9, 184
strategic asset seeking FDI, 14, 42, 47, 51, 183–4, 186, 191–4, 196, 199
Sun Microsystems, 31, 38, *39*
suppliers, 29, 33–5, 54, 67, 92, *97, 100, 102,* 104–6
  dependence on, 30, 44, 49
  lower tiers, 89, 96, 99–101, *101,* 103–6
supply chain management, 35, 40, 42–3, 63, 100, 233
Supply Chain Management Center, 41
supply chains, 29, 51, 53
  disruption, 48–9, 54
  integration, 89, 92, *95*
Swenson, D.I., 143
Synopsys Inc., 45

Taiwan, 7, 12, 14–15, 21, 40, 49, 54, 59, 94, 183, 185, 214, 218
  FDI, 102, 199, 201n15
  ODMs, 62, 69, 89, 91–2
  PC industry *see separate entry*
Taiwan Ministry of Economic Affairs, 102
Taiwan Semiconductor Manufacturing Company (TSMC), 67
taxation, 278–81
Tay, A., 272–3, 279
TCL group, 183, 189–92, 195–7, 199, 206–7
TD-SCDMA standard, 62
technology

capacity, 26, 50, 167, *168,* 185, 199–200, 222–4
diversification, 8, 61–4, 74, 297
global markets for, 73–4
telecommunications industry, 171–3, 189, 196–7, 200, 205–6
Telefonos de México, 171–3
territoriality/extra-territoriality, 272
Texas Instruments (TI), 62, 68, 206
textile industry, 179
Thailand, 40, 54, 212, 218, 237–8
third country investment, 237, 239, 253, 257, 259–60
third-party logistics industry, 26, 37, 40, 43, 51–4, 91
Thomson Group, 197, 199, 207
3G wireless communication systems, 60, 62, 69, 152–3
Thursfield, David, 44
Tianjin Development Area, 51
tobacco industry, 172, 179–80, 295
Toffler, A., 1, 4
Toshiba, 91, 104
total factor productivity, 13, 15, 141, 150, 156–60, 164, 166
Toyota, 30, 33, *34,* 35, 198
trade and FDI, 141–3, 150–60, *152*
trade press, 41–2, 53
trade unions, 276
TradeNet System, 54
transaction costs, 30, 34–5
transaction economics, 29–31
transfer pricing, 277, 279
transport and distribution, 29, 53–4
Trewin, R., 280
triple bottom line, 281, 285
tsunami (2004), 296
TSYS, 47

UAI, 190–1
UN Comtrade, 150, 210–11
UN Conference on Trade and Development (UNCTAD), 6, 64, 183, 264
UN Global Compact, 285, 301

UN Industrial Development Organisation (UNIDO), 6
UN Statistics Division, 150
uncertainty, 104
United States (US), 3, 12, 14–16, 18–19, 21, 29–30, 33–8, 47, 234, 237–8, 293
automobile industry, 27–35, *34,* 53
and China, 53–4, 187–8, 193–4, 196–8, 205–6, 223, 226
governance, 53, 61, 75, 176, 268–9, 273, 278–9
innovation, 59–61, 63–9, 72–3, 75–6, 80–2
and Japan, 126–7, 132, 136, 222, 278
and Mexico, 127, 164–7, 169, 171–80, 212
and South Korea, 141–6, **149,** 153–4, 156–7, 159–60
and Taiwan, 91–2, 96
university-industry linkages, 80–1, 181
Unocal, 188
upgrading, 61–4, 78, 81, 92, 139, 174, 179, 214
Urata, Shujiro, 51, 136
US Information Technology Office (USITO), 103
US Patent and Trademark Office, 62

Valenciana de Cementos, 176
value network, PC industry, 90–2
value-for-money products, 196, 200
venture capital, spread of, 72
Verizon Wireless, 43
vertical disintegration, 89
vertical FDI, 141, 143, 156, 232–3, 235, 257
vertical integration, 3, 9, 26–31, *32,* 34–5, 45, 49–50, 66–7, 71, 146, 151, 209
vertical intra-firm trade, 127–32
vertical production networks, 141–2
vertical restraints, 272
vertical specialisation, 66–7, 71–4, 227
Vietnam, 8, 20, 76, 191, 193, 197, 201n13, 207, 211, 214

virtualisation, 9, 26–7, 31–43, *32,* 47, 49–50
Vitro, 178–9
Vodafone, 6
Vogel, D., 293
voluntary codes and standards, 276–7, 298–9, 302

Wagner, J., 141–2
Wal-Mart, 36, 38, 49
Wang, Yu-liang, 186
Wanxiang Group, 190–1
Ward, H., 277
websites, 38, 46, 99–100, 102–3, 105
Weichenrieder, A., 279
Weiss, M.Y., 143, 161n6
welfare, global and domestic, 271–2
White, L. Jr, 26
Whitehouse, L., 285
Wijckmans, F., 270–1
Willman, G., 272–3, 279
Wipro Ltd, 41
World Bank, 6, 54
World Bank Corporate Social Responsibility Practice, 276
World Investment report (2005), 114
World Trade Organization (WTO), 15–16, 18, 165–6, 186, 198, 238, 270–1, 274, 279, 298
Wu, F., 195

Xilinx, 67
XML, 94–6

Yangtse River Delta, 91–2, 102, 110
Yano Research Institute Ltd, 43
Yeats, A., 211
yen appreciation, 115–16
Yoshida, J., 45

Zach, R., 272
Zhang Ruimin, 195, 201n8, 204
Zhou, W., 193–4
Zweifel, P., 272